FEARFUL
SYMMETRY

MAR. 2005

To Ann
With best wishes
and fond memories

Critical Issues in

PSYCHOANALYSIS

clp₃

Editors:

Steven J. Ellman, Ph.D.
Arnold Wilson, Ph.D.

Editorial Board:

FEARFUL
SYMMETRY

The Development and Treatment of Sadomasochism

Jack Novick, Ph.D.
and
Kerry Kelly Novick

JASON ARONSON INC.
Northvale, New Jersey
London

This book was set in 11 pt. Bodoni Antiqua Light by Alpha Graphics of Pittsfield, New Hampshire and printed and bound by Book-mart Press of Northbergen, New Jersey.

Library of Congress Cataloging-in-Publication Data

Novick, Jack.
    Fearful symmetry : the development and treatment of sadomasochism / by Jack Novick and Kerry Kelly Novick.
      p. cm.
    Includes bibliographical references and index.
    ISBN 1-56821-652-1 (alk. paper)
    1. Masochism. 2. Masochism—Case studies. I. Novick, Kerry Kelly. II. Title.
RC553.M36N68   1995
616.85'835—dc20   95-31774

Manufactured in the United States of America. Jason Aronson Inc. offers books and cassettes. For information and catalog write to Jason Aronson Inc., 230 Livingston Street, Northvale, New Jersey 07647.

CONTENTS

DEDICATION

The hundred years since Anna Freud's birth in 1895 encompass
the life span of psychoanalysis. We first met Anna Freud in 1964,
when she was nearly 70 years old. At a time when most people
are ready to retire, she was entering her most productive period.
We were fortunate to spend the next thirteen years at the Anna
Freud Centre as students, research associates, staff members, and
supervisor. We knew Anna Freud in her various roles as a clinician, teacher, theoretician, and researcher.

Anna Freud's clinical genius had at root the simple impera-
tive to see the world from the perspective of the child, with child
psychoanalysis providing the ideal materials for fostering a capacity for empathy. To her, each person held a story; every case
had a beginning, a middle, and an end, achieved through the
overcoming of conflicts and the transformation of infantile modes
of gratification. The techniques she espoused were remarkably
flexible, creative, and humane. She emphasized that transference
defined only one aspect of the treatment relationship. As a teacher,
Miss Freud's clarity and concision were legendary. She not only
influenced generations of psychoanalysts, but extended knowledge
of psychoanalysis to educators, pediatricians, lawyers, jurists, and
many others.

A powerful influence on all who studied with her has been what
we would describe as Anna Freud's theoretical style, with its
emphasis on multidimensional understanding, its rootedness in
psychoanalytic history, its empirical base, and its assumption that

child psychoanalytic experience is integral to the training of psychoanalysts and the growth of psychoanalysis. With gratitude and the wish to honor her work and life, on the occasion of the centenary of her birth, we dedicate this volume of work to the memory of our teacher, Anna Freud.

ACKNOWLEDGMENTS

The work described in this book draws upon many sources. In the thirty years since we began our psychoanalytic training, our thinking has been stimulated and enriched by dialogue with teachers, colleagues, students, patients, friends, and family. While we take full responsibility for limitations or confusions in our formulations, we are deeply grateful to all those—at the Hampstead Clinic (now the Anna Freud Centre), Brent Consultation Centre/ Centre for the Study of Adolescence, British Psycho-Analytic Society and Institute, Cassel Hospital, Michigan Psychoanalytic Society and Institute, New York Freudian Society, Hanna Perkins School, and Allen Creek Preschool—who helped us along the way.

INTRODUCTION

The chapters in this volume derive from our work of the last twenty-five years; some were published in different versions in journals, some in books no longer available, and some chapters contain material that has never been published. Psychoanalysis has changed greatly in that time, and our thinking has also evolved. Nevertheless, we find that there are four consistent and interlocking themes: an emphasis on the necessity for a metapsychological approach to all psychological phenomena, the importance of the developmental point of view, an assumption that child and adolescent analytic material and observation of infants and children have much to contribute to the understanding and technique of work with adults, and an increasing conviction about the role of sadomasochism and its omnipotent core in all pathology.

METAPSYCHOLOGY

Metapsychology has been understood in two ways: as an overarching abstract theory, and as a multidimensional description of phenomena. American psychoanalysis has predominantly focussed on the abstract formulation, systematized by Rapaport and Gill (1959). Metapsychology as a grand theory of the mind has been criticized by Holt (1981, 1982), Klein (1976) and others as derived from outdated nineteenth-century physical science concepts, and as too distant from daily clinical work. As a result, there has been a de-

cline in emphasis on metapsychology. Rather than the classical
equilibrium of a multidimensional description of psychic phenomena there has been a skewing towards a near-hierarchical theoretical model, with the structural point of view preeminent, and a
splintering of the metapsychological points of view into rival theories, each based on emphasizing one particular part of the whole,
resulting in overabstraction and oversimplification.

The alternative usage—of metapsychology as a multidimensional
description of phenomena—continues in Anna Freud's formulation
of metapsychology as the "language of psychoanalysis" (1966). Her
concept of a metapsychological understanding included the specifically psychoanalytic view of the complexity of the many influences
from inside and outside, the contributions of the different components of the mind and mental functioning, and the interaction of
past and present in the formation of the personality. Her use of
metapsychology found application in the "Metapsychological Profile" (1965). Throughout this book, we have tried to understand
complex psychological phenomena on the basis of Anna Freud's
metapsychological perspective, that is, as multi-determined and
serving multiple functions in the personality.

THE DEVELOPMENTAL POINT OF VIEW

The developmental point of view has always been at the center
of psychoanalytic thinking. Freud wrote in 1913, "from the very
first psychoanalysis was directed towards tracing a developmental process" (p. 183). Freud's 1926 description of the developmental sequence of anxieties and the subsequent work of Anna
Freud (1936, 1965), Hartmann (1939, 1952), Hartmann and Kris
(1945), and Erikson (1950, 1968, 1982) all contributed to a view
generally held in the middle years of the twentieth century that
psychoanalysis was above all a developmental psychology.

Recent years have seen a decline in the application of the
developmental point of view as an element of a full metapsycho-

logical description. As the papers in this volume indicate, we understand the developmental point of view not as a school of thought or a theory, but rather as a way of organizing clinical data, providing a context or ground within which particular phenomena may be examined. As such it can encompass any theory, forming a substratum to formulations as disparate as those of Melanie Klein, Anna Freud, Margaret Mahler, Heinz Kohut, and Daniel Stern.

The developmental point of view demands examination of antecedents and consequences, and thus precludes oversimplification or overemphasis on any one factor. Any clinical phenomenon must be understood in relation to what has led up to it and what will be the sequelae. The continuities and transformations that inhere should be explicated.

Exploration of clinical problems has led us to the idea that no one phase has preeminence over any other, that earlier experiences are not necessarily more important than later ones. Each phase influences and is influenced by each other phase of development, including the development that continues through adulthood.

We have also found it heuristically useful to apply the developmental point of view to the course of treatment. It has allowed us to think of psychoanalysis in terms of phases, therapeutic tasks, and assessment of accomplishment of those tasks—outcome of therapeutic interventions—at any given point in the treatment.

APPLICATION OF CHILD
AND ADOLESCENT PSYCHOANALYSIS
TO PSYCHOANALYSIS OF ADULTS

The chapters in this book contain a great deal of material from child and adolescent analyses and from infant and child observation. The importance of clinical data for generating theoretical ideas and then testing theory and technical concepts in the clinical setting has been a central value in our work. This derives directly from Anna Freud's "natural science," empirical approach to theory-building. In a reminiscence of Anna Freud we noted that "she took no pleasure in abstraction for its own sake; she eschewed both mysticism and arid intellectualization. Her need for theory stemmed directly from observations in and out of the consulting room, and theory had to have application to those observations" (Novick and Novick 1993, p. 59). Our earliest papers make use of observational and psychoanalytic child data to clarify concepts derived from adult work, such as projection, therapeutic alliance, and beating fantasies. This led to technical suggestions for therapeutic work with adults.

SADOMASOCHISM AND OMNIPOTENCE

The impetus for writing these papers was our need to understand better the problems of clinical work with difficult patients. Each paper describes people who were generally diagnosed as very disturbed, highly masochistic, borderline, severely obsessional, and the like. With each attempt to understand their pathology, we came across commonalities in the technical problems, etiology, and underlying fantasies that cut across nosological lines. We were drawn to explore the sadomasochism of these patients, the beating fantasy as its essence, the delusion of omnipotence as the core of the fantasy, and externalization as a major mechanism in its development and functioning. Through the chapters in this volume, we trace the evolution of our conclusion that sadomasochism is not a separate diagnostic category, but an integral part of all pathology.

These four themes may be discerned in all the papers selected for this book. We have grouped them, however, according to considerations of the development of sadomasochistic pathology, the mechanisms involved, some clinical manifestations of severe sadomasochism, and technical interventions that we have found helpful.

PART I
DEVELOPMENT

1   BEATING FANTASIES
IN CHILDREN*

The classic study of beating fantasies written by Freud (1919) was based on reconstruction from adult analytic material. This work reaffirmed Freud's views concerning the importance of the Oedipus complex; perversions as well as neuroses were seen as precipitates of this central complex of childhood. The beating fantasy was said to be "the essence of masochism" (p. 189) and represented both regressively debased genital love for the father and punishment for incestuous wishes.

From adult analytic material Freud reconstructed the sequential vicissitudes of the beating fantasy in boys and girls. He suggested that the fantasy first appears in the preschool years and no later than five or six years of age. It has three phases in girls:

1. "My father is beating the child whom I hate." Freud questions whether this can be called a fantasy and notes that it may represent rather a recollection "of desires which have

---

*This chapter was originally presented at the 27th International Psycho-Analytical Congress, Vienna, 1971.

arisen" (1919, p. 185). The motive for this first phase is the child's jealousy of and rivalry with a sibling. Freud doubts that this first phase can be described as sexual and gives its full meaning as "My father does not love this other child, he loves only me."

2. "I am being beaten by my father." According to Freud this second phase is the result of a profound transformation of the first phase. Although the beater remains the father, the one being beaten is invariably the child producing the fantasy. This fantasy is of an "unmistakably masochistic character" (p. 185) and represents both debased genital love for the father and punishment for incestuous wishes. This phase of the fantasy is never remembered, is a construction of analysis and, Freud adds, "in a certain sense has never had a real existence" (p. 185).

3. "A (father substitute) teacher beats children" (usually boys). This phase, like the first, is consciously remembered. Unlike the first phase, but like the second and thus linked with it, is the strong and unambiguous sexual excitement attached to it.

Freud expected but did not find a parallel sequence in the beating fantasies of boys. He described the third (conscious) phase of the fantasy in males as "I am being beaten by my mother (or other woman)." This is preceded by the unconscious fantasy: "I am being beaten by my father." This corresponds with the second phase in girls and thus the beating fantasy in both sexes has its origin in oedipal attachment to the father. Freud did not find evidence of a first phase in boys in which the beating bears no sexual significance but is motivated by jealousy. However, he felt that further observation might reveal that boys too have such a first phase.

Freud outlines the differences between the two sexes, and it is clear that the beating fantasy is more pathognomic of severe disturbance in the male than in the female. The male cases used for his study had "gross injury to their sexual activities" (p. 196) and "included a fairly large number of persons who would have to be described as true masochists in the sense of being perverts" (p. 196). Freud warns against pressing the analogy between boys and girls and says that the sexes should be considered separately. Although the fantasy stems from the Oedipus complex in both sexes, the girls' fantasy starts from the "normal," whereas the boys' starts from the "inverted" oedipal attitude. Furthermore, despite changes in the person doing the beating, the boy retains a passive feminine attitude in all phases of the fantasy. Since Freud, except for Marie Bonaparte's discussion (1953) of beating fantasies as a normal step in girls' psychosexual development, most authors have tended to neglect the difference between the sexes in their formulations on beating fantasies.

In Freud's later writings, additional factors were described. Beating fantasies represented not only oedipal wishes but also a confession of masturbation (1925), and they came to stand for castration, being copulated with, or giving birth to a baby (1924). This trend towards increasing the number of determinants and functions of the beating fantasy has continued in the work of authors after Freud, with a shift to emphasis on the preoedipal rather than the oedipal determinants of the fantasy (Bergler 1938, 1948, Schmideberg 1948). Work by Kris and others (Joseph 1965) has stressed the ubiquity of the beating fantasy, its multiple determinants and functions, the varied manifest forms and latent meanings of the fantasy, and the range of diagnostic groups in which it can occur. But this work, like that of others, has been largely based on reconstructions from adult analytic material. There has been no systematic study through the method of child analysis in this area where many formulations deal with the vicissitudes of the beating fantasy in childhood. Therefore, using the abundant child analytic material available at the Hampstead Clinic in the form of case material recorded in the Hampstead Psychoanalytic Index (Sandler 1962), Diagnostic and Terminal Profiles (A. Freud 1965), and weekly clinical reports by therapists, we have undertaken a study of the role of beating fantasies in normal and pathological development. Here we will present only a description of the beating fantasy as it occurred in children treated at the Clinic.

We found that beating fantasies rarely played a significant role in the analytic material of children. For example, only six out of 111 indexed cases were said to have beating fantasies. This does not preclude their being universal, but it does indicate that beating fantasies play a significant or visible role in only a minority of cases. No beating fantasies were reported in prelatency children, and the later incidence was about evenly divided between pre- and postpubertal children.

The question of incidence may turn in part on the definition of fantasy. We have found it helpful to follow Schafer (1968) in using a limited definition of the fantasy as conscious daydream. We distinguish among types of mental content such as instinctual wishes, theories, and fantasies. An instinctual wish may find discharge along a developmental continuum from action to fantasy, with games and play occupying a middle position.

In relation to beating fantasies our distinctions may be applied as follows: the beating wish is an instinctual representation that may or may not reach consciousness and can be defended against, sublimated, or appear in derivative forms at varying distances from the original impulse. The beating fantasy is the fulfillment in the form of conscious or preconscious thought of the sexualized wish to beat or be beaten.

We have applied these formulations to material from children observed in the nursery school and children treated in analysis and have found a distinct sequence of beating wishes. These children were normal or neurotic, without signs of severe disturbance. There is a stage in which almost all children form their concepts of relationships in terms of power and control. Hitting and being hit is a major avenue of discharge for aggressive and hostile impulses; an adult who frustrated one child's wishes was subjected to a hail of blows, accompanied by shouts, "I'm going to bash you, I don't like you." Dolls and toys often bear the brunt of these impulses, with fiendish punishments devised by their small owners. Active discharge of aggressive impulses to beat, hit, or overpower in this way is linked with the anal phase. This stage in the development of the beating wish is similar to the first phase of the beating fantasy as Freud described it: the important characteristics are that it is aggressive, not sexual, is discharged in action, is appropriate to the anal phase, and occurs in both sexes.

It is generally accepted that children form a sadistic theory of intercourse (Freud 1908), and our observations indicate that this is a "persistence" and "generalization" of anal phase concepts of relationships to the impulses of the phallic phase (Freud 1933, and see Chapter 5). It is via the sadistic theory of intercourse that the beating wish becomes sexualized. At the phallic stage both boys and girls were seen playing hitting games or chasing and catching games, all accompanied by intense sexual excitement. In treatment, many children played school games or hospital games, in which the therapist was asked to personify, for example, "Miss Mary who smacks the baby," or the cruel doctors who mistreat their child patients; cowboys chasing and shooting Indians, and policemen capturing robbers appeared often.

In these games the children alternated between active and passive roles, playing both attacker and victim. Diffuse sexual excitement and masturbation usually accompanied or followed the games. Freud (1919, 1924) talked about the necessary factor in both beating fantasies and masochistic perversions that the victim not be *really* injured; children playing a game reassure themselves that "it's only pretend." In this way drive gratifications are made acceptable. It may be that adult masochistic perversions involve a fixation at the stage of phallic beating games. In the roles assigned in the games it seemed immaterial whether the beater was male or female, because women were still regularly conceived of as phallic. For example, one child described intercourse as "Daddy spanks Mummy and she spanks him back."

With the awareness of the difference between the sexes, being beaten acquires a further meaning. From the anal phase it carries the meaning of punishment and loss of love, from the early phallic phase it comes to represent parental intercourse, and, at this point, with differentiation between the sexes, it represents castration and the passive feminine position in intercourse. Here we regularly find a divergence between boys and girls. Boys begin to struggle against passive wishes and the wish to be beaten. In their games they increasingly took the active role. Early in the phallic phase, for example, one boy was equally excited playing Batman or the "baddie" who was beaten up and thrown in jail. Later he insisted on taking only the role of Batman and the therapist or an imaginary figure was the "baddie."

Girls who had particular difficulty in accepting the lack of a penis either gave up beating games entirely and regressed to anality, or denied the lack of a penis and adopted the active role in the beating games. One girl repeatedly played that she had a magic sword and used it to smack all the soldiers coming to invade her land. In contrast, the increasing ability to take the passive role in beating games indicated a move towards the positive oedipal position.

The beating wish, sadistic intercourse theory, and phallic beating games could be seen in some form in all the young children in our sample and thus appear to be universal. Variations among children are the result of differences in intensity of the beating wish, the contribution of experience, for example, primal scene observation, and their environment's reaction to expression of instinctual impulses.

With some resolution of the Oedipus complex and the formation of the superego, these children moved into latency, and it was only at this point that what we would call the beating fantasy proper emerged in a few of the girls. It seems that the importance of the beating wish in the oedipal conflicts of the individual girl determines whether a masturbation fantasy involving beating will be formed in latency. When it did occur, it clearly represented both oedipal strivings in regressed form and punishment for them, as Freud described, but it did not appear in the vague third-person form he found in adult patients. Again the beaten victim of the fantasy consciously personified the child herself, as for the little girl who imagined herself to be a slave beaten every four hours by an emperor, whose first slave had been beaten to death, and replaced by the patient. Gradually sexual excitement and masturbation were divorced from the fantasy and the wishes appeared in increasingly distanced forms, the content elaborated with material borrowed from reading and schoolwork. Cinderella, Snow White, and the Sleeping Beauty were favorite sources of inspiration and they demonstrate the link between beating fantasies and the "typical" latency fantasies of the family romance and of rescue. One little girl told "dying stories" with great pleasure; the "dying" variation was due to her equation of death with yielding in sexual intercourse. She told of a "Snowflake Lady" who was sought out by the "King of the World"; when he found her he lifted her in his arms and she melted away. When seen again for follow-up in adolescence, there were no signs of excessive masochism in these girls, and it seemed that the beating wish had been adequately sublimated in the development of appropriate feminine passivity. Despite this benign outcome, it is possible that a beating fantasy may emerge in adulthood as a derivative of regressively intensified beating wishes.

If we compare this development with the reconstructed stages of the beating fantasy described by Freud, we find that the sequence is very similar: the child moves from an aggressive beating wish to a sexualized wish to beat or be beaten and then on to a wish-fulfilling masturbation fantasy involving beating or a derivative of beating. The timing of this evolution in the childhood material differs from that suggested by Freud, in that the beating fantasy *per se* arises only after the oedipal phase. Similarly, the wish to be beaten, standing for the oedipal wish, is or can be made conscious at that time. The ease with which the beating fantasy of latency could be transformed, elaborated, and distanced from the beating wish of the oedipal phase, coupled with the subsequent good development of the girls in whom it was found, leads us to the conclusion that this beating fantasy is a normal transitional component of postoedipal development in girls and may be more common than is generally supposed.

We did, however, find another group of children in whom a beating fantasy appeared against a background of severe disturbance. This group contained nine boys. Although these children showed different degrees of interference in their functioning, all presented a picture of multiple fears, intense anxiety, often leading to panic attacks or tantrums, passivity, and clinging dependence in an over-close sadomasochistic relationship to the mother. We could find no constant relationship between actual experiences of being beaten and the presence of beating fantasies in these children.

Sadomasochistic relationships were reproduced with peers and in treatment, where several of these children became management problems. One boy regularly attacked his therapist in an attempt to provoke retaliation; another raged, shouted, and threw objects out of the windows. It was often difficult to contain these children in the treatment room: frustration or noncompliance with his wishes produced panicky rage in one boy who raced around the clinic; another invaded the offices and would not stay put until provided with a typewriter for his own use. Isolated incidents like this, although rare, would not ordinarily mean much, but this disturbed difficult behavior persisted in children in this group for lengthy periods. One therapist summarized the first 2½ years of treatment as a "constant physical battle." Her patient pleaded to be tied to a chair and beaten, alternately wanting to tie up the therapist. Although the content of this material resembles the phallic beating games described earlier, this boy's therapist, and others faced with similar material, noted the lack of accompanying sexual excitement and conceptualized the behavior as anxiety-driven, almost as if the child literally wanted to "tie the object down," to retain the object and cling to it for safety. Painstaking analytic work was necessary before anxiety became manageable and drive impulses could be contained in thought.

The beating fantasy itself appeared only after substantial change had occurred, with a significant decrease in the sadomasochistic `behavior both in and out of treatment. The fantasies emerged along with the appearance of phallic-oedipal impulses, and in all cases this was at puberty. The following illustrates the link between the beating fantasy and phallic-oedipal wishes in a 13-year-old boy:

> After his first emission, the boy reported a masturbation fantasy in which he first thought of undressing a girl in his class; the girl changed to an older woman and then, as his excitement mounted, the image changed to that of his mother. As he reached a climax the fantasy shifted to the boy's father walking in, holding him down, and beating him on his buttocks.

In contrast to the transitory beating fantasy described earlier, the beating fantasy in this group of disturbed children was crude, monotonous, and repetitive. The subject was always in the passive role, and the beater was invariably a person who figured in the child's real life, often the father or someone drawn from the class of father-representatives. These characteristics may be seen in one boy's fantasy of being held down by two older boys from school and beaten on the buttocks. For the next two years, the fantasy remained basically unchanged, unlike the constantly elaborated imaginative productions of the more normal group of children, in which the characters were drawn from anywhere but real life.

The beating fantasy in the severely disturbed children can be called a *fixed fantasy* to contrast it with the more normal transitory beating fantasy, and to underline the fact that, once it is formed, it remains a relatively permanent part of the child's psychosexual life. The transitory beating fantasy had a brief duration and was usually spontaneously modified or easily gave way to interpretation, but the fixed fantasy seemed impervious to years of interpretive work, and in cases where follow-up evidence was available, the beating fantasy persisted after termination.

Presentation of the details of the background and treatment material of these children would provide the basis for an understanding of the factors which make this a fixed fantasy. Here we can only state that the fixed fantasy, in contrast to the transitory one, does not follow the pattern traced by Freud in "A Child is Being Beaten" (1919). It more nearly approaches formulations in the literature on adults where the beating fantasy is placed in the context of severe masochistic pathology with accompanying ego disturbance (Bak 1946, Ferber and Gray 1966, Rubinfine 1965). In reporting the beating fantasy the children usually stopped at the point where they had been beaten, as if that were the end of the fantasy. Further work, especially by means of the transference relationship, usually revealed that there was more to the fantasy, and this remainder contained the main libidinal and narcissistic pleasure of the fantasy—hence the reluctance of the children to disclose it. It stood for an early masochistic tie to the mother. In this extension, someone important, often a woman, felt very sorry for the beaten child, comforted him, and in many versions, the child was then regarded as a very important and special person. One child fantasied that the beating would be followed by both parents apologizing and the mother putting soothing lotion on his bottom. In another child's fantasy, after he had been cruelly beaten by schoolboys, the headmaster told the assembled students, "He is the outstanding boy who has been treated badly. We have never had another boy who has gone through so much." Although it is clear from our material that the beating fantasy is not formed until the phallic-oedipal stage is reached, the primary determinants of the beating wish which is discharged in the fantasy are preoedipal.

SUMMARY AND CONCLUSIONS

In our study of the role of beating fantasies in normal and pathological development we found it helpful to define fantasy as conscious daydream. It is of course arbitrary how one employs a concept, but we believe our approach demonstrates the value of maintaining distinctions among types of mental content and narrowing the referents of the term fantasy. Thus we found that beating wishes and beating games are universal, whereas the beating fantasy itself occurs infrequently. Further, we found that our material then fell into two sets, with significant differences between the sexes as to the functions and determinants of the fantasy.

In girls the sequence of a beating wish at the anal phase leading to a phallic beating game and then, in some girls, to a beating fantasy in latency paralleled the sequence reconstructed by Freud (1919); like Freud, we found that passive beating wishes and beating fantasies in girls represented both positive oedipal strivings and punishment for incestuous wishes. For girls the passive beating wish and even the beating fantasy of latency are often transitional phenomena. Although the presence of a beating fantasy in a girl signifies the persistence of intense libidinal wishes towards her father, if forward development is not too much interfered with, the beating fantasy may act as a second opportunity for some girls to establish the passive-feminine position and then move on to age-appropriate derivative wishes.

Although the beating fantasies could be seen in the context of normal development in girls, we failed to find any such fantasies in our group of normal or neurotic boys. We did, however, find beating fantasies arising at puberty in a group of severely disturbed boys. In these boys we saw that the beating fantasy became the permanent focus of the child's psychosexual life, and this was due to the multiple functions and determinants of the fantasy. The beating fantasy was rooted in an early sadomasochistic relationship to the mother, and we concluded that a beating fantasy in a boy was indicative of severe disturbance in ego and drive development. This study of beating fantasies in children has led to distinctions between different types of mental content, the separate examination of male and female development, and the hypothesis of an essential link between masochism and the beating fantasy. The application of these findings to adult development and perversion is delineated in Chapters 2 and 3.

2   THE ESSENCE OF MASOCHISM

Despite putative shifts in the types of pathology presented to the modern psychoanalyst, our caseloads are in fact very similar to Freud's, since he too grappled with masochistic phenomena of varying intensity and pervasiveness in his daily work. The male cases cited in his paper on beating fantasies (1919) "included a fairly large number of persons who would have to be described as true masochists" (p. 196) and there are references to suicide in all of Freud's published cases except Little Hans (Litman 1970, and see Chapter 8, this volume). The difficulties in conceptualization and technical handling of masochism led Freud to repeated revisions of his formulations and ultimately to fundamental changes in psychoanalytic metapsychology.

Since Freud, a vast literature has accumulated around the theoretical and clinical problems of masochism. Good summaries of the classical view are provided by Fenichel (1945), Loewenstein (1957), Bieber (1966), and Ferber (1975). Maleson (1984) says that masochism has acquired a "confusing array of meanings," with "little consistency or precision in its current usage" (p. 325). For Freud, all masochism was ultimately based on erotogenic masochism. The linkage of erotogenic and moral masochism takes place via the beating fantasy; morality for the masochist represents an unconscious, resexualized wish to be beaten by the father. In this way "the Oedipus complex is revived and the way is opened for a regression from morality to the Oedipus complex" (1924, p. 169). Thus Freud reemphasized his earlier tenet that the beating fantasy is the "essence of masochism" (1919, p. 189).

If Freud's statement is valid, a detailed study of beating fantasies should help us to understand more fully the complex phenomena of masochism. In "The Economic Problem of Masochism" (1924) Freud sketched the genetic point of view; Loewenstein (1957) used a developmental perspective; and we too will apply this perspective to a study of beating fantasies to elucidate a developmental line of masochism.

A major finding of our study of beating fantasies in children was that there were two types of beating fantasies, a normal transitory one and a *fixed fantasy*. As we described in Chapter 1, the transitory fantasy was more often found in girls, was usually spontaneously modified, or easily gave way to interpretation, whereas the fixed fantasy became the permanent focus of the child's psychosexual life and was often impervious to years of interpretive work. In this chapter we use the development of the fixed beating fantasy as a model to explicate aspects of the developmental line of masochism.

We use data from the cases of eleven children with beating fantasies as a framework. Further material from infant and toddler observation and from the psychoanalyses of children, adolescents, and adults is included. We delineate the epigenesis of masochism as an *adaptation* to a disturbed environment, a *defense* against aggression, and a *mode of instinctual gratification*. Further, we show that masochism is not only overdetermined but serves other ego functions.

INFANCY

The literature on masochism includes many controversies; one major issue devolves on the genesis of masochism in the preoedipal or oedipal stages. In the previous chapter we described material from child analyses and observations that showed that organized beating fantasies were formed only postoedipally, while the determinants could be traced to earlier phases. The beating wish, sadistic intercourse theory, and phallic beating games could be seen in some form in all the young children. The transitory beating fantasy seen in some girls arose postoedipally and represented, as Freud had described, both regressed oedipal strivings and punishment for them. In each instance, the dynamics followed the classical formulation of oedipal conflicts leading to regression to anal-phase fixations around aggression and the beating wish.

In contrast, the preoedipal determinants of masochistic behavior in those children with fixed beating fantasies derived from disturbances in the earliest months of their lives.

Mark, who entered analysis at 8½ years of age, was later found to have a fixed beating fantasy. He was the second of two children. His mother described her "obsessive concern" during pregnancy with the older child's potential jealousy. Her concern intensified after Mark's birth to the point where she felt compelled to interrupt any ministrations to Mark, including feeding, whenever she thought of her first child. She described Mark's first year as extremely unhappy, the feeding as totally unsatisfactory, and Mark as a fussy, crying baby. Like other mothers in the sample, she described herself as depressed and preoccupied, unable to take any pleasure in her baby.

Such descriptions of a mutual lack of pleasure on the part of both mother and baby were universal in the fixed beating fantasy sample and have recurred in all our subsequent cases of masochistic pathology where social history data have been available.

This finding contrasts strikingly with the histories of the children who were found to have a transitory beating fantasy. In that group, despite reports of various pathological interactions early in the child's life, there were nevertheless sources of available pleasure for both partners in the mother–child dyad.

Emma's mother, for instance, said that she started her 3-week-old infant on solids and she continued a pattern of premature demands throughout infancy. Emma's precocious positive responses, however, provided intense gratification for her mother, which was returned to the child as loving praise and pleasure. Derivatives of this mutually pleasurable interaction may have formed a component in the transference relationship of pleasant working together which Emma was able to enjoy in her analysis at age 4.

While we should be extremely cautious in attributing later manifestations directly to experiences of early infancy, it is important to note the unanimous report of the therapists of the children with fixed beating fantasies that the treatments were arduous, joyless, and ungratifying for a long time.

Disturbances in the pleasure economy between mother and infant appeared in the histories of all the children with fixed beating fantasies, and were recreated in more specific forms in the transference relationship during analysis. Clinical material from child analyses suggests the links forged in very early life between the experience of lack of pleasure or unpleasure and the age-appropriate developmental needs of the infant. But in the transference relationships of adult patients the multitude of transformations which take place in the course of development to adulthood make discernment of the deviations of early infancy very complicated.

Mrs. S., a tall, attractive divorcée, sought analysis to deal with issues of unresolved mourning for her father. Although outwardly very successful, she was finding it increasingly difficult to reconcile the demands of her profession with the needs of her three children and her own social life. Early in the analysis, Mrs. S. described a beating fantasy which she used in order to achieve orgasm. In the fantasy she imagined her father telling her that she was bad, putting her across his knee, and spanking her. She only became conscious of the fantasy just before orgasm, and then habitually forgot it. The fantasy surfaced in treatment in the context of sexualized pleasure in the joint analytic work, which was accompanied by pains in her lower back. After the interpretation that the pains seemed to be the condition under which she could experience pleasure, Mrs. S. remembered her beating fantasy and realized that she had "always" had it.

Subsequent material centered on her overstimulating relationship with her father and her unresolved oedipal conflicts and neurotic compromises. After these were worked through in the transference, successful mourning could be accomplished. After two years of work, when her presenting symptoms had abated and she was functioning apparently well in all areas, Mrs. S. wanted to finish her treatment. Despite the many positive changes, the analyst disagreed, because the beating fantasy was still central to Mrs. S.'s sexual life. She had strenuously resisted all attempts to relate any analytic material to her relationship with her mother, particularly in the transference.

During the course of her analysis, Mrs. S. had visibly gained weight and the analyst interpreted this as self-feeding to defend against her wishes and fears over reexperiencing the maternal relationship in the transference. Mrs. S. responded with stories about her childhood hitherto unreported because she considered them "irrelevant." She had been told by her mother that she had been a "poor feeder" from birth, had difficulty sucking, and had not gained weight for the first four months of her life. This history of her own failure-to-thrive had later been repeated when Mrs. S. became a mother and found the relationship with her own infant daughter unsatisfying and tense, with the outcome that Mrs. S.'s daughter was diagnosed failure-to-thrive at four months. Work on this previously omitted material revitalized the analysis, and the vicissitudes of her early painful relationship to her mother emerged in the transference and were understood as the first layer in the formation of masochistic relationships.

Reconstruction of the early mother–child relationship from analytic data can always benefit from corroborative evidence, so we will examine here some material from infant observation which pertains to pleasure and pain in infancy. From very early in life, the infant can differentiate among others via a wide range of perceptual modalities. Included in these capacities is the ability to differentiate between self and nonself at the body boundary of the skin. This takes place at the point where the skins of mother and child touch and are felt as separate, contiguous entities. Under normal circumstances, stimulation of infants occurs through multiple channels; but in a disturbed mother–child relationship, a reduction in possible channels occurs. One that may remain is skin contact, since this is not dependent on psychological or emotional synchrony, as are, for instance, eye contact, talking, or smiling.

We have been following the development of two infants who became hair-pullers. It appears that the development of this pain-seeking symptom represents an adaptation to a disturbed mother–child relationship. Both children were born to single adolescent mothers; both children were diagnosed failure-to-thrive at 4 months, when the mothers each went through a period of depression and withdrawal from the babies. While the etiology of failure-to-thrive is complicated and varied, some clear factors emerge from detailed observations, films, and interviews.[1]

---

1. These cases were selected from an ongoing study of adolescent mothers and their babies. We are grateful to the other members of the study group, Drs. B. Kay and Linn Campbell, Connie Silver, A.M.L.S., and Donald Silver, M.D.; the views presented here are our own and do not necessarily represent those of the group.

In films of feeding before 4 months, Nicole attempted to engage her mother in social interactions between bites. After each bite, Nicole's mother literally scraped the smile off Nicole's face with the spoon, until the sixth bite was followed by a frown. This is a good example of what Tronick and Gianino (1986) have called the failure to repair a mismatch between mother and baby. In our observations we could see the next step, in which the mother externalized her feelings of failure onto the baby: the mother then made clear that she found Nicole an unpleasant girl. Soon thereafter the mother's depression coincided with Nicole's failure-to-thrive.

Through the intervention of staff at the institution where they lived, useful feeding was reestablished and Nicole gained weight. But the effect of the sustained experience of dissynchrony persisted. Tronick and Gianino have found that infants of depressed mothers decrease their engagement with people and things and deploy more coping behaviors aimed at maintaining self-regulation. The child moves away from signaling the mother to self-comfort, such as rocking, withdrawal, or aversion. Nicole began to pull her hair, tweaking and twiddling it until it broke, just at the back top quarter of her head, the spot where her head rested in the crook of mother's arm, the one remaining point of contact with mother. For many months the spot was nearly bald; at 2½ years Nicole's hair was noticeably shorter and ragged at the same place. Despite excellent progress in both mother and child, this symptom persisted, appearing at moments when, for example, the nursery teacher failed to answer Nicole's question.

The hair-pulling in Nicole and the other infant is an example of pain-seeking as an adaptation to a pathological situation. Pain-seeking behavior represents an attempt to substitute for the withdrawal of cathexis by the mother. In Nicole the need for the object overrides the need for pleasure. For the children with beating fantasies or for the hair-pullers, safety resides in an object that `induces pain rather than pleasure. These are mothers who, for a variety of reasons, cannot pay attention to their children's needs. In our sample of children with beating fantasies we found a preponderance of mothers who were unable to absorb (Orgel 1974) or contain the infant's helplessness, neediness, and rage, but blamed the child and externalized their own infantile affective states. Tronick and Gianino make the point that successful joint repair of mismatches by mother and child is experienced by the child as "effectance," and this may be what Winnicott (1953) and others have called the child's normal phase of omnipotence. Winnicott suggested that a child needs a long enough stage of normal omnipotence before it can be relinquished. It is possible that extended periods of discomfort and dissatisfaction experienced in infancy by all the children with beating fantasies may have disrupted their normal stage of omnipotence prematurely. These children may have become aware too soon of their dependence on their mothers and felt deeply their inability to exert any control over the social realm. They turn to pathological solutions as an adaptation to this dilemma, as did the 11-month-old described by Loewenstein (1957) to illustrate his "proto-masochistic" maneuver of "seduction of the aggressor."

The type of intervention with both mothers and infants described by Brinich (1984) and by Peter Blos, Jr. (1985) in his discussion of intergenerational pathology could correct this pattern; however, in our sample, it appeared that the mothers themselves experienced such difficulty in relation to activity, dependency needs, and feelings of helplessness that they attempted to resolve them by externalization of these hated, devalued parts of themselves onto their children. Abel's mother was cold and irritable, withdrawn emotionally from her crying baby whom she saw as a pathetically helpless child. Eric's mother denied her own feelings of castration and passivity by externalizing these aspects of her self representation onto all her male objects: thus her husband and her infant Eric were seen as damaged, hopeless, useless people.

Rather than a relationship based on the sensitive mutual repair of inevitable moments of mismatch, the infants who later
developed masochistic pathology grew up in a milieu of painful
externalizations. We could speculate that externalization of blame,
failure, and devalued aspects of the self onto the child served as
a major and early mode of relationship and may have become
the "primary fault" (Balint 1968) leading to the evolution of
masochistic structures. We suggest that the first layer of masochism must be sought in early infancy, in the child's adaptation to
a situation where safety resides only in a painful relationship with
the mother. Glenn (1984) too found the roots of his patient's
masochism in the relationship to a "parent associated with pain"
(p. 72). Valenstein's description of "individuals whose attachment to pain signifies an original attachment to painfully perceived objects" (1973, p. 389) applies also to the patients in our
1972 sample (discussed in Chapter 1) and to those we have seen
subsequently. Their beating fantasies encapsulated and perpetuated the painful relationship to the object, not only historically,
but also in their clinging to unhappiness through all stages of
treatment.

Mark, whose early history was referred to above, was typical
of the group of children with fixed beating fantasies in our 1972
sample. His beating fantasy appeared against a background of
severe pathology. He was referred for frequent tantrums, periods of overwhelming anxiety, multiple fears, and being bullied at school. Once he overcame his initial anxiety, he presented a picture of chaotic drive development with little or no
phase dominance. Impulses from all libidinal levels coexisted:
his anxieties were often oral in form, with fears of being poi-
soned or eaten; he said, "in intercourse the lady eats the man."
Anal sexuality was manifest in excited preoccupation with feces,
bottoms, and nose-picking. Mark, like the other children in
the sample, was of superior intelligence and functioned adequately in school. In treatment, however, it soon became

clear that his reality perception was distorted in relation to self and object representations. Mark, a slender boy in treatment with a plump woman, complained of being fat. His feelings about himself fluctuated between grandiose delusions of omnipotence and a sense of abject worthlessness.

As with the other children in the sample, the first two years of Mark's treatment were marked by immediate discharge of wishes into action. His analyst said, "His behavior was wild and uncontrolled and there were long periods when I could make no contact with him. He would, for example, charge into the room with a pellet gun, shout, 'All right: I'm going to kill you!' and fire the pellets at me. One moment he would be lying on the table, licking his snot, telling me he has no friends and the next moment he would shout at me, 'You fat pig, you'll die for this!'" As words could increasingly be linked to feelings and the range of affects broadened to include pleasure, Mark said, "When I'm feeling good, I feel all alone; when I'm feeling bad, I'm with my mother."

The need for pain seems to be at the core of the personalities of these patients; it arises early in life, whether from environmental causes or constitutional factors, as some have proposed (Olinick 1964), persists throughout development, and can be seen to be at work even in the end phase of analysis.

Mary was an 18-year-old referred after a suicide attempt. We will meet her many times throughout this volume, as aspects of her development, pathology, and treatment have immeasurably enriched our understanding of work with sadomasochistic problems. Different segments of her history and analytic material are salient to topics addressed in various chapters; sometimes the same piece of material is helpful seen from a different perspective, although we have tried not to impose too much repetition.

At the end of Mary's first year of analysis the analyst described her as totally dependent on her mother, spending weekends and every evening in her room, sitting silently at meals; other than studying, her only activity was rearranging furniture in her room, or spending hours trying to decide which side of the desk to put her pencils on. She was physically inhibited and looked like a prepubertal boy. At the time, the major concern was that she would become psychotic or kill herself.

After six years of analysis, she had graduated from the university with highest honors and had a full scholarship to graduate school, where she was doing outstanding work. She looked very feminine and attractive, had many friends, and had a long-standing relationship with a very suitable young man. They had arranged to share an apartment and were planning marriage. She had confronted her parents numerous times and had forced a change in the relationship, which they enjoyed. Things were going well on all fronts, the end of analysis was in sight, and only one problem remained. The overt manifestation of the problem was Mary's continued difficulty in maintaining pleasurable feelings, especially with the analyst. As the suicide risk had receded, it had become apparent that Mary's primary pathology was not depression but an underlying severe masochistic disorder that subsumed both her depression and suicidal behavior. It became clear that her suicide attempt was an enactment of a fixed beating fantasy. As the determinants of Mary's underlying masochism were worked through, she could experience and maintain pleasure for longer periods of time outside of her therapy. She could feel pride and joy in her skills and competence and take pleasure in her attractiveness and in sexual activities. The conflicts around pleasure became centered almost entirely in the analysis. She would feel happy, proud of some achievement, until she walked in the door and then would feel gloomy and bad. Mary explained her need to feel unhappy with the analyst: "When I'm happy I feel I'm not with you"; "To be unhappy is to be like you, to be with you, to sit quietly and depressed with the whole world right here in this room"; "I tell you about something funny that happened in class and then I think, oh, you should have been there, and I realize you weren't there and I feel sad and lonely"; "I sometimes think of my suicide as the best time. Everyone was with me, and loved me, and felt sorry for me."

Throughout this chapter, we will be examining the transformations through development of the child's involvement with pain, but what we are describing at the earliest level is a learned association. The clinical material of our masochistic patients supports Stern's (1985) view, based on infant observation, that "it is the actual shape of interpersonal reality, specified by the interpersonal invariants that really exist, that helps determine the developmental course. Coping operations occur as reality-based adaptations" (p. 255). As Mary said, "Feeling bad is something I know; it's safe; it's the smell of home."

Tronick and Gianino demonstrated the stability of the child's early coping styles, and Escalona (1968) has shown that it is maladaptive infant behavior which tends to persist. Thus the association of mother and unpleasure leads to the early adoption of an autoplastic, rather than alloplastic, mode of dealing with internal and external stimuli, which sets a pattern of discharge via the self which will affect all later developmental phases.

TODDLERHOOD

From the perspective of masochistic pathology, the toddler stage is crucial in determining the quality of aggressive impulses and in fixing the pattern of dealing with them. The normal developmental tasks, activities, and wishes of toddlerhood provide an opportunity to establish constructive defenses; a sound sense of self accompanied by feelings of effectance, joy, and safety; a loving relationship to constant objects; and an exponential expansion of ego control of motility and cognition. All of these are

dependent on adequate drive fusion. In discussions of masochism, the concepts of fusion, libidinization, and binding are often
used interchangeably, even by Freud. We feel it is important to
differentiate them, as fusion denotes transformation of both drives
by a mixture in which aggression is neutralized to some degree
by libido, with resultant energy available for other purposes, such
as defense formation or sublimation. Libidinization occurs in the
formation of masochistic pathology, when aggressive impulses or
painful experiences become sexualized; no transformation of
either drive occurs. Binding is the structural inhibition of direct
discharge. A striking feature of all the children with fixed beating fantasies was the extent of primitive aggressive behavior,
apparently unfused by libido.

Throughout the first year of his analysis, Mark threw the toys
all over the room, down the stairs, or out of the window. He
would write on the wall, try to force open the files and lock-
ers, and generally try to destroy the room. His uncontrolled
behavior provoked the therapist to restrain him, which led to
bitter accusations of attack. His mental world seemed dominated by fantasies of attack and counterattack, as he filled his
sessions with complaints of being picked on by teachers, peers,
his brother, and his parents.

Mary presented with alternating states of blank silence and
overwhelming experiences of omnipotent rage. Her fantasies
were characterized by primary process organization and her
dreams were dominated by images of uncontrolled, explosive
destruction. For example, the central image in one dream was
of stabbing a man over and over until he was reduced to a
mound of indistinguishable flesh and blood. In a later dream,
a room full of babies was shotgunned to the point of indiscrimi-
nate mess. Later in her analysis, when Mary became able to
associate to these dreams, a repeated latent theme was anal
explosiveness that would destroy her mother, who in reality

had spent an inordinate amount of time scrubbing the bathrooms.

As Furman (1985) emphasized, the mother as auxiliary ego protects the child from excessive libidinal and aggressive stimulation. Our data confirm the findings of others (Brinich 1984, Orgel 1974, Rubinfine 1965) that mothers of masochists seem less than normally able to contain their children's aggression and thus promote fusion. The result for the children is unfused, primitive, omnipotent aggression. Rather than containing and modifying the children's impulses and anxieties with the help of their own libidinal investment, each mother in the beating fantasy sample intensified the child's aggression by bodily intrusiveness, constraint of normal moves toward independence and autonomy, and interference with pleasure in messing and exploration.

Further, the mothers' own conflicts over instinctual impulses were dealt with by externalization onto the children. With Mary's mother this was a lifelong process, which continued even throughout Mary's treatment.

For instance, Mary's mother insisted that family members and guests always enter through the back door and remove their shoes to protect the pale carpeting from any dirt they might bring in. She cleaned constantly, reproaching others for their dirtiness and mess. Once Mary "forgot" to remove her shoes and was overwhelmed with feelings of shame, which were linked via associations to having soiled her pants as a young child. During the intake interview following Mary's suicide attempt, her mother's sole complaint was that Mary had accompanied a group of girls four years earlier as they threw eggs at an abandoned house. Despite the passage of time and the intervening near death of her child, Mary's "vandalism," as she termed it, was the focus of her attention. In analysis, Mary recounted her continuing feeling of badness over the incident and her persistent fear that the police would still come after her.

Mrs. S.'s mother had a history of flamboyant sexual relationships with men who were unacceptable to her own family. Mrs. S. reported that, as a child, she masturbated openly. Though she had no recollection of her mother's reaction at the time, she described her mother's current practice of giving friends laughing accounts of Mrs. S.'s "extreme uncontrollable childhood sexuality." From early adolescence, Mrs. S. was promiscuous, imperiling herself with sexual exploits, which she recounted to her mother. In analysis, it became clear that Mrs. S.'s sexual behavior in childhood and adulthood represented an internalization of her mother's lack of control of impulses; the result was that Mrs. S. hated herself and contemplated suicide.

Mary and Mrs. S., like the children with fixed beating fantasies, already had a proclivity developed in infancy toward autoplastic solutions to stress. It is in the toddler phase that the earlier use of the self to restore homeostasis joins with the mother's externalizations to create the mechanism of turning aggression against the self.

We found that all of the children in our sample dealt with their aggression by denying any sign of hostility between themselves and their mothers and struggled to maintain an idealized image of mother as loving and perfect. This included denial of the mother's castration, which Bak (1968) considered an important factor in perversions. Refusal to face imperfections in the mother was linked to omnipotence of thought, as mother's failings were attributed to the boy's own aggression.

Mark felt that his penis was not his own; if his mother did not have one, it must be because he had stolen it from her. He felt his own defecation was a dangerous aggressive act (a result of his own wishes and his mother's attitude), and insisted that his mother could not do anything so terrible as defecate—he must be the only one in the world, and the worst person of all, to do so.

We see the defensive aspect of the underlying masochism expressed in the beating fantasy as following upon and reinforcing the child's prior submission to a threatening environment. What was initially an acceptance of the mother's externalizations (messy, dependent, aggressive) in the service of retaining the object becomes an active internalization used by the child to maintain the image of a loving, protective, perfect mother, safe from the destructive rage of his anal sadism. From the point of view of defense, the masochism can be seen as an attempt to defend against destructive wishes from each level of development, directed against the mother, utilizing the mechanisms of denial, displacement, internalization, and, via the internalization, turning of aggression against the body.

The operation of all these defenses can be seen in the form of the later beating fantasy. All the beating fantasies contained, implicitly in that they involved punishment or explicitly, the statement, "I am a naughty boy." Mark imagined that his strict paternal aunt entered the room; he took off his clothes, said, "I am a naughty boy," and then she spanked him. Despite the evidence from the boys' material which demonstrated that their mothers were experienced as threatening objects, and the fact that the mothers were often the punishers in real life, the beater in the fantasies was usually the father or a father representative. Here we see a displacement of aggression from the more frightening, but more important, primary object to the father.

In reporting the beating fantasy the children usually stopped at the point where they had been beaten as if that were the end, but further work revealed that the main goal of the fantasy was to force the object to meet the preoedipal, libidinal, and narcissistic needs of the patient—hence the reluctance of the children to disclose it. Analyses of adolescents who have attempted suicide show that the fantasied response by the object is crucial to the goals of the suicide (see Chapter 8). Mary imagined that, after her suicide, she would hover around to see how sorry everyone was, how they would feel guilty and turn their full attention to her to gratify all her wishes. The defensive efforts to rid the mother–child relationship of omnipotent aggression by means of displacement and turning aggression against the self are the child's contribution to the joint attempt to create a "purified pleasure dyad" (see Chapter 12).

The mothers of children who created a beating fantasy were psychologically intrusive, via their externalizations. Through hypercathexis of their children's bodies well into prepuberty or adolescence, for active gratification of their own needs, they were also physically intrusive. Anna Freud (1960) commented on the increased impact of parental disturbance when the pathology is not contained in thought but moves into the realm of activity.

> For example, one mother constantly checked the child's anus and feces for signs of worms. Mark's mother wiped his bottom until he was 11 years old; she stopped only after three years of analytic work with Mark enabled him to resist her intrusion into the bathroom.

> In her analysis, Mary occasionally displayed a cognitive uncertainty that contrasted markedly with her high intelligence. Work on these states allowed for recovery of a memory of a voice asking, "Are you sure?" This phrase became a pointer to her symptomatic uncertainty at many levels, but specific associations led to the reconstruction of her mother's handling of her toilet training. Mary experienced a confirming shock of recognition when she saw her mother constantly asking her toddler grandchild if she had to go to the bathroom. When the child said "No," Mary's mother said "Are you sure?" and then peeked into the grandchild's diaper while remarking to Mary, "You have to make sure."

In normal development, the self representation emerges out of and contains the body representation. This integration starts with the experience of pleasure in one's body at the hands of a loving object. The children with beating fantasies were unable to achieve integration of body and self. They experienced their bodies as owned and controlled by their mothers, and so preoedipal omnipotent aggression toward mother was defended against and expressed by attacks on the body.

> Mrs. S. was always ashamed of her breasts and had such antipathy to this part of her body that she was unable to breastfeed her children. When this was explored in analysis, there seemed no reality basis for her negative feelings, as her breast development had been normal in all respects. Later in analysis, it emerged through dreams and associations that Mrs. S. did not feel that her breasts belonged to her. Her lack of pride in her own body and her inability to feed her own children was her way of expressing her rage and disappointment at her own mother's inability to breastfeed her.

Autoaggressive behavior in infants as reported by Cain (1961) and the study of suicide cases confirm this finding (see Chapter 8).

A further effect of the intrusive pattern of interaction is the hypercathexis in the child of the receptive mode. This touches upon a major conceptual puzzle—the relation of masochism and passivity. Maleson (1984) notes that many analysts continue to equate the two, as Freud did originally. It might be helpful to distinguish between passivity and receptivity. We see passivity as an ego quality linked in its pathological extreme manifestations to the experience of an inattentive caretaker. An adolescent boy who had suffered from infancy from parental inability to sustain attention to his needs and feelings showed no signs of masochistic pathology, yet demonstrated extreme passivity in all areas of his life. Masochists are highly receptive and are ready to take in any stimuli from the outside world, ranging from subtle shifts in mother's moods to what one homosexual patient described as his wish for a "fist–fuck." Masochists are very active in their pursuit of pain and failure, in part to maintain the receptive relationship with an intrusive object. For example, Mary at 19 endured taunts because she wore her hair cut so short that she looked like a schoolboy; she revealed after years of analysis that she went to her mother for her haircuts.

We have discussed the ways in which the toddler's aggression is intensified by failure in the mother–child relationship to promote fusion and integration. Further, the normal impulses toward separation and independent functioning that arise in the anal phase are experienced as aggression by both mother and child. The struggle for autonomy first takes place in the realm of bodily activity; the mothers of the children in our group opposed independence and reacted to normal assertion as attack. These children lost the battle for autonomy and felt that their mothers needed them only as helpless anal objects. Mother and child had become locked in an intense relationship that was experienced by the child as one in which each partner needed the other for survival and gratification. The child not only feared loss of the mother, but his guilt resided mainly in his normal wishes to separate from her and function independently. As Mark said, "Whenever I do something good without my mother, I think she is going to die." The beating in the fantasy formed later could then also be seen as a punishment for wishes to separate from the mother. In the fantasy the naughtiness for which they were beaten was usually left vague, but we have often found that the fantasy followed age-appropriate behavior, independent wishes, or achievements.

> Mark, at 14, was about to leave on a school trip and worried that his mother would be sad and upset, which she became. He hoped that he would be able to flirt with the girls, and at first he managed to talk to a girl he liked. Before the trip was actually under way, however, Mark created a fantasy that the school superintendent would cane him for flirting, and he spent the rest of the time preoccupied with this fantasy to the detriment of any of the social activities.

Although this appears very similar to punishment for an oedipal wish, the subsequent material clearly indicated that Mark's flirt-

ing represented a breaking of the object tie to his mother, and it
was for this disloyalty that he was being punished.

Similarly, other age-appropriate activities throughout development were experienced as aggressive attacks on the mother and
could be performed only under conditions that counteracted any
normal moves toward independence and separate functioning. For
example, in adolescence several of the boys, including Mark, could
not masturbate with their hands but rubbed their genitals against
the sheets leaving the mess for their mothers to see and clean
up. Instead of gratification in a private act that excluded mother,
genital impulses were discharged in a form recreating an anal
mode of relating to their mothers. The dependent receptivity
which is central to masochism and the beating fantasy can then
be seen as a defense against the aggression attributed to activity,
separation, and independent functioning.

Thus the child's pain-seeking adaptation to a pathological early
relationship continues in the anal phase as the prime mode of
attracting and retaining the object. The aggressive impulses of
the anal phase are dealt with by the defense of turning the
aggression against the self, which prevents destruction of the
object and allows for discharge of aggression toward the internalized hated mother. In our view, the adaptive and defensive motives for the masochism that underlies the beating fantasy are
preoedipal; the masochistic behavior of the child is not as yet a
sexual pleasure in itself but a means by which he attempts to
survive and gratify other passive libidinal wishes. The clinical presentation of all the children in the 1972 sample was preoedipal.
They entered treatment displaying a persistence of anal-phase ways
of functioning, with excited preoccupation with seeing, smelling,
and wiping bottoms, thoughts of defecating on people and smear-
ing. One boy of 9 years still played with and hid feces, and several of them masturbated anally. The egos of these children had
little ability to control discharge of the anal drive impulses; the
defense systems were severely impaired, with predominant, often
exclusive use of primitive defenses, such as denial and the vari-

ety of externalizations, including drive projection. Battling relationships were the norm at home, school, and in treatment. It is evident that these children carry into the phallic-oedipal phase the preexisting pathology; for this reason they will experience it very differently from the normal child. The phallic-oedipal period is crucial for the sexualization of masochism.

PHALLIC-OEDIPAL STAGE

The nature of the child's theory concerning parental intercourse has a profound effect on the development of masochism and the later beating fantasy. Sadistic intercourse theories are universal, but in normal children they coexist with other theories, whereas for the children we are discussing the notion that in intercourse the parents beat or hurt each other is the safest theory available to them. Just as being beaten represents the safest form of relating to the object in the beating fantasy, so the sadistic intercourse theory is preferred to more frightening ideas, such as chaotic uncontrollable happenings (Niederland 1958), mutual mutilation, castration, and so forth. This view is in line with Niederland's suggestion that the sadistic intercourse theory and the beating fantasy serve to structure unorganized, terrifying primal scene experiences and ideas. For these patients the primal scene is not a reconstructed hypothesis or a metaphor for the universal exclusion from parental activities but an ongoing reality, as parents of patients with masochistic pathology seem unable to protect them from repeated exposure to overwhelming experiences. Indeed, they often seem to inflict them on the patients. On the eve of a 13-year-old's entry into analysis, the parents happened to leave the bedroom door open. The boy walked in to see his parents in the act of intercourse, mother on top of father. The following day, preceding his first session, the patient broke his arm playing ball. Analysis revealed that this was but the latest in a series of events in which his mother had exposed him to traumatic situations which were invariably followed by self-injurious behavior. Furman (1984) has noted the role of parental pathology in the exposure to traumatic situations of suicidal patients.

The phallic excitement of this phase and the wish to participate in sadistic parental intercourse turn what had been a means to an end into an end in itself. To submit, to suffer, to be beaten, to be humiliated now come to represent the feminine receptive position in parental intercourse. The wish to be in this position becomes the instinctual motive for the masochism, the spur and the accompaniment to phallic masturbation. A crucial transformation occurs during this phase, when the painful experiences in the preoedipal parent–child interaction become libidinized and represent for the child participation in parental intercourse.

To the powerful motives for masochism of the earlier phases is added the circumvention of the normal oedipal exclusion, humiliation, and rage. Often the parents collude at each level in the development of the pathological relationship. Their involvement in the lack of resolution of the oedipus complex contributes to the maintenance of what we have called the "delusion of omnipotence." This ego defect is an important factor in the characteristically high level of anxiety in masochistic patients.

In the children with beating fantasies, drive material from all levels of libidinal development was available in consciousness. The children were convinced that these impulses could not be controlled by themselves or by anyone else. They felt sure that their drive aims could and would be gratified; reality contradiction did not seem to affect this conviction. Mark, at 13, was convinced that his mother wanted to have intercourse with him. One of the sources of this attitude was the absence of an adequate system of defenses, which meant that internal controls were insufficient; none of these children had reached the stage of developing a structured superego. External controls were also missing, in that the fathers of these children were all particularly unsuitable to serve as strong, protective objects for identification. Two fathers had died, two fathers had psychotic breakdowns, and two were absent in the army during their children's early years. The others seemed to play no positive role in the family, showing undue dependence on the mothers. Conversely, the mothers were all described as powerful, domineering women, who ruled their families more or less overtly.

There was also a high degree of parental collusion in the gratification of inappropriate wishes. Several of the children in this group were allowed into the parental bed until ages of 11 and 12; others were helped with toileting up to 7 or 8 years; most ruled the house with their tantrums and rages, and in two cases there was danger of the child causing serious harm to a sibling.

Mark regularly ousted his father from the parental bed, to which father's response was a depressive withdrawal. When Mark began displaying an interest in girls in adolescence, his father became acutely anxious and then announced that he was homosexual, although this apparently resulted in no action.

Throughout her childhood, as far back as she could remember, Mrs. S. spent long evenings lying on her parents' bed watching television while her father stroked her body. She reported her childhood notion that mother had relinquished father to her while keeping the other children for herself.

Rubinfine (1965) has suggested that such parents are unable to limit and contain the child's aggression, a point amply confirmed by our material.

When it was suggested to Albert's mother that firmness might help control his wild behavior, she refused on the grounds that she did not want to risk upsetting the boy. In his teens, when his father became annoyed at Albert's resentment of his claims on his wife, one solution proposed by the family was that Albert and his mother should move into a flat together, leaving the rest of the family behind.

Both the delusion of omnipotence and the libidinization of painful experience persist in the pathology of adult patients. For example, a neurotic professional woman who lived out her beating fantasy in numerous unsuitable relationships reported a dream of marrying her father. In her associations, she revealed that she still thought that she really could marry her father and that no one could stop her from fulfilling her wishes. A male graduate student with beating fantasies had undergone frequent enemas as a child. For many years in analysis he recalled the enemas with enjoyment and remembered his older sister looking on with what he imagined to be jealousy. He said he felt special because he was the only one in the family to enjoy this exclusive relationship with his mother. His wish for an enema from the analyst figured as a central transference theme; only after many years of work could he begin to acknowledge and experience the rage he felt at his mother's gross bodily intrusion. In his early adolescence his mother bought him some bright purple shorts, which he described as the token of their exclusive relationship. Only after working through his libidinization of the enemas could he also recall that he was teased by the other boys for wearing the "faggy" shorts.

TRANSITION TO LATENCY

Fantasies and anxieties about pain and suffering are universal, as is the beating wish. With some resolution of the Oedipus complex and the formation of the superego, children move into the latency period. Only at this point did a transitory beating fantasy emerge in some of the girls in our sample. When it occurred, it clearly represented both oedipal strivings in regressed form and punishment for them, as Freud described. Gradually sexual excitement and masturbation were divorced from the fantasy, and the wishes appeared in increasingly distanced forms. In our study we concluded that this transitory beating fantasy was a normal transitional component of postoedipal development in girls and may be more common than is generally supposed. Female patients who present a beating fantasy may have regressed in or out of treatment to this postoedipal moment in development. As described above in the case of Mrs. S., it is only with clinical criteria of persistence and centrality of the fantasy, as well as the quality of the transference relationship, that the differentiation between a transitory and a fixed fantasy can be made.

In contrast, those children who later developed a fixed beating fantasy had no latency period to consolidate ego development and spent those years either in the enactment of preoedipal and oedipal sadomasochistic impulses or under the restriction of crippling inhibitions and severe obsessional symptomatology. For example, a potentially intelligent and creative woman with a fixed beating fantasy who sought analysis originally because of repeated work failure reported that she stopped learning in her school years and spent her time preoccupied with fantasies of imminent destruction which she contained by ritualistic repetitions of magical phrases.

PUBERTY AND ADOLESCENCE

The emergence of the fixed fantasy in the group of disturbed boys coincided with the onset of puberty, in all cases following the first emission. Pubertal changes in general give the stamp of reality to fantasies of gratifying infantile impulses. It was only because of the structural development fostered by years of analysis that the children in our sample could develop a fantasy outlet as an alternative to action. The capacity to contain impulses in fantasy represents an achievement. Less fortunate adolescents act out their impulses in self-injurious behavior or suicide.

Our children and adults used the fixed beating fantasy for important ego and superego functions which should have developed in latency, if these patients had been able to achieve a latency phase. These functions were control of anxiety, stablilization of the "representational world" (Sandler and Rosenblatt 1962), and defense against direct drive discharge. The *transitory* beating fantasy found only in girls became progressively distanced from frightening oedipal wishes. The *fixed* beating fantasy, on the other hand, represented the most innocuous form of the wish; variations on the theme often involved more ominous fantasies of suicide, self-mutilation, and death.

Abel had fantasies of being beaten by older boys, pop singers, and football players, but also masturbated with fantasies of having his penis and testicles burned or otherwise damaged. Further masturbation fantasies involved death and suicide; indeed, in late adolescence, some years after the termination of analysis, Abel attempted suicide.

In the cases of Abel and the other boys with a fixed fantasy, we could see a diminution of anxiety when the beating fantasy was employed, whereas fantasies of death or mutilation soon became anxious preoccupations and led to feelings of overwhelming terror. One might say that in place of a fear of being destroyed or damaged, they created a pleasurable fantasy of being beaten, that is, anxiety had become libidinized.

In the early phases of treatment of these children, it was often unclear who was standing for whom in the constant flux of externalizations, internalizations, and confusions with the object. In a brief sequence a child could become both the powerful attacking object and the victim of the attack. In the beating fantasy, however, there was a clear differentiation maintained between self and object. The subject was always the victim and the beater was invariably a person who figured in the child's real life, often the father or someone drawn from the class of father representatives. These characteristics may be seen in one boy's fantasy of being held down by two older boys from school and beaten on the buttocks. For the next two years, the fantasy remained basically

unchanged, unlike the constantly elaborated imaginative productions of children with transitory beating fantasies, in which the
characters were drawn from anywhere but real life. We would
suggest that formation of the fixed fantasy not only required a
modicum of stability of representations, but also seemed of itself
to contribute to maintaining stability in the usual chaos of the
representational world of these children.

Despite positive changes in these cases the "delusion of omnipotence" seemed unaltered. After six years of treatment Mark
remained convinced that his death wishes would destroy the
object. The work of Lamb (1976), Abelin (1980, 1985), and others has underscored the importance of the father in the preoedipal
development of the child. Through each stage in the development
of the children in the fixed beating fantasy sample, the fathers
failed to perform their necessary functions. As R. Furman (1986)
so clearly describes, the father's initial role is to protect and support the primacy of the mother–child relationship. Mark's father
reacted to his wife's pregnancy with intense jealousy, confirming
the mother's pathological fantasies about the effect of the new
baby on the other family members. Mary's father retreated into a
busy professional life during the pregnancy and her first year,
emerging periodically only to criticize mother's handling of the
baby. During the toddler phase, Furman describes the importance
of the father as a source of additional love for the child and support for the adult ego of the mother.

Mark's father was as messy and uncontrolled as his toddler son;
rather than taking pride in and fostering Mark's emerging
autonomy, he joined with his wife in externalizations of the
devalued anal aspects of his personality. By the time Mark
reached puberty and his analysis had helped him to approach
the possibility of oedipal-level impulses, he had no loving,
consistent parental relationship to draw on as an internal resource in his struggle to control his incestuous wishes. After
each achievement, which he experienced as an aggressive at-

tack on the object, he immediately had to find out whether the analyst was still alive.

It is in relation to this "delusion of omnipotence," the continuing lack of internal and external controls, that one of the important functions of the beating fantasy could be seen. From the material of these children, the timing of the emergence of the fantasy, and the content of the fantasy, it was evident that the beater in the fantasy represented a wished-for ideal father, a strong male who would limit and control the fulfillment of omnipotent libidinal and destructive wishes. The fathers of all these patients were particularly unsuitable to serve as strong, protective objects for identification. In the fantasy the beater was a father or father representative who was always a powerful, assertive figure punishing the child, often to stop him from gratifying a forbidden wish. Mark's fantasy was of attempting to go to bed with a middle-aged woman visitor, but before he could do so, his father stopped him, held him down and beat him. In reality his father was a passive, ineffectual man who did not stop him from entering his mother's bed whenever he wanted to. Thus instead of internalizing a representation of a strong father, to build a superego and defend against unacceptable impulses by means of age-adequate mechanisms such as repression, reaction formation, displacement, and especially sublimation, these children used the beating fantasy to control and limit drive discharge and gratification of omnipotent wishes. The fixed beating fantasy functioned in place of a superego, which would normally be formed in latency.

We have seen a similar outcome, arrived at by a different path, in the females with fixed beating fantasies. The fathers of the girls continued and intensified their denigration of the mothers and actively involved themselves in overstimulating relationships with their daughters from the oedipal phase on, with the result that a component in the masochistic pathology of the females was intense bisexual conflict and severe penis envy. The girls, like the boys, were unable to internalize an autonomous superego. In addition, the denigrated mother was not used as a feminine ego ideal. Mary entered treatment looking like a boy and declared her three vows—not to have a boyfriend, not to marry, and not to have children.

TECHNICAL IMPLICATIONS

Freud wrote to Jung in 1909, "In my practice, I am chiefly concerned with the problem of repressed sadism in my patients; I regard it as the most frequent cause of the failure of therapy. Revenge against the doctor combined with self-punishment. In general, sadism is becoming more and more important to me" (cited in Bergmann and Hartman 1976, p. 33). In his last work, Freud still comments that we are "specially inadequate" (1940, p. 180) in dealing with masochistic patients. We may note that the Wolf Man had a fixed beating fantasy and would have qualified for inclusion in our sample (Blum 1974).

All of the children with fixed beating fantasies had many years of analysis. The change in the overt behavior and functioning of some was quite remarkable. Obvious manifestations of sado-masochistic relationships with peers or adults disappeared; they seemed to be coping well and even functioning quite independently. Frequently it was near termination that the child would first hint at and then disclose the existence of a beating fantasy. Analysis had fostered the development of certain ego functions, especially those necessary for the use of fantasy as a discharge channel, and had addressed some of the preoedipal determinants of the masochism. The formation of a beating fantasy at puberty was achieved on the basis of these gains. However, on follow-up, we found that some of these boys suffered psychotic breakdown in later adolescence, some attempted suicide, and others remained tied in a submissive, dependent relationship with an overpowering mother. Our findings on the various determinants of the fixed beating fantasy and the multiple ego functions it served suggest certain technical approaches that may improve the outcome of these cases.

For example, the fact that the beating fantasy served in lieu of important ego functions suggests that interpretation of the drive determinants will not be effective until concomitant work has been done on the ego pathology. Specifically, focus on the "delusion of omnipotence" would be important; if the patient could internalize and experience a capacity for controlling drive discharge, the necessity for a masochistic fantasy might diminish. Work could then turn to the determinants of the underlying masochism with special attention directed at the three aspects emphasized in this paper—the adaptive, defensive, and instinctual motives. The patient's masochistic behavior and fantasies would then be seen as a threefold attempt to (1) maintain a preoedipal object tie to his mother, (2) defend the object against his destructive wishes, and (3) participate in a sadomasochistic sexual relationship.

As noted earlier, Mark's mother reacted with increasing distress and ultimately depression to his adolescent moves towards separation. Extensive analysis of his omnipotent aggressive fantasies was not sufficient to help Mark separate from his mother without work on his denial of the reality of her pre-existing problems around being left. When he saw her intense reaction to his brother's departure for college, he could not avoid recognizing her own hostile need to control those around her. The work could then return to his wishes to invite her control, thereby maintaining the narcissistically gratifying illusion that his mother clung to him out of love.

During the first two years of Mary's analysis, when she was 18 to 20 years old, she was completely dependent on her mother. During this time much of the work focused on Mary's hurt and rage and her many ways of defending against the experience or expression of anger at her mother. The subsequent shift in her defense system, especially the infantile dependence,

enabled her to become more active and self-sufficient. After
an extended period of work, Mary managed to confront her
mother over her intrusive behavior. Mother reacted by crying,
and running away for several hours. Mary eventually moved
to her own apartment and, when she first returned home for
a weekend visit, her mother retreated to the attic and refused
to come down to greet Mary. The accumulation of such incidents breached Mary's denial and she began to talk more in
sessions about mother's "weirdness." When she turned to her
father for reality confirmation, he did not validate her perceptions and support her healthy ego growth, but rather told her
they must be involved in "some mother–daughter game." At that
point she realized that the whole family had colluded for years
to cover up mother's pathology. Mary moved then into a period
of pleasure in her independent activity; she talked of "building
a wall" between her and her mother, so that she could assign
feelings to the appropriate person. She had earlier described her
terror during electrical storms, but during this phase of treatment Mary realized that it was not she, but her mother who was
so terrified. Mary herself actually enjoyed watching the lightning.
Once this distinction had been made, it was much easier to work
on Mary's contribution to the persisting infantile tie.

The ongoing preoedipal tie is the greatest stumbling block to
progress. In order to break the tie the patient will have to become aware not only of his internal conflicts but also of his
mother's pathology, especially her hostile opposition to progressive development. He will not only have to face his own destructive wishes but also relinquish his denial of his mother's hostility
toward independence. Unless the preoedipal tie between mother
and child can be broken, little change in the patient's underlying
disturbance can be expected.

Work on the underlying motives must be accompanied by work
on ego pathology, such as the persistence of omnipotent thinking and the inability to fuse drive impulses.

For some time during the fourth year of Mary's analysis, material emerged that demonstrated the many ways she worked to maintain the delusion of the power of her wishes. If something she had wished for did not occur, she convinced herself that she had not wished her hardest. Habitually, on reaching the corner of the street, she looked at the stoplight, willing it to change color; when of course it did, she experienced a feeling of exultation in her power. This work prepared the way for material to emerge regarding another determinant of her experienced omnipotence. This was the lack of fusion of her aggressive impulses, which left them free to rage unchecked. Thus, any angry feeling in thought, fantasy, or dream instantaneously led to total bloody annihilation. For many years her dreams were filled with images of mutilation, horrible death, and destruction. After her love for her younger brother was acknowledged, she dreamed about a baby, which led to a fantasy of saying to her angry baby, "It's all right, I still love you."

In hindsight, looking at the timing of the emergence of the beating fantasy in the child sample and the follow-up data, it becomes apparent that some of the cases in the original group were terminated prematurely. The very achievements that contributed to the capacity for fantasy formation obscured the continued operation of masochistic pathology encapsulated in the beating fantasy. This attempt at a solution to needs from all levels of development could not stand up to the internal and external demands of life. Thus, indications for termination should be carefully scrutinized in these patients.

CONCLUSIONS

In elucidating a developmental line of masochism we have been working toward a definition of the term. Valenstein (Panel 1981) noted that a discussion of masochism can easily "be obscured in a sea of words" (p. 674). Grossman (1986) surveyed the history of the concept and concluded that the term has only a restricted application. Maleson (1984) presents a broad definitional possibility which accepts existing usage and refers to all behavior, thoughts, fantasies, and symptoms or syndromes characterized by subjectively experienced pain or suffering which seems unnecessary, excessive, or self-induced. Unfortunately, this definition demands a judgment as to what is unnecessary or excessive pain. It also leads to the view that the choice of any experience or activity that may include pain, such as childbirth or self-sacrifice, is necessarily masochistic. We do not find any necessary relationship between feminine functions and masochism.

In addition to being too inclusive, this definition ignores the significant difference between a normal and a masochistic relationship to pain. For adaptive growth, a child must learn to tolerate pain within a certain range. Paradoxically, masochists who actively seek painful and humiliating experiences find ordinary levels of real pain intolerable.

But Maleson also suggests a narrow definition which would confine the label to states of physical or mental suffering in which a clear linkage to sexual, genital excitement is demonstrable. The experience of pain or suffering does not in itself warrant a conclusion that the behavior is masochistic, nor does the existence of genital excitement. We think it is possible, based on the work we have described here, to come to a more satisfactory definition. Masochism is the active pursuit of psychic or physical pain, suffering, or humiliation in the service of adaptation, defense, and instinctual gratification at oral, anal, and phallic levels.

Masochism is a clinical concept, and the definition requires some concrete observational referents to be of any value. We are suggesting that the data base of the definition is the transference and counter-reaction of the analytic situation. The patient's persistent search for pain or humiliation will be figured forth in the transference, often in subtle responses to interpretations. The counter-reaction of the therapist may provide the first clue of an underlying masochistic fantasy in the patient. The therapist may feel the impulse to be sarcastic, impatient, or teasing. Less subtle reactions may take the form of being late, forgetting appointments, falling asleep, forced termination, and so forth. The epigenetic layering of masochism and its multiple functions emerge within the transference relationship, and must be dealt with in that context.

There has long been controversy over whether the determinants of masochism are preoedipal or oedipal, and whether the underlying conflicts primarily concern drive gratification or relate to maladaptive modes of coping with traumatic objects. By examining the development of beating fantasies in particular, we have tried to throw light on the determinants of masochism in general. In our view, not only are derivatives of each phase discernible in masochism, but the pain-seeking behavior which starts in infancy alters and is altered by each subsequent phase, including the oedipal and postoedipal. Postoedipally, masochistic impulses are organized as conscious or unconscious fantasies that are fixed, resistant to modification by experience or analysis, serve multiple ego functions, and take the form, although not necessarily the content, of the beating fantasy. In the fantasies the subject is an innocent victim, who achieves through suffering reunion with the object, defense against aggressive destruction and loss of the object, avoidance of narcissistic pain, and instinctual gratification by fantasy participation in the oedipal situation. Suicidal pathology, masochistic perversions, certain forms of hypochondriasis and psychosomatic illness, and moral masochism have in common an *underlying fantasy structure*. In our view, this fantasy structure is the "essence of masochism" (Freud 1919, p. 189).

3   MASOCHISM AND THE DELUSION OF OMNIPOTENCE FROM A DEVELOPMENTAL PERSPECTIVE[1]

Freud was not the first or foremost Victorian explorer of human sexuality in general or of the perversions in particular. Krafft-Ebing published his *Psychopathia Sexualis* in 1886 and much of what Freud said about sadomasochism in his essay on the sexual aberrations (1905) can be found in Krafft-Ebing. But, at the end of that essay Freud explicitly took a developmental point of view and so staked out a distinct and original perspective on the subject. The usefulness of the developmental approach is clear in the work of Loewenstein (1957) and, more recently, that of Cooper (1988), Glenn (1984), Galenson (1988), Panel (1985), Sugarman (1991), and Valenstein (1973).

We too have found it helpful to approach masochism from a developmental point of view. Using the development of the fixed beating fantasy as a model to explicate aspects of the development of masochism, we arrived at a definition that emphasized the complexity of masochistic phenomena and asserted that maso-

---

1. An earlier version of this chapter was presented at the Midwinter meeting of the American Psychoanalytic Association, New York, December 1988.

chism can be best understood as the result of a multidetermined epigenetic sequence of pain-seeking behaviors that start in infancy and result in fantasies, modeled on the beating fantasy, which serve multiple functions. Brenman (1952) and Brenner (1959) described the importance of conceptualizing masochism as having multiple determinants and functions. Brenner noted that many authors take a "one sided approach" (p. 202) to masochism and he demonstrated the technical value of the multiple view or metapsychological approach for the treatment of such disturbances. Consistently with these metapsychological views of masochism, we would not regard the multitude of approaches as evidence that masochism is an outmoded or useless concept (Grossman 1986, Maleson 1984), nor would we suggest that the many different determinants and functions proposed in the literature on masochism should be assigned to different diagnostic groups ranging in severity from normal masochism to the masochism of the psychotic, as proposed by Kernberg (1988), Simons (1987), and Maleson (in Panel 1991).

Analyses of masochistic patients are long and arduous because of the self-destructive character of the pathology and its complex roots in every phase of development. In a recent book Helen Meyers said:

> [T]he treatment of masochistic character problems has long been considered one of the more difficult analytic challenges. The fixity of masochistic trends and their self-defeating nature in life and treatment, as well as the related countertransference reactions, are major constituents of this difficulty. [1988, p. 17]

Change and growth seem harder to achieve in work with these patients, which leads us to wonder about the nature of the resistance. In our studies of masochistic patients, we have found derivatives of each phase, but, like a thread linking knots of fixation points at oral, anal, and phallic-oedipal phases, there is a delusion of omnipotence that infuses the patients' past and current functioning. We will explore the relation of the delusion of omnipotence to masochism, and suggest that omnipotence of thought and deed constitutes a major component of the resistance so prominent in masochistic patients.

Any discussion of omnipotence should begin with Ferenczi's paper "Stages in the Development of the Sense of Reality" (1913) in which, following Freud's metapsychological formulations concerning the two principles of mental functioning (1911, 1915, 1917), he said, "All children live in the happy delusion of omnipotence, which at some time or other—even if only in the womb—they really partook of" (p. 232). Ferenczi's formulation has influenced analysts from Mahler to Melanie Klein. Mahler placed the peak of omnipotence in the practicing period; she described the pain of the child's recognition in the rapprochement phase that he is not magically omnipotent, but relatively small, helpless, weak, and lonely (Mahler et al. 1975). This formulation followed Freud's view that the child is forced to acknowledge the reality of the external world by the repeated experience of disappointments, frustrations, and delays of gratification. Ferenczi referred to "this almost incurable megalomania of mankind" (p. 231), and Freud said that the dominance of the reality principle occurs only "when a child has achieved complete psychical detachment from its parent" (1915, p. 220). This seems to refer to the completion of the adolescent process, a point made by Pumpian-Mindlin (1969). Thus, the psychoanalytic view has been that the child is born feeling omnipotent and only gradually and reluctantly, under the impact of failure of the magical omnipotent system, turns to and accepts reality. Currently most psychoanalysts speak of infantile omnipotence as a state of mind characteristic of the first eighteen months of life, the period Piaget called the sensorimotor period (1952, 1954).

There is a curious discrepancy between the state of omnipotence attributed in theory to the infant and the adult clinical manifestations of fantasies of omnipotence. The happy, contented infant, safe in mother's arms and surrounded by adoring adults, is said to be in a state of infantile omnipotence, a happy delusion that he is the center of the universe with the power to make everyone meet all his needs. But when we refer to fantasies of omnipotence in our patients we do not mean such blissful daydreams; rather, these are hostile fantasies of total control over others (Kernberg 1988, Panel 1990, Panel 1991b), relentless denial of and refusal to accept reality constraints. Omnipotent fantasies are often validated by overt or covert hostile actions. Chasseguet-Smirgel presented a summary of her views on perversion at the 1988 panel on masochism and described omnipotent fantasies as "the murder of reality." She was referring, for example, to the pervert's refusal to accept generational differences and the constant need to destroy father's potency, to reduce the phallus to an anal stick, to idealize pregenitality in order to keep father's genitality repressed (Chasseguet-Smirgel 1984, 1985). Rather than the image of the secure, smiling infant referred to by Freud as "His Majesty The Baby" (1914, p. 91), the image we get from analysts describing omnipotent fantasies of adult patients is of a raging, hostile tyrant whose behavior is fueled by envy and is a compensation for feelings of helplessness and shame. Reconstructions from adult clinical material have led to speculation concerning infantile forms of omnipotence and the transformations that lead to the adult fantasy. However, there has been no systematic study of the epigenesis of omnipotence using child analytic material from the preschool years through adolescence, in addition to infant and toddler observations and clinical material from the analysis of adults.[2] Using such material we will suggest a preliminary description or working model of the epigenesis of omnipotence.

---

2. The analytic data base for our work on masochism is six of 111 indexed cases treated at the Anna Freud Centre, five further cases at the Anna Freud Center, eleven cases treated through the Centre for Research in Adolescence, and nineteen cases of children, adolescents, and adults treated privately by the authors. All of the above patients fit our definition of masochistic disorder and were treated in four or five times per week psychoanalysis.

We have found that all our masochistic patients—child, adolescent and adult—exhibited the ego defect of a pervasive delusion of omnipotence. By the time they came for treatment the unfused primitive hatred and overstimulated, excited libidinal impulses of these patients had interacted with a fragile defense system and a deficient superego to produce the delusion that only they themselves were powerful enough to inhibit their omnipotent impulses, and then only by resorting to severe masochistic measures such as killing their feelings, provoking attack, or attempting to kill themselves. Through their long analyses, with the untangling of conflicts from every stage of development, we could trace the thread of the vicissitudes of their omnipotence.

DEVELOPMENT

Common experience and the work of infant observers through the ages combine to give us a description of the contented, joyful affective dialogue of the "good enough" mother–infant pair. The "good enough" mother has available sufficient supplies of ordinary devotion to her baby, while the "good enough" infant can respond differentially from birth to the real salient features of the caretaking environment. The neonate has an inborn capacity to elicit preprogrammed empathic responses from the caretaking person. This sets in motion a complex infant–mother transactional system in which attachment is fostered by "contingent responding by the caregiver" (Demos 1985, p. 556, Silver 1985). Many factors can interfere with the establishment of such a system. Colic, physical illness, or disability in the infant, depression, anxiety, psychosis, or distraction in the mother can all disrupt pleasurable interaction between mother and child. The infancy of the severely masochistic patients we have seen was marked by significant disturbances in the pleasure economy from birth. In many cases this was first reconstructed from an extended, painful, frustrating, confusing patient–therapist interaction in which the analyst was pushed to a position of feeling hopeless, incompetent, and ineffective. This was often the first indication of a history relevant to the formation of a delusion of omnipotence.

Ordinarily, the child's real capacity to elicit the appropriate response from the caregiver is the root of feelings of competence, effectance, and reality-based positive self-esteem. The capacity of the mother–infant couple to repair inevitable breaches in the empathic tie is an equally important source of feelings of competence and positive self-regard. A range of positive feelings from contentment to joy becomes associated with these competent interactions and comes to instigate, reinforce, and signify empathic interaction. Thus pleasure is dependent on and regulated by the capacity of each partner for realistic perception and interaction with the other, which leads in turn to the experience of having an actual effect on the other. When our patients were infants, their inborn capacities to elicit needed responses were often ineffectual. All the masochistic cases were intermittently loved and cared for, but in a way which undermined confidence in their ability to evoke a response. Their wide-eyed gaze was not met by a mother's adoring, joyful look but by a blank, depressed deadness. Their mothers smiled only when they emerged from their depressed or anxious state and felt like smiling, not in response to the child's smile. The only constant in their unpredictable lives was the experience of the range of dysphoric feelings and so, as Glenn (1984) and Valenstein (1973) have noted, these patients came to associate their mothers with pain. As one patient said, "Unhappiness is the smell of home."

Under the impact of such extreme and frequent disappointment, these patients in infancy turned away from their inborn capacities to interact effectively with the real world and instead began to use the experience of helpless rage and pain magically to predict and control their chaotic experiences. The failure of reality-oriented competence to effect empathic attunement forced the child into an imaginary world where safety, attachment, and omnipotent control were magically associated with pain.

The toddler period is a time of exponential expansion of opportunities to develop and exercise skills and controls, as the child
becomes increasingly competent in regulating tension states, feeding, dressing, and protecting himself, and establishing bowel and
bladder control. Parents' capacities to channel assertive impulses
appropriately and "absorb aggression" (Furman 1985, Orgel 1974)
are crucial to the toddler's growing confidence and pleasure in
his new skills. Our masochistic patients not only entered the toddler period with little confidence in their own capacities, but
further opportunities for competent interaction were blocked and
frustrated. Because assertions were experienced and labeled by
parents as aggressive, and channels for appropriate discharge were
not made available, the frustrated child did indeed become aggressive. Attempts at effective steps toward self-reliance were
experienced by these mothers as stubborn battles for control, and
through externalizations and physical intrusiveness the children
were never allowed to be in charge of and own their bodies.

In the toddler period of the masochistic patients, aversive or
angry responses to mother's lack of empathy occasioned ever-
increasing spirals of rage, guilt, and blame so that in the end these
children were made to feel omnipotently responsible for mother's
pain, anger, helplessness, and inadequacy. The intensity of the
rage generated in both mother and child was a constant affirma-
tion of omnipotence, and, since mother was felt to own the child's
mind and body, attacks on the self became a powerful weapon
for attacking mother. The continued failure of the caretaking
person to meet the child's appropriate need for competent interactions created a feeling of intense helpless rage in the toddler,
which was defended against by omnipotent fantasies of control,
rescue, and potential destructiveness.

The child's dawning awareness that there are mysterious parental activities from which he is excluded and in which he is not
equipped to participate is a narcissistic hurt to all children. But
those children who enter the oedipal phase with positive self-
regard—based on lifelong feelings of competence from effective

interactions with the real world—are not devastated by oedipal disappointment. They have moved beyond possessive clinging to mother and are capable of pleasurable interactions with father, other adults, siblings, and peers. They enjoy and take pride in physical and cognitive activities, have begun imaginative play, and can happily amuse themselves for considerable periods of time. Their capacity to defend against and relinquish infantile wishes creates an internal distinction between repudiated baby wishes of the past and more grown up, current and future-oriented wishes of the nursery child; that is, they attain a sense of growth over time, a sense that they are on a "path of progressive development" (A. Freud 1965, 1970). With such a feeling the child can begin to delay, defer, and accept the notion that displaced oedipal wishes can be gratified in the future. In a paper on child-bearing and child rearing one of us (KKN 1988) illustrated the little girl's capacity to handle oedipal defeat and humiliation by making an adaptive shift from childbearing to child rearing wishes enacted in doll games with peers. The caretaker's capacity for empathy, and the sensitive mutual repair of and negotiations over inevitable disruptions continue and prove to be at least as important in the oedipal phase. Parents must protect the child from excessive stimulation; they set appropriate limits and impart sexual information at a time and in a form the child can assimilate. The loving respect the parents have for the child and for each other helps to modify the aggressive infantile sexual theories all children create out of their own bodily experiences. So, for normal children, oedipal failure, though painful, will not be traumatic, but will serve as a spur toward continued developmental progress.

In contrast, the masochistic patients had no cushion of self-esteem nor were there reliable adults they could turn to. These children remained exclusively and anxiously tied to their mothers, with the feeling that safety and survival depended solely on their mothers. Fathers were usually absent or too disturbed to function as alternative objects. Oedipal exclusion, which forces recognition of the real physical differences between the sexes and between children and adults, was experienced as yet another failure to evoke the wished-for response from objects and revived all the earlier failures, leaving the child in a helpless, terrified rage. Lichtenberg (1989) described the infant's "aversive response" to painful experience; in later phases the child turns from mother in anger. This flight or turning away has an inner representation as a forerunner of denial of painful reality. Denial was a major defense in our masochistic patients. It was maintained by omnipotent fantasy in which everything painful was turned into a sign of special favor, uniqueness, and magical power. Inappropriate physical handling of the child, such as frequent administration of enemas, cleaning and checking of anus and stools, bathing and washing genital areas, and sleeping with the child, all well into the school years, was transformed in fantasy into a triumphant oedipal victory, a sign of the omnipotent force of the child's demands and his power to coerce mother into gratifying any and all needs.

Concurrent information regarding parental difficulties with children, which was available to us for many of the child patients, confirmed that the parents could not set limits or refuse inappropriate demands. Rubinfine (1965) suggested that such parents are unable to limit and contain the child's aggression, a point amply confirmed by our material and consonant with the reconstructions from adult treatment by Chasseguet-Smirgel and her colleagues (1985). She wrote of the "very frequent occurrence of an attitude of seduction and complicity on the part of the mother toward her child" (1985, p. 12).

There are many complex factors that serve to intensify, libidinize, and organize masochism at the phallic-oedipal phase, but we want to emphasize here those that affect the aspect of omnipotence. Parental collusion with the child's need to deny oedipal exclusion not only confirms the feeling of omnipotent power but adds a quality to omnipotence that will become a standard by which all achievements are measured. The omnipotent oedipal triumph feels quick and effortless; henceforth any achievement that requires time and effort is devalued. The conviction that things should come easily becomes a signficant component in the formation of the ego ideal and forms a kernel of reality in the latency fantasy that there really was a time when all wishes were instantly gratified, that mother and child were really a "purified pleasure dyad" (see Chapter 12). Smith (1977) called this the "golden fantasy" and he described the various ways it could become a significant resistance to treatment.

Even the most fortunate child finds the transition into latency somewhat painful and difficult as infantile objects and wishes have to be relinquished, defenses have to be established, controls internalized, and responsibility accepted for a much wider range of activities. Latency is the time when the child can become firmly established in enjoying the endless possibilities of competent interactions in the real world. Still smarting from the oedipal defeat, the normal child will have fantasies of glory and fame to fill the gap between his real and his ideal self. Such daydreams lead the child back to competence as a source of pleasure and self-esteem. Pleasure is experienced not only in achievements but also in the exercise of those ego functions leading to achievement, that is, work becomes as pleasurable as the prize. It is through these competent interactions that the child forms sublimations, the most adaptive and gratifying defense available.

None of the masochistic patients we studied had a normal latency period, and even those with considerable achievements derived little pleasure from them. The important latency tasks of internalization of controls and sources of pleasure were not accomplished and opportunities were missed for transforming infantile wishes into acceptable sublimations. For these children, the gap was not between the real and the ideal self but between the real and the ideal mother–child relationship. Fantasies were aimed not at enhancing the real capacities of the self but at denying and transforming the pain and inadequacy of the mother–

child relationship. Unable to make use of real capacities to elicit appropriate responses from mother, these children fell back on omnipotent fantasies of control to maintain their self-esteem.

In *Totem and Taboo* (1913), Freud informed us that he adopted the term "omnipotence of thoughts" from an obsessional patient and said, "It is in obsessional neurosis that the survival of the omnipotence of thoughts is most clearly visible . . ." (p. 86). He was referring to the Rat Man (Freud 1909), and it is interesting to note that the severe outbreak of obsessionality in this patient, and in the Wolf Man (Freud 1918), occurred in the latency period. Both cases show interesting parallels with the history and symptomatology of our masochistic patients. We know that the Wolf Man had a fixed beating fantasy (Blum 1974); the Rat Man had suicidal compulsions that he barely mastered. It would be interesting to explore the connection between obsessional symptoms and masochism. One link appears to be the delusion of omnipotence, manifested during latency in our patients in primitive religiosity and related obsessional thinking. Many of the children were initially referred because of being bullied or teased, and presented as very inhibited, with a host of obsessional rituals and compulsive symptoms. The obsessionality was an attempt to defend against rage and death wishes experienced as omnipotent. In many instances the obsessionality involved a "bargain" with God, whereby, in return for keeping mother or father alive, the child promised to do something or say something in a particular, usually painful, way. Often the ritual also involved a sacrifice; in a number of cases the child made a deal with God to trade his own life, or to subtract years from his own life to keep one or both parents alive. Many of our adult masochistic patients described similar obsessionality in middle childhood. In the case of the children, these obsessional mechanisms broke down soon after the start of treatment, and they were swamped with overwhelming rages.

The apparent discrepancy between the wild behavior of the children and the relatively well-functioning or over-controlled behavior of adult masochistic patients described in the literature disappears when we examine the latency of our adult masochistic patients. As noted, our adult patients described similar obsessionality in middle childhood, but they usually also presented a picture of childhood in which they were innocent victims, unfairly treated by peers, siblings, and adults. We would suggest that in many cases this view of their childhood is shaped by the power of their adult masochistic fantasy in which it is essential that they be seen as innocent victims of sadistic attack. The reality of their latency period was probably similar to that of the children seen in analysis during school years, where obsessional rituals alternated with periods of wild behavior and hostile thoughts.

The literature on re-analysis contains confirmation of these views. Tyson (Panel 1983) reported the analysis of a 28-year-old graduate student who appeared depressed, stymied in a relationship with a woman, and blocked in completing his thesis. He frequently blamed himself for everything bad. Sylvia Brody had analyzed him as a child and was struck on reading the case by the patient's omission of reference to his extreme impulsivity in childhood. There had been a troubled early mother–child relationship, and he showed disturbed behavior and functioning from early on. He was wild, uncontrolled, greedy, sadistic, and enuretic; at kindergarten, psychological testing indicated that his impulsivity carried the threat of psychosis. A similar account was given by Ritvo (1966) of the re-analysis of Frankie, whom he described as a withdrawn, joyless adult with severe limitations in his capacity for love and a fixation to his infantile relationship to his mother. Bornstein (1949), who analyzed him as a child, described how Frankie was swept by waves of wild uncontrolled behavior in which he would attack people and scream, "Don't grab me, I surrender!"

A further distortion of memory determined by the operation of masochistic fantasies in our adult patients is that things had probably not been as bad in childhood as they would currently like to imagine. As noted earlier, their parents were sometimes caring and giving, although only intermittently so, and usually in response to their own needs rather than the child's. This robbed the children of the experience of effectance, but provided some source of libidinal supply. Despite the patients' inability to own their achievements, many showed considerable capacity and talents but derived little pleasure from these accomplishments. Most relevant to our topic is that by the time these patients were in latency, they had become so firmly established in a magical omnipotent system that any achievement, display of talent, or positive parental action was interpreted as due to their omnipotence, rather than to work. Thus, as noted earlier, work was discounted, its efficacy denied, and achievements were measured by how easily others could be coerced to do the work. When such standards and goals had been consolidated in the ego ideal, particular effects emerged in relation to the working alliance in treatment. In our adult masochistic patients we have found variously a reluctance to work, or the apparent expenditure of enormous effort with little result, or the tendency to pervert the work so as to seduce the analyst into doing it all. These tenacious forms of resistance all spring in part from the operation of the delusion of omnipotence in the formation during latency of those parts of the personality that regulate self-esteem. As the expression of omnipotent forces, achievement then also represented destructive annihilating triumph over others, and, as such, was often followed by provocation of punishment and inhibition.

For those children analyzed during latency and into adolescence, the formation of the masochistic fantasy represented an achievement, an alternative preferable to enactment in suicide or other self-destructive behavior. A vivid example of regression from this position occurs in Blum's (1980) description of a patient who became acutely paranoid when he could no longer maintain his beating fantasy. The masochistic fantasy, as an organizing, conscious masturbation fantasy, followed the first emission for the boys. The conscious fantasy had a stabilizing effect and adequate functioning could be maintained for a while during early adolescence. Every one of our masochistic patients, however, whether treated as a child or adult, went on to have an extremely disturbed later adolescence. The sequence of manifest pathology usually followed failure to separate from mother but was built on failure of the earlier adolescent tasks of ownership of the body and integration of mature sexuality into the self image (Laufer and Laufer 1984). Study through psychoanalysis of the suicide sequence (see Chapter 8) in a group of teenagers demonstrated that in each case there was a conscious omnipotent fantasy that through self-destruction all wishes would be gratified. Further studies might test the hypothesis that the adult form of the masochistic fantasy, with its omnipotent component, is not consolidated until adolescence.

There is more to a masochistic fantasy than omnipotence but the delusion of omnipotence is a necessary part of it. The classical view is that the failure of omnipotence forces the child to turn to reality. In our view it is the failure of reality that forces the child to turn to omnipotent solutions. Competence is rooted in the attunement between the child's signals and the caretakers' responses. Repeated failures are frustrating and, as research with infants has demonstrated, soon lead to expressions of helplessness and confusion (Papouseck and Papouseck 1975). Within a month from birth, it can be observed that such failures produce signs of discomfort or psychic pain and are soon followed by signs of anger such as gaze aversion. This is followed by denial of the source of pain; denial is maintained by the transformation of pain into first a sign of attachment, then additionally a sign of specialness and unlimited destructive power, then a sign of equality in every way with oedipal parents, and omnipotent capacity to coerce parents to gratify all infantile wishes. By school age the magic omnipotent system has been established and the possibility of an alternate system of competent interactions with reality is undermined by the child as each realistic achievement is experienced as being due to omnipotent magical behavior.

During latency this delusion of omnipotence can be maintained, but in adolescence it becomes increasingly difficult to deny, avoid, or distort reality without resorting to escalating self-destructive behaviors, which adolescents may use to shore up the crumbling omnipotent fantasy. Once having attempted suicide the patient may cling to the potential of such an omnipotent act for many years. In fact, it is doubtful that it is ever entirely given up. In the final week of a successful eight year analysis of a teenager, the patient reported "old feelings and thoughts coming up." These related to the near fatal car crash which first brought him into treatment.

Analysis of masochistic adolescents reveals that the greatest threat to the omnipotent system is the experience of competence and pleasure, especially in separate, gender-differentiated adult activities such as genital sexuality. Pleasure has no place in the omnipotent system, except as secret moments of sadistic triumph, and leaves the masochist feeling, as one patient said, "like a row boat pushed out to sea." Pleasure leaves them feeling ordinary and not special. The experience of adult pleasure threatens the long-standing denial of differences between children and adults and opens the floodgates of primitive envy and helpless rage. Adolescence is a time of leavetaking, and the necessary task of relinquishing infantile objects and wishes is a painful and slow process. The masochistic patient is challenged throughout treatment to relinquish his omnipotent self. A major resistance to change and to termination is the need to cling, to the very end, to an omnipotent delusion. Working on and working through the determinants of masochism at every level are insufficient unless the thread of the delusion of omnipotence is also followed back to its roots and the patient can begin to construct an alternative system of gratification from competent interactions.

In this section we have attempted to describe the development of fantasies of destructive omnipotence, and how the delusion of destructive omnipotence becomes simultaneously a defense against feelings of helpless rage and humiliation and a pathological source of self-esteem. As such, it contributes to the masochist's resistance to change through experience or analysis. This conclusion is consistent with an emphasis on the narcissistic elements of masochism (Bergler 1949, Cooper 1984, 1986, 1988, Eidelberg 1934 [Panel, 1956], 1958, 1959, Freud 1919, Lampl-de Groot 1937). However, we see this as but one function among many of the masochistic disorder.

This is a preliminary description of the epigenesis of omnipotence and its relation to masochism. As such it should be tested against clinical material, and we expect this will lead to further modifications of the model. We have applied this multideterminate model of masochism and omnipotence to work with children, adolescents, and adults, and in recent work other authors have found the model applicable to the analysis of a severe masochistic perversion (Wurmser 1990, 1993), to work with women with subclinical eating disorders (Lerner 1993), to multiple personality disorder (Lerner & Lerner 1995), to the analyses of two cases of neurotic depression (Blos 1991), to the understanding of depression (Markson 1993), to work with self-mutilators (Daldin 1988), and as applied to literary criticism (Hanly 1993), and performance issues in musicians (Nagel 1994, 1995). The question does remain, however, whether this formulation of masochism applies only to one segment of the diagnostic spectrum, in particular the more disturbed masochists, such as the sadomasochistic personality disorders (Kernberg [Panel 1991a], Maleson [Panel 1991a], Simons 1987). Cooper summarized the 1991 panel on sadomasochism as illustrating the nosological as opposed to the dynamic-economic approach. Our conceptualization of masochism implies an underlying dynamic common to all forms of masochistic pathology.

TREATMENT

In adult patients, the omnipotent derivatives from all levels of development, which form an important component of the masochistic fantasy, are a major source of resistance throughout analysis. At the beginning of treatment, resistance to acknowledging and verbalizing aggressive and libidinal drive derivatives occurs in a wide range of patients, for familiar reasons of guilt, anxiety, or shame. But for the masochistic patient there is additional anxiety and guilt arising from the deep conviction that these impulses are omnipotent and will really lead to destruction of object or self.

> Mrs. T. was a slight, pale 30-year-old divorcée who had spent most of her adolescence in the hospital after having made three serious suicide attempts. At times of stress she stopped eating, pulled out clumps of her hair, and thought she could see evidence of hostility in everyone around her. Early in analysis she fluctuated between helpless tears and self-righteous rage. When the rage was directed at the analyst, Mrs. T. would clutch her body, clench her teeth, and sometimes beat her thighs rather than talk about her anger and what had caused it. The analyst took up her fear that her anger was so powerful that no one could stop her. Mrs. T. said that she was indeed powerful, that she had driven her mother to suicide, and, if she wanted to, she could pick up the couch and throw it through the window. Mrs. T. was using this fantasy image of an omnipotent self to defend against terror and helplessness to control the analyst in the transference and, historically, her mother's mental illness. In these early sessions she was giving up the real possibility of effecting change by examining the causes of her anger for the sake of maintaining omnipotent fantasy control of herself and the analyst.

At the mid-phase of analysis, when significant change occurs, the resistance will focus on the danger of pleasure and the threat this poses to the omnipotent system. This is more than a negative therapeutic reaction, that is, guilt because of success, it is a desperate clinging to pain. Pain is the affect which triggers the defense of omnipotence, pain is the magical means by which all wishes are gratified, and pain justifies the omnipotent hostility and revenge contained in the masochistic fantasy.

Ms. A. was a brilliant single woman in her mid-thirties who came to analysis because her professional and personal lives seemed to have reached a dead end. It soon became evident that she was provoking a negative response from suitable male companions and supervisors at work, both male and female, thus destroying the possibility of advancement and of a permanent relationship. The first three years of her five times per week analysis consisted of complaints about how she was mistreated, misjudged, and misunderstood by everyone, including her analyst. The masochistic presentation of herself as innocent victim of the aggression of others contained many elements, including projection of her own hostile impulses. But it also served nicely as a cloak for her omnipotent fantasy control of others: when she manipulated the direction and impact of aggression, she felt safe and strong, invulnerable to the terrifying narcissistic humiliation she feared when she risked seeing herself or others as they really were. Eventually she began to assume some responsibility for the way people reacted to her and began to behave differently; positive results occurred in her professional and social lives commensurate with her high-level capacities and her attractiveness. However, as the successes continued, her face and body began to appear strained, her voice became flat, and she spoke of wanting once again to destroy everything. She said that she felt like Cinderella at the castle. She was married to the handsome prince, the presents were flowing in, but, as each gold brick was stacked up, she felt increasingly miserable; something was missing. She missed the torn, dirty, tattered dress, she missed having to serve the wicked stepsisters and stepmother, she missed sleeping by the ashes. This was a reversal of the theme of the Cinderella story in which the humiliation and suffering of the first part leads to the rescue and joyful triumph of the happy ending. In her version, the happy ending made her feel lonely and vulnerable. She yearned for the safety, comfort, and power of being the victim. All her successes and the pleasure she was beginning to feel about her work and relationships made her feel vulnerable, helpless, and out of control. She said pleasure depended on other people, but misery was entirely in her control. Being a victim, like Cinderella, made her feel powerful. In that position her anger was justified and she had a right to do whatever she wanted, especially in the transference, where the victimized pain kept her tied to the analyst, made her one with the masochistic transference mother, defended against rage at her mother, and transformed her humiliation and feeling of being unloved into a triumph of being special at each developmental level. At this point in her analysis, Ms. A. was reexperiencing the choice she had faced many times earlier in her life when she had tried to deal with internal and external threats to her narcissistic equilibrium. The Cinderella fantasy represented an omnipotent defense of her self-esteem. The next stage was for her to experience internally the conflict between the competing sources of gratification, pleasure, and narcissistic satisfaction, that is, between the masochistic omnipotent fantasy and reality-based competent achievements.

It takes years to work through the many determinants and functions of masochism, and the start of a termination phase is often resisted in order to retain, at least in treatment, the delusion of omnipotence.

Mr. M. started his analysis by lying on the couch and begging the analyst to beat him and get it over with. He lived in a state of constant physical and psychic pain and there was not one area of his life where he functioned adequately. Ten years later, he was, by all customary analytic and external criteria, ready to terminate, but he resisted actually finishing for years. He felt that he was the analyst's oldest and hence favorite patient. Further, the sacrifices he made to be in analysis and open up his feelings were essential to the analyst's well-being and happiness. As he had in childhood with his depressed mother, he imagined he held the magical key to the analyst's heart—how could he even consider leaving when he was so needed? He felt that he didn't need analysis for his problems any longer, but there was no reason to end a situation where he enjoyed feeling so important and benefited from the analyst's wisdom. He completely denied any real cost in time and money; as there had been no increase in fee for several years it seemed like coming for nothing. Although analysis took a third of his take-home pay he considered it a necessary irreducible expense like the cost of food. Through a split in the ego, a simultaneous denial and acknowledgment of reality, the patient had turned his analysis into a sadomasochistic perversion. Mr. M.'s belief in his crucial importance to the analyst was the omnipotent strand in his sadomasochistic fantasy, and he used this image of his omnipotent self to ward off the helpless terror and panic he felt at the idea of meaning nothing to the analyst. Maintenance of the delusion of omnipotence superceded for him the real cost in time, money, and lost pleasure involved in staying in analysis. Despite all the gains in his outside functioning, a termination phase could not be started until the analytic work fostered and addressed the development of an internal conflict between the real and the omnipotent fantasy sources of self-esteem. His resistance to the idea of working towards termination yielded only when gradual interpretation of the deep anxieties and rage around his early relation to his mother could be made in terms of the omnipotent defense.

Earlier we described two distinct systems of regulating feelings of self-esteem. Each system starts in infancy, alters and is altered by each subsequent phase. The normal or reality-attuned system rests on the satisfactions derived from the infant's competent interactions with the caretaking person and evolves into a mature reality-based system in which actions are assessed within a context of testing and accepting the limitations and potentials of the self and the external world.

The other system is developed in response to experiences of

helplessness, frustration, and rage, and includes the delusion of omnipotent control in the context of a sadomasochistic fantasy. Hostile, omnipotent fantasies in adults stem, in our view, from these infantile roots. The initial passive experience of dysphoric affect is mastered and transformed into a fantasy of triumphant power. The omnipotent delusion includes the idea that the individual can use his pain and suffering to control the actions and feelings of others and to deny and avoid reality constraints such as gender and generational differences, the passage of time, and the inevitability and permanence of death. One of the aims of treatment is to help the patient become aware of the system he is using, to face the way in which the omnipotent system destroys the reality of his capacities and achievements, and ultimately to realize that relinquishing the omnipotent source of self-esteem will not leave him with nothing. As the patient laboriously gets in touch with the alternative sources of self-esteem available through competent, empathic, and loving interactions with others, a conflict arises between the systems. At this point, the analysis can more nearly resemble work with classical neuroses, despite the propensity for frequent regressive recourse to the sadomasochistic patterns.

Joyce McDougall (1985) distinguished between libidinal problems where the person strives for the forbidden, and narcissistic problems where the person strives for the impossible. She described the latter striving as an omnipotent attempt to control other people's thoughts and actions, to deny the undeniable, to reconcile the irreconcilable, to destroy and yet retain the object, to die and yet live forever. How to help someone accept the impossibility of omnipotent fantasies is a major and often insurmountable obstacle in work with masochistic patients. They believe that taking away their magic leaves them with nothing. Shengold (1989) described King Lear's magical expectations that he could have the unattainable, that his daughter Cordelia could become his perfect mother. Her refusal to meet his omnipotent demands brought the response, "nothing will come of nothing" and, as Shengold noted, "Lear reacts by hating and disowning her" (p. 230). Shengold's beautifully written explication follows classical lines, but we might add that Lear's resurgence of omnipotence occurred in relation to feelings of helpless rage in the face of death. To deny the inexorable power of time and death he gives away his real kingly powers. The whole action of the play can be seen as his continued attempt to deny the necessities of reality and, with his final acceptance, he became once again a mature man who acknowledged the value of what he had and accepted the superior force of nature and the pain of irreversible loss. Shengold (1989) captured the transition in his comments:

> In the most moving lines in the play—and perhaps in all literature, Lear laments the dead Cordelia. Through his deprivation and suffering he has attained a full sense of what it is to love—and thus can feel loss as a man and no longer as an infant. Lear says to Cordelia's corpse:
> '. . . thou'lt come no more,
> Never, never, never, never, never!'
>
> The five iterations of "nothing" in the first scene, full of destructive rage and denial, have been transmuted by love and acceptance of tragic reality to the five iterations of "never" in the last scene. The repeated "never" hammers home the poignancy and terror of irreversible loss. . . . [p. 233]

Just as omnipotence is a defense that keeps the subject related to others, the sadomasochistic fantasy as a whole also defends against a complete withdrawal from objects to a state Krystal (1988) terms alexithymia, which the patients often describe as "being dead." This state is more dangerous than masochism, and so perhaps we may also attribute the difficulties of grappling with the masochistic character, and the omnipotent resistances it enlists, to the survival value it has had for the patient.

4 POSTOEDIPAL TRANSFORMATIONS: LATENCY, ADOLESCENCE, AND PATHOGENESIS[1]

The Piazza Signoria in Florence is a beautiful Renaissance square, surrounded by palaces and paved with stones from the fifteenth century. For recent visitors, however, the beauty has been obscured by scaffolding and fences surrounding construction work. In the course of repairing the pavement, workers discovered medieval, Roman, and pre-Roman paving stones. Florentines have split into factions, each vociferously advocating the importance of one particular historical level above the others. At a dinner party of psychoanalysts in the hills above Florence, we were given a beautifully engraved invitation to a demonstration championing the restoration of the Renaissance pavement by covering up all the others. This is not an unusual controversy for analysts to be involved with; indeed, in our own field, particular analysts at particular times have argued for the overriding importance of specific developmental phases. So we have oedipalists, and preoedipalists, among whom

---

1. This chapter is dedicated to the memory of Robert Kabcenell, M.D., under whose chairmanship an earlier version was presented as the Annual Child Analysis Lecture at the New York Psychoanalytic Society, February 1991.

we can find champions of early infantile influences, issues of early toddlerhood, such as separation–individuation, or later anal phase conflicts. Like the tourists who now avoid the Piazza Signoria, there are also those analysts who want to deny developmental issues altogether and focus strictly on the here and now.

Memory has always been a preoccupation of psychoanalysis, from the earliest attempts to abreact troublesome relics of the past to current discussions about the nature of the transference neurosis and the relevance of reconstruction (Blum 1980, Curtis 1983, Friedman 1983, Reed 1990, 1993, Renik 1990, Sandler 1992). But, throughout, a central tenet has been that the past lives on in the present. But which past are we talking about? In 1914 Freud said that he and Breuer had initially intended to focus on the current conflict and the exciting cause; however, because of the process which he termed regression, the patient's association moved back from the current scene and began to occupy itself with the past. "At first it seemed regularly to bring us to puberty; later on, failures and points which still eluded explanations drew the analytic work still further back into years of childhood which had hitherto been inaccessible to any kind of exploration" (p. 10). So, starting with Freud, the analytic quest has led further and further back. In 1978 Anna Freud described the psychoanalytic theory of pathogenesis as it "veered, rather wildly, from the oedipal period as the responsible constellation to the mother– infant relationship at the beginning of life; to the separation–individuation phase in the second year (Mahler); to the disturbances of narcissism (Kohut); to the developmental frustrations and interferences (Nagera)" (pp. 98–99).

Valenstein said that the widened scope of psychoanalytic practice has turned our attention to the "inchoate neonatal and infantile period of development" (1989, p. 434), and that infant observational data has made this period more accessible to reconstruction, a view shared by many. Those who dispute this view, for example, Arlow (1991) and Rangell (1989), tend to stress development at the oedipal phase.

Although Freud progressively assigned importance to oedipal and preoedipal phases, he retained the idea that crucial determinants of adult pathology occur postoedipally. Freud repeatedly described postoedipal transformations of early experience. In the "Three Essays on the Theory of Sexuality" (Freud 1905) the section on adolescence was called "The Transformations of Puberty"; it is both the concept of transformation and the retention of the importance of postoedipal change that are lost in the infinite regression to primary causes.

The effect of the search for ever earlier causes combined with the view that postoedipal development is a recapitulation of infantile experiences relegates adult memories of latency and adolescence to serving mainly a defensive screen function. This conceptualization has a profound effect on technique. If, alternatively, we retain Freud's earlier view that important transformations occur in latency and adolescence, how would this affect our understanding and handling of the adult patient's material?

Here we focus on those transformations, normal and pathological, which occur during latency and adolescence. We want to emphasize that this concentration is chosen within the framework of a model in which each phase from infancy through old age makes important contributions to normal and pathological development. This model was used in our work on masochism and in our more recent study of masochism and omnipotence, where we stressed the layering throughout development of omnipotent solutions to the conflicts of each phase (see Chapters 2 and 3). For us the determinants of adult pathology are not to be found in a big bang occurring at the beginning of time but in a series of transformations which both alter and retain earlier determinants.

First we will look at those transformations which occur in middle childhood, in order to define more clearly their role as the resultants of preoedipal and oedipal development and trace their impact on the subsequent course of adolescent and adult growth. To do this, we will first use material from a child who began his analysis at the age of five and thus provided us with a window on the very transformations under examination. Then we will describe the role of latency and adolescent memories in the analyses of some adult patients, in order to suggest some of the technical ramifications of what we have learned from the postoedipal development of the child.

Oliver was an English boy of 5¾ years of age who came for analysis at a time when his parents were in the midst of an acrimonious custody battle. He was the second of two children and seemed to be showing severe reactions to the separation and especially to the custody dispute. He was a very bright, likeable fellow who told the analyst that he needed help because his parents had divorced and he had feelings about it. He said his main feeling was that he wanted to spend more time with his father and that a boy should do so. However, whenever the conversation turned to his father, he very deftly changed the subject. If confronted with his resistance he would turn an innocent face to the analyst and say, "1+1 = 2, 2+2 = 4, 4+4 = 8," and so on. His curiosity and superior intellectual endowment could be readily enlisted as allies in the therapeutic work and, before long, he had volunteered to be the analyst's assistant in exploring not only the planets, but also inner space. He counseled the animal hand puppets in their difficulties with their warring and separated parents, and wrote out lists of his associations to his dreams, trying to find the main themes. At the same time, this brilliant boy could not sit still; he circled the room touching the walls, leaping from the furniture and holding his penis whenever he talked about himself. He was highly tense, anxious, afraid of monsters, and apparently unable to control his behavior at school, home, and sometimes in his sessions. His intellect was that of a 12-year-old but the intensity and inability to control himself were like those of a toddler. Furman (1980) has written about the centrality of externalization as a defense in latency; this process marked most of his behavior. He could seldom talk directly about his feelings, but rather expressed them through a daily game with animal puppets in which the mother, the father, and the 6-year-old puppet played out his current conflicts. Oliver himself acted like a toddler who could deny intentionality, desire, or responsibility. He seemed to suffer no shame, guilt, or remorse.

Oliver named the boy puppet Fred; the first resistance faced by the analyst and his assistant Oliver was that Fred could not acknowledge the slightest negative comment about his father. Fred, the 6-year-old puppet, would change the subject at these moments, get angry at his mother instead of his father, or have them remarry so that he wouldn't be torn between their demands on his loyalty and allegiance. The loyalty conflicts were overwhelming. Oliver said he thought this was what made Fred so angry at his parents, especially the father puppet, who was so critical of the mother. Oliver told Fred he would help him by making a sign which read, "Everyone should be on Fred's side," to which he then added the large motto, "Everyone should agree!" Further work on Fred's fear that his hate would overrun his love and his anxiety over father's retaliation allowed Oliver to share with Fred that he too was very angry with his father.

But his admission of his angry feelings was at first too much for Oliver. After a long vacation with his mother Oliver had a dream of a Monarch butterfly. He told his analyst that the dream was very upsetting because the butterfly's wings came off in Oliver's hands. When his associations led from "monarch" to "king" to "daddy" Oliver became completely overwhelmed. He ran frantically around the room, screeching in panic that he had wings coming out of his back. The analyst could barely make out what Oliver was saying, but eventually understood that Oliver felt himself to be the butterfly daddy, the innocent victim of the terrifying therapist, who was being experienced as the mean boy who kills daddy butterflies. After some time, interpretation of the projection of death wishes calmed Oliver enough to allow him to work on his intense anxiety and recover from his traumatic experience of the dream.

Oliver began to contain his ambivalence and spoke of his "plus-minus" feelings for his analyst and his father.

A component of Oliver's idealization of his father had been his view that only his father could control and contain his wild behavior; if his father were no longer perfectly powerful it was up to Oliver to control his own behavior. A schoolmate was mean to Oliver and he told the boy that they were no longer friends. The teacher who overheard his remark told Oliver to apologize as his words were very unkind. Oliver promptly slammed his head against a door. For a short period this became his reaction to the slightest reprimand from teacher or mother. Oliver told his analyst that he was punishing himself before anyone else could, and that he deserved to be so harshly punished. At this point a new animal character appeared in Oliver's analysis. He was a judge, but he was a very poor judge. He condemned people not only for their criminal deeds but also if they merely had angry thoughts. Oliver said that the judge puppet should go back to judge school to learn the difference between thoughts and deeds.

During this period of work Oliver also learned about the importance of having an "inner policeman" and the difference between a good and a bad policeman. He began to defend his mother against father's continuing criticism and suggested to father that he too should go to an analyst to help him with his angry feelings. Father did not take kindly to Oliver's recommendation and soon the boy felt put in the position of having to choose between his therapy and his father. His father told him not to talk to his analyst about his feelings, that these were matters which belonged only in the family, but Oliver found a way to sidestep what he felt was father's incorrect instruction. He simply continued the animal puppet play, but acknowledged with no disguises that the puppets represented his feelings about his parents. The game had shifted from serving as a defensive externalization to an adaptive maneuver protecting his emotional well-being.

For a while Oliver was able to avoid a direct confrontation, but soon his father precipitated a crisis by refusing to help facilitate Oliver's legitimate wish to join a sports team. The struggle was long and painful. Oliver's monsters returned and his regressions were frequent and severe. In the sessions and at home he externalized his superego, trying to provoke the analyst to control and contain his infantile behavior. Eventually he reinternalized a superego, which seemed capable of differentiating between appropriate and inappropriate parental injunctions. His superego had become more adaptive, less tied to his objects, and he told his father he thought he was not doing anything wrong in playing cricket.

Soon after this Oliver told his mother that he had something to confess: for the last three nights he had continued to read past his bedtime. He was not in a state of panic, he did not hurt himself or say that he wished to die as he had done before. He just felt bad about breaking the rule. This was shortly before his annual summer vacation with his father. In the past, Oliver had returned from these visits tense, anxious, regressed, and provocative; his father often used the time alone to criticize both mother and analyst. But this time Oliver returned happy and loving. For the first time he talked of the fun he had with his dad, but also of how happy he was to see his mother and his analyst.

This material from the analysis of a latency child illustrates an evolution of structure and function that involved profound changes in Oliver's personality. He had suffered from the effects of parental discord from birth onward. His father had always competed with his mother, interfering with her ministrations, disrupting intimacy and bonding between mother and child. This pattern persisted throughout his childhood, with serious consequences for his object relations and sense of himself.

At the oedipal phase, Oliver's conflicts were unusually distorted. His love for his mother was not in imitation and then in rivalry with his father, but rather represented for Oliver an abandonment of his father, which in turn threatened to evoke a retaliatory abandonment by father. This interfered with identification with his father and internalization of the superego.

With the analysis of his death wishes, more realistic perceptions of his parents, and integration of his ambivalence, Oliver entered latency, and we could see the transformation brought about by the action of his coalescing superego. What had been a passively experienced, environmentally imposed loyalty conflict became a self-generated vehicle for his aggressive impulses, an internalized conflict, and hence a source of intense guilt. We could then see in Oliver's material the centrality and pervasiveness of superego formation and conflict during this phase.

From the data of infant research and increased attention to preoedipal development it has been possible to identify superego precursors; contingent learning and internalization of parental prohibitions begin in early infancy. But with the convergence of cognitive, emotional, and social developmental achievements between the ages of 5 and 7 a qualitatively new crystallization of self-regulation emerges. R. and P. Tyson (1990), after summarizing the literature about early internalization of prohibitions, concluded that "more is required to reach superego autonomy than identification with parental punishing introjects" (p. 219). They emphasized internalization of parental values and moral codes, and identification with these internal codes. Along the same lines we would add that the postoedipal child begins to appreciate the protective and self-enhancing value of holding to an internal set of abstract principles. The preoedipal child does not want to get into trouble; the postoedipal child wants to be fair and do what is right. As one 9-year-old said, "It feels good to be good." In a sense, the mind may be likened to a passport: once a border is crossed, the passport is ineradicably stamped with the port of entry. Having entered latency, the psychic apparatus is permanently transformed to include elements of intentionality, choice, responsibility, and guilt. Any subsequent mental activity is marked by this transformation, which must always be taken into account.

In Oliver's case, interpretations had first been directed toward the preoedipal anxiety he experienced in relation to his impulses. He feared that his mother or father would abandon him or that his father would retaliate in kind for his death wishes. He did not feel like a bad boy, but rather was terrified that his wishes, if discovered or revealed, would lead to disaster. Eventually this work allowed for developmental progression and consolidation of his superego. Postoedipally, these impulses led to internalized conflict and interpretation had to include guilt feelings and defenses against them. When he stayed up reading too late, Oliver was worried that his defiance would lead to his mother's anger. But he was more upset at having broken the rule, and he dealt with this guilt by externalizing the blame, accusing his mother of setting his bedtime earlier than his friends'. It was only after entry into latency that his experience included a knowledge of right and wrong and conflict stemming from an identification with internalized standards.

This is not a new concept; indeed, it has been an ordinary assumption of our theory since Freud and continues to be elucidated by some modern authors, notably in Furman's discussion of externalization in latency (1980) and Shapiro's (1977, 1981) reassertion of the Oedipus complex as the nuclear conflict. Yet, as already noted, there is also a powerful countertendency to look ever earlier and neglect the impact of latency and adolescent experiences and transformations on the analysis of adults. In those theories which hinge on early trauma, the role of choice, intentionality, and guilt in neurosogenesis and later pathological functioning is denied or ignored.

However, most analysts do not ignore manifestations of guilt. Superego conflicts have long been a staple of analytic work. But we are suggesting that interpretations of choice, intentionality, responsibility, and guilt are most effective, indeed may only be effective, when made in the context of latency phase material.

Interpretations of conflict derived from earlier impulses will be valid, but may miss crucial internal aspects if undertaken prematurely or considered complete without the stratum of latency experience and development. Let us illustrate this point with material from some adult cases.

Ms. A. was a 33-year-old divorced woman who had suffered repeated family convulsions in her preschool years. Her masochistic fantasy of being the innocent victim of disturbed parents was woven around the parental divorce that occurred when she was 2½ and her mother's lengthy hospitalization for severe depression when Ms. A. was under 3½ years of age. Other associated stories of being victimized added to her central masochistic fantasy. In particular, she told of a beloved warm-hearted Irish nanny who was fired because Ms. A.'s mother thought the nanny was working secretly for the father to help him sue for sole custody of Ms. A. For a long time the analytic work centered on the multiple determinants and functions of her masochistic pathology, resulting in significant changes in her functioning.

Despite years of interpretive work, including detailed analysis of her superego conflicts, Ms. A.'s reactions to separations remained problematic. These were variously interpreted in relation to her loyalty conflicts and guilt for loving someone other than the analyst, for loving the nanny rather than the analyst mother. Both the analyst and the patient felt that these interpretations were accurate as far as they went, but that there was still something else, a missing element.

During a later period of the analysis, in response to the analyst's linking her stilted style of associating to a possible inhibition of play in childhood, Ms. A. began to recall how and with whom she played as a child. Her reminiscences led to memories of happy play with the Irish nanny. Earlier, Ms. A. had been vague about the timing, implying that the nanny had been hired when her mother first went into the hospital, when

Ms. A. was around 3 years old. The analyst noted the age discrepancy between these memories, and Ms. A. confirmed that the nanny had been hired during her second grade year, when Ms. A. was 7. The analyst repeated the earlier interpretations about her guilt for loving the nanny instead of her mother, but added, "And at age 7 you knew better."

Ms. A. seemed to freeze, held her breath, then relaxed and cried for ten minutes. When she regained her composure, she recalled that she had known that all her friends loved their mothers, even those who had also loved their nannies. She had felt awful and mean for loving Mrs. Riley instead of her mother and wishing her mother would go away again. The effect of the interpretation was profound. Hitherto, all her memories of childhood had been consistent with her masochistic fantasy of being the innocent victim of her mother's sadistic attacks. From this point on she began to recall times when she had provoked her mother into a furious rage. She had known exactly what would drive her mother and older brother mad and she began to remember the feeling of power and glee as they lost control.

A month later she had her first successful separation. She wrote to the analyst, "I was thinking yesterday about writing you a letter to let you know how I'm doing. I've been doing and feeling really well—I've been feeling very proud of how things have been going this time for me. I feel like we talked about some things this time, Mrs. Riley/guilt, etc.—that really are central to what happens to me when I don't see you—even for one day."

As we saw, for Oliver, intense loyalty conflicts and death wishes produced feelings of guilt only after his entry into latency. The point of this vignette from Ms. A.'s analysis is not only that latency puts the stamp of guilt on preoedipal experiences but also, perhaps more crucially, that the interpretation of guilt is most effective in the context of the recovery and reconstruction of postoedipal events. As long as Ms. A. restricted her associations to preoedipal events and issues she could effectively defend against her superego conflicts. In the case of Oliver, interpretations of guilt were irrelevant until he had entered latency. The adult patient, Ms. A., had passed through latency and had struggled with her superego strictures during that phase. Transference interpretations of her superego conflicts made sense to her only after typical latency defenses, such as externalization of the superego, had been addressed. Further, Ms. A.'s distorted memory of her childhood confirmed our finding (see Chapter 3) that adult patients' memories are shaped by the defensive transformations of latency and adolescence, which in turn serve a defensive function in their adult pathology.

Developmental transformation is implicit in the classical psychoanalytic concept of a derivative, and for us a complete interpretation has always included the origins of a conflict, the developmental and defensive transformations of it, and its current manifestations in or out of the transference. Oversimplication can lead to assumptions of one-to-one correspondence between early and current experience. This clearly untenable assumption is one of the causes of the debate over the epistemological basis of reconstruction and has led many to reject what has been a cornerstone of psychoanalytic technique. Curtis (1983) noted the decline of attention to reconstruction and elegantly described the complexity of the technique of reconstruction, the many questions it raises, and the hazards in either misapplication of reconstruction or exclusive attention to the present. Sandler (1992) has summarized the continuing trend to focus on construction of the patient's style of mental functioning in the present, instead of on reconstruction of the past. Rather than rejecting reconstruction, we suggest that knowledge of the developmental transformations appropriate to each phase—as we saw in the case of Oliver's latency development—can help the analyst to refine reconstructions, so that, as with Ms. A., current manifestations of conflict may be elucidated and linked with their past roots, memories may be recovered, and an improved veridical life history attained. Reed (1993) described the importance of increased specificity, and Blum (1980) not only stressed the clinical value of reconstruction, but suggested, as we do, the inclusion of postoedipal experience.

Mr. C., a professional man in his thirties, spent much of his time both in and out of analysis protesting his innocence and pointing out the sadistic behavior of others. His memories were all of being rejected and abandoned. One poignant story was of being left on the doorstep while his mother went shopping. The neighbor's dog was killed by a car while chasing a ball, and Mr. C. was blamed for letting the ball roll into the road. In his sessions he often reported extremely sadistic fantasies about the analyst, but they dropped passively from his lips like a ball falling from the unsteady grip of a toddler. Mr. C. said that these fantasies were like a landscape seen from inside a fast-moving train, and that he was just telling what he was seeing in the landscape of his mind. Something in his passivity, his disavowal of hostile intent, and, perhaps, in the analyst's own annoyance, led back to the story of the dog. The analyst wondered how old Mr. C. was when it happened. Mr. C. was vague, saying, "Sometime before I started school." But then, as he visualized the street and the house, he realized that the family had moved to that house near the end of first grade. "I couldn't have been younger than 6, perhaps I was 7." The analyst noted that the memory had originally been set at a time when he couldn't be held responsible, but that at 6 or 7 years old he had understood the consequences of his action. Mr. C. responded by recalling that he had hated the dog. He was jealous of it because he felt that the neighbors loved the dog more than his parents loved him. He had been told not to throw the ball into the road, because the dog might chase it and could get killed. He had done it deliberately to get his revenge on all those who were mean to him, including the dog. With the accurate placement of this incident in latency, Mr. C. could no longer deny his sadism or his own guilty reaction to his sadistic wishes, and the work could proceed.

In summarizing the sequence of Oliver's latency-age struggle with superego conflicts, we described a moment when his ego was overwhelmed and he was in a state of trauma. This was in reaction to his dream of the Monarch butterfly. Was this a revival of an earlier trauma? Death wishes and hostility had surely been present before latency, and he had started treatment highly resistant to any uncovering of negative feelings about his father. Had rage and death wishes at some time overwhelmed Oliver's more fragile preoedipal ego, and was the occurrence in analysis a transference repetition of a preoedipal trauma? This possibility would be consistent with the idea that what occurs earlier is more potent, that infantile trauma is what we look for, and that postoedipal traumata are repetitions of the earlier ones. However, in Oliver's case, there was no evidence of early trauma. Most significant was that, while criticism and anger at the father and the analyst had emerged in treatment considerably before the dream, there had been no sign of a traumatic reaction. It was only when separation fears and death wishes arose after the consolidation of a superego that the trauma occurred.

Before Freud described infantile sexuality, his theory of neurosogenesis hinged on the idea of deferred action. Initially he used this theory in relation to puberty. Briefly summarized, the idea was that an experience in childhood may have little impact until the memory becomes linked with later sexual impulses. In his "Project for a Scientific Psychology" (1895) Freud wrote, "We invariably find that a memory is repressed which has only become a trauma by deferred action" (p. 356). Freud later used this theory to explain the relation between the Wolf Man's anxiety dream at 4 years of age and his primal scene observation at 1½ (1918). In answer to the doubt that a child at 1½ could understand "the process as well as its significance" (p. 37) Freud said in a footnote, "I mean that he understood it at the time of the dream when he was four years old, not at the time of the observation. He received the impressions when he was one-and-a-half, his understanding of them was deferred, but became possible at the time of the dream owing to his development, his sexual excitations, and his sexual researches" (pp. 37–38). The theory of deferred action is now seldom mentioned or used in American psychoanalytic literature, but in 1989 Modell included both deferred action and what Freud (1886) called the "rearrangement" and "retranscription" of memory in his theoretical examination of the multiple levels of reality in the psychoanalytic setting. Earlier, Greenacre (1950) used a similar idea in her paper on prepuberty trauma in girls. In discussing one such case she said, "only under the influence of later events did it become charged with the anxiety" (p. 217).

We suggest that the ego in latency may also be vulnerable to being overwhelmed traumatically, as superego formation provides for an additional powerful source of noxious stimulation. Parents may act as buffers against the impact of potentially traumatic external stimulation, but they can do very little to alleviate internal attacks from the superego. In the case of Ms. A., work on her guilt for loving Mrs. Riley instead of her mother led her to reformulate her life story. She began to wonder if the traumatic event in her life was not the parental divorce at 2½ or her mother's breakdown and hospitalization at 3, but rather her overwhelming guilt at age 7. As important as the early painful events were in shaping her history and personality, the momentum of development had persisted to a certain extent as her ego continued to grow, and she could recover new memories of pleasure with her grandparents and others. It may be that the earlier experiences of loss and rage did not completely overwhelm the ego until guilt was added to them in latency. The sequel to this trauma was that she could not undertake the important developmental tasks of latency. In her analysis this understanding of her history allowed for a shift from the masochistic position of being the innocent victim of traumatogenic parents to one where she could accept the idea that, whatever had been done to her, it was now her job to do the work of latency and adolescence and so return to the path of progressive development. Oliver's material provides us with examples of some of the adaptive transformations of the latency period. As noted earlier, superego formation is one of the major tasks of latency. The goal is the establishment of a relatively autonomous and reasonable source of regulation and self-esteem. The latency period provides a safe arena for experimentation and negotiation with the superego, as the physically immature child is confined to gratification of drive impulses in fantasy and play. Oliver sent his conscience, the puppet, to judge school so that he could learn to be a more reasonable judge.

Modern evidence (cited by Shapiro and Perry 1976) shows that there is a steady growth in hormone levels and genital development in latency. But resolution of the Oedipus complex and entry into latency does provide for changes in the channels for discharge of drive impulses. A major part of this process is an increase in fusion and integration of aggression and libido. Partly through identification with his analyst and other empathic objects, Oliver could absorb his anger into his loving feelings. He told Fred, the 7-year-old puppet, "It's all right to be angry at your father, you still love him."

All developmental psychologists and psychoanalysts describe extraordinary changes in cognition in latency. Mahon (1991) has stressed the "cognitive revolution" (p. 628) taking place in the developing psyche at this time. We have written about changes in sources of self-esteem, from omnipotent manipulation of objects to pleasure in the exercise of cognitive capacities; later in latency, work and play become sources of pleasure in their own right, irrespective of results (see Chapters 3 and 13). Oliver's cognitive endowment was evident well before latency, but it was drawn into his loyalty conflicts. He constantly displayed knowledge he had acquired from his father, but resisted learning in areas of father's ignorance or lack of interest. Oliver showed little

pleasure in learning and used his high level intellectual capacities in the service of maintaining an idealized image of his father.
He could pursue his own interests only after the analytic work
led to a decrease in intensity of the loyalty conflicts. Normal latency shifts in the meaning and use of cognitive competencies
could then take place.

Latency is also the time when the child moves from the relatively exclusive tie to parents to important relationships with peers
and other adults. The power of new object relations is such that
even a seemingly stalemated therapy of a latency child can still
produce change. All the above-mentioned normal transformations,
superego formation, changes in drive organization, cognitive
growth, and new object relations, allow for profound transformations in the type and use of fantasy, the capacity to tolerate delay
and frustration, an increase in resilience, and the capacity to grow
rather than disintegrate in the face of adversity.

There are many ways in which sensitivity to the transformations of latency may help the analyst of adults. We discussed first
the timing of interpretations of guilt, suggesting that these are
most effective when made in the context of emerging latency
memories. Secondly, we noted that earlier pathology becomes
transformed in latency, such that latency pathology is not a direct
recapitulation of earlier disturbance, but a transformation of such
prior elements into a new, usually more complex pathological
structure. At times the transformations of latency may bring earlier pathogenic stress experiences to traumatic intensity.

There is a third aspect that merits the attention of the analyst
of adults, and this is the extent and power of the adaptive, progressive transformations of latency. Sometimes, even without
therapy, earlier pathology can be transformed into more adaptive ways of functioning (Anthony 1987). At the very least, latency
provides alternatives to pathological functioning that were unavailable earlier. Child analysts find it helpful with parents and technically crucial with children to be sensitive to progressive forces,

noting that there is assertion within the latency child's aggression, love in his hostile messiness, and strength in his stubborn silence.

Mr. G. was a brilliant scientist with a worldwide reputation in his field, but he was, as he put it, "a selfish, obnoxious pain in the ass." He was a tyrant to his wife, children, and employees, and seemed to enjoy his sadism without guilt, remorse, or conflict. He entered analysis only because his wife threatened to leave him if he did not undergo treatment for his abusive behavior. He was like an unsocialized child who saw no reason to act otherwise. His preschool and school-age memories were all of doing sadistic things to his younger brothers, his mother, and his teachers. One day he was gleefully recalling jumping on beds until they broke, an activity he engaged in well into the school years. The analyst chose not to comment on the obvious sadistic triumph, but on the kinesthetic pleasure of jumping up and down. Mr. G. seemed startled, as he had expected a comment about his destructive behavior, but he then recalled, for the first time, school-age experiences of rolling down a grassy slope. His voice became soft and warm as he talked of the smells, the sun, the blue sky, and the pleasure of joining in with other children. This latency memory of an alternative source of pleasure, one which would not leave him lonely and hated by others, was a crucial entree into his hitherto seemingly impervious sadistic defense.

It should be no surprise when we say that Mr. G.'s sadistic behavior proved to be a defense against feelings of helplessness dating back to infancy, nor that during latency earlier defenses were organized into a rigid complex defense system that became part of his character, an essential component of his self-image, and a source of self-esteem. From early on Freud and his colleagues viewed latency as synonymous with defense consolidation and character formation. It is a psychoanalytic truism that the resistances of adult patients draw upon the defense system and character traits consolidated during latency. This being so, analysis of resistances should include attention to latency phase phenomena, but this is seldom the case. As stated earlier, the importance of postoedipal transformation has always been acknowledged but then seems to be forgotten. We are not inventing or reinventing the wheel, but simply pointing to its existence. Gray (1982) wrote about a developmental lag between analytic knowledge about defense analysis and the use of this knowledge in actual treatment. Busch (1992, 1995) wrote about the resistance to analyzing resistances and stated that analysts seem much to prefer the use of dramatic deep interpretations of unconscious wishes. We can apply his idea and suggest that there is a resistance to analyzing latency, the period during which many defenses are consolidated, with a corresponding preference for interpretations and reconstructions of early infantile configurations. Or, to use the language of the Sandlers (1984), there is a tendency to bypass the present unconscious and try to interpret the past unconscious.

We are suggesting a correspondence between adult resistance and latency defense systems because the analysis of latency children consists primarily of defense analysis, with occasional dramatic interpretations or reconstructions. These defenses can be classified as alloplastic, as in externalization and provocation, and autoplastic, as in massive repression bolstered by arid obsessionality. The analyst's counterreaction to externalization tends to be rage, and the counterreaction to withdrawal of cathexis is often boredom and overwhelming sleepiness. These are deep responses to narcissistic insult, difficult to integrate with our analytic stance. Winnicott (1965) may in part have been referring to the analysis of latency defenses when he said: "In doing psychoanalysis I aim at: Keeping alive, Keeping well, Keeping awake . . ." (p. 166).

A fourth reason to understand the contributions of latency to our patients' development is that in our clinical experience the progressive transformations of latency are essential to the adaptive passage through adolescence. We turn now to a brief discussion of the transformations of adolescence.

Scattered in the literature are comments noting the importance of addressing the adolescent experience in adult patients (e.g., A. Freud 1958, Jacobson 1964), and recently there has been a resurgence of attention to this issue (e.g., Feigelson 1976, Goettsche 1986, Isay 1975, Jacobs 1987, Renik 1990). Some of our earlier work has highlighted how adolescent patterns of termination may appear as a component of the termination phase in the analysis of adults (Novick 1982b, 1988, 1990). We have described this in terms of the adolescent task of relinquishing the omnipotent self.

Even the normal solutions of preoedipal and oedipal conflicts involve the formation of typical latency fantasies, based on limited knowledge and capacity. Unrealistic, omnipotent fantasy solutions may be maintained through the latency years, but adolescent changes make it increasingly difficult to deny, distort, or avoid reality. The reality of adolescent growth, with the capacity to put wishes into action, demands transformation of earlier fantasy solutions. The accomplishment of the adolescent task of taking ownership of the mature body requires relinquishment of the fantasy that one can be both a man and a woman. The experience of genital pleasure makes untenable the notion of oedipal equality and requires acknowledgment of generational differences. Coalescence of a separate identity contradicts the fantasy of indispensability to the primary object. Acceptance of the realities of time, choice, and personal limitations necessitates abandoning the fantasies that one need never grow up, grow old, die, have to choose, or give anything up. All of the developmental tasks of adolescence require a transformation of the relation to reality and fantasy, as part of the integration of the mature body and self. Failure at this stage will have a profound impact on adult functioning. We shall briefly describe some material from the end of an adolescent analysis to illustrate these issues as they appeared, and then return to a later phase of Ms. A.'s treatment to examine the impact of failures of adolescent transformations on her later development.

When Terry entered analysis in late adolescence, she was depressed, overweight, and abusing alcohol and drugs. After a tumultuous, occasionally alarming, but ultimately successful analysis lasting four and a half years, she entered a termination phase by mutual agreement with the analyst. She had worked hard throughout the analysis on her pervasive tendency to react to any conflict or frustration with magical thinking, and during the last year there was abundant oedipal material in displaced, derivative, and transference forms. Despite the substantive work accomplished and her enormous gains in reality testing and richness of emotional life, there remained almost to the very end a sense that Terry clung to some secret fantasy which she wanted untouched. She began the last week of analysis reproaching the analyst for not conducting the termination properly, for not giving her what she wanted and, indeed, being just like her mother after all.

The following day Terry came in with a grievance about having to do all the work of the termination; she said she was tired of setting not only her own boundaries, but also the analyst's, by controlling her curiosity. Her associations to this feeling revealed a series of fantasy thoughts about the analysts's spouse and children, her awareness of conflict over her potential jealousy, and her resentment that she had had to inhibit her curiosity and oedipal transference wishes. The analyst took up the remaining omnipotent fantasy—her holding on to the last bit of magical control in the thought that it was only her inhibition that prevented her taking over the spouse, rather than the reality that, no matter how her figure looked or what she did, her wishes could not change the fact that the analyst was the person married to that individual. Terry was using this magical fantasy to defend against being overwhelmed by helplessness in the face of the reality of the ending of her treatment. With this acknowledgment, she felt free to experience her sadness as an appropriate emotion and reflected that what she would miss most about analysis was precisely that permission to feel her feelings.

This material from the last week of Terry's analysis exemplifies many of the issues of reality noted above, and work in this specific domain of ego development has been crucial for the restoration to progressive development of all our analysands in this age group. Let us turn now to our work with adult patients in order to examine how derivatives of adolescent conflicts over reality appear and how we may consider approaching them technically.

In the case of Ms. A., the 33-year-old divorced woman who had suffered significant preoedipal developmental interferences, we noted how the placement of superego interpretations in the context of a latency-age experience seemed to prove useful.

Near the end of her analysis, Ms. A. began actively preparing for entrance to professional school. She was doing very well in her studies, but as the date of the entrance exam approached she regressed significantly both in and out of treatment. The regression was marked by a rageful attempt to relinquish ownership of her body and mind and to attribute responsibility for her actions to the analyst. This was not new, as externalization of blame, intentionality, and responsibility had been major defenses throughout her analysis, but the resistance was more intense than previously experienced. Her rage was palpable as she lay on the couch, legs quivering and jaw clenched. She accused the analyst of being uncaring and unsympathetic. To protect the analyst from her intense fury and to bolster her externalizations, she reinvoked her image of her mother as erratic, intrusive, depressed, and controlling. Her memories were of childhood, but the clue that the immediate precipitant was a derivative from adolescence was the recurrence of suicidal fantasies. These fantasies referred back to her three serious suicide attempts when she went to college at 17 years of age. The analyst suggested that the current entrance examination represented a reality confrontation with her omnipotent convictions, just as going away to college had done. Her breakdown during adolescence had been her way of avoiding the central task of integrating her childhood fantasies with her adolescent reality. At first Ms. A. responded with what she called a temper tantrum and studiously avoided talking of her adolescence. She referred everything back to childhood.

Then, after weeks of painfully difficult sessions, Ms. A. came in and said, "I felt better yesterday—it was a good session. Talking about reality helps." Her subsequent associations confirmed that facing the reality that her analysis would end as she left for professional school in the foreseeable future highlighted and challenged her omnipotent fantasy convictions. As work continued on the adolescent task which had been avoided, she began to experience the conflict between the magical and reality systems of thought. She still felt and lived in her magical world, but she also began to step back and say, for example, "It's crazy—who am I hurting with screwing things up—not you or my mother, only myself." She then said of her adolescence, "My only reality at that time was a need to be perfect. Now I know what that meant. It meant being in control of everything, stopping time, stopping change, staying a little girl who thought she knew how to control her mother's feelings."

With these illustrations we are emphasizing the role of reality in the adolescent transformation of latency fantasies. Further, we are suggesting that a major determinant of adult personality can be found in whether the reality of adolescent development was denied, distorted, or integrated. In his characteristically poetic way, Winnicott captured the impact of the reality of physical maturity at adolescence when he wrote, "It is valuable to compare adolescent ideas with those of childhood. If in the fantasy of early growth there is contained death, then at adolescence there is contained murder" (1969, p. 752).

Over the years, we have tried to demonstrate that child and adolescent analysis is a rich source of contributions to the further development of psychoanalytic technique and theory. In all our work we have emphasized the contributions of preoedipal, oedipal, and postoedipal phenomena. In this chapter, we focused on latency and adolescence. We have tried to show how alertness to latency elements can affect both the timing of interpretations and the understanding of neurosogenic factors and the forces for health available in the patient's personality. Alertness to adolescent phenomena highlights the adult patient's difficulty in integrating adolescent realities with his childhood fantasy solutions to preoedipal and oedipal conflicts. The outcome of the adolescent struggle with reality appears in adult pathology in overt symptoms, such as perversions, or in covert fantasies and expectations about analysis. Our clinical findings from this and other work have reinforced our assumption that no one phase has preeminence over others, that earlier is not necessarily more important, and that there cannot be pure recapitulation, revival, or "reanimation" (Freud 1925) of the past in the present.

The past transforms and is transformed by the present. We can never know the past directly, hence the persistent devaluation of reconstruction. Here we have tried to demonstrate that a knowledge of the transformations appropriate to each phase in the past—from infancy through adulthood—gives us additional access to the determinants and functions of the patient's pathology in the present, increases the specificity of genetic interpretation, and gives both patient and analyst greater conviction about the accuracy of the essential analytic work of reconstruction.

When the frescoes in the Sistine Chapel were restored, there was enormous controversy over the accuracy of the colors. A similar debate delayed the cleaning and restoration of the Masaccio frescoes in the Brancacci Chapel in Florence, as there was no way of knowing who was right about the original tints. While the work was being prepared, an altar was moved away from a window in the chapel. This exposed two painted medallions on the window frame, which had been protected through centuries of dirt and discoloration and thus shone in their original colors. One was painted by Masolino, the other by his brilliant student, Masaccio. The original colors were displayed, and the transformation in style between the Gothic and the Renaissance was revealed. Child and adolescent analysis can be our medallions.

PART II
MECHANISMS

5   PROJECTION AND
        EXTERNALIZATION[1]

Projection was one of the first concepts developed by Freud and
a detailed analysis of the topic can be found as early as 1895. It
is a measure of the complexity of the subject that despite the long
history of its usage there remains considerable confusion and
disagreement as to the meaning and applicability of the term.
Projection is one of the more frequently used terms in psychoanalytic literature, especially in clinical presentations. It is seen
by some authors as basic to all clinical work. Rapaport (1944),
for instance, states that the fundamental psychoanalytic postulates of psychic determinism and continuity require a concept like
that of projection.

In the current literature it is used as a portmanteau term en-
compassing such diverse processes as displacement, generalization,
transference revival, externalization, and some processes of adap-

1. An earlier version of this chapter was presented at the annual meeting of
the Association of Child Psychotherapists in London, March 1969, and the
present version was presented at a meeting of the Hampstead Clinic in July
1969.

tive mastery. A host of phenomena is described as subject to projection: drives, introjects, aspects of the self, affects, sensations, and structures such as superego and id. Projection is said to be manifest in such varied areas as play, artistic creation, religion, projective tests, and persecutory delusions. Used in this way the term lacks explanatory power, and significant clinical distinctions are blurred. Rycroft's definition (1968)–"viewing a mental image as objective reality"–reflects the current broad application of the term. This definition is a resurrection of a preanalytic usage (Feigenbaum 1936) and epitomizes the degree to which Freud's specific psychoanalytic formulations and differentiations in this area have been lost.

There have been attempts to differentiate some of the processes subsumed under projection. In particular the concept of externalization has been the focus of increased attention (Brodey 1965, Rapaport 1944, 1950, 1952, Weiss 1947). However, this has added a terminological difficulty since those who write about externalization tend to use it synonymously with projection, and it is not clear whether externalization is viewed as a subspecies of projection, as a process distinct from it, or as a more general process with projection as a subspecies. The current state of affairs can best be exemplified by quoting the definitions of projection and externalization given in the glossary of psychoanalytic terms (Moore and Fine 1967):

> *Projection*–is a process whereby a painful impulse or idea is attributed to the external world. [p. 24]
> *Externalization:* A term used to refer in general to the tendency to project into the external world one's instinctual wishes, conflicts, moods, and ways of thinking (cognitive styles). It is evident in young children who are afraid of monsters in the dark, in the savage for whom the jungle is populated by evil spirits, and in the paranoiac who sees persecutors all about him. The capacity for externalization may be used constructively in art, poetry, literature, etc. It is also the basis for the Rorschach test. . . . [p. 39]

Our interest in this topic stemmed from the fact that clinically we were making distinctions that we were unable to encompass and clearly communicate within the current terminology. The conceptual difficulties can be traced, in part, to the many misunderstandings that exist concerning Freud's use of projection. Freud himself felt that this concept was unclear, and he repeatedly stated his intention to devote a separate study to it (1911a, 1915b).[2] Illuminating as this study would have been, there remains in Freud's extant writings on projection a major source of confusion, which continues to affect current usage. Freud used the term in two distinct ways, which we describe as the psychological and mechanical referents of projection. "Projection" is a pre-analytic term, with major referents in other fields. The literal meaning is "to throw in front of"; hence its usage in relation to the mechanical process by which an image is thrown onto a screen. This usage of projection in relation to psychic processes is a metaphorical application of the mechanical model. It is as if the mind is likened to a cinema projector and said to project internal images onto the blank screen of the external world.

Parallel with the continuing elaboration of a psychological concept of the "process or mechanism" of projection, Freud, from his first to his last usage of the term, employed the descriptive mechanical metaphor. This can be seen, for instance, in his paper on "Screen Memories" (1899). In relation to the "amalgamation" of two sets of fantasies Freud states, "You projected the two phantasies on to one another" (p. 315). Similarly in 1936 he writes, "but these two motives are essentially the same, for one is only a projection of the other" (p. 242fn.). A final example will illustrate Freud's explicit use of the term in a descriptive mechanical sense and not as a psychic mechanism or process. In the *Introductory Lectures* (1916–1917) he writes of melancholia as follows: "the object has been set up in the ego itself, has been, as it were, projected on to the ego. (Here I can only give you a *pictoral description* and not an ordered account on topographical and dynamic lines.)" (p. 427, italics added).

---

2. Strachey suggests that this may have been one of the "missing" metapsychological papers.

The above quotation emphasizes the fact that when Freud used projection in the mechanical sense, he was describing and not explaining the phenomenon in question; in contrast, the psychological concept of projection was meant as an explanation. The mechanical-descriptive and the psychological-explanatory uses of projection are frequently employed in the same paper, and unless one distinguishes between them the theory presented is ambiguous and frequently contradictory. When they are differentiated, it becomes clear that the two referents of the term are used for different purposes. As we shall demonstrate later, the psychological concept undergoes progressive modification so that finally it refers to mechanisms of defense. The mechanical referent of projection remains a "pictorial description" used largely to highlight evidence for the fundamental psychoanalytic assumptions of psychic determinism and continuity. This is especially so in relation to the phenomena Freud subsumed under the projection of "endopsychic" percepts. In 1897 Freud wrote to Fliess:

> Can you imagine what "endopsychic myths" are? They are the latest product of my mental labour. The dim inner perception of one's own psychical apparatus stimulates illusions, which are naturally projected outwards, and characteristically into the future and a world beyond. Immortality, retribution, the world after death, are all reflections of our inner psyche . . . psychomythology. [p. 237]

The accent here is on projection not as the explanatory process but as a synonym for "reflection." In subsequent discussions of the projection of endopsychic percepts (1901, 1909, 1911b, 1913) Freud emphasizes the nondefensive "transposition" of the structural conditions of the mind into the external world (1913, p. 91). In each instance he traces the inner source of the external manifestation, using the term projection only to stress that these are reflections of inner phenomena. For instance, the doctrine of reward in the afterlife "is nothing more than a mythical projection" of the endopsychic impression made by the substitution of the reality principle for the pleasure principle (1911b, p. 223).

This use of projection is similar to its current application to the areas of art, religion, projective tests, children's fantasies, indeed all surface manifestations of inner phenomena. It is this reflection of the inner in the external world which Rapaport (1944) refers to as "the projective hypothesis." It is legitimate to use projection in this way, but it should be emphasized that this is a preanalytic, nonpsychological, and mainly descriptive usage. We would therefore suggest that this usage be discontinued since it leads to a situation where all surface manifestations are subsumed under projection, which entails the loss of the specific psycho-analytic referents of the term and strips the concept of any explanatory value. Instead of the "projective hypothesis" one could speak of an "expressive hypothesis" to underline the existence of causal and genetic links between surface expressions of the individual (fantasies, behavior, creative acts, and so forth) and "the hidden structures, functions and contents of the mind" (A. Freud 1965). It should be stressed that surface manifestations may reflect or express any or all psychic processes, including defenses among which may be the defense mechanism of projection. The main theme of this paper is the clinical importance of distinguishing between the various psychic processes since each requires its own technical approach. To speak of all these surface expressions as projections, as is currently done, obscures the fact that defenses require different technical handling than manifestations of other inner processes.

There are further clinical and theoretical reasons to make the distinction we have suggested. Although the distinction between projection as a description and projection as a psychological explanation is relatively clear in Freud's writings, this is not so in the current literature. Thus surface reflections of inner processes not only are described as projections (which, as noted above, is a legitimate but confusing usage) but also are explained as being due to projection. This is particularly evident in the area of empathy, where communication between infant and mother, between patient and therapist, is attributed to processes of projection (Jacobson 1964, Klein 1955). This leads to an equation of expression and communication, which in our view obscures recognition of the patient's resistances to communication. Understanding of the mental states of the infant or patient on the part of the mother or therapist need involve neither the child's intention to communicate nor the use of the mechanism of projection. Correct inferences can frequently be drawn from external expressions before the infant develops the capacity to communicate and despite the patient's intention to avoid communication.

A related issue is the conceptualization of the projective process in terms of instinctual modes and aims (Abraham 1924, Jaffe 1968, Malin and Grotstein 1966). Communication is said to occur via a projective process in which the patient spits out or evacuates something which the therapist then ingests. This is a concretization of a process that, as Freud (1913) repeatedly emphasized, takes place in the perceptual system, and thus involves a delusional or fantasy representation. To say to a patient that he has put something *into* the therapist (e.g., Klein 1955, Lush 1968) is to collude with his omnipotent fantasy, give it the stamp of reality, and provide the therapist with a rationalization for the acting out of countertransference feelings.

Returning to Freud's views on projection, once we have excluded the mechanical usage discussed above, we find a psychological theory of projection and related mechanisms which is further advanced than much current thinking on these topics. Under the general heading of projection Freud subsumed five interrelated but distinguishable applications of the concept. We have described the areas of application as follows:

1. Projection as an early mechanism basic to the development of the self
2. Generalization, an aspect of animistic thinking
3. Attribution of cause or responsibility to the external world

4. Externalization of aspects of the self
5. Projection of the drive, or projection proper.

In our view these differentiations should be incorporated into any attempt to conceptualize mechanisms involving the subjective allocation of inner phenomena to the outside world. We would thus achieve a historical consistency the lack of which leads to misunderstandings. More important, the differentiations made by Freud are based upon clinical distinctions which are obscured when these phenomena are subsumed under a portmanteau heading.

In this section we shall summarize Freud's views on the first three categories noted above, and we will comment on their applicability to current clinical and theoretical issues. The second section will focus on the importance of the distinction between externalization of aspects of the self and projection of the drive.

PROJECTION AS AN EARLY MECHANISM BASIC TO THE DEVELOPMENT OF THE SELF

It is generally accepted that among the major tasks confronting the developing organism are those of integration and differentiation. Specifically, the child must gradually differentiate the self and the outer world. Writers in the field of developmental psychoanalysis and psychology have put forward a number of suggestions concerning ways in which, at various stages, this differentiation might be made. There is, for instance, the action-oriented mode of differentiation (Piaget 1936), and Freud describes differentiation on the basis of the pleasure principle (1915a). From the adult observer's point of view, such modes will initially lead to faulty, unrealistic differentiation of self and object, but normally this is gradually corrected by experience.

Many authors, especially those of a Kleinian orientation, refer to this initial faulty differentiation as projection. They see pro-

jection as a process that occurs from birth on and, with introjection, as a primary mechanism leading to structure formation
(Heimann 1952, Klein 1932). Whether projection can occur prior
to structure formation, especially minimal differentiation of self
and external world, is a major controversial issue. Waelder, for
instance, states that "conclusive evidence for these early manifestations [of projection] is still wanting" (1951, p. 169). Anna
Freud, as early as 1936, pointed out the logical problems created
by the Kleinian theory of projection, when she stated, "we might
suppose that projection and introjection were methods which
depended on the differentiation of the ego from the outside world.
The expulsion of ideas or affects from the ego and their relega-
tion to the outside world would be a relief to the ego only when
it had learned to distinguish itself from that world" (p. 51).

Proponents of the theory of projection as a neonatal mechanism cite the authority for their view in the writings of Freud,
especially "Instincts and Their Vicissitudes" (1915a), and "A
Metapsychological Supplement to the Theory of Dreams" (1917).
During this period Freud did in fact view projection as an important process in the early development of the self. Under the dominance of the pleasure principle objects which are a source of pleasure are "incorporated," and "a part of its own self" that causes
unpleasure projected into the external world, thus creating the
"purified pleasure ego" (1915a, p. 136).

However, writers on both sides of this controversy fail to take
into account two important points. First, in all genetic statements
concerning projection, Freud posits at least minimal structure
formation or ego organization prior to the occurrence of projection. The purified pleasure ego, which is created by projection
and introjection, is *not* a primary ego state. Originally, according
to Freud, there is a primal pleasure ego, one which is cathected
with instincts and capable, to some extent, of satisfying them on
itself. It is indifferent to the external world. This primal pleasure
ego, "as a consequence of experience" is then forced to take account of reality, thus leading to the "original reality ego." This

reality ego "*distinguished internal and external by means of a sound objective criterion*" (1915a, p. 136, italics added). It is only after the development of the capacity to distinguish between internal and external that the processes of projection and introjection come into play in order to create the third phase of the ego, the "purified pleasure ego."[3]

Secondly, most authors fail to note that in his later writings Freud explicitly differentiates the early process from projection proper. In *Beyond the Pleasure Principle* he described this same process not as projection, but as "the origin of projection" (1920, p. 29). In his many later investigations in the area of early ego development he does not employ the term projection but uses phrases such as "ascribe to the external world" (1930, p. 66f).

Since any statement concerning the earliest stages of development must be seen as hypothetical, the question of the occurrence of projection prior to structure formation is essentially a theoretical one. We can add little to Freud's clear formulations, but would stress that to speak of processes involving the subjective allocation of inner phenomena to the outer world before the development of the self and the differentiation of inner and outer is meaningless and confuses cause and motivation (Rapaport 1960).

GENERALIZATION

With the differentiation of the self from the external world, the child's view of the external world, and especially of his objects, will be partly determined by what he knows and feels about himself. Thus as the child becomes aware of himself, he *naturally* ascribes similar characteristics to the object. This is a primitive animistic mode of thought, appropriate to his relatively egocen-

---

3. Even in an earlier paper (1911b), where he described the replacement of the pleasure ego by the reality ego, Freud posited the existence of minimal structuralization ("devices") in order to account for early defensive processes.

tric stage of development. In the current literature, it is frequently described as a result of projection (Eidelberg 1968, Fenichel 1945, Jacobson 1964).

In 1901, Freud explicitly correlates "anthropomorphic" thinking with projection, the dynamic mechanism he discovered at work in paranoia. He continued this line of thought in *Totem and Taboo* (1913), which contains his most detailed examination of animism. The attribution of primitive man's own characteristics to the external world is said to be caused by projection. However, we find in the same work another, more detailed, explanation of animism that does not require the mechanism of projection: animism is a "system of thought" (p. 77), natural to primitive stages in mankind and the individual. It involves the attribution to the external world of those internal characteristics *consciously perceived* by the primitive mind. The animistic system makes use of the technique of magic and is intimately linked with the narcissistic phase of libidinal development and the principle of the omnipotence of thoughts (p. 85).

It seems to us that Freud opts for the latter alternative, because in his later writings on primitive thought he makes no use of projection as a dynamic explanation. In fact, in 1927, he states that projection is not an explanation, but merely a description of what occurs. His clearest description of the process involved in animistic thinking is in "The Unconscious" (1915b) where he refers to it as an "identification":

> Consciousness makes each of us aware only of his own states of mind; that other people, too, possess a consciousness is an inference which we draw by analogy from their observable utterances and actions, in order to make this behavior of theirs intelligible to us. (It would no doubt be psychologically more correct to put it this way: that without any special reflection we attribute to everyone else our own constitution and therefore our consciousness as well, and that this identification is a *sine qua non* of our understanding.) This inference (or this identification) was formerly extended by the ego to other human beings, to animals, plants, inanimate objects and to the world at large

and proved serviceable so long as their similarity to the individual ego was overwhelmingly great; but it became more untrustworthy in proportion as the difference between the ego and these 'others' widened. . . . But even where the original inclination to identification has withstood criticism—that is, when the 'others' are our fellowmen— the assumption of a consciousness in them rests upon an inference and cannot share the immediate certainty which we have of our own consciousness. [p. 169]

In the interest of terminological clarity, we would call this process "generalization."[4] Following Freud, we see this process as a natural mode of thought, not the defense of projection proper — the child retains conscious awareness of that which he has attributed to the external world. Generalization is the child's major mode of apprehending the unknown and persists to some extent throughout life. Examples are legion: for instance, the infantile sexual theories described by Freud (1908) provide clear illustrations.

The differentiation between generalization and projection is of theoretical importance in many areas,[5] but in our view its major

---

4. We recognize that the usage of this term in mathematics, philosophy, and academic psychology usually connotes abstract secondary process thinking. However, the dictionary definition of "generalization" conveys precisely the sense of the process we are discussing:
   a. The process of generalizing, that is of forming general notions or propositions from particulars.
   b. Quasi-concretely: a general inference.
   c. The process of spreading over every part.
In our view, generalization occurs at every level of mental functioning. What differentiates animistic thinking from sophisticated logical inferences is the operation of other functions such as judgment and reality testing.
5. For example, it is often assumed that Freud saw projection as playing a central role in superego formation. This is not the case. Freud ascribed the severity of the superego not to the projection of aggressive wishes onto the subsequently introjected object, but to three other factors, one of which was the *natural assumption* on the part of the child that he and the father had similar aggressive wishes toward each other. This is spelled out most clearly in *Civilization and Its Discontents* (1930, p. 128ff.)

importance lies in the clinical and technical implications. Extensive manifestations of generalization beyond a certain age usually reflect a weakness of the ego due to immaturity, faulty development, or deterioration.

For example, Kevin was an 11-year-old boy referred to a child guidance clinic for a variety of obsessive-compulsive rituals. He was diagnosed as a neurotic whose major conflict centered around aggression. In psychotherapy he very soon showed conscious fears of being attacked by his therapist. These were seen and interpreted as projections, that is, as a further attempt to defend against the awareness of his own aggressive impulses toward the object. The child soon became totally unmanageable and was referred to the Hampstead Clinic for intensive treatment. Soon after the start of analysis it became clear that the fear of being killed by the therapist was not based upon a projection but upon a generalization of his own conscious wishes toward all his male objects; that is, wishing to kill an envied male object, he simply assumed that the object had the same wishes toward him.

Diagnostically, this use of generalization alerted the therapist to other signs of ego deviation, and finally a diagnosis of "borderline" was confirmed. This new perspective on the case led to modifications of technique. Despite positive changes that occurred during the first year of analysis, the use of generalization persisted. At a certain point it became possible to focus on this pathological mode of functioning. The therapist then helped the child to develop those structures necessary to inhibit generalization. By using the therapist as an auxiliary ego Kevin slowly came to accept that he could not know the object's thoughts or feelings (unless these were communicated to him in some way) and that the object was therefore not necessarily like himself and might have thoughts or feelings different from his own. It should be noted that with the inhibition of generalization Kevin remained conscious of his own aggressive wishes, but there was a significant change in the intensity and quality of his anxiety. Only much later in treatment, after considerable ego development, did Kevin make use of projection proper to defend against the conscious awareness of his own aggressive impulses.

While in this example we have emphasized the contrast between a mode of functioning and a defense, that is, generalization and projection, we are aware that after structural inhibition of early modes has taken place, they may be re-employed for defensive purposes. As a defense, generalization is frequently used to stave off the painful affects attendant upon separation and represents a fantasy fusion of self and object representations. For example, Kevin, at a later stage in his analysis, insisted that the therapist had the same wishes and thoughts as he did himself. It emerged that this insistence represented a fantasy defense against loneliness. Kevin said, "Oh, I wish you did think the same, because then I wouldn't be alone."

Manifestations of the defensive use of generalization are frequently referred to as projections, not only by Kleinian authors but also by more classically oriented writers, such as Jacobson, who states, "the terms introjection and projection refer to psychic processes, as a result of which self images assume characteristics of object images and vice versa" (1964, p. 46). This view obscures an important clinical phenomenon. In the fusional or merging fantasies, what is said to be projected is not a painful personal characteristic that must be divorced from the self and attributed to the external world, but is rather a conscious inner experience which is extended and *shared* with the object.[6]

---

6. It would be interesting to examine the possible genetic relationship between generalization and projection. We suggest that the capacity to generalize is a necessary precursor to the later use of the defense mechanism of projection.

ATTRIBUTION OF CAUSE OR RESPONSIBILITY

During the long period of the child's dependence on his parents, he often attributes to them the responsibility for his thoughts, actions, and feeling states. Gradually the child becomes aware of his growing capacity to execute his wishes in action, to alter both internal and external conditions, and thus assumes or internalizes responsibility for certain of his own actions and thoughts. Anna Freud's description of the developmental line toward bodily independence provides a model of the necessary steps for the internalization of responsibility (1965).

The first type of projection discussed by Freud is the attribution of cause to the external world, and this remains for him a major category (1895, 1909, 1910, 1911a, 1918, 1925). He applies it to the defense against self-reproach, or, in later structural terms, guilt or shame. In his examples we can see that the idea or impulse is retained in consciousness, but the responsibility for it is allocated outside.

There are many examples of this in clinical practice, especially in work with children. It frequently occurs after a period of defense analysis and, as the drive derivative emerges in action or thought, the child may say, "You made me do that," or "You put that thought in my head." For instance, the phallic-oedipal wishes of an adolescent boy emerged in the following form: "You want me to look at my mother's legs." It is striking that there is little discussion of this category of projection: it is a common clinical phenomenon, and represents Freud's first conceptualization of projection as a defense.[7]

---

7. This category is important enough to warrant a separate study. The internalization and externalization of responsibility can be seen most vividly in child analysis. A starting point might be Anna Freud's discussion of "The Child Analyst as Object for Externalization" (1965, p. 41). A study of this nature would involve discussion of the relations between transference and externalization, the treatment alliance and the internalization of responsibility, and the externalization of structures such as id and superego.

In the previous section, we focused on the theoretical and clinical importance of distinguishing between the applications of projection to defensive and nondefensive processes. Concerning Freud's use of projection, we wished to emphasize the line of progressive limitation in the application of the term, the exclusion of phenomena which had initially been subsumed under projection, and the increasing characterization of projection as a defense. We believe it would be helpful if the term "externalization" were to be accepted as the general heading for all those processes which lead to the *subjective allocation of inner phenomena to the outer world.*[8] As a general term "externalization" would refer to processes that might be normal or pathological, adaptive or maladaptive. Such usage would parallel the current general usage of "internalization" under which we subsume a variety of processes: introjection, identification, and so forth.

Freud differentiated three types of defensive projection. We have already discussed the defensive externalization or attribution of cause. In this section we shall focus in particular on the differentiation we derive from Freud between the externalization of a drive and the externalization of an aspect of the self representation. We would suggest that the term "projection" be reserved for the former process—that is, *drive projection.*

Although we are aware that the distinction between drive and self representation is an arbitrary one, since these two elements are intimately interrelated—aspects of the self representation are, for instance, "colored" by the drive—we still propose that on balance one can say whether a specific phenomenon is related more to the drive or to an aspect of the self representation. For example, there is a difference between the statements, "I am an angry person" and "I am angry at (I hate) you." The former

---

8. This is a modification of the view advanced in an earlier report on this study (Novick and Hurry 1969) where "externalization" was restricted to defensive processes.

is an evaluation of the self representation, the latter a drive expression.

From 1911 onward Freud's most consistent and major use of the term projection was to denote a reflexive defense against the drive. Thus, in the Schreber case, he described a paranoid defense against homosexuality in which *unconscious hate* was projected. The unconscious proposition "I hate him" became transformed into the conscious thought, "He hates (persecutes) me" (1911a, p. 63). In later writings (notably 1913, 1922), Freud linked drive projection with defense against ambivalent conflicts. The last time Freud used the term projection in this sense was in 1931, when he explained the girl's fear of being killed by the mother as due to the projection of her own hostile wishes.[9]

Although the Schreber case is the major reference for most discussions of projection as a defense, it is not generally recognized that, in the same paper, Freud explicitly differentiated another type of defensive projection. He wrote that the proposition "I [a man] love him" could also be contradicted by the formula, "It is not *I* who love the man—*she* loves him." By means of "the change of the subject who loves, the whole process is in any case thrown outside the self. The fact that the woman loves the man is a matter of external perception" (1911a, p. 64). We would term this type of projection "externalization of an aspect of the self representation."[10]

We shall discuss the processes of externalization of aspects of the self and drive projection from two points of view, the devel-

---

9. References to projection also occur in 1936, when it is used in the mechanical sense described above. See also the posthumously published notes (1941).

10. This is a cumbersome phrase and in the section that follows we often use "externalization" as a shorthand. The context should make it clear to the reader that we mean here the specific defensive process of "externalization of an aspect of the self representation" and not the general heading under which we subsume all the different types of externalization.

opment of the individual, and the effect upon him when he is used as a target for the externalizations of others.

EXTERNALIZATION OF ASPECTS
OF THE SELF REPRESENTATION

With the emergence of the self from the state of "primal confusion" the child faces the extremely difficult task of integrating the various dissonant components of the developing self. When one considers the rapidity of the physical and mental changes which take place in the child between 8 and 18 months, one realizes that the demands made upon his relatively weak integrative function are far greater than at any other period of life. In addition to the integrative demands made by his own physical and mental growth, the object's expectations of the child also undergo rapid changes, and these expectations are transmitted to the child. (Only in adolescence does the individual have to cope with changes that make integrative demands of a magnitude approximating those of infancy.) The earliest conflicts confronting the child in his attempts at integration relate to the existence of dissonant, seemingly incompatible aspects of the self. These conflicts are intensified as some aspects become narcissistically valued through both the child's own pleasures and, more importantly, the parents' response to one or other aspect of himself. Those aspects which are not so valued may become dystonic. Their retention within the self representation will lead to a narcissistic pain such as humiliation. The toddler who falls often cries not only because of the physical pain but also because of the humiliation of seeing himself as unable to walk. One solution is to *externalize* that aspect of himself, for instance, to make the doll or the baby the one who is incapable of walking, thus avoiding the narcissistic humiliation. At this stage of development such externalization is both normal and adaptive.

It is adaptive in that the intensity of the current conflict is decreased sufficiently to allow progressive development to occur. When the child's self image is stabilized at a higher level (through the consolidation of ego skills, the reinforcement of pleasure in functioning, and a general decrease in the intensity of the earlier drive derivatives), he is then able without threat adaptively to integrate many of those aspects previously externalized. Thus the child who is fully capable of walking can again allow himself to crawl without humiliation.

Externalization may also be adaptive in many other ways. It may, for example, be used as a stepping stone on the way to identification.[11] The self is constantly reshaped by changing ego capacities and drive aims. New shapes of the self may be externalized onto contemporaries, in play, onto imaginary figures, fictional characters, and so on. In addition to its defensive aspect, this process allows for what may be termed a trial reality test in which, via the object of externalization, the child can assess the effects of and reactions to this new shape of the self. In the light of these effects and reactions he may then be able to accept this new aspect of himself.

Thus, as a transitory phenomenon externalization is a normal defensive process and can be adaptive, particularly at certain phases. However, the extreme or persistent use of this defense at any period of life may have serious pathological effects. It may result in a very restricted personality with important aspects of the self permanently split off and unavailable.

It is a defense not *primarily* directed against the drives or against object-linked anxieties, but is aimed at avoiding the narcissistic pain consequent upon accepting devalued aspects of the self. Object relations are only secondarily involved in this process, and in fact externalization can be used as a defense against object relationships.

---

11. We are here following a suggestion made by Anna Freud at a meeting of the Clinical Concept Group.

PROJECTION PROPER

The defense of *projection proper* is fundamentally different. It is motivated by the sequence of fantasied dangers consequent upon drive expression. It is a defense against a specific drive derivative directed toward an object and thus considerable structural development must take place before it can or need be employed. Among other things there must have been a channeling of drive energies into a specific aim and the establishment of the capacity to relate to a whole object. In addition, there must be sufficient ego development to allow for the integration of drive derivatives with ego capacities in the formation of fantasy expressions of object-directed wishes. Thus we would see the use of projection as becoming possible at a later stage than that of externalization—at a stage, in fact, when the capacity to manipulate objects in fantasy has developed to the point where a drive derivative originally directed at an object can be subjectively allocated to that object, while the self is experienced as the target of that drive derivative.

As a transitory phenomenon the use of projection may be normal at certain points of development, but in contrast to other processes of externalization it has relatively little adaptive value. It may be seen as adaptive insofar as it represents an attempt to attain, retain, or regain object ties, albeit in distorted form, and thus may presage the emergence of an object relationship. As Freud (1911a) noted, projection could represent an attempt at recathexis of objects following upon a psychotic withdrawal. But from the point of view of the observer projection as a defense is remarkably inefficient for the avoidance of anxiety, except insofar as it makes possible actual or fantasied flight from the apparent source of danger. In contrast to externalization of aspects of the self, which can effectively do away with painful affect, projection may leave the subject a constant prey to anxiety. Whereas externalization of aspects of the self can be seen as a *relatively* simple one-step defense, projection is often the last step in a series of defenses and may in itself occasion the use of further defenses, such as reversal of affect.

CLINICAL AND TECHNICAL IMPLICATIONS

Anna Freud's (1965) discussion of externalization and especially of the technical implications of distinguishing between externalization and transference phenomena contributed greatly to our thinking on these topics.

It was primarily for clinical and technical reasons that we earlier made the distinction between mode of functioning and defense. For similar reasons we believe it essential to distinguish between the two types of externalization outlined above. Extensive use of either defense relates to, and results in, serious ego pathology. However, externalization is more closely bound up with impairment in the integrative function, whereas projection relates to a weakness in the defense system vis-à-vis the drives. Extensive use of externalization of aspects of the self would indicate severe narcissistic disturbance with a very early fixation point; extensive use of projection would indicate severe conflict over drive expression, with a later fixation point, possibly related to the anal phase.

A transitory use of both processes, however, is frequently seen in treatment. While at times it may be difficult to differentiate, from the surface manifestation, which process may be at work, it is usually possible to do so on the lines of the distinctions we have made. Thus a child may say that the therapist is a messy, uncontrolled person. Given that this represents an externalization rather than a generalization, a displacement and so on, it is of value to ascertain whether it is predominantly the messy aspect of the self representation which is being externalized, or whether it is a drive derivative (such as the wish to mess upon the therapist) which is being projected. One can note whether the defense leads to anxiety or relief on the part of the child. The former would indicate the working of projection with the drive allocated to the therapist and the child experiencing himself as the object of the therapist's wish to mess. Here there would be no relief, but the anxiety-driven wish to flee from the situation. In contrast, there is relief when the externalization is the result of the child's need to rid himself of a narcissistically painful self image, for here he will perceive the object as unrelated to himself, as different from himself, and as something which may be ignored, derided, or treated with contempt.

We chose this example to underline the difficulties which may arise in the course of distinguishing between the processes which may be at work, and to point to the child's consequent feeling state and attitude as a valuable indicator. Very often, however, especially in child analysis, the processes can also be separated on the basis of the degree of fit between the externalization and the reality. In the case of projection there is always some degree of fit; that is, what is projected always has somewhere a basis in reality. There is, for instance, no relationship without ambivalence, so that the child's projection of hostile impulses will always touch upon a core of truth—and in fact the child will frequently hang the projection upon some real event such as a canceled session. In contrast, there may be a very small, or even no degree of fit between an externalized dystonic self representation and the reality. Thus the preschool child who claims that the therapist is stupid and cannot read or function independently is clearly denying the reality of the therapist and simply using him in order to externalize an aspect of himself.

Once the differentiation has been made it follows that interpretation of externalization of aspects of the self must focus upon the need to defend against narcissistic pain, whereas interpretations of projection must focus upon the need to defend against the anxiety related to drive expression.

Michael, a 14-year-old boy, spent much of the first phase of his analysis being extremely condescending, sarcastic, and derisive toward his analyst. The material would be purposefully presented in a confusing manner so that the analyst was often left in the dark or made errors in relation to the factual material. This could have been taken as a direct expression of aggression by the patient, or an attempt to ward off anticipated attack from the analyst, an anticipation based on projection. However, Michael's affect and the subsequent material clearly indicated that he was identifying with the powerful, arrogant father and was externalizing the "Little Mike" who had often been laughed at, ignored, and left confused.

The analyst successfully handled this defense by first verbalizing the manner in which he was being viewed by the patient: how he was being seen as a stupid, little boy, and how painful it must be to be treated in this manner. Michael responded by saying, "Like a retard 8-year-old" and could then recount the earlier narcissistically painful experiences at the hands of a condescending father who laughed at him for his ignorance. The therapist could take up the persistence of this image in Michael's current self representation and his attempt to defend against a recurrence of humiliation by externalization. The use of this mechanism then decreased significantly. Michael could accept the fact that he could be ignorant of something without being humiliated and, most important, he could begin to relate to the analyst as a real object.

With the emergence of object-directed wishes toward the analyst, we had the manifestation of projection proper as a defense. Michael's material, and especially his nonverbal behavior, clearly indicated a fear of attack. It should be noted that when Michael was externalizing aspects of the self, he reacted not with anxiety, but with relief. "You've got problems, not me," he would say, but he seemed to look forward to the sessions. However, when projection was used to defend against his hostile wishes, the analytic situation became one fraught with anxiety and Michael would frequently run from or miss his sessions completely. During the hour he would focus on those reality factors which could be experienced as signs of hostility on the part of the therapist, such as the cancellation of a session, the unwillingness to change an hour, or the seeming attack of an interpretation.

The analyst did not disagree with the patient's understanding
of these reality events; accepting them as within the realm of
possibility, he suggested that what was feared was not just dislike or lack of consideration on the part of the therapist but an
actual wish to hurt, possibly kill, the patient. Michael readily
agreed that this was his fear, and the analyst could then take up
the magical equating of wish and deed as a major factor behind
the intensity of the anxiety. This work on the omnipotence of
thought led to a significant decrease in the patient's anxiety, the
establishment once again of the therapeutic alliance, and the
gradual emergence into consciousness of Michael's own aggressive wishes. Subsequent focus on the emphasis on only one side
of the therapist, the hostile side, allowed for the uncovering of
Michael's intense conflicts over ambivalence and with this the
projections themselves disappeared.

IMPACT OF PARENTAL EXTERNALIZATIONS
AND PROJECTIONS UPON THE CHILD

Externalizations and even at times projections are fairly common
occurrences within families. It is the extensive and rigid use of
these mechanisms by the parents that indicates that pathological
processes are at work. In what follows we shall examine the impact upon the child of the pathological parental use of either
externalization or projection. This is a subject of great complexity, and here we illustrate only some of our main findings through
selected aspects of two cases.

1. Tommy's mother was a woman who could not integrate her
view of herself as castrated, damaged, messy. Throughout her
life she searched for objects upon whom to externalize this
dystonic aspect. Thus all her male objects, including her hus

band, were extremely messy, damaged, and inferior individuals. From the moment of Tommy's birth until he came into
treatment at the age of 11, the mother perceived him only as
a damaged, messy, stupid child. This view of Tommy was not
dynamically related to the vicarious gratification of her own
primitive impulses. On the contrary, she had little involvement
with the child, distancing him from her as far as possible and
at times forgetting or even losing him.

At the time of referral Tommy was a prime illustration of
what is frequently referred to as "the self-fulfilling prophecy."
There was an exact fit with the patterns of the mother's externalization. Despite indications of normal intelligence on psychological testing, he was retarded in all school subjects.
He was a regressed, soiling, snot-eating child with little control over drive expression. Most striking was the relative absence of anxiety or guilt in relation to drive expression. What
clearly emerged was the presence of a severe narcissistic disturbance with mental pain and conflict rooted in the acceptance of the devalued self and the inability to integrate positive aspects with this conscious self representation.

Outside the immediate family environment he defended
against the narcissistic pain almost exclusively by means of
externalizations. Despite Tommy's evident relief after having externalized the devalued part of himself, he still could
not see himself as clever, competent, and so forth. A fluctuating and relatively adequate level of functioning could be
achieved only by means of a conscious imitation, a type of
pseudo-identification with those contemporaries who could
manifest the positive qualities he could not accept in himself. Thus, as he later verbalized, "When I pretended I was
John I was able to score a goal, but when I was myself I fell
in the mud."

Within the family there was little need to externalize the
degraded self since the role of the devalued, damaged object
was compatible with the needs of all members of the family,

especially the mother. The main reason for accepting the mother's externalization lay in the realization, at some level, that despite the mother's distancing maneuvers she needed such a devalued object and that failure to comply with her need would leave him prey to the primitive terror of abandonment.

The father played an important role in Tommy's pathological development by offering him no alternative solution. He constantly reinforced the effects of the mother's pathology by using the same mechanisms along parallel lines. The father viewed Tommy as stupid, girlish, and damaged, and frequently said so to him. Psychiatric interviews with the father revealed the extent to which this view was based upon externalizations of dystonic aspects of himself.

As Tommy began to progress, one could clearly see the extent to which his acceptance of the parental externalizations had been a vital factor in the maintenance of the family equilibrium. Slowly, Tommy became consciously aware of the fact that, in his words, "They put the bad onto me and they feel good." As he gradually overcame the primitive fear of abandonment and could begin to integrate positive aspects within his self representation, his material centered mainly on the sadness of the mother, the chaos in the home, the madness of the family members, and, related to this, his own intense feelings of guilt. It should be noted that he was guilty not about the newly attained level of functioning per se, but about having deprived the family of a needed vehicle for externalization. To a certain extent this material related to Tommy's own feelings, fears, and fantasies, but to a marked degree it also reflected the reality.

As Tommy's positive development became unavoidably apparent, the family was thrown into a state of disequilibrium and chaos. The father took to his bed in a state of panic and confusion. The mother became depressed, disheveled, and totally disorganized. She consciously viewed herself as useless and unlovable and made a desperate search for a new object upon whom she could re-externalize.

There was another child in the family, George, three years older than Tommy. Until the time when Tommy began making significant progress, George had seemed like a boy with a well-structured ego who functioned efficiently in many areas. In the eyes of the family, including Tommy, George was a near genius. It was George who was chosen as the mother's new target for externalization of dystonic aspects, and very soon the family equilibrium was restored on a reversed basis, with Tommy now seen as the near genius and George as the stupid, messy, damaged child.[12] Tommy, no longer fulfilling his mother's most pressing need, now had to cope with the fact that he was an outsider in his own family. As he said, "I feel the odd man out. I feel good, but nobody notices me."

2. Molly's mother was a woman who had never been able to tolerate her own aggression. From childhood on projection had played a major part in her battery of defenses. Her response to all objects was one of fear, and she was obsessed by the thought that her parents would murder her. In relation to her own child she made use of projection even before the birth, being consciously afraid that the unborn baby was killing her and eating her up inside. She continued to project throughout the child's development. A most pathogenic feature in her projections was the extent to which they were hooked onto the reality of Molly's phase-adequate aggressive impulses; Molly's early development intensified the mother's phase-linked aggressive conflicts. Thus, when Molly was in the oral phase, the mother feared that Molly wanted to devour her. When Molly reached the positive oedipal stage, the

_____

12. The changing roles of the two brothers represent a highly complex phenomenon related to many factors in addition to the family use of externalization. A more detailed report on the two brothers can be found in a paper by Novick and Holder (1969).

mother's continuing projection of death wishes now took the form of the fear that Molly wanted to kill her in order to possess the husband.[13]

The extensive use of projection left the mother prey to the constant fear that Molly only hated and wanted to kill her. This image of the child acted as an additional stimulus to aggressive wishes, thus further threatening the mother's defenses. She therefore needed secondary defenses, which could be maintained only provided that the child utilized the same mechanisms, that is, denied her anger, displaced the hate onto other objects, and reactively stressed the "loving" aspects of the relationship—and this Molly did. She and her mother spent much of their time in mutual assurances of love, the frequent exchange of propitiatory gifts, and the mutual denial of aggression on the part of either partner. Frequently they would discuss their dislike for a shared displacement object.

Unlike Tommy's father, Molly's father did not, on the whole, reinforce the effects of the mother's pathology. Indeed, so close was the bond between mother and Molly that the father remained a relative outsider.

Molly was referred to the Clinic at the age of 12 for school phobia and for sleeping and eating difficulties of marked severity. When Molly was seen diagnostically, all observers were struck by her identification with the mother's defenses. The major conflict related to the aggression toward the mother. Despite the severity of the pathology, there were no indications of a primary ego or narcissistic defect.

---

13. In this chapter we are focusing solely on the role of projection in the pathological mother–child relationship. It is evident that the relationship is one of great complexity involving other elements, such as the revival of the mother's past object relationships, especially the infantile relationship to her own mother. In general, it is important to distinguish between phenomena related to the revival of past object relationships and projection proper (A. Freud 1965, Waelder 1951). In this case, however, projection was a major defense utilized both within and outside the framework of the revived object relationship.

Very soon after the start of treatment one could see how ineffective and brittle the defense system was. Primitive aggressive breakthroughs began to occur, each time followed by the intensification of the defenses shared with the mother. It was only with the analysis of the shared defensive system that Molly could become aware of her fear of aggression; at this point the role of projection in her pathology became increasingly apparent. While Molly's own aggressive wishes remained relatively defended, the fear of being destroyed by the mother intensified, and with panic in her voice Molly would say, "She hates me, she'll kill me, she'll eat me alive." Further analysis clearly revealed the largely projective nature of these fears.

This case involves a paradox which can be understood by taking into account the pathological impact of the mother's projections. Molly's ego and superego development had been precocious; for example, verbalization (including complete phrases) occurred by 11 months of age. Despite such precocious development Molly's defenses remained completely dependent upon the presence of the object and formed no more than a brittle superstructure overlaying primitive and peremptory aggressive wishes. But this could be seen as a direct consequence of the mother's extensive use of projection. By projecting her aggressive wishes onto the child, she constantly revived, intensified, and drew Molly's wishes into the child's consciousness. The normal, developmental evolution of drive expression from direct and primitive to more distanced and less conflictual forms was grossly interfered with. The development of autonomous and adaptive defenses was impeded, and the child was left with no alternative but to use primitive defenses (such as projection itself) and to accept the defenses forced upon her by her mother.

With the working through of pregenital and oedipal hostility toward the mother Molly began to function independently. The mother reacted to the positive changes in her child by making repeated attempts to reestablish the old, shared defense system. When these failed she became extremely disturbed, continued to project her hostile wishes onto the child, but now was increasingly aware of her own aggression. She became terrified that she might act upon her wishes and kill the child. She became consumed with guilt, increasingly disturbed, and made a number of suicidal attempts. A period of treatment reduced the intensity of the disturbance, but she continued her basic pattern of projection onto Molly despite the changes in her child, unlike Tommy's mother, who reacted to his positive changes by shifting the object of her externalizations. Furthermore, whereas Tommy's change affected the entire family equilibrium, Molly's affected the family only secondarily via the effect of the mother's increased distance.

Study of the treatment of these and similar cases has led us to the following general conclusions:

1. Children who are the objects of parental externalizations, as in the case of Tommy, manifest relatively little anxiety or guilt over drive expression. Rather, they show a severe narcissistic disturbance with mental pain and conflict rooted in the acceptance of the devalued self and the inability to integrate positive aspects with this conscious self representation. There is a primary impairment of the integrative function of the ego, the maintenance of self-esteem, and the development of an adequate self representation.

On the other hand, in children who are the objects of projection, as in the case of Molly, ego functioning and narcissistic cathexis are only secondarily involved in the pathology. They are subject to intense anxiety and guilt in relation to drive expression. The drives are constantly reinforced by the parental projections, and the development of an autonomous and adaptive defense system is hindered. A brittle superstructure, based on an identification with the primitive superego and defense system of the projecting mother, is created.

2. The extensive use of either projection or externalization by these children can be seen as a generational effect which goes beyond identification with the parental defenses.

3. The use of either of these mechanisms by the parents relates not only to severe pathology in the parents but also to a differing pattern of family dynamics. The extensive use of externalization relates to a pathological balance in the family, a closed system (Brodey 1965) in which all members of the family play interdependent roles. A change in any one member of the family directly affects each of the others and produces a complete disruption of the family equilibrium. Projection, on the other hand, indicates an intense dyadic bond, usually between mother and child. A change in the child directly affects the mother and has only secondary effects upon the other members of the family.

SUMMARY

This has been an initial attempt to sort out some of the problems in an area of great complexity: the subjective allocation of inner phenomena to the outer world. We first separated processes which may have similar surface manifestations, such as displacement, transference, and processes of early differentiation from externalization. Within the category of externalization, we made a further distinction between modes of functioning, for example, generalization and defenses. Among defensive externalizations we described the attribution of cause, externalization of aspects of the self representation, and externalization of drives, that is, projection proper. The latter two were discussed in detail, and the differences between them were examined from the point of view of individual development and family dynamics.

6   VARIETIES OF TRANSFERENCE
IN THE ANALYSIS
OF AN ADOLESCENT*

Continuity and change are two prominent strands in the complex fabric of the life cycle, and writers on this topic frequently emphasize one or the other. Those who focus on change characterize development as a series of discrete phases or stages, each stage being a necessary prerequisite for subsequent ones but different from all others. This emphasis on the differences among stages of development is balanced, at times by the same writer, with the view that there exists a basic continuity between past and present, between child and adult. The importance of the past in determining later behavior is an axiom of psychoanalytic theory, and the notion of continuity in development is intrinsic to such clinical concepts as fixation, regression, and, most crucially, to the concept of transference.

The two strands of continuity and change, of similarity and differences in the developmental phases, create a tension within the growing individual and a synthetic task for those writing of

*Presented at the 32nd International Psycho-Analytical Congress in Helsinki, July 1981.

such issues. Although psychoanalytic theory can, and has, encompassed both views, there often is a tendency to emphasize one or the other position. At the extremes each view can lead to untenable assumptions. The view that development is continuous and few fundamental differences exist between adult and child can lead to an uncritical application of adult techniques to work with younger people. Anna Freud questioned Melanie Klein's assumption that the child's play can be equated with the adult's free association, and Freud's failure with Dora has been attributed by some to his application of adult techniques to an adolescent case. At the other extreme, there is a current tendency to overemphasize the developmental differences so that intensive therapeutic work with children and adolescents is considered to be something totally different from psychoanalysis. It is noted by many that a majority of adolescents withdraw early in treatment. Those who stay are said to be unable to form a workable transference or transference neurosis and very few adolescents reach a point of mutually agreed termination. Blos (1980) summarized his years of experience with adolescents with the statement that a transference neurosis cannot be formed until the close of adolescence, a remark which echoes a view stated earlier by Berman that "the adolescent does not have the capacity to regress and develop a transference neurosis" (Panel 1972). This generally held pessimistic view is highlighted by the remark attributed to Anna Freud that "we might have to face the fact that adolescents are not truly analyzable" (Panel 1972, p. 135). It should be recalled, however, that Freud's revolutionary discovery of the central role of transference in analysis was based on the treatment of Dora, an adolescent. In his supplement to that case, Freud presented the theory of transference which is still used in the psychoanalytic treatment of adults.

We will present clinical material from four and a half years of five times per week analysis of a 15-year-old boy to facilitate a discussion on transference and the similarities and differences in the psychoanalysis of adolescents and adults.

Daniel, the youngest child of South African parents, was said to have been a lively, normal boy until his mother died when he was 10 years of age. From the start of his analysis Daniel complained that his parents and sister kept things secret from him and deceived him. This had in fact been his experience of his mother's death. She had been ill for some time but all his questions and concerns had been dismissed and the seriousness of her illness denied. Just before her death he was sent to relatives, not told why, and not told of her death until after the funeral. His own grief and mourning were unsupported for, as he said, "Who cares about the feelings of a snot-nosed 10-year-old?" It seems that there was little opportunity for anyone to mourn. As reconstructed from the analytic material, then confirmed by father, the year following mother's death was one of chaos and breakdown in family life. Father traveled frequently on lengthy business trips, leaving the children with relatives or babysitters. Many of Daniel's symptoms appeared at this time, such as his sleep disturbance, compulsive rituals, and frequent somatic complaints. He also adopted his mother's religious rituals and attempted to impose her strict orthodoxy upon other members of his family. The symptoms diminished or disappeared after a permanent housekeeper was employed and accepted by Daniel. She seems to have been an attractive, talented, and loving person. After a period of initial reluctance Daniel became very attached to her. When he discovered that she and father were having an affair he felt deceived and betrayed. The affair had been going on since her arrival but kept secret from Daniel. According to him, when he began to voice his suspicions they were dismissed as childish imaginings. Two years before the referral Joan, the housekeeper, left without warning or explanation to Daniel. Soon after, at 13 years of age, Daniel had the first of two operations for a severe hydrocele. This combination of traumatic events in early adolescence seems to have shattered completely Daniel's tenuous hold on normality and resulted in a neurotic regression, symptom formation, and widespread disturbances of functioning.

When first seen, Daniel was a tall, very thin, red-haired 15-year-old with regular but delicate features. He was awkward in his movements, walked with head thrust forward and shoulders stooped. His clothes were shabby, uncared for, and unflattering. He described himself as "stupid, dense, weak, a physical freak." Despite his high intelligence and hard work Daniel had failed five of the ten ordinary level high school exams and barely passed the others. He doubted his ability to pass the advanced exams and gain entrance to a university. Daniel's severe learning inhibition, his depression, total isolation, and frequent somatic complaints were the main reasons father and son initially sought psychiatric consultation. In addition, father was very concerned by Daniel's seemingly uncontrolled, thoroughly offensive and somewhat bizarre behavior at home. He had driven two housekeepers away because of his rudeness and abuse and father was terrified that he would do the same with the current housekeeper.

Daniel said he wanted analysis and was eager to start so that he could get rid of his problems, especially the numerous compulsive rituals which intruded upon, and interfered with, every part of his daily routine. His isolation was due to a defiant withdrawal of positive feelings for any person past or present. He said that he almost never thought of his mother. "It's as if I never had one," he said. "I remember her only as angry and bad-tempered." He called the housekeeper who had been so important to him a hypocrite and said he felt nothing for her any more. He had no friends and "there is a barrier between me and the blokes at school." This barrier started to crumble as soon as he started analysis. The first week on the couch he began to talk of his mother and he recalled that initially he had missed her and had resented others having a mother. He went on to say "I wish I knew what she was really like, her character. In early photographs she looks happy." Soon he began to talk about Joan, the housekeeper. He said that at first he didn't like her and resented her taking Mother's place but "then I felt affection for her. She taught me to read. I used to read only comics before.

She was someone to talk to." He went on to recall that "She added life to the house. Without her the place is dead." He even began to express positive feelings about analysis. He enjoyed the work he was doing with the analyst and he was beginning to feel a little better, less hopeless, and starting to make friends at school.

The emergence of positive feelings led to longings for more. He began to complain of being hungry, of needing filling foods such as potato pancakes but "the food at home is lousy and that thick woman is a terrible cook." He complained of being hungry in the sessions and wanted the analyst to "lay on something, like a bag of chips." The longing for supplies became intense and left him feeling deprived, lonely, and vulnerable. At the end of the first month of analysis he wondered if what he really wanted was sympathy. He felt that nobody cared whether he lived or died and he didn't blame them since he had accomplished nothing. The next Monday he said that after having left on Friday he had had the shivers, the shakes, and had been depressed all week-end. "I had shouting fits, I almost cracked up. I was staring out of the window like an autistic. I'm not going to say anything any more. I have to protect myself." After further talk he wanted to know if there was some other quicker, less painful way. The work on his fear of depression was quite fruitful but intensified his fear that as the longed-for but powerful person the analyst would lie to him, confuse him, keep things secret and laugh at him, humiliate him by treating him in a condescending way, and, finally, reject him. When he talked of this distrust he said, "Once bitten, never again."

He had come to treatment with severe learning difficulties and very soon his intense conflicts about knowing and finding out became and remained central to the analysis. He was unable to concentrate and fell asleep while reading his schoolwork. He often felt a weight on his head, something pressing down and not allowing him to be happy. He said that about a year after his mother had died he had felt as if there were another person inside him. "I felt like it was someone else, I called it my conscience. If I wanted to go to the bathroom or something else, it wouldn't let me." This weight or conscience soon came into treatment as a major transference resistance. He was not allowed to know and the analyst became the one who forced him to know or the father who used knowledge to overwhelm and humiliate Daniel.

In the fourth week Daniel missed a session but told the analyst "not to fret." Later in the week he came two hours late and the analyst met him on leaving after the last patient of the day. He started the sixth week with one foot off the couch. The next day he sat up, and by the end of the week he was sitting at the end of the couch with his back to the analyst. The next week he was off the couch, pacing the room, moving ever further away, finally leaning out of the window as he shouted that the analyst was just like his father, a fascist, a tyrant, and a capitalist. The rude, abusive behavior father had complained about became a central feature of treatment and remained so for over a year. Any comments were shouted down with cries of "Rubbish, rubbish, we heard all that before." He would argue, distort words, mock, and mimic the analyst. He began to miss sessions and come late. When he came he would stand in the doorway and say defiantly, "Well?" Near the end of the third month he came on two of the five days and was deliberately silent. He then failed to show up at all. After a brief absence he returned in response to a letter and asked if he would become schizophrenic if he didn't come. This had been a concern of Daniel's since the start and the analyst suggested that the future breakdown he feared had in fact occurred, that he had experienced moments of madness before. "How do you know, who told you? Do I have to come five times a week? Can I come once every five weeks?" He became less abusive but it emerged more clearly that though he accused the analyst of being like father, he had in fact externalized the vulnerable, hungry little boy and the curious little boy who was forbidden to know and humiliated for the little he did know. The analyst had become for him the "snot-nosed 10-year old" overwhelmed, confused, made helpless and humiliated by uncaring adults, and finally abandoned. Daniel kept things secret, told parts of events and dreams, and withheld other parts. He would promise to come and then fail. Anything the analyst said was "rubbish, rubbish, irrelevant, drivel." The analyst began to focus on the internalized conflict as presently experienced in the externalizing transference. According to Daniel it was the *analyst's* wish to know; his own internalized prohibition was directed outward in attacks for what he called the analyst's presumption in wanting to know and stupidity for not knowing. He would not associate to dreams or make any attempt to reflect on his material. This was the analyst's job. "Get weaving" he would say. "If old Siggy were here he'd have a thing or two to say, eh what!" The analyst suggested that this was Daniel's way of getting around the prohibitions. He was not allowed to find out; if the analyst found out, Daniel could then dismiss the knowledge as rubbish. "But," he added, "then I would know and probably think about it."

The sarcasm, abuse, and condescension continued but a glimmer of something else also began to appear. Once again, as at the start of treatment, he occasionally asked for food. This of course was "just a joke," and he "would rather walk from one end of town to the other" than accept anything. He peppered the analyst with questions, with the obvious intention of confusing and overwhelming, trying to trap the analyst in a contradiction. "There!" he would say triumphantly, "I caught you in a lie." But some questions carried a different quality, a plaintive request for help. Amidst a torrent of sarcastic questions which definitively proved that the analyst was "stupid, thick, and a moron," he asked "Why do I always think of funerals when I've never been to one?" A short time later he asked exactly what his problems were. He had been told before but this time he listened. The next day he said, "I've been thinking a lot about what you said and about the things I do. It was as if I didn't notice before but now I do. I see that I do have a mental illness." One of the things the analyst had told him was that he suffered from a tyrannical conscience; later the analyst could empathize with his experience by telling him what it felt like when he turned the analyst into the little Daniel and he became the powerful attacking superego. In response to this Daniel recovered a series of memories. He recalled mother censoring the comics he read and not allowing him to read any that depicted rebelliousness against parental authority. He vaguely remembered father explaining that the reason Daniel wasn't told the nature of his mother's illness was because they thought he would tell her. "I can't be trusted to know, that's it, isn't it?" The analyst told him how helpless he often felt when attacked by his superego and how he could understand that Daniel must feel that whatever he does is wrong. Daniel recalled that mother frequently took taxis and told him to keep it secret from father since they could not afford such an expense. "Like being between the devil and the deep blue sea," he said. "Guilty if I keep the secret and guilty if I don't." He could re-internalize the conflict and, at least for a while, work together with the analyst on some of the determinants of the strict superego. Soon after he announced that he had "overthrown" his religion. He said that he had defended analysis in a discussion with schoolmates. That same week he had left his laundry in the waiting room and when the analyst wondered about this he said "I trust, I trust." The worst was not over—he still missed many sessions or he came late. Externalizations were still frequent but less intense and often an object of analytic inquiry rather than a reality to be endured.

He started the second year of analysis more trusting and more accepting of his need for help. He felt proud of having stuck to analysis for a year and he thought of the many changes which had taken place in that time. He said that he had been thinking about "this trusting thing. I find it difficult to trust. I feel I'll be taken in by people. But then things happen and it's better to trust too much than not at all." The next week when the analyst commented on the fact that he still kept his sexual activities secret from the analysis, he said "It's Custer's last stand." However, the last stand turned into a prolonged battle. The resistances increased, he again missed many sessions, somatic complaints reappeared, he could not concentrate on his schoolwork, and he felt tired and lethargic. In the sessions the analyst again felt confused, overwhelmed, and excluded as Daniel withheld information, told parts of events, and often sent the analyst up the wrong path. The return of the externalizing transference became most apparent when he once again began openly to attack and accuse the analyst of lying, being evasive, and holding back. This time neither felt the need to keep the conflict externalized and Daniel responded with relief when the analyst said that battling represented an internal fight. He asked if the analyst knew what he felt guilty about. His father was about to remarry and for weeks Daniel had spoken with contempt and derision about that "thick woman who has such appalling taste." He wished she would just leave him alone. The analyst suggested in a general way that his guilt might relate to this woman and his father. He said, "You don't mean Oedipus, do you? It can't be. You mean that I'm Oedipus? Impossible! I mean, she's so ugly. I don't want to . . . er . . . well, I mean I have my own girls. I don't need my father's woman. Are you accusing me of being Oedipus?" When the analyst suggested that it was his conscience making this accusation, he said "Well, that's ridiculous." After a brief silence he went on. "But you may have something there. You know I'm always alluding to death, undertakers, and things like that. Well, I also think of Oedipus. Yes, you may have something there." He then said that he had had a dream but had repressed most of it. *It was about death, people dying, being carried off, and it was very frightening.* He then said, "Well, what about this dream about loss . . . er . . . death?" When the analyst referred back to his slip he said, "I know, I know. I'm sharp, you know. Nothing passes me. I noticed that slip. I probably put those things together."

He could by this time contain and experience the internalized conflict, the battle between his wishes and his prohibitions. He felt vulnerable, anxious, but also strong enough to join in looking for the roots to his conviction that his thoughts and behavior would result in loss, death, and retaliation. "The fight's on!" he said. For the first time he apologized for coming late and said he felt guilty when he missed a session. As parts of himself were re-internalized and integrated the analyst could become a separate person to him. As a separate person he not only had concern for the other's feelings but also could experience the analyst as the oedipal object he envied, desired, competed with, and feared. With this recovered capacity for an oedipal transference there was a sounder basis for a treatment alliance. First via dreams he could begin to look at what had once overwhelmed and traumatized him. Daniel was 17 at this time, nearly a year and a half into his analysis, and it was just prior to the second Christmas vacation. The dreams led first to the operations he had been subjected to at the beginning of his adolescence. He referred to these events as "the big cut," the retaliation for his thoughts and actions. Further dream images led, he said, back to early childhood memories of toilets and blood. Following a defense interpretation linking his sleepiness, missed sessions, and forgetting, Daniel recovered a forgotten portion of a dream. *It was an image of a large bed, a man and woman in the bed laughing, probably laughing at him.* He had the feeling the man was his father. Following the vacation Daniel said he was now keeping two diaries, one for everyday events and one for dreams. There were dreams of *hills, water, trains going in and out of stations, and being chased.* "I wonder what water means to me," he said, and via a series of associations, starting with mother's anxious concern that Daniel would wet his bed, he recalled being sent away to a holiday camp a year and a half after mother died. Joan, the housekeeper, was then at home and he said, "I was sent away while Joan and the old man were making out at home." The transference link to having been sent away over Christmas brought confirmation of the guess that he had been subjected to repeated primal scene exposure. He recalled that up to the age of 8 or 9 he had slept in the parental bedroom. At the end of this week Daniel said, "This is an historic occasion, what does it augur for the future, what does it signify?" Although presented in a somewhat self-mocking tone, he was in fact proud of the work he had done and he was specifically referring to the fact that for the first time since the second month of analysis he had come to all five of his sessions. The next week he presented an overwhelming mass of dream material. He said it was obvious the analyst couldn't get the main point and that was probably why he had given so much so quickly. "Perhaps it will come to you when you're sitting on the crapper," he quipped. The analyst suggested that the overwhelming profusion of material was not only a defense but also a way of remembering the experience of being overwhelmed by things he was forced to see and hear. He said that he knew there was something important in the dreams but he could also feel that there was something frightening underneath. He recalled that terrible weekend early in the analysis when he said something about his mother. The analyst said he could take it at his own pace. He said "thanks," and then began to work on his dreams. His associations all led to sex, the bed, the color of mother's nightdress, a rose color, the color of lipstick in a dream. "Was the lipstick a phallic symbol?" he asked. He then looked at the analyst and said, "You have an idea, don't you?" The analyst assented but suggested that it was just his own idea and that he would wait for Daniel, who then said, "I think you're right." He went on to say, "Could it be? No, it couldn't. I would be in bed before they came in and I would wake up before they would. I mean, could it be? No, it couldn't. Was I there at the vital moment? Could it be?" The analyst said that it could be. "No," he said, "it couldn't, but it feels right. I think you're right. I think I was there at the vital moment." As he was leaving he said that he had the feeling that the "vital moment" was the major piece in the puzzle, the thing that held everything else together.

The analysis now had its own momentum, an unfolding drama which Daniel and the analyst at various times facilitated, observed, participated in, or obstructed. With the primal scene at the center, the material moved back into anal battles with the mother, forward to a current persistence of the sadistic intercourse theory, and a continued involvement in parental sexual activities as he shamefacedly said that he often listened to his father and new wife having intercourse. The main theme which was being played out in its countless variations was Daniel's intense guilt over his assertive activities. Assertion was equated with sexual activities and sex was hostile, leading to death and abandonment by the woman or to "the cut," retaliation by the powerful father. The death of his mother was the unique element in his typical progressions into, and regressions from, the oedipal position. The death of his mother was the reality confirmation of his sadistic wishes. Sexual activities, including masturbation, looking, listening, finding out, and knowing were felt to be hostile acts, vehicles for sadistic fantasies that did come true. Death of the mother also created further powerful determinants to the negative oedipal position. By identifying with the dead mother he could deny her death, placate his conscience, and fill the emptiness by becoming his mother. He said that he slept under such a mountain of blankets he could hardly move. He agreed that this stopped him from masturbating but it also made him feel safe and comforted. He said it felt like having mother in bed with him.

Initially, as in the work with his dreams, the analyst functioned mainly as the protective parent. He brought his outside activities for exploration and was kept, he said, on the right track, not letting his guilt, anxiety, or grandiosity get out of hand. He was exercising his new-found ego capacities and discovering, first with surprise but then with pleasure and pride, that he could be witty, intelligent, and respected by his peers and elders. For a time much of the work revolved around his current social interactions but as the work began to deepen the conflicts increasingly began to appear in the transference. The transition from current external reality to the transference neurosis was marked by his first symbolic acknowledgment of his mother's death. On the anniversary of her death he visited her grave for the first time and noticed that he called the visit "going to the funeral." His outside activities became much less subject to sudden drive vicissitudes but remained a source of self-esteem and pleasure. In treatment he could begin to acknowledge a feeling of dependency; then, with more conviction, a fear that the analyst would leave him. Near the end of the second year of treatment he reacted to the spring vacation with a panic attack. He called asking for an extra appointment because he was "cracking up." He said that he had become ill with terrible "migraine, colic" and he had thrown up. He felt terribly weak but the "quack" couldn't find anything physically wrong with him. The intense ambivalence and death wishes in the transference could be approached via his dream *of being chased, then turning around and choking the person chasing him.* A further dream *about a train* led to his sexual sadism. He said that only after talking of the fact that he equates sex and violence did he notice that whenever he sees a pretty girl he says "Put the boot in." This was something he had felt compelled to write on a card to his girlfriend without realizing why. With interpretation of his preoedipal and oedipal anger at the analyst for abandoning and rejecting him, Daniel's somatic complaints could be understood as a masochistic appeal for maternal care, a defense against his own sadistic masturbation fantasies, and an identification with the analyst's body, damaged due to his having "put the boot in."

With this work within the transference there was significant improvement in all areas of functioning. Most symptoms had disappeared or were much less intense and of limited duration. He had pleasure and pride in his work and social relations. He was working effectively on his advanced level college entrance exams, he was respected by his friends, had a number of girlfriends, and seemed to have become sexually active. Even his relations with his family had improved and father had told him that he seemed completely cured and should stop his analysis. The guilt, anxiety, and conflicts were now almost completely in the transference, a fact he could acknowledge and confirm. He felt good in all areas but worried what would happen to him. The worry, he said, was mostly in the treatment. Was it a worry that the analyst would attack him, he wondered. Was it a worry about the "big cut"? He struggled to control his anger, his ambivalence and rivalry. He wondered why he should be angry with the analyst. "Why should I fight you when my power is through you?" What if he let go, what if he beat the analyst, he wondered. "I would be left a nothing."

Within the transference neurosis much was worked on and worked through but a major piece of work related to Daniel's passive, masochistic, feminine identification. At the start of his third year of analysis Daniel said that he planned to enter university the next autumn, but after January, he might work or travel. He did not know as yet. With this assertive challenge, this expression of his wish to leave, he became anxious and began to express his fear of loss and retaliation for what he considered to be his "selfishness, immorality, and thieving." It was all a question of morals, he said. He was concerned that his ambition would lead him to be selfish and greedy. For example, he said, if he wants some peaches he very carefully divides the tin in half and goes to great lengths to ensure the two portions are exactly equal. "The irony is," he said, "when I finish my dish I go on and eat the other dish." He was referring, of course, to something more important than peaches. There was a young woman, somewhat older than Daniel, with whom he had become very friendly over the summer, as had his father. The woman was living in their home now while looking for a flat of her own. The woman worked for father but Daniel's relationship with her was a secret from his dad. He said that the old feelings were coming back, memories of mother and father. Although the rivalry seemed to be with the contemporary father it was in fact with father of the past, now re-experienced in the transference. He was very anxious in treatment, afraid of attack and humiliation, and it emerged that his success with the young woman consisted of playing the role of the therapist. She confided in him, told him of her early difficulties, and had cried. He was succeeding with this older woman, stealing her and defeating the analyst. Over the next weeks his

successive defensive moves to avert jealous attack were interpreted. First there was the "poor Arthur" defense, a masochistic
display in which he drew attention to his bedraggled appearance,
accentuated his failures, and omitted his successes. He protested
that he was not liked and that no one cared for him. Coupled
with this was the loss of his excellent wit and instead there appeared the alternation of open sarcasm with clowning. As these
defenses against his anger and rivalry were interpreted, his anxiety became more intense. The analyst was not only experienced
as the jealous father who would retaliate but also as the maternal
provider who would leave him without supplies. He again complained of being hungry. On the way to the session he had found
a sign and he put it on the desk. It read "We give Green Shield
stamps." A girlfriend of a classmate became interested in Daniel
and he found himself talking to her about analysis. He told the
analyst, "She is very interested in coming to see you."

He was giving everything away, his girl, his wit, his masculine
drive, and presenting himself as a passive, damaged person. The
analyst suggested that he was being a woman and he said, "Don't
try to pin that on me." That night he awoke from a nightmare and
felt nauseous, "like a pregnant woman" he said. The next night he
had a dream which led to his envy of his stepmother. When the
feminine identification was verbalized not only as a defense but
also as a wish for father's love, he nodded gravely and said, "I think
there's something there. During my hard times I used to wonder
what it would be like as a girl. Would it be easier, it couldn't be
much worse." He then wondered what his mother would have
thought of his girlfriend. He thought she would have disapproved
since his girlfriend was "not of the faith, right? Of a different class,
right?" Thus to be a woman would also mean to be his mother, to
be loyal to her and to her faith. All this work took place in the first
twelve weeks of his third year in analysis. It was as if he had become enveloped in old anxieties and conflicts and, as the various
determinants of his passive, masochistic, feminine defense were
brought into the light, he began to relate to the analyst and others

with a newfound clarity. First, he talked of his father and with genuine feeling spoke of the good times they used to have, of father's capacity to be a good person but how father allows himself to be overtaken by his anger, competitiveness, and viciousness. For the first time Daniel spoke with anger about his mother and he blamed her for many of his difficulties, as he would later blame the analyst for having failed. But for now he was determined to fight and get to the bottom of his problems. "Things are at a head," he said. "This is the last stand. We are right near it, aren't we Doc?" The regression of the transference neurosis allowed a surge of development. "Come to Novick's and grow two years in four days. Cut-rate offer," he said in a jokingly affectionate manner. The re-emergence from the regression was evident in his changed perception. He saw not only an analyst, he said, but also a person with feelings, someone who had a past and another life. He appreciated how hard the job was. It was evident that he also appreciated how much he had changed. He had just turned 18 and he said, "I feel like I'm starting over, a rebirth. It's a new card game, only this time I'm the banker. I worry over whether it will last. Will my luck run out?" This was a period of working through and there was a constant interplay between analytic and current life events. The continued importance of the transference relationship was most evident at a time of extreme crisis in his outside world when his stepmother nearly died. He began to regress until the analyst noted that he was avoiding talking about the seriousness of her condition. It emerged then that the analyst represented the father who denied, hid, and lied about mother's illness and opposed Daniel's adaptive attempts to deal with the situation. Stepmother took a turn for the worse and following work together Daniel could do some independent analytic work linking her illness with mother's death. This relieved the headache he was developing and though he still felt concern about his stepmother he could go out to a party and have a marvelous time.

Daniel was by this time firmly established in the phallic-oedipal phase and regressive moves were, as he put it, "intolerable."

There was but one direction—working through, and termination of, infantile longings and oedipal object ties. This is always a point of danger in analysis, a point of transference/countertransference collusion in which a proper termination is often avoided. What frequently goes unnoticed is the shift back from a differentiated to an externalizing transference in which it is not the analyst as real and transference object who is relinquished and mourned but a part of the self, often the infantile self, which is guiltily discarded. The adolescent becomes the powerful parent who leaves the lonely, helpless child behind. Daniel began talking about terminating analysis. Together with friends he began to plan a long and somewhat risky camping trip through the jungles of South America. He planned to stop a month early and proposed, if things went well, to end treatment at that time. His progressive moves and his increased independence were acknowledged but the analyst suggested that the situation should be assessed on his return from vacation.

He started the fourth year of analysis in high spirits. The camping adventure had been a great success and he was now preparing to attend a fine university within commuting distance of the office. These sessions were initially more like social visits and Daniel said that he felt ready to terminate. However, the day Daniel moved into his own room near the university he had a severe anxiety attack and had to return home. He recounted that he was in a panic, depressed, and terribly frightened. He seemed overwhelmed with the feeling that he would be completely alone but equally that being alone he could be sexually free. The landlady had told him that he could bring anyone he wanted into his room. A number of his symptoms had returned and he said that he was losing everything. He was losing his gloves, his books, his confidence, and his ability to concentrate. Analysis continued for another year and a half. Within a few weeks the acute anxiety and depression receded; he could leave home and adapt reasonably well to university life. The analytic work became very intense and the anxieties and conflicts were contained mainly within the transference. The view was amply confirmed that the recent attempt at a unilateral termination was a defensive avoidance of crucial developmental tasks.

The final year and a half may be summarized by saying that within the bounds of a mutually agreed termination the transference neurosis could intensify and be adaptively resolved. Oedipal and preoedipal conflicts were interpreted and worked through and intense oedipal rivalry was transformed into acceptance of strengths and limitations in himself and his analyst. A major accomplishment during this termination phase was the final relinquishing of Daniel's denial of his mother's death. He said that he had never quite accepted that she had died. He always felt that she was there with him and he would wonder how she would react to such things as his having a motorbike and his sexual activities. In talking of his need to bury his mother he began to experience sadness over the loss of his mother and his analyst. In a number of sessions he cried, something he had not been able to do as a child. The mourning for his mother eventually allowed a complete involvement in school and with contemporaries. The learning difficulties disappeared and he did well in essays and exams. It was time to end, to leave each other not out of fear or vengeance but out of mutual respect and a painful awareness that we each had to go our separate ways. His twentieth birthday was approaching and he said that this was the end of an era, the end of his teens. He was moving into young adulthood.

Despite his current uncertainty about the future of his relationship with his girlfriend, he felt in general very happy. He said that he was pleased with his work, eager to read, to learn, to grow, and looking forward to the future. He felt, he said, that the pain he was currently experiencing with his girlfriend was part of growing up. He couldn't expect the analyst or anyone else to take it away from him. He was grateful for what the analyst had done and felt that he was not only ready to leave but also ready to come back should the need arise. He thought he would be able to tell when he could no longer analyze his problems or cope with them in some other way and would need help.

The analyst saw Daniel again three years later at his wedding. He had completed university and he and his bride were heading for postgraduate work.

Transference can be thought of as an amalgam of images from different historical periods. The final image of Daniel is part of the analyst's transference. The 15-year-old, hobbling, awkward, and not of or in his body, is superimposed on the image of the young bridegroom, happy, confident, and graceful as he danced at his wedding.

CONCLUSIONS

In this discussion of Daniel's analysis, we have tried to highlight the ways that understanding of certain transference issues can help clarify similarities and differences in the analyses of adolescents and adults. The first year and a half of intense anxiety and resistance was understood in relation to the difference between an externalizing and a differentiated transference. We see the externalizing transference not only as a resistance, but often as a necessary step in the formation of integrated self and object representations that are needed for a differentiated transference relationship. The next phase of Daniel's analysis was a transitional one in which the analyst provided "coverage," that is, was experienced by Daniel as a benign presence in the transference who accompanied him in his beginning exploration of his inner world via dreams. The dreams led to Daniel's recovery of primal scene memories.

In the third phase, the sustained, differentiated transference led to Daniel's experience of the analyst as an object who could protect against and mitigate the effects of repeated traumata by verbalizations and interpretations. This allowed for a surge of psychological growth eventuating in Daniel's move to a phallic-oedipal level of functioning, both in and out of treatment. At this point he could and did develop a transference neurosis. Next came a phase of working through, with constant interplay between analytic and current life events. The analyst was experienced as the oedipal transference object, both maternal and paternal, and also as a therapeutic ally in Daniel's continuing struggle for mastery.

Following this phase, Daniel attempted a premature resolution of the transference neurosis by a unilateral termination of his treatment. The analyst registered the progressive aspect of Daniel's wish, but allowed for the necessary continuation of treatment. Finally, a mutually agreed-on termination phase allowed for the full formation and adaptive resolution of the transference neurosis. The analyst as a transference object was relinquished and mourned and Daniel identified with the analytic functions necessary for continued growth. It was only during the termination period that he could fully experience and mourn the death of his mother.

Implicit in this chapter is our attempt, evident throughout this volume, to balance emphasis on continuity and change in development. With examination of the vicissitudes of transference in Daniel's analysis we see that psychoanalytic principles and techniques are applicable and that psychoanalysis can be the treatment of choice for a much larger number of adolescents than is often thought possible.

7 Externalization as a Pathological Form of Relating: The Dynamic Underpinnings of Abuse

Child abuse is currently so much talked about that we might tend to think that, like AIDS, it is a late twentieth-century phenomenon. *The New England Journal of Medicine* of December 6, 1990 stated, "Over the past two decades the incidence of child abuse and neglect has increased dramatically, with 2.2 million cases reported in 1987." There is no doubt that there has been a dramatic increase in our awareness of and sensitivity to child abuse. In many states, mental health workers are now required to take courses on abuse. But there is some question whether the actual incidence of child abuse has increased. In a recent survey of the literature on sexual abuse the psychohistorian de Mause predicated the universality of incest. He asserted that "it is incest itself—and not the absence of incest—that has been universal for most people in most places at most times. Furthermore, the earlier in history one searches, the more evidence there is of universal incest, just as there is more evidence of other forms of child abuse" (1991, p. 125). In his seminal 1974 paper de Mause presented a wealth of data to demonstrate that "the further back in history one goes . . . the more likely children are to be killed, abandoned, beaten, terrorized and sexually abused" (1974, p. 1). Kahr (1991) found evidence for widespread abuse of children throughout history and concluded: "Thus I submit that the actual extent of abuse in history has been more grave than we can even understand" (p. 207).

More traditional historians have arrived at similar conclusions. John Boswell, in his book *The Kindness of Strangers* (1988), detailed child abandonment throughout the history of Western civilization, citing rates even in prosperous countries of between 20 and 30%. Greven, in his book *Spare the Child* (1991), focused on the religious roots of child physical abuse, demonstrating, as Alice Miller did earlier (1983), that a range of abusive practices was sanctioned as good for the child. Biblical authority was found, for instance, in Proverbs 23:14, "Thou shalt beat him with the rod,/And shalt deliver his soul from hell."

Nineteenth-century intellectuals and reformers were well aware of the extent of child abuse; writers such as Dickens vividly portrayed abuse and exploitation of children. Freud's traumatogenic theory of adult neurosis was part of this nineteenth century sensitivity to child abuse. Contrary to the assertions of Masson (1984) and others, Freud never repudiated or suppressed the fact of childhood sexual abuse but modified his seduction theory and placed the reality of sexual abuse in the framework of a more comprehensive theory based on his new discoveries of the intrapsychic world of fantasies, wishes, and conflicts (Hanly 1987, Shengold 1989).

Mental health writers seem now to have come full circle. Rather than having made new discoveries which invalidate or supercede psychoanalytic insights, they have returned to the nineteenth century awareness of child abuse and many propose methods of treatment remarkably close to the cathartic method first employed by Freud to abreact the affects associated with trauma. Just as an exclusive focus on the intrapsychic led many to neglect environmental factors, there is a danger that emphasis on the concrete events of sexual or physical abuse may lead us to negate the dynamic underpinnings and sequelae. Years of accumulated psychoanalytic knowledge have led us to the understanding that each person processes external events to give them unique internal meaning and psychic representation (Solnit 1994).

The complex interplay of external and psychic realities has been a central psychoanalytic concern from our very beginnings. Even Freud's early seduction theory was not a simple one of cause and effect between a reality event and symptom formation but posited a transformation of repressed memories by "deferred action" (Schimek 1987, and see Chapter 4). In a chapter entitled "Did it Really Happen?" Shengold (1989) looked at this issue from the perspective of the sexually abused child. He noted that this burning question for the victim of soul murder has a long philosophical history and is a current controversy in psychoanalysis with the poles represented by Masson (1984), who denied the pathogenic power of fantasies, and Spence (1982), who denied the importance of historical truth. Many psychoanalysts approach one or the other extreme. For example, de Mause (1991) said that Abraham, Jung, Melanie Klein, and Kernberg tend to avoid the topic of childhood sexual abuse in contrast to Freud, Ferenczi, and many women analysts who accept memories of incest as real. Our position is well expressed by Shengold when he concludes, ". . . it does make a difference whether something actually happened but this does not deny the pathogenic power of fantasy" (1989, p. 38). Here our emphasis is on the complex matrix of relationships that allows for the occurrence of abuse. Since abuse is trauma which could be avoided there are two questions that are central. First, how is it possible for parents to allow abuse to occur? And, second, what role does the child's personality play in the occurrence and sequelae of abuse?

We think that at least part of the answer lies in the conceptualization of abuse as a symptom of a pathological relationship between parent and child, a relationship which in itself is assaultive and intrusive, whether or not concrete instances of physical contact occur. Such pathological relationships all revolve around issues of power and submission; in fact, they can be described as sadomasochistic. Sadomasochism has been at the center of psychoanalytic interest since Freud's early discoveries and clinicians have continued to struggle with the many theoretic and technical issues involved. We have written about sadomasochism from a developmental point of view, emphasized the complexity of these phenomena, and said that sadomasochism can be best understood as the result of a multidetermined epigenetic sequence of pain-seeking behaviors which start in infancy. In our sample of masochistic patients we identified externalization by the parent as a major determinant of the pathology.

In Chapter 5 we described externalization of aspects of the self representation as a defense aimed at avoiding the narcissistic pain consequent upon accepting devalued aspects of the self. On the basis of child analytic material we concluded that children who are the objects of parental externalizations show a severe narcissistic disturbance with mental pain and conflict rooted in the acceptance of the devalued self and the inability to integrate positive aspects with the conscious self representation. These children have a primary impairment of the integrative function of the ego, the maintenance of self esteem, and the development of an adequate self representation. Extensive use of externalization relates to a pathological balance in the family, a closed system (Brodey 1965) in which all members of the family play interdependent roles. A change in any one member of the family directly affects each of the others, producing a complete disruption of the family equilibrium.

We have come to think that externalization by the parent is in itself a form of psychological assault on the personality of the child and is central to the pathological relationship in which abuse can occur. In this chapter we will present a series of child, adolescent, and adult cases, each of whom was sexually abused. We will use this material to try to understand the nature of their relationships in the past and the present and, on that basis, to make appropriate technical suggestions.

Mrs. N. was 45 years old when she sought help to leave an abusive marriage. She presented as a helpless, victimized person, unhappy in all her relationships and suffering from multiple physical complaints. In the first interview, she recounted that, some years earlier, she had broken down when her new boss accused her unjustly of unethical behavior at work. Unable to stop crying, she was eventually hospitalized and was put on antidepressant medication. Although her response clearly indicated an extreme reaction, the therapist first remarked that she must have felt justifiably angry and betrayed at that time, and then wondered whether such a thing had ever happened to her before.

She then said that she had been sexually abused by her mother's brother. The events had occurred repeatedly between ages 4 and 6. When Mrs. N. finally told her mother, she was slapped and called a liar. It soon emerged that the uncle was also abusing his daughter. Mrs. N.'s aunt, his wife, packed up her children and left immediately. The extended family was in turmoil; the maternal grandmother went into mourning and joined the mother in blaming Mrs. N. for causing the whole disaster. From that point on, the grandmother singled Mrs. N. out by giving her different presents than the other grandchildren, presents like costume jewelry and see-through blouses, more appropriate for a sexually active adult than a school-aged girl.

After a period of analysis, Mrs. N. progressed sufficiently to leave her inadequate, cross-addicted and violent husband and initiate divorce proceedings. Her family reacted in a way that confirmed Mrs. N.'s memory of their response to the childhood abuse. Her parents and her siblings blamed her for the breakup of her marriage, accusing her of being selfish, destructive, and sexually uncontrolled. With the support of her analyst, Mrs. N. asked her older relatives about her parents' histories and discovered that both her mother and her uncle had been sexually abused as children. Mrs. N.'s mother was said to have been sexually promiscuous before and after her marriage.

This sounds like the typical history of a multigenerational dysfunctional family in which abuse has occurred. When faced with histories like these, there is so much pathology that it is sometimes hard to know where to begin understanding or intervening. For instance, we have not even mentioned the role of Mrs. N.'s father and the interference of his pathological jealousy with her appropriate adolescent intellectual and social ambitions. However, we would suggest that looking at parental externalizations can help us to clarify the pattern of pathological transmission of abuse from one generation to the next. Externalization is an abuse in itself, as it violates the child's selfhood. This is the mechanism of what Shengold (1989) and others have called "soul murder."

What was externalized on to Mrs. N.? Both her mother and grandmother appeared unable to take responsibility for and integrate their own sexuality and attributed to Mrs. N. their illicit and uncontrolled sexual wishes and the helpless, victimized aspect of their own self-representations. This pattern of attributing unwanted parts of the self to the child began long before the actual sexual abuse occurred. The crucial parental function of protecting the child was counteracted by the process of externalization. Thus in this case the sexual abuse occurred against the backdrop of longstanding abuse in the form of mother's externalizations.

The treatment material allows us to explore the ramifications of this abuse in the development of Mrs. N.'s personality and pathology.

Mrs. N. was a very bright, competent person who had become a successful midlevel manager, despite the active opposition of her husband and her parents. At work she provided her employers with detailed, complex, analytic operational reports, but, from the start of her analysis, she presented herself in treatment as a helpless, overwhelmed, and victimized person who had no capacity to protect herself from a long series of physical and emotional exploitations by authority figures. Initially she saw her analyst as one more idealized person who would provide her with suggestions and solutions, in effect, control and regulate her life. Mrs. N.'s parents had indeed been unable or unwilling to meet her basic need for psychological and physical protection. Did her apparent confusion and inadequacy represent a primary deficit that the analyst should attempt to repair? The analyst's feelings were the clue that the desired interventions were not simply a helpful human response to Mrs. N.'s basic needs, but rather an interaction forced and subtly molded by Mrs. N.'s externalizations. Mrs. N. was very grateful and highly complimentary; instead of the usual sense of low-key gratification from doing a good enough job in a difficult and frequently frustrating line of work, the analyst began to feel like a wise, all-knowing guru. There was an increasing awareness of the impulse to rationalize unusually active technique, which covered up a tinge of guilt for crossing some habitual boundary and anger at feeling pressured to do so. In fact, Mrs. N. had recreated an abusive relationship by becoming the helpless, dependent child her parents had externalized onto her and maintaining that role by allocating her high-level ego capacities to the analyst. By identifying with her externalizations (Sandler [1976] called this "role responsiveness") the analyst became a participant in her perpetuation of her abuse. This was part of the patient's lifelong defensive effort to "normalize" parental abuse.

Mrs. N.'s mother buttressed her externalization of guilty sexual excitement onto Mrs. N. by allowing the abuse to occur. Mrs. N. defended against her perception of her mother's inadequacy by allocating all blame to her uncle. This had to be reinforced continually by generating abusive relationships with all subsequent men. We would suggest that some such pattern explains the typical finding that someone other than the mother often inflicts the concrete abusive acts.

Confirmation of this view came in Mrs. N.'s furious response to the analyst's attempt to focus attention on the defensive nature and purpose of the relationship she was trying to create in treatment. Not surprisingly, the analysis then entered a tumultuous period of complaints, accusations, threats to leave or kill herself. Although Mrs. N. had always attributed her problems to the sexual abuse, the experience of reenacting an abusive relationship in the transference made her aware that her difficulties sprang from the abusive externalizing relationship with her parents. In the treatment she realized that she had not only internalized the parental externalizations of helplessness and damage, but had also identified with the family style of defensive externalization. She had learned to deal with her conflicts by externalization. Gradually her attribution to the analyst of qualities and responsibilities which really were hers was understood as a forcible violation of the analyst's role, similar to her experience when her childhood self had been burdened with helplessness, which contradicted her actual competence, guilty responsibility when she was an innocent victim, and grown-up sexual demands when she was a little girl.

This work allowed for exploration of what had led her to accept the externalizations and then to perpetuate them. For instance, when the analyst did not respond to her demand for an interpretation, but asked Mrs. N. to think about her dream, she became enraged. She accused the analyst of being malicious and withholding. Her stream of criticisms continued to the point where the analyst became aware of the provocation to respond in kind and was therefore able to interpret her anticipation of mutual fury. The underlying fear of abandonment came through in her preemptive withdrawal. This led to memories of hiding alone in the barn to avoid being attacked and rejected by her parents. Threatened by her intelligence, they frequently called her stupid. This memory brought her back to the transference dilemma, in which she feared that having her own associations to her dream would threaten the analyst's competence. Such sequences recurred whenever she was called upon to use her mind in the analytic work. Thus it became clear that she felt she had to externalize her own excellent ego capacities and identify with externalized parental incompetence in order to maintain attachment, defend against mutual destructive rage if she repelled the externalizations of others, and deny parental inadequacy and pathology. It was this work in the transference which helped her to integrate her ego functioning with the rest of her personality. This enabled her to end her abusive marriage and withstand her family's furious manipulative reaction to her assertion of autonomy.

Externalization is intimately linked with an inability to tolerate the separate existence of another. So, for children who are targets of parental externalizations, separation becomes defined and experienced as a hostile act. This can be very clearly demonstrated when we turn to work with adolescents, whose developmental task is to define a separate identity.

Mary, whom we describe in detail elsewhere as suffering from a severe sadomasochistic disorder (see Chapters 2, 3, 8, 13, and Novick 1990), came into analysis at the age of 18, following a serious suicide attempt. What is relevant here from her treatment is that both her suicide attempt and the occurrence of two years of sexual abuse by her older brother were the result of extreme longstanding pathology in her relationship with her parents. The most striking feature of the initial presentation was the disparity between the family's description of Mary as a high-achieving, well-behaved person, generally well-adjusted and happy, with many friends, and the analyst's perception of Mary sitting with her teeth clenched and her legs trembling as she held in a rage that she later described as so powerful that it would overwhelm everyone. Through the first year of analysis, the parents' denial of Mary's lifelong distress emerged. Long periods of unhappiness in childhood seemed to have gone unnoticed, as did her severe menstrual dysfunction, which was ignored for some years until frequent fainting spells from loss of blood necessitated medical intervention. Her mother, an overly conscientious housewife, was ever vigilant about household matters. However, the intrusions of Mary's older brother into her bedroom and the noises of scuffles and sexual activity apparently aroused no suspicion. The mother denied any knowledge of the continual sexual abuse that occurred when Mary was between the ages of 13 and 15. Mary's inability to remain away from home at university was not seen as indicative of any problems.

At the end of a year of analysis, Mary was still alive, but the analyst's main concern was that she might become psychotic or kill herself. The parents, however, expressed their pleasure at her progress and their feeling that she was back to being a normal girl and suggested that she stop treatment. The parental denial of her distress had been obvious from the beginning of her treatment; more subtle but increasingly apparent was their denial of everything individual about her. For instance, she had never had a birthday celebration of her own, but had always "conveniently" shared her party with a family member, whose birthday was a week later. The gifts she received bore no relation to her tastes or interests. Each year, the approach of her birthday intensified her conflicts; indeed, her suicide attempt had been made just after her eighteenth birthday. Mary's mother always said that she and Mary were just alike. As the scale of her denial of Mary's individuality became apparent, the analyst and Mary began to understand that the mother was attributing to Mary her own actual or wished for characteristics, irrespective of Mary's own personality. As the work of analysis freed Mary to begin developing along her own lines, it became inescapably clear that she was in fact very different from her mother in temperament, cognitive style, energy level, interests, and talents. The mother reacted irrationally to each of Mary's progressive moves: for example, when Mary moved to her own apartment, her mother became busy cleaning the attic and would not come downstairs for hours when Mary made a weekend visit home; Mary's independent decision about her hairstyle precipitated her mother's tears and running out of the house. With Mary's continued growth the family's pretense of normality crumbled. Her mother's condition deteriorated; she became severely depressed and suicidal, eventually entering treatment. The parents separated and the father precipitately left his secure and prestigious position to move to another locale.

This disruption of her family's pathological equilibrium confirmed the understanding that her growth involved rejecting her parents' externalizations (Brodey 1965). In Chapter 5 we described a subtype of externalization called generalization, a mode of thinking typical of early childhood, in which a person ascribes to the object characteristics similar to his own. We noted that as a defense, generalization is frequently used to stave off the painful affects attendant upon separation and represents a fantasy fusion of self and object representations. Thus we could see that the mother's externalization was an attempt to deny separateness. Her abuse of Mary for her own emotional needs superseded her maternal protective function and made Mary feel that she could neither turn to her mother for help, nor turn away from her to help herself, without risking complete abandonment.

During the termination phase of Mary's analysis, the pressure of imminent real separation brought to the fore her own feelings connecting externalization with leaving and being left. She brought into the transference the push to be the same as her depressed mother. As we have described in other discussions of Mary's analysis, she told the analyst, "When I'm happy, I feel I'm not with you. To be unhappy is to be like you, to be with you, to sit quietly and depressed with the whole world right here in this room." This material allowed work on Mary's motives for accepting her mother's externalizations and then using externalization herself as a mode of attachment to the analyst.

With Mrs. N. we saw how, in an adult, externalization interfered with integration; Mary helped us to understand how externalization interfered with the adolescent task of identity formation. Now we will look at material from the analysis of a child to see what happens earlier.

When Taylor first came to analysis at 5 years, 1 month, she could not remember her games from one session to the next and, although she was a very bright, verbal child, seemed to have difficulty maintaining or following a logical sequence in school and in treatment. After some time in treatment, it became apparent that her superficial way of relating, playing, and thinking reflected a massive defense against being surprised or attacked. She began to talk of her need for advance warning, so that she could prepare herself for any eventuality.

Taylor had been brought for treatment because of her parents' concern over her apparent fascination and fearful excitement at sexual matters, and a lag in reading readiness. Although Taylor had not even begun primary school, her intellectually ambitious father was worried that she might not pass her grammar school entrance exams at the age of 11. Mother and daughter quarrelled continually and seemed to be locked in a sadomasochistic interaction. The parents presented a vague possibility that Taylor had been molested by her cousin Kenny, who was eleven years older. In fact, her mother had witnessed many instances in which Kenny grabbed Taylor's buttocks and nipples, licked her genitals and climbed into her bed at night from infancy on.

After six months of treatment, Taylor began to play out with little dolls Kenny's visits to her bed when she was younger. By this time, he had been sent away for residential treatment, for which Taylor felt guilty responsibility. Day after day in the sessions she set out the configuration of the bedrooms and the dark of nighttime, but initially warded off any attempt by the analyst to talk about what was happening, even to the dolls. She also began to have nightmares and bouts of enuresis, and became increasingly restless. Her newfound capacity to be present emotionally and cognitively receded in treatment and her teachers reported renewed intermittent "tuning out" at school. Her games took on a sinister component of inflicting gory genital damage on all the little girl dolls. At this point interpretation addressing the relations and confusions among her own excitement and masturbatory impulses, her wetting, and fears and fantasies of castration began to take hold. Taylor was learning to read and wanted to make a "word-book" in her session. Her choice of words to illustrate each letter included "a for asshole, b for beat it, f for fatness, h for hitting Taylor, l for lick, m for mommy mad, t for tapping you," and so on. Taylor began to talk of Kenny's excited behavior and we could clarify the real and fantasied effects of his intrusions and her attempts to reenact these in the transference. Taylor's primary and secondary defensive interference with ego functions of integration, memory, and impulse control is typical of children who have suffered abuse in the preschool years. Abuse interferes with all ego functions, particularly reality testing and maintaining differentiation between self and other. At the age of 6, Taylor was truly unsure whether the children dressed in costumes for Guy Fawkes Day were really monsters. In games and in interactions with the analyst it was often hard to tell who was doing what to whom. Not only was Taylor confused, but there were times when the analyst was made to feel confused. After a year-and-a-half of treatment Taylor made great improvements, particularly in her ego functioning. She almost never presented the withdrawn, confused, unintegrated appearance of the early days. Her massive defensive disruption of her synthesizing function and memory had yielded to interpretation and verbalization, and her relationships and cognitive functioning reflected these gains. But, as Taylor continued to reject the externalizations of helplessness, confusion, and lack of self-protection, the family began to show signs of disruption, with parental discord increasing markedly.

The concrete sexual abuse had taken place in the context of a long and complex history of family dysfunction, in which externalization played a prominent role. Taylor's father had first married a very disturbed woman, who abused their children physically and sexually and eventually committed suicide. He then married Taylor's mother, who, at the age of 19, weighed two hundred pounds; she herself had been sexually abused by an uncle in early childhood. Subsequent interviews with father substantiated the inference that he related to women as damaged and defective. The line of externalization came also from the maternal grandmother, who was preoccupied with the idea that her daughter should be exactly the same as she, to the point where she urged Taylor's mother to dye her hair to match her own hair color. By the time treatment began, Taylor's mother had become slender and begun to pursue graduate work, while Taylor was overweight, confused, and sexually abused.

The analyst worked with the mother throughout Taylor's treatment, and, during the period of Taylor's working through her feelings about the events with Kenny, mother was able to reduce the overstimulation of scary movies, outings which were inappropriately exciting, intrusive and confusing lack of privacy in bedrooms and bathrooms, and so on. And yet her unconscious participation in exposing her daughter to abuse persisted; for example, she bought Taylor a dress which said "Tickle me" all over it. In the interview when this outfit's message was called to her attention, the mother talked extensively about maternal grandmother's pressure on her to be like her. The analyst asked about the maternal grandmother's reaction to mother's childhood sexual abuse; the grandmother had been vague and denied that it really could have happened. In a similar way, while she was fully aware that Kenny was impulsive and had himself suffered sexual abuse, the mother nevertheless denied the clear indications that he was abusing Taylor. At this point the analyst interpreted the mother's need to protect the maternal grandmother from her own rage and reproach by doing to Taylor what maternal grandmother had done to her, that is, externalizing her own helplessness, confusion, and uncontrolled excitement onto the child. The interpretation seemed to have a strong impact. Within two weeks, Taylor's mother had resumed her own analysis, and seemed genuinely to have changed the tone of her interactions with Taylor.

In therapy Taylor was able to use her restored ego functions to acknowledge her anger at her mother and complain about her being controlling, bossy, and smothering. Both Taylor and her mother began to reject the externalizations which had thus far maintained the marriage. This work and the impact of the mother's own treatment further disrupted the previous pathological family equilibrium. The parents were on the verge of divorce; under this threat of abandonment, the mother could not continue her support of her own and Taylor's progressive development and Taylor's treatment was interrupted. Soon after termination of Taylor's treatment, the parents nevertheless decided to divorce and Taylor insisted on coming to tell the analyst. She drew a picture of her family, all with sad faces and tears, and then crossed out the image of herself. Taylor felt obliterated and disregarded.

Using material from adult, adolescent, and child analyses, we have tried to show that instances of concrete sexual abuse occur in the context of and subsequent to the establishment of an abusive externalizing relationship. This understanding of abuse as a broader relationship issue allows us to look beyond particular events both historically and clinically. In each of the cases we have described, parental externalizations violated the patient's selfhood long before the sexual abuse. Infant observational material allows us to examine the earliest stages of such an externalizing relationship.

From 1981 to 1991, we were part of a research project that studied the development of relationships between adolescent mothers and their babies. We followed eighty-five pairs through their two-year stay in a residential center, which provided schooling, therapy, medical and social supports for the mothers, and medical and day-care services for the babies. Research data included periodic videotaping as a developmental record, therapy notes, cottage observations, medical and social history records, and case conference discussions. Here we will describe selections from the films of one mother and baby pair between the ages of 3 and 15 months.

Mother, whom we will call S., was one of twins, who had both been sexually abused by a relative in childhood. She witnessed a murder when she was a little girl and her beloved older brother was sent to prison for the murder of a neighbor girl at the time S. became pregnant. As soon as the pregnancy became known, her extremely religious family rejected her completely. S. said that her mother was a controlling and manipulative person, and S. herself was described in the cottage as hostile, irritable, and demanding. The first film, of a feeding situation at 3 months, shows that her baby Freddie was a healthy, active, related infant. Observations at this time noted S.'s love for her baby, but there was concern about her rough handling and apparent use of him for her own needs. For instance, she had difficulty sleeping and kept the baby awake with her until late into the night, when she would take him into her bed in order to go to sleep.

Film sequence 1: baby is 3 months old. S. and Freddie in feeding situation. S. is affectively engaged with her baby, who drinks her in with his gaze. He sucks vigorously, then plays with the bottle with his tongue and lips. S. reacts by attributing mischief to him and begins to tease him with the bottle, brushing it on his lips and cheek. She remarks "Feeding time at the farm," that is, he is a pig. S.'s affect varies from cheerful engagement to solemn distraction or withdrawal, as well as a teasing provocation.

Film sequence 2: baby is 9 months old. S. has been instructed, "Be with your baby." She has filled the floor with toys, and engages Freddie in hectic play. He begins repeatedly to explore toys with his hands, eyes, and mouth, only to be immediately interrupted by mother's presentation of a new stimulus. He cannot complete a play sequence without disruption, cannot experience competent, effective play. S. offers him a toy bunny, grabs it back saying, "Don't eat bunny," then bites it herself. When Freddie puts a rattle in his mouth, S. pulls it away, asking "Can I have some?" Throughout there is intrusion and interruption in his nascent ego functioning; his age-appropriate assertion and exploration is misinterpreted and greed and oral aggression are attributed to him.

Film sequence 3: baby is 1 year old. Again S. has been instructed to "Be with your baby." At the beginning of this play sequence she pushed him to perform on a toy piano. When he began to try it himself, she fetched a beach ball and began the game we see in the film. At the beginning of the game, there is a joyful interaction between them, with Freddie crowing in delight and S. praising his performance. Then she happens to hit him on the head with the ball. She apologizes, but then repeatedly bounces it off his face and head on purpose. S. also begins to call him derogatory names, like "Fat belly, old man, slobbery," and so forth. Freddie begins to look bewildered, but tries to continue the game. S. persists in hitting him with the ball. Eventually Freddie, confused, looks away, then hits himself in the head.

This is a crucial sequence. For Freddie there is a shift of affect from joyful achievement to resigned acceptance of his mother's externalization of badness.

Film sequence 4: baby is 15 months old. Freddie and his mother are at the table for snack. He is now very competent at self-feeding. This snack should be pleasureable for him, as he is being offered sweet cupcakes and there is no nutritional pressure. Nevertheless, the film begins with S. trying to make him eat, feeding him as if he is a helpless baby, which he resists. The next segment, moments later, illustrates the escalating tension between them. Freddie responds angrily with distinct aversion of his gaze and S. sighs in angry discouragement. In this fourth clip we see continuing refusal to look at his mother; Freddie only feeds himself when angrily blotting her out. S. tries unsuccessfully to enter his field of vision, and reacts with helpless anger to his stubborn refusal to comply.

In these film sequences, covering a year of Freddie's life, we see his change from a happy, engaged infant to an angry and withdrawn toddler. His joyful competence is no longer evident; instead we see a retreat to either bewilderment or sulkiness with his mother. Material from S.'s therapy revealed the oral demanding nature of her aggression, a quality she attributed to Freddie from his birth. She succeeded in externalizing this aspect of herself onto Freddie, as he became a biter in the nursery. S. tried to control the externalized aggressivity by keeping him an incompetent infant, but, as we have seen in the last eating film, he was still resisting this as a toddler.

It seems clear that concrete sexual abuse often occurs in the context of a pre-existing abusive relationship with the parent. By its nature, externalization constitutes an abuse since it violates the child's existing and developing personality. When a patient describes instances of abuse, an underlying pathological relationship may be assumed. Whether or not concrete abuse occurred or is remembered, an abusive relationship from childhood may first be picked up by the operation of externalization in the transference. In a phenomenon as perverse, pervasive, and complex as child abuse, it is obvious that externalization is only part of the explanation. Externalization is a general term for a variety of mechanisms and, when a child is the object of externalization, he too becomes an externalizer, with that process gathering layers of determinants and functions through the course of development. Externalization is a mechanism leading to and forming part of the adult sadomasochistic character, which is a frequent clinical outcome of childhood sexual abuse. By the time the patient enters treatment, externalization has become a dominant mode of relating.

In what we have called the "externalizing transference" (see Chapter 6) the patient attributes to the analyst a part of his own mental apparatus and then forms a relationship on that basis. Mrs. N. focused her attention on the uncle as the abuser, but the underlying abusive externalizing relationship with her mother emerged only when the analyst took up her externalizations in the transference. The analyst was alerted to the externalizations by his own affective responses. Children externalize in an obvious way, calling the analyst messy, smelly, stupid, or disgusting. Adults may be more subtle, but, when the analyst feels violated in his professional or personal *self,* when he feels over time that he is being gaslighted, misunderstood, misinterpreted, ignored, rendered ineffectual and helpless, furious yet guilty, when he feels trapped in a static situation where interventions are repeated without insight or growth yet any attempt to alter the interaction is met with vigorous resistance, then he should consider the possibility that the patient has established an externalizing transference, based on childhood abuse by an externalizing parent.

Technically, once the externalizing transference has been recognized, its various motives and effects must be dealt with. As we saw with Mrs. N., the adolescent Mary, and Taylor the school-child, the patient has internalized the externalization in order to remain attached and not feel abandoned, to contain rage at the externalizing mother, to keep the relationship from disintegrat-ing in a mutual explosion of fury, and to maintain a feeling of being essential to the mother. This omnipotent conviction is validated in the reaction of the parents when the child begins to reject the externalization, as we saw in each of our cases.

Externalization does not operate alone, but calls upon and leads to other defenses. Two are particularly important: turning aggres-sion against the self, and denial. Turning aggression against the self, a crucial element in the whole range of self-destructive ac-tions, including provoking or tolerating abuse, is a defense that builds upon the internalization of an externalized aspect of the parent. In normal development, the self representation emerges out of and contains the body representation. Integration starts with the experience of pleasure in one's body at the hands of a loving parent. Externalization interferes with the sense of ownership and integration of body and self. These patients experienced their bodies as owned and controlled by their mothers, and so aggres-sion towards the mother was defended against and expressed by attacks on the body. When Mary tried to kill herself, she was try-ing to murder the mother inside her.

Denial operates first to avoid the perception that the mother is an abuser. Secondly, denial is used to avoid the pain and dis-appointment of acknowledging that mother is neither an ideal-ized saint nor a persecuting monster, but rather an inadequate parent, unable to fulfill the ordinary good-enough protective func-tions. Shengold's (1991) study of the pathogenic impact of pa-rental weakness is relevant in this regard.

Work on these motives for defense must be accompanied by attention to the severe damage they have done to all the func-tions of the ego. Mrs. N.'s integrative capacity was severely com-promised by her need to externalize; Mary's compliance with her mother's externalizations interfered with all her ego functions, but especially those needed for independent action; because of her internalization of her mother's externalizations, Taylor could not use her memory or her reality testing. In Freddie's case the externalization led to a corruption of his psychic economy and self-regulation shifted from a base in pleasure to one in pain and anger.

The goal of the therapeutic interventions at this stage of treatment is to help create conditions for the reinternalization of the externalized parts of the self. Then the patient can experience an internal conflict and face the pain of dealing with developmental issues, which have thus far been avoided by living within the narrow confines of an unchanging externalizing relationship. Rage, sadness, loss, and mourning come into the center of the treatment.

As has been pointed out in Chapter 5, the clinical phenomena we have been describing in terms of externalization and internalization are often formulated, particularly by those influenced by Kleinian theory, as examples of "projective identification." As our earlier discussion makes clear, our usage is not simply a matter of taste or politics, but involves substantive conceptual objections to labeling complex interactions as projective identification. The term was complex when first introduced by Melanie Klein (1946), and later additions by authors such as Meltzer and colleagues (1975), Rosenfeld (1965), Bion (1958), Ogden (1979), Grotstein (1981), and others have given the term such an array of meanings, some of them contradictory, as to render it useless. Grotstein (1981) listed at least twelve varieties of projective identification. Kernberg (1987), whose writing has made the concept of projective identification palatable to American psychoanalysts, said that its "meaning has become blurred; it has been used to mean too many different things by too many different people under too many different circumstances" (p. 93).

Projective identification is a pivotal concept in the Kleinian account of normal and pathological development and, as such, is a cornerstone of Kleinian technique. Many analysts have also applied the concept to diagnostic differentiations. We are reluctant to use a concept that implies a specific diagnostic category, points to a particular developmental phase, and legislates for a specific technique. In contrast, the classical concept of externalization is mainly descriptive of a mental process, carrying no additional developmental, diagnostic, or technical implications.

Projective identification seems to be used in a way that condenses a sequence of defenses and reactions within both the subject and object. This may not only be confusing but also risks oversimplification. Important steps can be missed, some with crucial technical implications. For example, in our films of Freddie, labeling the interaction as "projective identification" would miss the rage that arises between the projection and the identification, or, as we prefer to term these processes, externalization and internalization. There is clinical gain from being able to follow with the patient each step of the sequence. Technically it is crucial to help the patient recover the feeling of rage, which follows externalization and precedes internalizing or identifying with the externalized aspect of the other.

Finally, in a field where clear thinking and free communication are both clinical and theoretical goals, we find it preferable to use a verb (to externalize) to describe the process rather than a noun. It is more direct and more elegant to say "A externalizes something onto B; B becomes angry and then may internalize it." If we say "By a process of projective identification A has projectively identified B with something and B in turn has identified with it" we lose the opportunity both to trace the affective steps in the sequence and to assign active responsibility for these processes.

When the externalizing transference is first linked to childhood abuse, patients often experience relief, clarity, and hope. Therapies that stop at this point of discovery avoid the conflict and resistance which inevitably ensue. Initial good feelings rarely last, as defensive confusion, doubt, and displacement of rage to others, including the therapist, are soon invoked. Considering the many determinants and functions that accrue to the role of the victim, it is not surprising that lasting change is strongly resisted.

What then can provide an impetus and motivation for change? Despite differences in age, background, and experiences of the three patients we have described, Mrs. N., Mary, and Taylor all lived lives devoid of pleasure. Pain and suffering characterized their relationships, their achievements, and their activities. Nothing was done for pleasure, nothing gave them pleasure, indeed the goal of their functioning was not pleasure but omnipotent control of others. In our discussion of omnipotence and masochism we described two distinct systems of self-esteem regulation. One is the omnipotent system, which stems from early and persisting experiences of helplessness, frustration, and rage. We said that those who live by the omnipotent system manifest a desperate clinging to pain because pain is the affect that triggers the defense of omnipotence, pain is the magical means by which all wishes are gratified, and pain justifies the omnipotent hostility and revenge contained in the masochistic fantasy. In looking at abused patients, we emphasize that a major mechanism of the omnipotent system is externalization.

Mrs. N., Mary, and Taylor were victims of externalization in childhood and they became externalizers, with the fantasy that they could use an externalizing relationship to control the actions and feelings of others and to deny and avoid reality perceptions and constraints. When we recognize the externalizing transference and help patients reinternalize parts of themselves, they can then take pleasure in functioning, pleasure in reality-attuned interactions with others, and begin to experience pleasure as an alternative basis for the regulation of self-esteem. In other words, therapeutic work on the patient's externalizations helps restore a normal system of self-regulation, one in which self-esteem comes from competent, realistic, empathic, and loving interactions with oneself and others. It is only when the patient has available this pleasure-based alternative to the externalizing, omnipotent system that he can experience an internal conflict between the two systems. The therapeutic work must address the price paid for living in the omnipotent system and restore the patient's capacity to choose.

The essence of the two systems is captured in our images of Freddie. We see him at 9 months, crowing with delight at his skill in catching the ball. At 15 months, we see him transformed into the initiator of hostile interactions. He turns away from his mother, looks right through her, gazes at the ceiling and at the cameraman, while she sighs in helpless frustration and rage. Through externalization, S. has turned Freddie into her angry, sadistic self. She and Freddie are tied together in a sadomasochistic relationship forged and maintained by externalizations. If, later, Freddie were to come to treatment, a central goal would be to help him reject externalizations and rediscover the joyful ball-player part of himself.

PART III
CLINICAL
MANIFESTATIONS

8 ATTEMPTED SUICIDE IN ADOLESCENCE: THE SUICIDE SEQUENCE

Soon after her 18th birthday, Mary drove her car down a steep embankment. The car was completely destroyed, Mary suffered severe internal injuries and nearly died. After recovering from major surgery, she told her psychiatrist that she had intended to kill herself. Mary and her parents met with the analyst soon after she left the hospital. Near the start of the interview Mother said, "I refuse to feel guilty," and remained fairly silent, as did Mary, for the rest of the session. Father, a tall, tree-trunk of a man, did most of the talking and the women nodded assent when looked at for additional comments. The whole family referred to the suicide attempt as "the accident," and apparently viewed it as an impulsive, rebellious bit of behavior to be appropriately punished and not repeated. The parents had insisted that Mary use her college savings toward paying for a new car as this would help impress her with the unacceptability of her actions.

Mary was the second of two children, with an older brother. The elder child had always rebelled, fought with the parents, and failed at school, whereas Mary was seen as a high-achieving person who had done well at school and was well behaved. She was said to have had many friends, to have played on the school teams and in general to have been well adjusted and happy, with a secure future in the professional career she had chosen. The parents said that they were completely surprised by the event. It was totally out of character and they could see no reason why she had done it. Even when seen alone, Mary had little to add to understanding her serious suicide attempt. She claimed that she too had no idea why she had done it, and said that while driving she had suddenly felt that it would be better if she were dead. She was having difficulty with her superior at work, and felt unjustly criticized by her but, at the same time, felt that she was not doing well enough. The referring psychiatrist had ruled out psychosis or a major biological depression, a view that concurred with the analyst's assessment and that of another psychiatrist called in for a second opinion and a drug consultation. So why had she made a serious suicide attempt? What was the risk of a further attempt? What was the treatment of choice?

When four-times-per-week psychoanalysis was recommended, Father went back to the referring psychiatrist to ask, "What kind of nut is Novick? Are they still doing psychoanalysis?"

Aside from his personal issues, which were then addressed, he did well to ask about psychoanalysis. Psychoanalysis is not commonly used with adolescents and almost never with suicidal young people.

There is a vast literature on suicide and attempted suicide, for, as Baechler (1979) comments, "It is probable that suicide is the most unremittingly studied human behavior" (p. 3). Except for the epidemiological data on suicide and attempted suicide that underscores the increasing incidence of the problem, the vast literature (Haim 1974, Otto 1982, Petzel and Riddle 1981) offers little assistance to the clinician. Given the nature of the topic, it is understandable that there are few studies based on clinical case material, but even research into attempted suicide in adolescence has relied almost entirely on demographic data, interview data obtained immediately subsequent to the event, and sometimes on clinical material obtained from brief interventions with suicidal adolescents. Hurry (1977) and Kernberg (1974) provide notable exceptions to the meager clinical literature on the topic.

The value of psychoanalysis as a research technique has often been questioned by those outside the field, and of late the research value of psychoanalysis has been put under very severe test by sophisticated arguments from within. Without entering into these stimulating and controversial issues, such as natural versus humanistic science, the search for meaning (hermeneutics) versus the explication of general scientific laws, nomothetic versus idiographic science, narrative versus historical truth, and so forth, we present here a research project on attempted suicide in adolescence conducted by analysts using five-times-a-week psychoanalysis both as a method of treatment and as a method of investigation. Mary's material is used to illustrate and amplify the research findings.

METHODS

Through the late 1960s and early 1970s, we were involved with colleagues at the then Brent Consultation Centre in a research project based on the psychoanalysis of adolescents who had attempted suicide. The summary report of that project has yet to be published in toto, but brief descriptions, summaries, and references have appeared in the literature (Hurry 1977, 1978, Friedman et al. 1972, Laufer and Laufer 1984, 1989, Novick 1977, and see Chapter 12, this volume). In that project, subsidized, five-times-a-week psychoanalysis was offered to nonpsychotic adolescents who had made medically serious suicide attempts. We were thus excluding those who made suicide threats, where the attempt did not require medical intervention to save the person's life, or where an ongoing psychotic process obscured the issue of intentionality.

The final sample consisted of seven adolescents, three females and four males ranging from 14 to 19 years of age. Analysts wrote detailed weekly reports on each case. These reports were circulated to the other members of the group, and all the analysts met weekly for two hours to discuss each patient and to evolve a conceptual and technical approach to the topic. We started with the assumption that attempted suicide in adolescence is always a sign of severe pathology. There are many who tend to romanticize suicide; to see it as an expression of free will. There have been best selling books in Europe and the United States on techniques of suicide. Alvarez (1971) traces the differing attitudes toward suicide and the attraction suicide has for the young and the creative. However, an earlier study on adolescents who came to a walk-in center found that adolescents who had made a serious suicide attempt showed more signs of current disturbance, a history of greater childhood disturbance, and a higher incidence of parental disturbance than the nonsuicidal adolescents who had come for psychological help (Hurry et al. 1976b). The psychoanalytic project on attempted suicide further confirmed this finding as each of the seven subjects proved to have been severely disturbed from childhood on. The same was true in Mary's case.

Near the end of her first year of analysis, Mary was attending college but did nothing more than study for her courses. She lived at home, totally dependent on her mother for everything from shopping to laundry. She turned down all offers of friendship and spent weekends and evenings alone in her room. When she was not studying, she stayed up late at night rearranging the furniture or spending hours trying to decide which side of the desk to put her pencils on. She sat silently at meals, hardly said anything to her father, and spoke only when asked direct questions. She was 19 years old, fully developed sexually but always dressed in bib overalls, sneakers, and loose-fitting sweatshirts. She wore her hair closely cropped and looked like a young boy. Her inhibited behavior and strange appearance were the overt signs of her disturbance; the analyst was more concerned about the continuing danger that she might either kill herself or suffer a psychotic breakdown and have to be hospitalized.

Nevertheless, at this point in her treatment her father, under pressure from mother, told Mary that he and mother were very pleased with her progress, that they felt she was now a "normal girl," that she seemed to be doing well and perhaps she should think of stopping her analysis or at least cutting down. They were intelligent, college-educated, professional people. Defenses, of course, have no respect for class or intellectual distinctions. Gross denial of pathology was the hallmark of this family, and a major focus of analytic work was Mary's view that only she knew that the story of her being a normal child from a normal family was untrue. If she were to reveal to anyone how disturbed she and her mother had been, and still were, terrible consequences would ensue. It is risky to base an assessment of parental pathology on the patient's distortions of memory and the selective acuity of projections, but Mary's description of mother as "weird" probably comes close to the mark. Mother's barely concealed hostility to her daughter and her extreme obsessionality were evident during meetings with the parents, and over the years the family had completely acceded to her pathological concerns with cleanliness and security.

Most striking, however, was mother's inability to tolerate the slightest sign of hostility. In her constant preoccupation with defending against both her own hostility and that of others, mother seemed completely out of touch with Mary's ordinary needs. This could be seen in many examples from current and past behavior and also in Mary's identification with an inattentive, unresponsive, affectless mother. Mary said that she had always considered herself as neuter, neither male nor female. Although signs of severe problems in sexual identity had appeared at puberty, including serious menstrual dysfunction of probable psychogenic origin, Mary's identity problem was more basic. As we learned from the analytic work, her choice was not between male and female but between life and death. Neuter did not refer to gender identity but to existence. Repeatedly, in treatment, Mary's response to stress was to "tune out, go blank, become a zombie." We came to call this "a little suicide" and she said that she could remember long periods of time, going back to childhood, when she would function like a robot, with no feelings. "When I tune out," she said, "it's as if I'm not there." Mary's memories of childhood showed signs of a lifelong difficulty in experiencing and maintaining feelings of pleasure in achievement. She had what Krystal (1978) has referred to as *anhedonia*—in treatment we called it the "big deal" response. She would work with enormous energy out of a near panic that she would fail. When she achieved her A or A+, she would feel a brief period of relief and then say to herself "big deal" and forget about her accomplishment. The disturbance in her ability to tolerate and experience affect and her feeling of being a "robot, a zombie" are typical signs of a posttraumatic reaction, which have led us to hypothesize that infantile trauma is part of Mary's history.

THE FOCAL RESEARCH

It does not require the effort and power of psychoanalysis to demonstrate that attempted suicide represents a breakdown in normal adolescent development and appeared, both in Mary and in the other adolescents in our research, in the context of severe, long-standing disturbance. As important as this finding may be, a psychoanalytic project should be able to tell us much more about attempted suicide in adolescence. In our project, an immediate obstacle—one shared by most psychoanalytic research projects—

related to the volume of material generated by psychoanalysis. We devised a method, called *focal research*, in part as a response to the challenge of dealing with large amounts of data. The weekly reports on each case contained many references to suicide. Most of these suicide references related to the actual attempt, some were threats or plans for further attempts, and some were intellectualized comments on the nature of death. Each suicide reference was extracted from the weekly reports and put on a separate piece of paper. It was noticed that these comments varied in frequency, and the focal research was an attempt to study both the content and the context in which these suicide thoughts appeared. Examples of such comments, taken at random from each of the seven cases, are as follows:

Female Case #1: "I had told my school friends that I wanted to kill myself but they didn't believe me."

Female Case #2: "When I took the tablets I felt nobody cared for me."

Female Case #3: "It may sound paradoxical but I think of suicide as my lifeline. Suicide is my way out. Without it I would become dependent on life."

Male Case #4: "Suicide people don't really believe they will die."

Male Case #5: "I always feel that it is something I might try again. I'm frightened of doing it again and frightened of the pain but it's something I can't give up."

Male Case #6: Patient reported that while at his parents' home for the weekend he had made a trial run, taking six aspirins to see if he could swallow them one after the other. The next day he tried to kill himself.

Male Case #7: "I think I must have been in a mad, insane mood. I can't even remember what happened or how I came to turn the gas on, so I think I must have been crazy."

On the same page as the extracted comment, note was made of the immediate context, the larger context and, finally, space was allotted for speculations. The immediate context included proximal interventions by the analyst, the patient's material and affective state prior to and subsequent to the suicide thought, and such events as an upcoming vacation, a weekend break, and so on. The larger context referred to events that took place over a span of time, such as the developing and predominant transference relationship, emerging changes within the patient, shifts in defenses, and the increasing dominance of certain phase-specific dynamics. The section on speculations allowed the analyst to associate freely to the material and to see whether certain hypotheses could be borne out by subsequent material. In doing the focal research analysts worked in pairs, each abstracting the suicide comment and content on the other analyst's case. A pilot study using pairs of analysts working independently on one case showed almost perfect agreement on the abstracted suicide items and on the immediate context for the emergence of these suicide thoughts. Surprisingly, there was also very high agreement between the analysts on the larger context for the emerging suicide thoughts.

As a further measure of the reliability of the findings, two measures of internal consistency were used. Each analyst wrote a detailed metapsychological portrait of the case in treatment. The sections and subheadings of this portrait were based on Anna Freud's metapsychological profile (1962) as extended for adolescents by Laufer (1965). The analyst who was doing the focal research could then check the dynamic picture that was emerging with the metapsychological profile written by the analyst of the case, and, finally, the analyst of the case would evaluate the focal research findings for consistency with his own clinical view of the case.

RESULTS

An immediate and striking finding of the focal research was the extent to which significant bits of information concerning the actual suicide attempt were not available until well into the analysis. For each case an enormous amount of additional information emerged during the course of analysis compared to what was elicited by direct questions soon after the suicide attempt. Often, the new information came in response to an interpretation, especially a transference interpretation. In Chapter 12 we refer to one of the seven cases, a 19-year-old who had claimed that his suicide attempt was precipitated by a rejection from the university of his choice. Near the end of his first year of analysis, interpretation of his attempt to force the analyst to reject him led to his remembering that he had applied to the university knowing that the deadline had passed. Similarly, in Mary's case the meager information available soon after the suicide attempt was considerably augmented by memories recovered following analytic intervention. For example, she recalled, in the third year of her analysis, that the car she had smashed was her mother's; mother had loved the car and Mary had hated it.

The focal research provided two sets of information: 1) suicide thoughts (which include memories of the actual attempt, attitudes and fantasies about suicide, and so forth) and 2) the context in which these thoughts emerged. We hypothesized that the thoughts and memories did not emerge at random but related to specific dynamic patterns discernible in the immediate and larger context of the flow of material. We found in all seven cases that suicide thoughts emerged in relation to: (1) fear of or feeling of abandonment, (2) fear of or wish for engulfment, and (3) fear of or guilt over what were felt to be omnipotent aggressive wishes toward mother. Our research also uncovered important distinctions between a suicide act and a suicide thought—and the multidetermination of such thoughts and acts. To present another of the major findings of the focal research—*the suicide sequence*—we return to Mary, the adolescent seen subsequent to the study.

THE SUICIDE SEQUENCE

Mary and her parents viewed her suicide attempt as an impulsive act, out of character with a previous well-functioning person-

ality and precipitated by some person or event outside the immediate family. This characterization of the suicide attempt is similar to the one presented by the adolescents in the research project
and is not an unusual view. In a syndicated newspaper article
(Shirley 1981), the reporter wrote of a 16-year-old boy who had
shot himself with his father's favorite shotgun. His father described him as "popular, played football, just a normal, teenage
kid." This view of adolescent suicide has attained the power of a
myth, and one of the major findings of the focal research was to
contradict this myth. In every case we found a consistent sequence
of psychological steps leading to a suicide attempt. The attempt,
rather than being a sudden act, was the end point in a pathological regression.

The focal research enabled us to combine the memories of the
suicide attempt with the dynamic context for the recall of these
events to arrive at a first approximation of the steps in the regressive sequence leading to the suicide attempt. Bearing in mind
all the limitations and controversies concerning the accuracy of
reconstructions, we now present the steps in the sequence (Hurry
et al. 1976a,b) and use the material from Mary's case to test the
findings.

1. For a considerable period prior to the suicide attempt, the
adolescents had felt depressed, sexually abnormal, and had suicidal thoughts. The focal research shows that depression and
feelings of sexual abnormality can coexist with suicidal thoughts
without in themselves motivating the act of suicide.

When Mary reached puberty her feelings of nonexistence
were expressed as feelings of sexual abnormality. She frequently constructed mental lists of "impossibles." The order
of "impossibles" changed during treatment, but for years the
top three remained unaltered—sex, marriage, and babies. Much
later in the analysis she admitted with embarrassment that
during junior and senior high school she sometimes had fantasies about boys, thought of talking to certain boys but was

sure that they would find her "weird and unattractive." Mary
was potentially an attractive young woman and as the analysis
progressed and she gathered courage to take charge of her own
body, there were times when she allowed herself to be quite
feminine and pretty. It was evident, however, that from early
puberty on she had felt sexually abnormal and incapable of
becoming a mature, sexual woman.

Regarding feelings of depression preceding the suicide attempt, Mary reported that she had been "feeling bad" for at
least four years. Her father, a professional, had accepted a
position in another part of the country, and Mary had to leave
her friends and her school. She said that she had felt "bad"
ever since and had never been able to make the kind of friends
she had before the move. "Feeling bad" was Mary's term for
an undifferentiated state of dysphoria; as she slowly became
able to differentiate and verbalize her feelings, she could talk
about her anger at her parents, especially her father, for not
having considered her feelings or her needs and for never
having talked to her about the move.

As to preexisting morbid fantasies and suicidal thoughts,
the material revealed that for many years Mary had been preoccupied with thoughts of death and dying. Father traveled
frequently and since childhood Mary had worried that he might
die. She was surprised when she had reached her eighteenth
birthday and realized that she had never thought of herself as
being 18. She felt this indicated that she probably thought she
would not live to be 18.

Some aspects of her memories regarding the actual attempt
were still unclear at that point but there is evidence for a pre-
existing suicide plan from another source. The year after the
start of treatment, just before the anniversary of her suicide
attempt, Mary was in a state of visible anguish and "feeling
bad." She was spending many hours in her room, not sleeping
at night, and defending vigorously against conscious awareness
of any angry feelings toward her parents. The analyst mentioned

the anniversary, the reemergence of suicide thoughts and, when Mary agreed that such thoughts were in her mind, asked if she were making concrete plans for such an event. Following extraction of wisdom teeth her dentist had prescribed a powerful pain killer. Mary said that she had been refilling the prescription for weeks and saving the pills for her next suicide attempt.

As we found with the seven adolescents in the project, so, in Mary's case, depression, feelings of sexual abnormality and suicidal thoughts could be present for considerable time without leading to an actual attempt. This finding suggests that there is a more complicated link between depression and adolescent suicide than usually noted in the literature. As will be demonstrated, it requires more than depression and a suicide plan to lead to a suicide attempt. Furman (1984) arrived independently at a similar conclusion.

2. The sequence leading to the suicide act is precipitated in all cases by external events which impose on the adolescents the responsibility of taking a step that represents to them the breaking of the tie to the mother.

In Mary's case the suicide attempt was preceded, first, by her leaving home to go to university, and then by her 18th birthday. Both these external events symbolized independence and adulthood, a phase she had never imagined entering. During the course of analysis, many external independent moves were seen to represent for Mary the complete severing of ties to mother, actions which she felt were totally unacceptable. Moving out of her house to a dormitory precipitated suicidal thoughts. Going to a party or even imagining buying her own television set was felt by her to be an act of extreme defiance which was followed by suicidal thoughts. In her third year of analysis she planned to return to the city of her childhood home in order to visit her old high school friends. She first arranged a change in her analytic schedule, then went through all the other necessary steps. On her way to the travel agent she realized that this final step would mean that she had done it all without her parents. She knew that she should feel pleased; instead, she felt terrible. "It wasn't right." When the analyst suggested that this was what she might have felt when she was away at college, she recalled a moment of panic when she had realized that her winning a scholarship meant she did not need her parents for anything.

3. In all cases the adolescents fail to make such a step. The external event and the experience of failure make the adolescents conscious of their dependency on their mothers.

In Mary's case the failure which occupied most of the first year of analysis was her inability to stay away at college. The college was highly competitive and she had attained a place and a full scholarship by beating out a long list of female applicants. The college not only symbolized independence from mother but would, in fact, have made her independent since she would not need them for any financial support. During the period of extreme difficulty at college, she felt very close to her mother and appreciative of mother's support. She felt that it was father who wanted her to stay. She left college after six weeks and returned to her parental home. Following the start of analysis, she attended a local college but remained at home and had her mother do everything for her from cooking to laundry. Mary felt totally dependent on mother, would panic at the thought of traveling to a different place without her, and allowed mother to select and buy all her clothes. It was only during her third year of analysis, at the age of 20, that Mary began to allow herself to shop independently.

A psychology of will and action must encompass the paradox of adolescent suicide. Mary's behavior underscores the fact that these young people are often incapable of the simplest actions such as buying clothes or going to a party. On the other hand, they are capable of self-destruction, an avenue of activity not open to other young people, even those who are otherwise seriously disturbed.

4. The failure to make the normal adolescent move away from the parent throws the adolescent back into an intense infantile relationship with mother, which on a descriptive level could be termed a sadomasochistic relationship. The female adolescent, terrified of being abandoned by mother, will submit to her and create situations in which she is repeatedly forced to do so. The preexisting relationship with the mother is very primitive and failure to separate and become autonomous throws the adolescent back into that primitive relationship.

The analytic material, especially during the periods of repeated suicidal crisis, allowed for reconstructing the relationship between Mary and her mother prior to the suicide attempt. It had revolved around Mary's total inability to contain the slightest negative thought about her mother:

> The anger was, as she termed it, a "hot potato." She dealt with her anger mainly by turning it against herself and displacing it onto some other object. Since childhood, anger at her elder brother had been an accepted outlet and often she and mother joined together to criticize and attack him. Prior to the suicide attempt, aggression was displaced onto her father and then onto the superior at work. In the analysis the analyst was frequently the recipient of her displaced aggression. This occurred concomitant with regression to a state of helpless submission in which Mary saw herself as totally inadequate and her mother as perfect.
>
> The state of total submission to a powerful, idealized mother who could do no wrong was epitomized in Mary's hairstyle. Mary wore her hair in a highly unusual style. It was shorter than that of most boys, clipped behind the ears and the back of the neck, a "short back and sides," reminiscent of the style

of haircut worn by men in the 1950s. Well into the analysis, in the context of talking about her inhibited exhibitionism, her wish to wear pretty clothes but her fear and inability to do so, the analyst inquired about her hairstyle, wondering if Mary was aware that it was cut unusually short. She said that her brother and father had said that her hair was very short. Her friends had also said so, but her mother thought it was a good length. Mary then smiled ruefully and said, "But she would, you know, since she cuts my hair."

The sadomasochistic battle centered on who owned Mary's body and it could be safely inferred that toilet training was achieved in a traumatizing, unempathic manner. Mary commented on mother's rough, "no nonsense" handling of her niece and said that mother would have been a good animal trainer but a bad child raiser. Mary's fear of making a mess was a focus of considerable work, and links could be drawn between her fear of losing bladder or bowel control and her severe constriction of affect and activity. At one point, when discussing her inability to tolerate ambivalent feelings, she said that she thought such feelings were messy. She said, "I always thought feelings should be neat and tidy."

5. In this state of heightened consciousness of their dependency, all sexual and aggressive preoccupations become a source of anxiety. There is evidence in the memories of the external event that these adolescents become at least dimly aware of the incestuous nature of their fantasies.

In Mary's case one could see repeatedly how her extreme dependency and submission served to defend against her primitive rage at mother. However, the dependency intensified her anger, which in turn made dependency more necessary but more unacceptable.

As she gradually learned to tolerate her feelings and began to recognize anger directed at her mother, she said often, "If I'm angry at someone else I still have mother, but if I'm angry at mother then I'm all alone." Regarding incestuous fantasies breaking through prior to the suicide attempt, it is evident that the oedipal situation was a source of enormous anxiety for Mary, especially because of the aggression involved in the rivalry. To take a minor example: Mary always performed extremely well at school, but seldom had any pleasure in the results. It was a problem focused on in the analysis and it was linked with her inability to dress in a pretty way, to take pride in herself, or to exhibit herself in an appropriate fashion. Following this work, she explained that when she brought back a good grade father was appreciative and seemed to understand the nature of the effort involved and the achievement in the grade. Mother, on the other hand, expressed her pleasure by immediately comparing Mary's high grades with her own academic difficulty when she went to college. Mary felt that there was a rivalry, that mother felt beaten, and then Mary began to wonder if this was why she could take only momentary pleasure in her academic achievements and then dismissed them as "big deal."

Clearer evidence of a link between positive oedipal fantasies and suicide thoughts emerged in what came to be seen as a repeated pattern in which good feelings about the analyst and Father emerged in the context of criticism of her mother. When she criticized her mother, she then felt good about the analyst. During one of these periods, she dreamed that she was going on a trip with her father and that her mother had floated off alone in a balloon. There was a period of about two weeks in which she and father shared giggly jokes and teased each other. She worked hard in treatment, and brought much material related to her feeling that her mother was "weird" and unusual. The situation then became unbearable. She began to "feel bad," she refused to talk in treatment, Father and the analyst became the "bad guys," and she again became totally dependent on Mother and highly suicidal. As this repetitive pattern was linked to the sequence preceding the suicide attempt, she at first denied that there had been any positive feelings for her father. But she then remembered that she had been able to make an important intervention in regard to the father's feelings about the elder brother, an intervention that Father still described as having been enormously important. Further, it seemed that Mary's intervention had altered the balance of forces within the family. It had brought Father, Mary, and elder brother close together and excluded mother. Mary had completely forgotten about this event, which had happened just before her actual suicide attempt.

As the work progressed, the influence of persisting sadistic sexual theories became explicit and were seen to have had an important influence on Mary's inability to retain positive oedipal fantasies. In her dreams, associations, and memories, sex involved sadistic attacks eventuating in death or destruction.

6. The next event in the sequence was the attempt, once again, to break away from their mothers by appealing to another person. The appeal took the form of a suicide threat. The appeal to the other person is an attempt by the adolescent to get out of a highly dangerous situation, one in which both sexual and aggressive wishes are threatening to break through to consciousness.

There is no evidence in Mary's case that she had threatened suicide and had appealed to some person outside the family for help. Mary's material both amplifies and clarifies the points in the sequence outlined from the suicide research. Her material indicates that the aborted move to someone outside the family is not simply an emergent step in the sequence but a repetitive pattern that occurs with increasing frequency in the adolescents' frenzied attempt to defend against aggressive feelings toward mother. There is an attempt to break away from the dangerous dependency, but very quickly the person toward whom they turn as an ally comes to be seen as an enemy. Disappointment, hurt, and anger toward mother are quickly displaced, and the person who could help them is seen as the person who drives them into a more intense dependency on mother.

This is what we describe in Chapter 12 as a "negative therapeutic motivation"; when it appears in treatment it becomes a means of displacing failure, blame, and anger onto the therapist and intensifying the primitive tie to the again idealized mother. Did this happen prior to Mary's suicide attempt?

Her memory was somewhat fuzzy, but repeatedly in the course of treatment each moment of suicidal crisis—and there were many—was preceded by just such a point in the sequence. Friends who seemed eager to help would be regarded with suspicion and anger. She would be invited away for a weekend and then imagine getting sick so that she would have an excuse not to go. Most ominous, and a sign that suicidal thoughts and wishes were in the forefront, was when the analyst became the "bad guy," when she would come to the session determined not to talk, when she deliberately kept things secret. During a session filled with stubborn silence she said, "I feel as if I'm a POW and you're trying to make me talk." It was at these times that the analyst's anxiety increased, and concern that she was thinking about and intending to kill herself could be verbalized.

The suicide research summarized this section of the sequence as a series of appeals to an outside object to take the adolescents away from the intense and dangerous tie to the mother. In Mary's case it was apparent that there had been a lifelong pattern of oscillation between mother and non-mother. During the analysis, one could see the oscillation occurring with increased frequency and intensity as, with each return to mother, Mary's anger at her intensified. Displacement as a defense was no longer sufficient. Mary's material revealed reasons for this. Even while locating all the negative feelings on the external object, Mary was aware that she was doing this for mother's sake. In Mary's view, and there seemed to

be some justification for this perception, it was mother who could
not tolerate separation, mother who could not accept or absorb any
aggression or criticism. Mary had been dimly aware of this before,
but, during analysis, she became conscious of an intense feeling
that all her sacrificing of an external life was done for mother. To
return to a submissive dependency on mother and still feel unattended to, unappreciated and unloved, intensified her rage even
further and led to an ever-increasing frequency of oscillation between mother and non-mother.

7. In the sequence of actual events there is a breakthrough of
aggressive feelings toward Mother by both girls and boys. In the
case of girls it is a breakthrough of conscious aggressive feelings
toward mother accompanied by extreme guilt reactions. The guilt
was intensified by an event which confirmed the girls' feelings of
omnipotent aggression. The girls experience a conscious choice
between killing themselves or killing their mothers. As a result
of the breakthrough of aggression, both boys and girls experience
a fear of loss of control over their impulses.

For much of the first year of her analysis, Mary denied that
she had been angry with her mother before the suicide attempt.
However, Mary's repeated pattern of dealing with her anger at
her mother during analysis made her aware of how she had
distorted her memory of the events prior to the attempt. During her sessions, any remark critical of mother would be followed, at times in the same session, by Mary "feeling bad,"
becoming highly self-critical, and "tuning out" or "becoming
a zombie." She would stop feeling and thinking. A voice in
her mind kept saying, "you've said enough, you've gone too
far, you better stop now." The next day Mary would be agitated and very anxious about school or angry about something
a friend had said. When the analyst pointed out the displacement and the fact that only the day before she had been critical of her mother, she would react with genuine surprise, having completely forgotten that she had said those things about

her mother. Eventually, the supposition that this "whitewash" might have occurred in relation to her feelings prior to the suicide attempt brought some confirming material. The most intense and sustained feeling of anger centered on her reactions to her birthdays. Her eighteenth birthday had occurred a week and a half prior to the suicide attempt; during analysis her reactions to her nineteenth and twentieth birthdays repeated the reactions before the suicide attempt. Mary and her brother had birthdays two days apart, and it was a family custom, initiated by mother, to hold their birthday parties on the same day. This was but one of the many features of her birthday that left Mary feeling unattended to, uncared for, and unloved. The birthday celebration and the presents seemed perfunctory, slapdash, and performed out of duty rather than caring. This young woman, who had a remarkable memory for academic subjects, could not remember what she had received on her eighteenth or nineteenth birthdays. During the analysis, the breakthrough of rage at mother immediately following the birthday was evident, expressed in the analysis and immediately followed by self-criticism, "feeling bad," agitated attempts to displace the anger, and then another suicide crisis in which she was overwhelmed by suicidal wishes and close to putting suicidal plans into action.

In relation to the issue of loss of control, Mary regarded everything in extremes. In her view she had to become a zombie (that is, totally devoid of wishes), or she would be swept away by impulses and move directly into omnipotent action. In her dreams she never just felt angry but continued to hit until the person was killed. The zombie reaction was termed a "little suicide," and the analyst suggested that she was killing a part of herself. She responded by saying that if she did not kill herself she would kill someone else. Regarding the finding that some external event confirmed the adolescent's fantasy of omnipotent aggression, there was no evidence by the third year of treatment that anything had occurred specifically in relation to mother just before the suicide attempt. What probably did occur was a breakdown in Mary's strenuous denial of Mother's "weirdness," her vulnerability, and the marital difficulties of the parents. The mother's increasing instability as Mary's functioning and reality testing improved indicated that the whole family had for years been protecting the mother and denying her pathology, accepting her externalizations of dysfunctional aspects of her self (see Chapter 6).

8. The adolescent will now feel in a state of intense panic and deadlock. Suicide thoughts which had been present for a considerable period of time will now become the solution. It is considered a positive, brave action. It is a solution to the conflict, a way out of the dilemma. Unable to make the normal adolescent moves, the wish to positive action is transferred to the suicide attempt.

In Mary's case suicide as a positive, brave action and a solution to an insoluble dilemma was addressed from the very beginning and interpreted as such. She confirmed the interpretation. When the analyst suggested that it would be wise if she handed over the pills she had saved for her next suicide attempt, she agreed, but said that she would hate herself for doing it. It was her only way out. It was a positive action, she said, one she could not think of giving up. She described her suicide attempt as an overpowering surprise to her parents, and it became clear that it represented, in part, an acting out in reverse form of the experience of having been surprised and thus unprepared and overwhelmed. Her parents had been completely shocked; she had kept all thoughts and suicide plans secret from them. During the analysis, the analyst felt especially uneasy at moments when the suicide crisis seemed to have passed. When this disquiet was first verbalized Mary said, "I was just thinking that this would be a good time to do it—I mean, everyone thinks the worry is over." It became apparent that suicide as an overwhelming surprise was a derivative of what Laufer (1965) has termed a "central masturbation fantasy" and, in turn, could be traced to repeated primal scene exposure and a persistent lack of parental protection from other overwhelming experiences. In this connection, E. Furman (1984) has written about the role of parental pathology in the exposure to traumatic situations and "the persistence (in the suicidants) of intense unfused early aggression in its sexualized sadomasochistic form. . . ." At another point, Mary agreed that her suicide was an attempt to change her parents and went on to say that she had achieved many of her aims by attempting suicide. For the first time, her parents had paid attention to her and had expressed their love and devotion. In fact, she was in analysis only because of her suicide attempt and the analysis was being supported by her parents.

9. Totally preoccupied with suicidal impulses, the adolescent turns once more to the outside world, not for help but in order to deal with guilt in reaction to aggressive feelings about mother. Material on the suicide event indicates that unconsciously adolescents provoke a rejection and the focal research shows that they feel compelled to do so. There is an unconscious need to take the blame away from mother and put it on some person outside the home. By provoking rejection at the hands of someone else, the conscious awareness that the suicide is an aggressive attack on mother is avoided. This is a decisive move because the blame is located on some external object, the guilt no longer acts as an inhibiting factor, and the suicide plan is put into action.

In Mary's case we know that consciously she experienced the suicide attempt as due entirely to a difficult relationship with a superior at work. She was critical of this superior and felt criticized by her. She felt that she was not living up to the expectations of the superior, but at the same time this woman had disappointed her. All her feelings of rage, rejection, and abandonment had been displaced from mother onto this female authority figure, and consciously the act was precipitated only by her feelings about this female superior. She had been pre-occupied with thoughts about her superior, anxiety about work, and self-hatred for having failed to remain at college. She had not thought of her parents or brother nor had she felt any pangs of conscience for intending to kill herself.

10. Consciously, at the time of the actual suicide attempt, the adolescents saw the event as producing multiple results. It would reassert their control over external events, over people, and over their bodies. The world would be sorry for having mistreated them and they would achieve a bodily state where there was no experi-ence of aggressive or sexual feelings.

Mary's fantasies about the effect of her suicide on other people and on her own impulses was a central theme from the begin-ning of her analysis; various aspects recurred repeatedly in her words, actions, and dreams. Most prominent was the fantasy that by killing herself she would make others "feel bad." She would force them to pay attention to her, to feel sorry for hav-ing neglected her and not having paid attention. Their reac-tion, she imagined, would be one of total surprise and guilt. They would say, "Oh, we never knew, we never suspected."

11. In the memories of the circumstances of the actual attempt there are many details to indicate that the adolescents had experi-enced an altered ego state, a psychotic state, at the time of the attempt. In all cases the adolescents did not experience any con-scious concern or feelings of guilt in relation to their parents. Fur-ther, there was a total denial of death as evident in the conscious fantasies that they would not only achieve their aims through the suicide but would be around to observe and to benefit from the changes effected by their deed. This denial of death was related to ever-increasing regression in which they had given up completely any feelings of ownership of their body; the body was something

which did not belong to them. It was a source of unwanted impulses, both aggressive and sexual, something intruded upon, controlled by, and belonging to mother. Finally, analysis showed that as part of the ego regression, the mother they wish to destroy becomes the mother who wishes them dead, and suicide then is not an attack but a submission to the wishes of mother. Thus, we see that the adolescents not only deny the reality of death but see it as a state of peace and of being at one with their mothers.

All this was very true of Mary; in her case projection of her death wishes seemed to fall on very fertile ground. Mary felt that her mother did not like her children, that she wished that she had never had any. As Mary became more observant and more capable of containing these observations and bringing them to treatment, there were many things which, as Mary said, "make one think." A particularly vivid example was the following: a psychiatric patient had committed suicide by jumping from a bridge. Within a day of the event, Mary's mother was driving Mary to a shopping center and took a roundabout route which passed over that bridge. Then, according to Mary, mother mentioned casually, as if commenting on the weather, that she had heard a rumor that a psychiatric patient had jumped off that bridge the other day.

12. In many cases the very choice of method will itself be of dynamic significance and not just fortuitous.

As noted earlier, Mary's suicide attempt was made with her mother's car, a car that Mother loved and Mary hated.

13. Immediately following the suicidal act the adolescent will feel a state of calm, of relief and release from all tensions.

This was true in Mary's case. She felt an enormous sense of relief and total calm while waiting for the ambulance to arrive. She knew that she would not die, she said. She felt that she had finally accomplished something. She had done a powerful, brave thing, something most people could not do. She had shocked everyone and forced them to pay attention to her and now everything would be different.

As we have seen, the material from Mary's case appears to confirm the results of the study of seven adolescents who had each attempted suicide. From the psychoanalytic material of Mary's case, we can replicate the finding that the suicide attempt was not a sudden act but the end point of a pathological regression. Suicide thoughts had been present for a considerable period prior to the attempt. The regression started with her experience of failure in the move toward independence from mother. Subsequent events then led to an intensification of her tie to mother and a displacement of the experience of rejection and anger from mother to an external object. Once the experience of rejection and blame was displaced, guilt was no longer an inhibiting factor, and the suicide plan was put into action. At the time of the attempt, Mary thought of suicide as a way to change the external world, mother, and self. Suicide was considered a positive, brave action, producing multiple results including the restoration of positive self-regard. Reality of death was denied and the death wish was projected onto mother.

In addition to replicating the findings from the psychoanalytic study of attempted suicide in adolescents, the material from Mary's analysis amplifies some of these findings. Here are some points in the suicide sequence as seen in the somewhat different light cast by the analytic material emerging in Mary's case:

RELATIONSHIP WITH MOTHER PRIOR TO SUICIDE ATTEMPT

The emphasis on the adolescent's fear of abandonment and engulfment, though correct, does not sufficiently emphasize the importance of primitive aggression. In Mary's case it was not rejection or abandonment in themselves that were crucial components, but her fantasy of the omnipotent rage that would break through if these events were to occur. Her intense anxiety consequent upon each developmental step was not primarily a fear of abandonment, but a fear of enjoying and preferring the non-mother to her own mother. This would break down her denial of her mother's pathology and unleash Mary's primitive and omnipotently experienced rage. For example, as a way of saving money mother provided only powdered milk at home. Mary could not remember having had whole milk until she was a school child and then she was shocked and thrown into a panic on finding out how much she loved milk.

DEPENDENCY INTENSIFYING ANXIETY

Although it is true in Mary's case that the experience of complete dependence on mother intensified fear of drive expression, especially hostility, her material underscored another, possibly more important, reason for the association between increased dependency and heightened anxiety over hostile wishes. Mary experienced her dependency as a giving up for mother. It was "a little suicide" with the same motives of self-sacrifice in order to change mother into a caring, loving mother. Mother's failure to change intensified Mary's primitive rage. Concomitant with defenses against the rage was an ever-increasing self-sacrifice of autonomy and feelings of separate existence, which made Mary even more dependent. Suicide was the ultimate sacrifice of a separate self, with the fantasy that this surrender to total dependency would create the wished-for *purified pleasure dyad* free of hostility from either partner.

PROVOKING REJECTION

Regarding the step in the sequence in which the adolescent provokes rejection, Mary's material emphasized that this was an old pattern of oscillation between Mother and non-mother objects such as brother, Father, and teachers. For her, there was a lifelong pattern of splitting the ambivalent feelings, displacing negative feelings onto some object other than mother, and thereby retaining the illusion of a blissful mother–child dyad. Such a history of intermittent involvement with others might be looked for in other cases.

PROJECTION OF DEATH WISHES ONTO MOTHER

Mary's material indicated that her conviction that mother wished her dead was not just a projection but had a substantial basis in reality. Mary's material should make us sensitive to the intense death wishes of mothers of suicidal adolescents. Looking back over the material of the seven suicide cases, there is abundant evidence that the intense hostility and death wishes of mothers played an important role in the suicidal behavior of the adolescents. Hurry (1977, 1978), in her excellent summary of suicide in adolescents and her detailed clinical presentation of one of the suicidal patients from the study, demonstrates the importance of this factor.

TURNING THE AGGRESSION AGAINST THE SELF

Although this mechanism in suicide was described by Freud in "Mourning and Melancholia" (1917[1915]) and noted in interim reports on the suicide study, we feel insufficient emphasis has been placed on this factor. In Mary's case the mechanism by which it was accomplished could be seen. It was via an identification with the hated part of the mother that the instinctual vicissitude of turning aggression against herself could not only defend against but also express her hostility towards mother. An important shift in the treatment was when these identifications could become a focus of the analytic work. As one of many examples: Mother had put the envelope containing Mary's grade reports in Mary's desk without showing them to Father. On the weekend, Mary discovered the grades in her desk and thought to herself that Mother did not want Father to see the grades. She said to the analyst, "So then I did the same as Mother did. I put them back into the desk." She then completely forgot about the grades and about the incident. That weekend she was "feeling bad" and felt angry and critical of herself for not doing what she imagined she should be doing for school.

Affect Regression

In cross-validating the regressive sequence with Mary's material we were struck by how much of the work centered on the history and vicissitudes of her feelings, especially her anger, toward her mother. In our attempt to conceptualize the material we were stimulated by the highly original views of Orgel (1974) and the series of critical papers on affect and trauma by Krystal (1978, 1982). Orgel postulates that the suicidant, in infancy (6 months to 15 months), has been deprived of a primary love object who could "absorb his waves of aggression." Krystal writes about a progressive response to trauma termed "lethal surrender." Starting with anxiety, it progresses to catanoid states, aphanisis, and potentially to psychogenic death (1978). It would be useful to look at the suicide sequence in relation both to its infantile roots and to the sequence described by Krystal.

SUMMARY AND CONCLUSIONS

The findings presented here emerged from a study using psychoanalysis as a research tool. But psychoanalysis is also a therapeutic technique, constantly refined by experience. This study led us to certain technical suggestions regarding the treatment of adolescents who have made serious suicide attempts. Initially, the family, the adolescent, and even the referring person may try to deny the seriousness of the attempt and may speak of it as a one-time occurrence totally out of character with the adolescent's usual good behavior. This should be addressed quickly with the adolescent and the family. The one action these adolescents are capable of is suicide. To the adolescent, suicide represents a positive, powerful solution to all conflicts and he will be reluctant to give it up. The aggression in the attempt should be verbalized, as this may produce some guilt in regard to the suicide attempt. Without guilt, there is little to stop the adolescent from repeating the attempt. The multiple motives in the attempt and the unreality in the fantasy that the adolescent will actually be around to reap the rewards should be taken up. The lifelong pattern of displacing negative feelings from mother to others may soon become a problem in the therapy. This will be especially true around weekends and vacations. If the adolescent can construe the analyst as the bad object, the one who rejects and abandons, then he is free once more to kill himself without guilt.

The finding that a suicide attempt is the end point of a regressive sequence was a major result of the focal research. Our subsequent work has been influenced by this result and we actively engage our young analysands in a search for the elements of the suicide sequence. In Mary's case it took almost three years to elucidate the crucial elements of the sequence. In her third year of analysis she could become conscious that the precipitating event of leaving home meant for her a sadistic oedipal triumph over Mother and, with her integration of this last bit of knowledge concerning the initial step in the sequence, the issue of suicide receded to make way for more pressing neurotic conflicts about becoming a mature, adult woman.

To undertake the treatment of an adolescent who has made a suicide attempt is a responsibility that entails a ceaseless struggle. Litman (1967) notes that there are references to suicidal symptomatology in all of Freud's published case histories except that of "Little Hans." Many of Freud's cases, especially his earlier ones, were adolescents, and Freud's experience with suicidal young people might be one of the factors influencing his shifting views on aggression and his final adoption of the theory of the death instinct. One cannot work with suicidal adolescents without being impressed with the power of their wish to kill themselves. The positive value they put on suicide and the power of this force is captured in a poem by Sylvia Plath, written in 1965, before she killed herself:

> Dying
> Is an art, like everything else.
> I do it exceptionally well.
>
> I do it so it feels like hell.
> I do it so it feels real.
> I guess you could say I've got a call.

To counter this force, we have to call on all our experience, our tolerance, and the support of our colleagues. In 1926, discussing a young patient, Freud said, "What weighs on me in his case is my belief that unless the outcome is very good it will be very bad indeed: What I mean is that he would commit suicide without any hesitation. I shall therefore do all in my power to avert that eventuality" (1963, pp. 101–102).

9 A "Boo Warning": Ego Disruption in an Abused Little Girl

We first described Taylor in Chapter 7, where material from her analysis was used to illustrate our discussion of the impact of parental externalization. Here we describe some different aspects of her treatment in greater detail, to understand more about the complex operation of trauma and memory in childhood and its interaction with her parents' pathology. When she began her analysis, just after her fifth birthday, she did not know how to pretend, but played mechanically, in a way that was deeply boring. Nothing in her games happened in an order that made sense to me (KKN), and Taylor did not seem to notice that sometimes the dolls ate breakfast before they went to sleep or arrived at school before they got into the car. She liked to line up and sort the toys, but could not communicate the basis for the categories. Taylor did only what she wanted, but she also wanted to know and perform what would placate the grownups. The puzzle was to understand the meaning and etiology of this appearance of profound dissociation and to help Taylor achieve integration of her developing ego, so that it might effectively mediate between her impulses and the outside world.

But the outside world had already impinged inappropriately on Taylor. Working with children can be very unlike our frequent predicament with adult patients who remember or suspect abuse in their past, or whose treatment uncovers such a possibility. With Taylor, the facts were clear: her history contained numerous evidences of abuse of different kinds. So, at the start, we had both definitive information and a child who was not functioning adequately. One of the tasks of evaluation and treatment was to understand the connections between Taylor's history and her current functioning. We knew much of what had happened to her, but we did not know what she thought about it and how her experiences had contributed to the picture she presented of a person who, at 5 years of age, could not make full use of her ego capacities.

Taylor's lack of symbolization and her difficulty in ordering and sequencing her experiences and thoughts were not the only signs of ego disruption. Her tendency to action instead of emotional experience and her problems of impulse control were both apparent from Mr. and Mrs. D's description of their daughter's intermittent timidity and avoidance of her father and other men, and her fearful excitement and preoccupation with sexual matters. Taylor stared and grabbed at people's genitals, fondled her mother's breasts at every opportunity, kissed her mother near her crotch. When her father stopped walking around the house naked—he was finally made uncomfortable by Taylor's curiosity—she often tried to invade the bathroom and snatched at the fly on his trousers. Taylor was described as a very articulate child who had no trouble being demanding and obstreperous about her wishes, but her parents felt she had trouble settling to activities and worried that her restlessness would interfere with learning when she started primary school. They were relieved, though puzzled, that none of this behavior extended to Taylor's preschool, where her teachers reported generally appropriate social behavior and good interest in her work. I (KKN) was equally puzzled by this disparity, but also relieved, as it indicated that Taylor had ego capacities that she could mobilize under certain circumstances, which therefore meant that we could rule out some ominous diagnostic possibilities.

When Mrs. D. brought Taylor for her first evaluation interview she insisted on speaking to me before I saw the child, even though this had not been planned, nor what Taylor had been prepared for. We settled Taylor to drawing in the playroom and repaired to the waiting room, where Mrs. D. offered a bit more information about the last week. Taylor complied with her mother's request that she wait in the playroom without visible protest or distress and accepted my joining her soon thereafter without comment. She had been drawing unrecognizable pictures, but did not seem very invested in them, although she brightened when I wondered whether there were a story in her picture. Rather than tell the story, she turned to dolls, dividing them into oddly assorted families, giving them different houses, and building a zoo for them to visit. The D.'s had described Taylor as an assertive child, and she did indeed have a determined expression on her face; yet she demanded very little explicitly and gave a curious impression of being disengaged from her play and from her interaction with me. The dolls too were merely going through the motions of their activities in the game, without really being made to interact with each other or progress through a story with any dynamic narrative. These games, which looked formally age-adequate, were too emotionally empty to hold either Taylor's interest or mine, and we turned to playing with blocks. As we built a playground that included a slide, Taylor suddenly became anxious and needed to go see her mother in the waiting room. She was quickly calmed by my remark that children often, especially the first time they come, need to check with their moms that what they are thinking and doing is okay. When I wondered if something in our game of building made her worried, Taylor agreed enthusiastically, but we could not figure out exactly what it was. It would be many months before this worry was clarified, but it was clear that Taylor needed to distance herself emotionally from much of what she thought and wanted.

As we came closer to the end of our first time together, Taylor became very curious about other children and the rest of the office. Many children express the wish to see where the grownups go or what lies behind the other doors, but few have made it so clear—without having a disorganized tantrum—that it felt like an absolute emotional necessity. Taylor was at her most related while saying she must see the other rooms. She insisted on exploring, lay down on the analytic couch in the grownup office, and said she was daydreaming.

In this chapter, I hope to convey the *feeling* of working with Taylor and her parents, and so I will describe some of the material in detail, as well as my concurrent thoughts and reactions. In situations of suspected or substantiated abuse, the feelings and reactions of the therapist are very strong; this can become an interference, but may also be used as an aid to understanding some of the dynamic forces at work in the complex relationships and background to the abuse. It is in the spirit of learning from looking at *all* the difficulties involved in working with patients who have been abused that I include the description of my own feelings, some of which were, at times, angry and judgmental, anguished and despairing. Thus I noted at the time of the first evaluation session how disconcerted I had felt by Mrs. D.'s unexpected change of procedure, and how her air of anxious preoccupation had tugged at my attention. I wondered if such experiences were common for Taylor. The puzzlement engendered in me by Taylor's affectless play, which also had the effect of leaving us disengaged from each other, presaged my frequent bewilderment and discouragement as I wondered if what felt like the scattered bits of this child would ever come together.

This initial material is significant in several ways. Themes and feelings that appear during evaluation often prefigure issues that remain important for the whole course of treatment. Taylor was no exception to this clinical axiom: families—where they lived and where they went, their members' lack of true involvement with one another, and their behavior to each other—occupied her analysis; her definitive insistence on *doing* continued to pervade her treatment and provided major technical problems. The concreteness of her "action mode" of relating to me was one aspect of the disturbance in symbolic thinking that was to emerge more clearly later, but could already be glimpsed in the emptiness of her doll play. There were no stories to the doll games; Taylor did not know how to pretend. This is a grave symptom in a 5-year-old.

Taylor's interest in my question about the story of her pictures sprang from her attempt to please me, to provide what she thought I wanted. The other side of her compliance was stubbornness that reappeared in our second meeting. She seemed docile, not contradicting anything I said or requested, but she went directly for what she wanted, apparently oblivious even to my presence. She appeared not to respond to any of my remarks, although she occasionally incorporated one of my suggestions, as if coincidentally. For weeks thereafter, when treatment had begun, she came straight into the room, set out the people dolls and blocks for their houses, then knelt or squatted on the floor, lining up little cars. All of her energy went into ordering the toys, setting up for a game that was never played. My contributions were limited at first to descriptive commentary—"Oh, that's the kitchen, and the front door's over there"—or questions of clarification: "Which ones live in this house?" As identical sessions followed one another, I was allowed to help build the house. Taylor corrected me very definitely whenever I placed a wall or a piece of furniture inaccurately. The house took on increasing importance as the

weeks rolled by, and Taylor spent less time lining up the cars
in their usual traffic jam. Her concentration was more and more
devoted to silent organization of the rooms and their occupants.
Eventually I realized that the very point of this activity was
its invariance. Taylor showed extraordinary single-mindedness
in her daily pursuit of an unchanging, predictable content in
her sessions. This also had the effect of controlling me. I began
to remark on how important it seemed to her to be sure of
exactly what we were going to do and exactly what each of our
jobs would be. This method of feeling safe with a new person
helped us to understand some of what worried Taylor. She
responded to this work on her controlling defenses against the
anxiety that accompanied unpredictable events with slight
relaxation of her rigidity, both in the game and in her face
and feelings. My sense of what was involved for her came both
from the form and content of the games and from the frustration and anger produced in me by being so tyrannized. The
hostility contained in Taylor's inflexible instructions was a clue
to the presence of a strong aggressive component in the conflicts underlying her disturbance.

Taylor began to have the people dolls who lived in the houses
do things, like have meals and take showers. In the context of
what had gone before, this was great progress—her games were
achieving some content. From the perspective of assessing her
development and pathology, Taylor's play was primitive, immature in its concreteness, and indicative of severe ego restriction and impoverishment.

By this time, when Taylor had been in treatment for several months, much of her symptomatology had abated in her
outside life. She was more relaxed with her father and other
males, less stubborn, better able to concentrate and complete
activities, and almost all of her compulsive, sexualized behavior disappeared. She had restabilized herself within the framework of rigid ego controls, including a rudimentary superego
that enforced an unsophisticated list of rules for proper be-

havior. Keeping everything predictable helped Taylor ensure that there would be no breakthroughs of disorganizing impulses from inside, nor any unpleasant surprises from outside. Controlling our interaction allowed her to use me as an auxiliary ego. Little by little Taylor incorporated some of my ego qualities of curiosity, flexibility, and safety. Her treatment became a place where she knew what she would find, what would happen, and what I would do.

Taylor began occasionally to talk about events in her daily life and bring difficulties to treatment as a place where problems would be understood and solved. She talked one day about not liking her day camp anymore. We wondered together about that, as she had enjoyed it until then. Taylor worked to think what had changed, which allowed us to note again how upset it made her if something was unexpected. The dolls in our game had a barbecue, but it was interrupted when the littlest doll got sick and had to be taken home. Taylor then told me that she and her parents had left the camp family cook-out early because she had been too scared to stay. It had gotten dark and a counselor had come up behind her and picked her up. Mr. and Mrs. D. confirmed that Taylor had cried hysterically at the campfire after dark, and that they left, feeling she was overexcited and overtired. Taylor began to talk in her sessions of how she especially needed to know what was going to happen in the nighttime, when it was too dark to see. Her mother reported that Taylor was having trouble falling asleep, saying she was scared, but unable to tell her mother or me what she was afraid of.

Over the next few weeks Taylor and I made a list of all the nighttime warnings she wanted to have in order to keep herself safe. One day she announced a new kind of nighttime warning. This was a "boo warning," which comes when there is a danger of being surprised in the night. Through this period Taylor alternated the house game, by this time almost exclusively consisting of organizing the bedrooms and distributing the people in many different combinations, with a school game, in which she was attempting to master some of her worries about starting primary school. Genuine though this effort was, Taylor's anxiety about school also served a defensive function, as it posed a lesser threat than the potentially overwhelming events of the night, for which she was never sure she would get a boo warning.

I struggled with a dilemma that may be peculiar to child work. It was clear that Taylor was working her way towards feeling able to allow memories of abuse to surface, while derivatives pervaded her material. Unlike the situation we face in the treatment of adults, however, I knew about the events she had conflicts over remembering. We were not struggling in shared ignorance of either the very existence of particular events or their nature, and grappling with lifting repression together. The technical problem was to facilitate Taylor's coming to grips with her past and finding ways to integrate it without breaching her defenses and re-creating traumatic experiences in the present.

By the time an adult seeks treatment, intervening development has reshaped childhood experience so drastically that it may be difficult or impossible to recover in a recognizable form. Tracing the vicissitudes of the transformations already underway in middle childhood can suggest the magnitude of the task of reconstruction in an adult treatment, and the pitfalls of too simple an attribution of direct correspondence between childhood events of abuse and later symptomatology or pathology. We can learn from Taylor's treatment that memories of her early experience had already gone underground by the time she was 5 years old. Memories had already been reworked and incorporated into the structure of her developing personality and disturbance.

At the time of the evaluation Mr. and Mrs. D. had conveyed their concerns about the impact of their nephew's disturbance on Taylor. Taylor's cousin Kenny, eleven years older, lived in the other half of their two-family house and was always in and out of their home. He had been physically and sexually abused by a psychotic caretaker early in his life. He was unhappy when Taylor was born and the family made a fuss about the first girl cousin. He sought her out in infancy for sexualized, aggressive interactions. When she was a little baby, Kenny frequently pinched her nipples and chest, chanting "boobie, boobie," or paddled her buttocks until his excitement escalated to the point where he ran off around the house. He bounced Taylor on his genitals, using her body to masturbate, and played a game of sliding her down his legs.

After Taylor began to toddle and play independently, Kenny often surprised her, interrupting her activities with a swoop from behind to squeeze her bottom or chest. When Taylor was 2, a neighbor discovered that Kenny had removed her clothes and diaper and was licking and kissing her genitals. The two families used each other for babysitting and thus the children often spent nights in each other's houses. Mr. and Mrs. D. were vague about how this had been arranged, but did remember that Kenny had often slept in the other bunk in Taylor's room. Kenny's family had moved to a distant city when Taylor was 4 years old; the D.s were relieved that they did not have to confront Kenny's increasingly uncontrolled behavior and felt that the problem was solved. The subsequent development of Taylor's symptoms puzzled them—why hadn't she reacted more at the time? It was hard for them to understand that such a little child had mentally reworked her memories.

As we approached the end of the first year of Taylor's treatment, she spoke increasingly in sessions about secrets. The little girl dolls in our games were very interested in their daddies and in finding out about babies. Taylor often tried to engage her father in excited games of chasing her and had insisted that she ride with him exclusively when they recently attended a fair. These were some of the indicators of her beginning to feel age-appropriate oedipal impulses. She also compared herself to her mother and me, discussing whose hair was longer, who was taller, and so on. Each day I found her "sleeping" on the waiting room couch when I went to fetch her for her session. She wanted me to guess things, played games where we each had to hide our eyes and wouldn't know what the other was going to do. At first she listened avidly when I talked about my discomfort and confusion hearing mysterious things in the dark that was created when I hid my eyes, and how it made me think of how it felt not to know what might come upon me when I was unprepared because I couldn't see, like a person at night. We repeatedly got that far and then Taylor would halt my monologue abruptly, declaring that not only could I not see, I also could not hear or talk. I had to be shut up, with my thoughts, feelings, and worries only inside where no one else could know them. Taylor then told me that she had a secret with someone that she could not tell me or anyone. I had the distinct impression that Taylor had recovered conscious memory of some of the events with Kenny and was suffering conflict over the many meanings of talking about them.

Both the surfacing of the memories and Taylor's conflicts were colored by the developmental phase she was in. At the time of the original events one of her responses had been to repress the memories. In the context of her libidinal wishes towards her father, and her sexual curiosity, the memories took on new meanings that affected her reactions and her defensive solutions. Strictures on talking about any of this took on a punitive quality related to her developing conscience.

Then outside events impinged on the internal pace of Taylor's work. Her father announced that Kenny would be visiting and her mother had her watch a television special on sexual abuse.

Taylor began having nightmares, tossing and turning in her sleep, and wetting the bed. The day following the television program, the repetitive school game that had occupied recent sessions changed to a doctor and hospital story. In the game, children had mysterious operations on their genitals, with blood tests. On the days Taylor built her old houses, the children were rapidly involved in car accidents and taken to the hospital, where the girls had their genitals cut in such a way that they were left with an open wound that would never, ever heal. On the third day after the program, Taylor wet her pants right before leaving school to come to her session. She claimed to be unaware of having done so, although she was wet from waist to ankles. She told her mother that she had been listening to her body, but in the session she talked about the girl dolls blocking their ears so that they wouldn't have to listen to anything—then they wouldn't have any feelings from anywhere in their bodies! In the following weeks, her teachers reported that Taylor was withdrawn in a way they had not seen for ages; one teacher remarked that Taylor seemed lost in her own world, as if she did not want to hear anything from anyone, and that Taylor was startled when spoken to in class. The regression pervaded each area of her life: she wet the bed almost every night, urinated several times in school, was clinging and demanding with her mother, and alternately over-excited and panicky with her father.

In treatment, Taylor's newly-achieved symbolic capacity, which had been demonstrated in her growing ability to use the dolls to play out her conflicts in displacement, receded. She insisted on concrete action to express feelings and thoughts. She could not pretend that it was the dark night, but insisted that we had to really turn the lights off as we practiced for Guy Fawkes. Taylor had always found Guy Fawkes Day particularly exciting and frightening, with its potential for surprises, but it was worse that year as she struggled desperately to keep reality straight in her mind. Masks and costumes threatened her reality-testing, as she poignantly conveyed her unsureness about whether they really changed children into monsters. Instead of giving operations to the little girl dolls, Taylor wanted us to play performing the operation on her. She lay down on the little table with her shirt pulled up, as if to prepare for an operation in the game, and became increasingly excited showing me her body. Then she played with her nipples in a form of apparent comfort-masturbation, trying to calm herself down by what turned out to be a characteristic self-soothing practice.

As we worked to sort all this out in treatment, Taylor was able to talk about her fantasies that masturbation would damage her and cause her to bleed forever, like grownup ladies. There were many examples of this kind of amalgam of information, fantasy, fears, and wishes, compounded by internal processes, overstimulating amounts of inappropriate information from adults and other children, and confused memories of experiences of abusive interactions with Kenny. She became preoccupied with making up stories and pictures of monsters. She named one "Tasha," the name she had always wanted for herself, saying he weighed 50 pounds too much and always had blood coming out; he licked people and then sat on a little chair and fell over. Taylor started a new game of "monsters in the dark," in which the monster touched someone all over in a way that felt both good and bad. In one session she had to interrupt that game twice to use the bathroom. When she came back the second time she said, "I think there's a body feeling telling us something from my vagina."

Taylor was using her treatment to differentiate her physical sensations and locate discrete sources of excitement, an ordinary developmental task of toddlerhood that had been interfered with by Kenny's exciting and overwhelming inflictions of sensation. At the oedipal phase, when vaginal sensations took on new prominence and significance, Taylor had to redifferentiate the feelings of the impulse to urinate and the genital excitement associated with masturbation. She worked also to differentiate reliably between herself and others through repetitive play about who was the monster—was it the person who felt the other or the one who was felt—and whose feelings were whose? Her sense of consistent self-representation was threatened by the combination of excitement from within and overwhelming stimulation from the outside.

During the ensuing months, Taylor worked through these issues, trying to come to terms with her past experiences and integrate her oedipal wishes, both libidinal and aggressive, so that she could move on into latency and turn her attention outward. There were intermittent regressions, triggered either by upsurges of wishes or external events, such as Kenny's visits to the family. Taylor continued to make progress, yet there remained a serious vulnerability in her ego's capacity to modulate her impulses without resorting to her old restrictions on herself.

Taylor's case presented me with the problem of understanding precisely how her experiences could have had so profound an effect on her development. Was it sufficient to say that sexual abuse that takes place so early is bound to skew subsequent growth? I think that is an important factor, but there are other problems, which this case illustrates, when we try to come to grips with the effects of sexual abuse in very early childhood.

Some of the problems are conceptual. A child does not exist in isolation and cannot be treated alone. Therefore we include the framework of the family in the assessment, treatment, and prognosis of the situation. When we are dealing with suspected or substantiated abuse, the events are never singular, but occur in the context of pathological functioning. Thus we are not surprised to find, as I did with Taylor, a background of overstimulation, lack of safety and protection, emotional pathology in other family members, and severe marital difficulties. We sometimes have to look hard, however, past our own blind spots from convention, stereotype, or prejudice, and through the smokescreen of defensiveness in adults, to discern the disturbed background to events of physical and sexual abuse.

We are accustomed to assuming that abuse is traumatic. Here too there is a conceptual issue to address. There are different formulations about what constitutes a trauma, for instance, one terrible event, or an accumulation of stresses and strains. These depend more or less on external description and miss the salient point that trauma is properly defined in terms of *subjective experience* of the ego being overwhelmed. The ego is likely to feel overwhelmed when the external event is cataclysmic, apt to make almost anyone feel helpless, as in natural or man-made disasters or persecutions. Internal states, such as chronic pain, catastrophic wounds or illnesses, may also be described as likely to overwhelm the ego because of their scale. A relatively weak, young, unformed ego has few resources, is unable to withstand much, and is thus also likely to be easily overwhelmed. Thus, even when we do not have access to the subjective meaning of particular events or experiences for an individual, there are times when we may estimate that there has probably been traumatic impact. For Taylor, who was overpowered, surprised, overstimulated, swamped with adult anxiety, hated, and violated, all from infancy on, we may therefore surmise with some confidence that she was a traumatized child. But we cannot be sure until we look more carefully at the meaning of her experiences for her, and their impact on her developing personality, and assess the availability of people and circumstances that did or did not work to help her recover from bad experiences. The only way to gain access to her subjective experience and understanding is in therapy that is intensive and long-term enough to allow different levels and aspects of her functioning to emerge.

What did she do with her traumatic experiences? We are never in a position to see the trauma. What we see are the patient's solutions to the problems posed by the effects of trauma. The solutions include the crucial ingredient of the particular meaning ascribed to the trauma by the child. There can be no understanding of her reactions without access to her private world; there are no general remedies for abuse. Taylor's story is by no means the worst story of abuse you will have read. It was, nevertheless, a difficult history; from Taylor's experience and mine in working together, we may gain an understanding both of what her life felt like *to her* and of the nature of the barriers I encountered in helping Taylor and her parents change. Perhaps our difficulties may also give some indications of what lies hidden in the life histories of those patients who come for treatment as adults, offering help with the technical problems we encounter in those very problematic cases.

When Mr. and Mrs. D. first sought consultation they did not say that Taylor functioned like an automaton without feelings. They were most concerned by her compulsive, sexualized interactions and intrusive sexual curiosity and afraid that she would not succeed at school if she were so distracted. Mrs. D. worried that her own hovering over Taylor in the effort to protect the child from Kenny had produced extra anxiety. They reported that Taylor had a normal birth and achieved developmental milestones somewhat early. Her mother's attempt to impose a feeding schedule in infancy failed when Taylor cried and cried, too tired to nurse and too hungry to sleep. A change to demand feeding eventually solved the problem.

There may have been no specific sequelae to this dyssynchrony between Taylor's needs and the environment's handling of them, but it does give us a provisional paradigm for unnecessary distress suffered by the child in the service of someone else's needs.

What are we to make of such a report? We always hear a patient's developmental history in the context of problems that arise later. While this may allow us the wisdom to discern early roots and precursors of pathology, it also tempts us to make facile equation of early experience with later functioning. Child and adolescent analysis may be of help in illuminating these complexities, because so much more information is available than is often the case in adult work. Parents and therapist share historical data, in which patterns may be seen; the participants pool current observations, while the child brings in the past in the form of memories and transferences and the present directly in explicit material and indirectly in transference of current functioning and relationships. Added to this are the analyst's perceptions of the relations between the parents and between the parents and the child. The observation of current family dynamics allows for evaluation of the patterns and strands discerned in the history. This is of help in understanding the core of Taylor's and her family's pathology, and in assigning weight to causative factors.

There is no doubt in my mind that Kenny's behavior was abusive; however, I think we must also give great weight to the parents' seeming inability to intervene in these attacks. So much is apparent from the outside and from the vantage point of an adult. But what did these experiences mean to Taylor at the time of their occurrence and subsequently? Was it these activities that traumatized her? The question is important for assessing and understanding Taylor's symptoms later on. It is significant also for what the answer may contribute to our knowledge of how such early experiences affect the growing child as they are transformed by the forces of health and pathology in the course of development. The course of these transformations affects what impact will be visible and how it will manifest itself in later life.

If we consider Taylor's ego development at the time of her abuse we may try to assess whether or to what degree she was likely to feel overwhelmed. Kenny's assaults began in Taylor's infancy and escalated when she was a toddler. That phase marks the transition in normal development between the body ego and the coalescence of the overarching ego structure that will integrate the body ego, the self-representation, self-esteem regulation, beginning defenses, reality testing, mediation between the inner and outer worlds, cognitive functioning, the synthetic and integrative functions, modulation of affect, the control of action, and the internalization of parental functions. During the extraordinary acceleration in development typical of toddlerhood, the child has need of parents to help her perform and practice many of her ego functions, to serve as an auxiliary ego that protects her body and self and keeps her safe from danger so that her development can unfold. The description of Kenny's activities suggests both the disruption to Taylor's developing ego and the adults' apparent ineffectiveness at protecting her from his assault, which interfered with their crucial auxiliary ego functioning. We begin to get a picture of a child whose ego was severely assailed and who lacked the supports she needed for normal development throughout her very early childhood.

> Taylor had more than her share of accidents and injuries. Twice during toddlerhood she needed stitches in her face and head. A tooth was broken in a fall; a year later, another was knocked out when a playmate pushed her over. Treatment for a broken shoulder the year before the referral made her afraid that her arm would come away with the cast. Here again the history revealed contradictory elements: Mrs. D. hovered anxiously over Taylor and yet the child was neither adequately protected from accidents nor taught to use reasonable caution to protect her own body from harm.

All of these elements made this an upsetting history to hear, but, to my ears, they also helped to make sense of Taylor's presenting problems. It seemed evident to me that Kenny's assaults were at least part of the cause of Taylor's disturbance of relations with males. Despite Mrs. D.'s detailed account, however, the connection was not obvious in the same way to Taylor's parents. So, before I had even seen the child, there were grave issues to consider as part of the assessment: the parents' reality testing appeared compromised. Mrs. D. described her awareness of the danger Kenny presented, yet she sounded as if she herself had felt powerless in the face of his impulses. She was more concerned with the impact of her own worries on the child than with Taylor's experience. She presented precise observations, but appeared to stop short of drawing any conclusions from them. Mr. D. heard his wife's story, and had witnessed many of the events, yet asked sincerely whether I thought his daughter had suffered any abuse and whether we would be able to find out from her what had happened. Both parents appeared unable to make inferences or draw realistic or plausible conclusions from the information they shared; they presented a picture of helpless dissociation from Taylor and her history. This split between their perceptions and their understanding was part of the family pathology that formed the background to Taylor's disturbance and created the context in which abuse occurred. My concern at the evaluation stage was how much their defensive denial would interfere with their capacity to focus on the child and her needs and to participate in the effort to help Taylor.

In treating children, we have the benefit of the opportunity to observe parental functioning and relationships. But in the ancillary parent work the analyst has no specific mandate to make direct use of these perceptions in interpretation or efforts toward change. At the beginning of treatment, we have no way to assess the significance of what we see. All parents are full of painful feelings when they bring a child for assessment and then therapy. They empathize with the child's distress to some extent, they feel guilty about and ashamed of the problems, and they have intense mixed feelings about the therapist. It is not surprising, therefore, to see simultaneous consciousness and denial on the part of the parents early in treatment. Regular work with the parents of a child in treatment aims for restoration or development of the capacity for constructive parenting that will help return the child to the path of progressive development. Along the way, the resistances that arise illuminate those pathogenic influences in the child's history that stem from parental problems.

Throughout the first year of Taylor's treatment, regular parent meetings with her mother, and occasionally with both parents, served multiple functions: I felt in touch with Taylor's daily life through the months of our stultifying house and people sessions and was thus able to assess just how desperately she was warding off feelings and trying to control her experiences; the strains in the D. marriage were evident and I wondered how much Taylor's disturbance was serving as a safety valve for issues her parents were reluctant to confront with each other; I could see that Mr. and Mrs. D.'s denial was not a short-term defensive reaction to the stresses of referral, but represented characterological pathology that interfered profoundly with their ability to see Taylor as a separate person and imagine her feelings and point of view; I was able to understand how, for different reasons in each of their histories, Taylor's parents used her as an object for externalization of unacceptable aspects of themselves.

Taylor's daily life was a whirlwind of excitement and overstimulation. The television and the radio were always on in every room of the house, she saw movies that were filled with sexual and violent content far beyond her capacity to understand or absorb, she was taken on wild big rides at every available fair, bathroom and bedroom doors were never closed, both parents slept nude, language contained pervasive sexual imagery, teenage relatives were in and out of the house night and day with overwrought displays of affection for their boyfriends and girlfriends—even just hearing about her life was overwhelming. The picture that emerged dovetailed with my own observations of Taylor's clothes always being too tight, her kisses with her mother too long and always on the lips, her mother's tapping, touching, and caressing of Taylor through all conversations, and her father's always holding his very big 6-year-old on his lap. Taylor's frequent storms of restlessness, excitement, and sexual actions made sense as I understood more about her environment, but her parents' need to keep it that way emerged only over time, in their inability to respond to my attempts to invite them to imagine the impact it was having on Taylor. Taylor carried their excitement, their lack of impulse control, and the helplessness they had experienced in their own lives in the face of overwhelming inappropriate stimulation from others. Far from protecting her from impingement, her parents had been the active or passive instruments of inflicting it upon her.

Thus, we must widen the field when we try to understand the nature of the traumata Taylor suffered. We cannot restrict ourselves to the particular events that occurred with Kenny, nor to the meaning that accrued with further development, but must include the environment that made them possible, the surroundings that perpetuated overwhelming stimulation, the lack of remediation and reparation after the fact, and the impact of the unavailability of adequate models with whom to identify.

Mrs. D., who was in her own therapy and came faithfully to parent meetings, responded positively when I finally confronted her with parental externalizations. She began to change her handling of Taylor, and as she reduced the amount of inappropriate stimulation in the child's life, Taylor calmed down and was able to work more effectively in treatment and in school. Ego capacities flowered as Taylor learned to read and write; she began to make books in her sessions. As we saw in Chapter 7, these books began as barely neutralized expressions of Taylor's impulses. Gradually she became able to use them for sublimation and brought her preoccupations in more manageable symbolic and derivative forms. We catalogued her favorite pop singing stars and copied pictures of costumes from characters on television shows. We talked about Taylor's thoughts, worries, confusions, and wishes about bodies and growing up, and she began to enjoy being responsible for taking care of herself. Taylor was increasingly able to modulate the maelstrom around her without regression or withdrawal. She began to look and feel more like a schoolchild and I felt hopeful about her treatment.

I also felt some continuing concerns. Taylor began many projects in her sessions, but never completed them: she colored the covers of her books, illustrated the first few pages, and then somehow the rest remained blank. Her pleasure never lasted long, but was swiftly overtaken with a kind of weary sadness or remote resignation. There had always been pressure from her parents to expedite the treatment, from Mrs. D. mostly in the form of wanting her anxious guilt relieved by a rapid recovery, from Mr. D. an unrealistic preoccupation with finances that masked his accelerating discomfort with dynamic changes in his daughter and his wife. He was able to understand intellectually that he and his wife were living out issues of their own at their child's expense, but he found it almost impossible to change, and Taylor's increasing autonomy threatened the pathological abusive equilibrium that the family had established. My experience of this period of Taylor's treatment included the tension of wondering how long her family could tolerate her treatment and the gains it was producing. Taylor began to take charge of her own eating, trying to control her weight, which had increased to the point where the pediatrician had remonstrated with her parents. Her mother became very anxious, dimly feeling that Taylor should not have to be doing this, but embarrassed that she herself had been so ineffectual. Her father, who was the continual source of illicit snacks and treats, became agitated and reproached Taylor with depriving him! Taylor reeled under the impact of this parental pathology, which assailed her boundaries and her growing wish to be in charge of a clearly-defined self. This renewed assault provided a clear demonstration of the traumatic effect the parents' pathological need to externalize had added onto Taylor's earlier experiences, giving a measure of what she would have to be able to withstand to preserve her progressive development. I had the task of coming to terms with limitations on my therapeutic ambitions and assessing realistically how much Taylor had been able to integrate into her restructured ego and how much more work she could do as a 7-year-old.

As we approached the end of the second year of Taylor's treatment, she talked sadly about the friction between her parents and we worked on her wishes and fears about her role in their marital problems. Taylor dealt with these by making an adaptive shift to planning how she would handle her relationships when she was big; she was able to relinquish her fantasies of legislating for her parents' lives. With this consolidation, I felt more comfortable about her future capacity to hold on to the gains from treatment. Before we finished, Taylor and I talked about, and I discussed with Mr. and Mrs. D., how future developmental transitions might be times of vulnerability for Taylor, when new impulses might revive old worries and leave her prey to feeling overwhelmed.

When Taylor was 14, she asked her mother if she might see me for a session or two, just to "talk a few things over," as she put it. Her father did not allow this, but Mrs. D. called me to recount that Taylor seemed to have used the idea of talking with me to restabilize herself. Thus, it appeared that Taylor may have been able to take away from her childhood treatment enough to be able to hold onto an internal sense of her own ego capacities, despite the stress of puberty. I think that she will need treatment in adulthood, but I am confident that she will seek it out.

What can we learn from Taylor's story, as it unfolded in the course of her treatment? We saw her at the beginning as a child whose ego had been profoundly disrupted by impingements from the outside. As therapy progressed and Taylor entered the oedipal phase, her experiences took on new meaning for her; her ego was overwhelmed from the inside and she showed a traumatic reaction. As Taylor began to change, her parents' disturbances were thrown into sharper relief and we could see their ongoing contribution to her skewed development and the traumatogenic potential of their pathologies.

We suggest that one may draw some conclusions from this account. First, children's personalities, even in the earliest years, are complex and capable of working and reworking experience. We must be wary of memories that purport to remain unchanged from infancy or early childhood. Taylor's memories of Kenny's incursions were all mixed up with fantasies derived from the impulses of the oedipal phase, which in turn had been influenced by the multitude of aggressive and sexualized experiences of her daily life. Were we to see her in adulthood, there would be further layers of developmentally-influenced transformations. Second, our descriptions and definitions of trauma must take that complexity into account. We must not be tempted into facile equation of singular external events with "trauma," but can only approximate accurate understanding by inclusion of internal meanings and developmental influences on the individual. Third, the therapeutic relationship with a patient who has suffered trauma is bound to reproduce not only the content of particular experiences, but the whole form and style of the surrounding environment of people; this environment must be understood as traumatogenic and be addressed in the treatment as a major focus for change. Taylor had been abused by being overpowered and sexually stimulated from earliest infancy, but this could not have happened outside the context of externalizations from her parents, which overpowered her personality-in-formation and stimulated maladaptive responses. In her treatment she strove to recreate such a relationship with the analyst. Work on her very concrete enactments of these wishes produced the greatest changes and allowed for growth and consolidation of her ego that had earlier been so disrupted. She became able to provide "boo warnings" for herself.

10 "I HATE YOU FOR SAVING MY LIFE": BORROWED TRAUMA IN THE ANALYSIS OF A YOUNG ADULT

. . . [The] prows [of the motorboats] would tear the water into a V shape that spread until it reached both sides of the canal. There the water would suddenly begin to lap up and down, even though the boat was already far away. Then the waves bounced back and formed an inverted V, which interfered with the original V, reached the opposite shore transformed, and bounced back again—until all across the water a complicated braiding of ripples developed which went on changing for several minutes, then finally smoothed out.

Each time, Anton tried to figure out exactly how this happened, but each time the pattern became so complex that he could no longer follow it. [pp. 5–6]

These lines from the Dutch author Harry Mulisch (1985) were read aloud by Felicity in the fourth year of her treatment, when she was 23 years old. She felt he had captured her experience of her analysis in his prologue to a novel about the power of repressed memories. In this chapter we will use material from April to June, the last three months of Felicity's nearly seven-year analysis, to try to describe how the process of termination brought together the major components of Felicity's conflicts, her neurotic solutions to them, the developmental history of her pathology, and the contribution of her family history to its formation. Literary critics have termed the activity of examining each element of a work for its denotation and connotations "unpacking." The process of unpacking the clinical material of the termination phase will illustrate historical and thematic aspects of the whole analysis.

In the middle of April Felicity brought two dreams that felt very important to her. In the first dream *her whole family had gathered for a photo portrait and each person had undergone cosmetic plastic surgery in preparation.* There had been regular family portraits made throughout Felicity's childhood and each had been the occasion for tantrums by the children and rages by the mother. In the analysis the photo sessions had become a metaphor for Felicity's experience of her mother's obsession with a facade of family happiness and normality and a disregard of the feelings of the older child, Felicity, and her brother Brett, three years younger. Later in the dream there was an episode in which *a black man slid effortlessly past another, who turned out not to mind.* A theme in the treatment had been the various attitudes of family members to their own identities and their social roles and positions; Felicity struggled with her angry reactions to her grandparents' and parents' prejudices. Further on in the dream, in *a scene where she sat companionably with her brother while the school principal lectured them about being Kenyans, the child Felicity joked, "Not from Kennebunkport, Maine."*

Felicity's associations to this long and complex dream led her to identify the two black men with the children in her family, each of whom felt marginalized—she herself as the underachieving elder, and Brett as a brilliant high achiever who had recently announced his homosexual orientation after a suicide attempt. With thoughts of a presentation about a black man's desperate search for ways to solve his identity conflicts, she recalled recently finding her own journals from when she was 12 and 13. Felicity recounted the stories she had written of motherless heroes, how

clearly she had articulated her anger at her mother and her longing for help to deal with her own and the then 8-year-old Brett's
wishes to die. Throughout Felicity's latency and early adolescence
her mother's response to any stress in the family was to smoke
marijuana. She had many memories in which her earlier sense
of her mother's depression merged into the image of her mother
sitting in the kitchen, stoned and inaccessible. One side of her
pervasive identification with her mother was this depressed, para-
lyzed, inactive person.

The second dream of that week in the middle of April was that
*Felicity had dropped and broken a teacup on the floor and her
father was screaming at her. She said she would clean it up.*
Felicity associated her father screaming to the fact that he never
did. She had always described him as a withdrawn, depressed
person, unable to relate to others. For the first four years of her
analysis, Felicity's father had been notable by his absence from
the material, appearing only in a recurrent, but isolated, encapsulated idyllic memory of building a bonfire at twilight to play
Indians. He had begun to appear in her material via Felicity's
noticing her preoccupation with control over eating. She attributed this not only to her mother's food issues, which had included
dieting and bulimia, but also to her father's uncontrolled gob-
bling. Thoughts about her father's fatness had ushered in a period of analysis of her confusions about pregnancy and obesity;
oral impregnation fantasies led to thoughts about bisexuality, and
Felicity struggled with her omnipotent wishes to have a "female
penis." Homosexual wishes in and out of the transference appeared at that time, but the primary link was between her terror
of abandonment at separation times and her omnipotent fantasy
solution of being able to be complete in herself, that is, incorporate the penis, grow fat and pregnant, and then have a baby to
keep her company. This would also enable her to identify with
the analyst in the role of mother. Identifications could then be
understood as posing a dilemma, as they protected Felicity from
aloneness, but threatened her own identity.

Analysis of the bisexual fantasies in the fourth year of treatment had led to further crucial material about her relationship with her father. Rather than identifying with his intelligence or interests—these seemed to be reserved for her brother—Felicity discovered that she had introjected his capacity to kill off feelings. She invoked a sense of "possession"—as if by an evil spirit with the same name as her father—to damp down her own perceptions and pleasures. Guilt and anxiety over her excellent capacity to see others clearly and her experiences of sensual and sexual pleasure were obscured in a vague, frustrated state of feeling unsure of her own identity, stymied by unknown forces of inertia. This defensive stasis had affected her functioning academically and continued to interfere with her career choices.

But enough work had been done by April of the seventh year that Felicity was well able to take responsibility for noticing the fluctuations of her own affects. On the Friday of the week of the two dreams, when she had also been able finally to fix on the end of June for termination, she reported that the dreams seemed to have some "weird sexual feeling in them." Putting together the dreams with the material about finding the journals from the time when she felt she still had a "voice," Felicity began to talk about "feeling 13." A major element of feeling 13 had been having sexual feelings and urges to masturbate, which Felicity had in part responded to with occasional nocturnal enuresis until she was 15 or 16.

Remembering these conflicts led to thoughts of the lakeside vacation, which had been a pivotal memory throughout the analysis. Felicity's father had broken down when she was 7, leaving the family for some months to go fishing with a male friend. On his recovery, and probably as part of a reconciliation process with his wife, the whole family went to the friend's lakeside cabin for a two-week vacation with the father, the friend and his wife, and the host's brother and girlfriend. Felicity's mother disliked the host, hated the country, and was terrified of swimming; nevertheless, she insisted that the six adults and two children were going to have a wonderful time in the two-room cabin. Felicity, at 7, was afraid that dangerous creatures from the bottom of the lake might bite her. Sent to the dock with Brett, she retreated from the edge, only to watch helplessly as her little brother fell into deep water. A passing stranger rescued Brett, but the parents blamed Felicity ever after for the accident.

Such had been the memory at each previous presentation throughout the treatment, with the emphasis on Felicity's misery and resentment and the grownups' ignoring of the children's needs and wishes. In the context of "feeling 13," however, Felicity brought new additions to the story. She remembered that the host's brother and his girlfriend had gone into the cabin and "had sex for hours." The children knew this was so because Brett had found a chink in the wall and they peeked. It had been titillating, partly because they knew it was naughty and they would get into trouble if they were caught. But Felicity remembered feeling guilt only in adolescence, when she and a girlfriend looked at *Playboy* magazines together and she felt intense excitement. Thus connections were established among feeling unprotected by adults from external dangers and internal impulses, guilt over her own sexuality, and conflicts about her death wishes and rage.

Felicity's sexuality represented not only forbidden libidinal impulses towards other people, but also a whole area of liveliness and activity denied to her in her times of rageful depression. A recurrent sequence early in treatment had been initial enthusiasm and excitement, for instance, for a new class, followed by doubt, inhibition, and loss of any zest or capacity to think, which rapidly deteriorated into suicidal thoughts. Felicity had first been referred at age 19 for depression; her suicidal tendencies were frankly expressed during the evaluation and remained a danger for several years. During the first year or two of her analysis, repeated experiences of her negative reactions to potential success had led to uncovering of her rage and rivalry with her mother and brother. She had then been able to make sense of childhood memories of going up to her room, breaking the furniture, and throwing herself around so that she banged into the walls. These tantrums had invariably followed quarrels with her mother; she had not felt understood in these quarrels, and could not bear her disappointment with her mother. She could not remember her parents ever intervening during these episodes, nor did they appear to notice the broken furniture, which she propped together herself and left unrepaired for years. Eventually Felicity became able to understand her defensive inhibitions and her wishes to kill herself—partly put into action only once as scratches on her wrist—as murderous impulses towards her mother.

On one occasion she was alarmed on a visit home when she felt the impulse to rip open the cat's stomach with the scissors she held in her hand, but such moments convinced her of the reality of her rage and the necessity of dealing with it. After long, painful, and tumultuous work she sobbed in her session, "There isn't really any other way. I'm going to have to feel these feelings. I *hate* you for saving my life." This came after two and a half years of treatment; it felt like a turning point in the analysis, but there was no way of knowing at that time just how much more of her history was contained in Felicity's passionate reproach.

Felicity's finalization of the termination date and her report of new memories of childhood sexuality were followed by her missing the first session of the following week, something she had not done in years. When she came in the next day, she broke a long silence to talk about her disappointment at attending a lecture given by a person she had greatly admired in the past, someone she had wanted to emulate, even become, because she had always felt that he had surmounted a terrible childhood to make order out of the chaos of his life. The lecturer had interviewed audience members; as Felicity was thinking about what she would say if questioned, she realized that she would have only her mother's life story to offer—she felt she had none of her own. She thought again of her parents who "weren't there" to raise her, how they "got different kids than they expected." As she said it, "If you put in eggs, oil, and flour, you get a cake. Put in fear,

self-doubt, and confusion, you get Felicity and Brett." The analyst took up her longstanding feeling of being caught in someone
else's scenario; the imagery she was using of not being raised by
her parents was *borrowed* from her mother's history. Felicity
responded with "three revelations." The first was that her parents were imposing their own ideas on her about her career path;
their assertion that copywriting for ads was the same as writing
stories not only negated her creative capacities, but reflected a
cognitive style of denial and doublethink that had bedeviled her
intellectual functioning in school and college. The second was
her intense relief at her conviction that she had not been responsible for Brett falling in the water, or for any other of the situations for which she had been blamed—it was her parents' problem that they were unable to take on their appropriate roles. The
third concerned her sense of being at last ready to face something sexual, as yet undiscovered and unresolved.

The next day Felicity talked desultorily, then began to reflect
on her difficulty in getting going. She felt she had been working
well and hard in analysis, more like other people did; it was not
easy but it flowed. But ever since her parents had pulled the plug
and she had fallen ill, she had been unable to focus. Felicity was
referring to the fact that she had been discussing termination the
previous autumn when her parents had suddenly announced that
they would support only a few more months of analysis. Thus,
just as Felicity began flourishing, working her way toward solid
life determinations about career and relationships, her parents
had preempted her independent decision about her analysis. This
pattern, so familiar from child work, usually alerts us to the possibility that the patient's illness may be serving some function in
the family's psychology. Recovery of independent healthy functioning might threaten a pathological equilibrium in the family.

Within a week after her parents' announcement, Felicity had
begun to suffer symptoms of headache, dizziness, and vertigo.
She had frightening sensations of falling and had become tempo-
rarily unable to drive or walk steadily. Sophisticated tests had

produced a diagnosis of labyrinthitis, with a prognosis of months of disability and the possibility of a chronic problem. This ailment was attributed to a viral infection of the inner ear. No cure was available, but physical therapy would help with symptom management. Much useful analytic time in the autumn had, of necessity, been spent on Felicity's feelings and fantasies about her medical situation, but neither she nor the analyst had felt fully satisfied by the interpretations achieved. However, in the lethargic session in April, a reaction to Felicity's partially successful attempts to break through to her own feelings and insights, the return of her vertigo on the couch, and her preoccupation with the thought of not being the lecturer she had heard aided a fuller understanding. More and more details of Felicity's pathology could be seen as *borrowings* from elements of her mother's traumatic life history, taken on as identifications to defend against rage at being deprived and assaulted with externalizations.

Felicity's knowledge of her mother's history had unfolded through the middle years of the analysis, after the work on her suicidal rage. "I hate you for saving my life," she had cried out in response to her transference dilemma of ambivalent feelings for the analyst. Over and over again she played out her transference fears that thoughts and feelings would be imposed on her, that she was helpless to resist the submissive dependence on the analyst that made each weekend and holiday break nearly unbearable. The prospect of termination was much more terrifying.

Felicity came from a family in which there were three generations of Holocaust survivors. Her maternal great-grandparents and grandparents, with her infant mother, had been forced by the Nazis to move into a ghetto in Eastern Europe. Under the pressure of imminent deportation, her grandparents had decided to put their 2-year-old daughter in the care of Catholic peasants in a country village. For two years the child lived as a member of a family who spoke a different language from her mother tongue, practiced a different religion, and enjoyed a different relationship with the occupying army. The foster mother carried the toddler with her at all times and they enjoyed a very close, loving relationship. After the grandparents' liberation from concentration camps, Felicity's mother, then 4, was reclaimed, again taken from a mothering person without warning or explanation, into the care of people she saw as strangers. Her response was to fall into what was described as a "coma," a state of extreme withdrawal that lasted for three days. After some months of unsettled conditions, the reunited family of three generations emigrated to the United States. Felicity's mother made a seemingly good adjustment, traversed adolescence, finished college, and married a young man of good family.

As work proceeded on the parallels between her mother's story and her own emotional situation, Felicity recovered her resolution to find her way to her own history. With only two months left in the analysis, the analyst struggled with the worry that there was insufficient time. But Felicity seemed revitalized by the understanding of her borrowing of her mother's conflicts. She began to experience consciously her own internal conflict between the lethargy induced by the operation of her defensive inhibition and the energy available in enjoying work and play. She looked up old friends, cleared out and sorted old letters and stories, felt she was "letting go." Connecting these feelings with her thoughts about her termination, she described a sequence: she had felt there was good work together. Then the analyst was away for two sessions and since that time she had felt nasty and withdrawn, had stopped working, and was ending before the ending while fearing her capacity to do that so automatically. She associated to a dream of *two old boyfriends, in which she felt she had to give up one so as not to hurt the other.* Angrily she exclaimed that even her dreams reflected her mother's issues—"I want my own imagery!" but she regretted that her stories seemed resistant to change. The analyst pointed out that her lakeside vacation story had changed only once she had allowed herself to recover the element of sexuality.

Felicity responded with a happy memory of dictating a story to her mother when she was about 5 years old. It was called "The Worm Who Could Do Anything," and concerned the adventures of a worm who eventually made a difficult choice by breaking into two. "Then there were two magic worms." We can see Felicity's struggle between what felt to her to be the only alternatives; she had either to give up one friend or opt for a magical fantasy connected with her mother. Despite her resistance to examining other possibilities, her associations drew her irresistibly forward into memories of adolescent sexual fantasies. These led to concerns about whether she would be able to be herself during an impending visit to her boyfriend's family in another city. The sense of holding back returned her thoughts to her mother's low estimation of Felicity's capacities and consequent limited expectations.

For the first time it occurred to her to wonder what her mother's ambitions had been. Felicity realized that over the years she had indeed heard a great deal about her mother's thwarted aspirations and the sense that the grandparents had limited her options, barely supporting her college attendance, much less considering professional training, while lavishing full support on the ambitions of Felicity's uncle. Felicity felt she had taken on her mother's sense of limitation and envy of the male. She didn't feel like a woman, but rather that she could be both male and female, and she did not want to give that feeling up. The analyst remarked that holding on to the idea of being both a man and a woman allowed her to be neither. It seemed that she could not imagine being a *woman doing* things, only a *man doing*, but then she felt like an inadequate man, not a super worm. The very idea of a woman being able to *do* felt new to Felicity, and she savored the possibilities it opened up. After the earlier work on her identification with her father and her bisexual conflicts, Felicity had stopped dressing in an androgynous style, but she continued to mask her attractive body with mildly unflattering and uninteresting clothes until the secret omnipotent kernel of the bisexual fantasy could be addressed. As work continued on her omnipotent ideas and how she was using them to ward off her feelings about termination, Felicity also developed an individual flair in her clothes; by the end of her analysis, she had an attractive feminine look of her own.

During the visit to his parents the next weekend, Felicity's boyfriend was hospitalized for a sudden acute but limited condition. This delayed Felicity's return to analysis for a week and during the subsequent week these events were still reverberating. Toward the end of May Felicity was due to return to her job after the long absence occasioned by her labyrinthitis. She began the week by filling her session with arid stories about work, complaining meanwhile about the interferences to her analysis imposed by her parents' deadline, her own illness, and her boyfriend's. The analyst interpreted her wish to obscure the issues around her own readiness for termination by figuring as the victim of these external events. It appeared that, just as Felicity had become ready to integrate images of both good and bad mothers in the transference, her mother had reenacted the drama of her own life by trying to snatch her away from the foster mother the analyst may have come to represent in her transference to her daughter's analysis. Felicity had defensively identified with her mother's loyalty conflict and the solution the mother had found of splitting her ambivalence between two mothers; by avoiding assessing her own capacity to resolve her ambivalence and terminate her analysis, she was continuing to make herself available for her mother's externalizations of rage. Felicity responded to this line of interpretation with material about what it might feel like to try to have an existence independent of her mother, which reminded her of her failed attempt two years earlier to apply to graduate school. Felicity could not specify the problem, but felt strongly that something dreadful had happened.

Indeed something dreadful had happened at that time when, in the fifth year of her analysis, Felicity seemed to be generating some momentum in her life. The analyst recalled with Felicity her enthusiastic work on her applications and her pride at surmounting her old writing inhibitions in starting the essays. She had brought in one composition to read. In fulfillment of the assignment to write something that would both demonstrate descriptive capacity and convey the writer's personality, Felicity had chosen to describe a photograph of her mother taken just after World War II. The first line of her piece was, "When I think of myself, I see a photo of my mother." The analyst had responded first with what seemed very mildly encouraging interest in her examination of her conscious identification with her mother. There followed a transference interpretation regarding her conflict over making a choice that would take her away from the analysis, yet allow her to stay with the analyst by identifying with the writing aspect of the analyst's work. When Felicity did not pursue the application process, both had attributed it to the genuine hesitations she had been experiencing around her choice of field of study. In the following months, she had experienced great difficulty working in the analysis, expressed through lateness, silence, and absences, but that too had been fruitfully analyzed in relation to the problems she was having in her relationship with a rather neurotic young man.

In retrospect, however, it became increasingly clear that there had been a complicated transference enactment, which had not been understood and to which the analyst had responded by participating rather than interpreting. Only now in May, some two years later, was the earlier interaction more fully examined. Felicity had felt the praise meant that the analyst had some stake in her application and acceptance to graduate school, that her functioning somehow served the other's emotional needs rather than her own. If the analyst had any wishes or feelings at all, it meant to her that the whole process became taken over. Felicity could no longer hope for anything for herself, as any achievement became the analyst's and left her a lonely failure. The pleased response to the work she had done on her application essay had been the analyst's lapse into the role of idealized mother. But Felicity could not allow anyone to give her what she had so longed for from her mother without facing her disappointment in her mother's shortcomings. Additionally, the idea of an alternative mothering figure had many extra charged meanings in this family. The work done on her borrowing of issues from her mother's history allowed finally for understanding more of the complex transference problem and the specific resistances generated by her defenses. This came with the help of additional associations to the dream of the two boyfriends and to another dream in which she had tried to sort out the different ways to be close to more than one person at a time.

The next week was a short one, because of Memorial Day; there was a month left before termination, and there had been a noticeable change in the tone and pace of the analysis. Felicity was much more active than she had ever been before; the analyst was correspondingly quiet, with a sense of keeping her company in her analytic work, as she noticed the fluctuations in her capacity to follow her own thoughts. She brought in two dreams she called "weird." The first was of *being in a session when her boyfriend, who really had the same name as her brother, burst in with two thugs, saying "I have to find my grade, I know it's here on my transcript." Felicity told him that grades weren't the point in analysis, but he and the others went through the door into the next room anyway, and rummaged around until they found the transcript. Brett was very upset to find that he had a B. Felicity again told him that grades were irrelevant, but she noticed that she received an A.* She went on to the second dream, which was of her boyfriend Brett and his older brother, Frank. Brett and Felicity had occasionally identified Felicity with Frank, who actually had the same name as one of the old boyfriends who had figured in the earlier dream of the two boyfriends. In the dream *Frank and the boyfriend Brett were boys at a fair in the grounds of Felicity's old high school. Frank told Brett "I forgive you"; they hugged and made up. Felicity was very moved and then the black man whose life had inspired her appeared and sang a song about a happy girl.*

Felicity's first association to these dreams was to report that she had been feeling renewed sexual attraction to Brett, as if something had been liberated through the dreams. She thought about Brett likening her to Frank and wondered whether she was finally coming to grips with her feelings about her brother Brett, that she could finally forgive him for being preferred and outshining her. Looking again at her graduate school applications, she realized that she could easily complete them. The thought that her brother Brett would be taking some graduate classes in the summer led to indignant memories of songs in which men go off to follow their dreams, leaving women behind to wait in frustration. What about women? Why not her? When the analyst suggested that it was time to deal with all the parallels between the two Bretts, as indicated by her calling the dreams "weird," which in her vocabulary suggested a sexual connotation, she bravely agreed. She recognized that her confusions about modalities of intimacy had interfered with the sexual side of her relationship with her boyfriend. Again the material led back to issues in her relationship to her mother at each stage of development, as she recalled on the one hand the lack of physical affection between them, but on the other the confusion and excitement of being pressed close to her mother's naked body in habitual joint showers until she was a schoolchild. Frightening dreams, recurrent throughout her life, of *her mother laughing in a sexualized way when stoned on marijuana and having affairs with other men*, could be understood as related to a confusion of oedipal wishes and anxieties with her intense separation fears.

By the end of the week of the two weird Brett dreams, Felicity was able to use the contrast between the childish attitude of the boys and her more "mature," reasonable understanding of analysis to bring in her own curiosity and wish to rummage in the private areas of the analyst's house. Felicity struggled with the dilemma of knowing what is considered appropriate while wishing for something else. She said ruefully that at times it was rather hard to have one's own conscience, that she guessed she wished for an A from the analyst, even while knowing that she would really value only her own sense of achievement.

June began with Felicity describing at length the sequelae to Brett's hospitalization. When she spent considerable time in the second session of the week with more overwhelmed complaints, the analyst took up the possibility that her pathetic speeches might be a way of dealing with other feelings about his illness. This released a flood of anger and the sense that she had dealt much more sturdily with her own illness than he was dealing with his. She was relieved to be back at work and did not want to spend the last month of her analysis discussing Brett's medical problems. Felicity's presentation of herself as the helpless victim was a twofold defense: it turned her critical perceptions of Brett's weakness away from him, just as she had dealt with disappointment with her mother by becoming an even more inadequate, incompetent person. It also diverted her from facing the feelings around her termination. Once her anger was expressed directly, her thoughts turned to the analyst.

Felicity began to cry, saying, "I can't reconcile the feelings of wanting to be done with my analysis and missing seeing you, I just can't put them together. Ever since I had the memory of the bright lights and no one was there and I was saying 'I want mommy,' I keep getting that feeling and I don't know how I'll be able to bear it." She was referring to a recently recovered memory of a tonsillectomy at age 4, when she had woken up and the nurse told her that if she cried she would not be able to see her mother. This memory had been connected in her thoughts to Felicity's grandmother telling her that she would kill her mother if she disturbed her nap just after she had come home from the hospital with the new baby Brett. Felicity had felt the same sense of lonely desolation when she arrived on the wrong day for an early morning session to find the analyst's house dark and the door locked.

Her boyfriend had remarked to Felicity that he thought she had a different relationship with her analyst than with anyone else, and Felicity cried as she said she felt liked. She thought of seeing the analyst's child walking to school every morning as she came for her session; she had realized that the children took a different route through the drive if she was already parked there. Felicity said she used to feel threatened by the children, but it had just occurred to her to wonder if they felt threatened by "all these strange people going in and out of their driveway. No, they look fine." Then she said, in a tone of revelation and with increasing vigor, "They have a different relationship with you . . . I don't have to miss you in the same way I wanted my mom." The session ended with a few minutes of relaxed, companionable silence.

For the rest of the week Felicity worked on the details of her thoughts about leaving and associated anxieties. She had a happy thought, then found herself wondering about the analyst's dying. This was differentiated from her masochistic need to spoil good feelings and achievements, which had been worked on repeatedly over the years, by a feeling she described as "a foreign body, something slapped on to me." She thought of how she had been frightened as a child by her grandmother's ring, worn to ward off the evil eye. She remembered the family story of how the maternal grandmother had repeatedly slapped her mother's left hand to make her write with the other one, and announced with relief, "They are the ones who are afraid to be happy. I feel so strongly now how those fears were laid on me and I don't have to go along. My grandmother's ring had an evil eye on it, but seeing isn't evil."

The following Monday Felicity brought a long dream which included *a gathering where her whole family was going from station to station and she realized that they were "already at station 5."* She worked on various aspects of the dream. On the last day of the week there was a 17-minute silence at the beginning of the session. Then she said, "I just remembered that when I learned to swim I did very well at it, and got to level 5 quickly." She went on to discuss this content, which involved issues about talent and work, and Felicity's lifelong feeling that no one had been available to teach her the techniques needed to get beyond a certain point in any area. She had always looked good, but did well only until the penultimate phase. There had been material throughout the analysis concerning her mother's practical incompetence and failure to teach the children ordinary life skills. But in this session she also looked at how she was using or not using the skills she had learned in her analysis. In fact, when she had trusted herself, her own head had done the work, her associations leading her to understanding her dream and the current issues it expressed. Felicity talked plaintively about how she could only do this with the analyst, who didn't rush her but rather let her sit with it until she had figured it out for herself, and that no one out in the real world would ever do that for her. The analyst reminded her that whenever she had described herself in this pathetic way in the past, it had masked a criticism of someone else. The week before, she had not confronted someone at work when it would have been appropriate—was there some disappointment or criticism about the analyst that she was not expressing? Felicity struggled with the contradiction between her sense that the analyst did think she was intelligent and her wish to hear it explicitly, to get an A for analysis.

During the penultimate week she continued to feel pulled in different directions by her many feelings about the termination. She brought many comparisons, to her disadvantage, between herself and her brother, and deprecated the significance of her own thoughts. With some internal difficulty the analyst refrained from intervening with interpretations of her defensive withholding of her good feelings and good functioning. It was important to see if she could work her own way out of doing this.

Happily, Felicity did, as she began the last week with a "stupid dream" about the analyst paying attention to something else at her session time. She had figured out that this was a worry about whether she would be thought of after she was gone, but, more important, it was an instance of her internalizing what she had come to call a "nonindigenous worry." She had spent the weekend working on an exciting project and had become aware that her own theme was emerging. Rather than risk coming in and talking about her excitement, pride, and enthusiasm, however, she generated an anxiety that negated her experience of the analysis. Under the pressure of the misequation of her competence with hostile separation, she had first turned the analyst into someone who could not pay attention, then identified with that and felt unable to understand herself.

After accomplishing this excellent piece of work virtually on her own, Felicity came late the following day. This partly represented a reversion to a past appointment time, but also a shortening of the session, as she felt she had nothing more to say, nothing worth starting with so little time remaining. She wondered if this was a usual feeling on ending analysis: Was it okay? Then there was silence. Eventually the analyst asked whether she was feeling shut down or having private thoughts. Felicity answered, "A bit of both." When asked what she thought about that, she referred to her difficulty in dealing with mixed feelings; it still felt so hard to have opposite feelings about termination. The analyst took up her persisting omnipotent fantasy that she could find a way to have no feelings as opposed to the reality that she always will have feelings. Her independent analytic work of earlier in the week had generated the perception that she didn't really need the analyst so much anymore; she had responded to the mixture of feelings this evoked with an attempt to obliterate all her feelings and thus force attribution to her of whatever feelings the analyst thought she should be having. Then both would be together again, joined in an unholy alliance of imposition and dumb resentment; the price would be giving up her experience of her own feelings. The following day she brought in a confirming story. She had been suffering, as she frequently did, from a terrible headache. Brett had remarked sympathetically that she must be upset, as it was her final week of analysis. Felicity had burst into tears, saying, "I'm sad," and the headache dissipated immediately. She realized that she had been feeling her sadness weeks before but had not been able to cry since then, as she had been so involved in warding off her glad feelings of readiness to finish her treatment. How hard it had been for her to have mixed feelings, to acknowledge what she herself cared about, as opposed to what she felt she was expected to feel! Felicity found it ironic and comforting to think that the analyst probably was not surprised by her reactions to terminating.

Before telling of how Felicity said her goodbye on the last day of her analysis, it might be useful to summarize the historical and thematic issues we have tried to highlight. In such a highly condensed form it is not possible to describe all of the complex areas of Felicity's personality development or pathology, but some features do stand out. These were the particular tenacity of her difficulties in experiencing pleasure in her body, mind, or feelings; her guilt over legitimate needs at every level, from basic protection to sexual fulfillment; the problem of rage; and the dilemma she faced repeatedly in that her identifications involved a choice between attachment and identity. Our task is to try to understand the origins and evolution of these issues and the mental mechanisms involved in their unfolding, both in Felicity's development and in the analytic relationship.

In the middle phase of Felicity's analysis, as the family history began to emerge, Felicity and the analyst were both struck by the almost uncanny correspondence between the details of her mother's actual experiences and those of Felicity's emotional life. The analyst turned to the literature on treatment of Holocaust survivors and their children. The search was both rewarding and frustrating. The rewards came in the appreciation gained for the extraordinary efforts of understanding and imagination that have been made by those who experienced the Holocaust directly and those who have tried to help with its aftermath. Work by Judith Kestenberg, Martin Bergmann, Milton Jucovy, and members of their research group (1982) identifies several characteristics that may appear in children of survivors and that seem to apply to

Felicity. One involves the mechanism Kestenberg called *transposition*. By this she means something more concrete than identification, rather a process by which a child ends up somehow living the life of its parents. This approaches the feel of Felicity's profoundly terrifying and inexpressible rage, and her overwhelming terror of abandonment, expressed in imagery that could have come only from her mother's experience. But we are still left with the theoretical question of the mechanism of transmission—how can one person's experience be transposed onto another's psyche—and the clinically crucial issue of motivation. What would impel a mother to inflict her experience on her children and why would they accept such mental content?

A second characteristic described by Kestenberg is a sense of closeness to death, which can create anxieties about drive development and growing up. Here too there are links to Felicity's intense conflicts about her drive impulses and her resistance to independent functioning. Yet we must supplement these ideas with understanding of the individual meaning of these issues for Felicity. Another area of common difficulty identified by all these writers concerned superego conflict with heightened or defensively diminished guilt about death wishes and rivalry. This applies to Felicity's guilty masochistic reactions and her breakthroughs of uncontrolled destructive rage. Krystal (1978) described a typical regression to psychosomatic diseases, and we may certainly discern a proneness to somatic expressions of affect both in Felicity and in her accounts of her mother's functioning, as well as close correspondences between the somatic modalities chosen by both. Yet these descriptions, accurate as they are, remain at the level of generalities.

Erna Furman, in her discussion of the impact of the Nazi concentration camps on the children of survivors (1973), stressed the need to study individual cases intensively to gain understanding and to avoid tempting generalizations. In their prologue to an issue of *Psychoanalytic Inquiry* on "Knowing and Not Knowing the Holocaust" (1985) Laub and Auerhahn discuss the prob-

lem of articulating and integrating for nonsurvivors. "If our ability to know is dependent on the language of the dead, which is
absent, and the language of survivors, which is inadequate and
incomplete, how can we know? We who lack direct experience
with the Holocaust must assimilate it through our imagination"
(p. 4). Felicity affords us an opportunity not only for the exercise
of our human and clinical imaginations, but also for another
avenue of assimilation, through the understanding of her identifications with her mother's reactions to her own experiences and
those of her parents and grandparents. Her analytic material
contains clues to a possible understanding of some of the family's
dynamics, which had interacted with the dramatic events of their
history and led to Felicity's pathological development. It was rather
unusual that three generations of Felicity's mother's family had
escaped and come to this country; in our experience it was unusual to have a young person in analysis who had access to her
parents, maternal and paternal grandparents, and maternal great-
grandmother, all living near each other and interacting regularly
throughout her childhood and adolescence.

Many features of Felicity's personality could be described as
sadomasochistic. Her depressed moods and suicidal thoughts at the
beginning of her analysis represented highly condensed adaptations
to and defenses against conflicts over drive impulses at all levels of
development. The experience of pleasure, whether in eating, activity, sensuality, sexuality, or the exercise of ego functions, at first
evoked almost immediate self-destructive responses, ranging from
car accidents and physical ailments to intellectual inhibition and
dullness of affect. Legitimate needs had gone unmet in childhood:
for instance, at 3 Felicity was sent on a visit to her grandparents'
distant vacation home with no explanations; at 5 she walked to the
first day of kindergarten unaccompanied; her persistent nocturnal
enuresis was never investigated.

By the time Felicity entered analysis, her own sense of her
needs brought dull resentment, confusion over what was normal,
and intense feelings of guilt when a need was articulated or met

by someone else. Of course this made friendships difficult to sustain and interfered with the development of appropriate heterosexual relationships. Work on these issues led Felicity to associate to stories of her mother's childhood soon after emigration. Felicity's grandmother was given to wild outbursts of rage over small infractions, "Did I save you from Hitler to leave your socks on the floor?!" At other times she belabored the children with the frying pan, shrieking that their ingratitude would kill her. When Felicity's mother was an adolescent, she was regularly greeted on the doorstep after a date with shouted accusations of prostitution. There were profound issues of guilt, responsibility, and rage unresolved in Felicity's grandmother, which devolved to Felicity's mother in due course, probably via identifications with externalized helplessness and the furious blaming that supported them.

Felicity's mother too was given to sudden storms of rage, which broke over the children unexpectedly. At other times her aggression was self-directed, as when she gorged to the point of severe abdominal pain and regularly vomited after meals. Felicity had identified with both these tendencies in her destructive tantrums, which alternated with states of sullen withdrawal. It began to seem in her analysis that rage was like a hot potato for the whole family—it was bounced from one person to another, one generation to the next. Something made aggression completely unacceptable on the one hand and too easy of access on the other. Family stories and current experiences reported in Felicity's analysis gave the impression that the extreme helplessness and inability to retaliate against murderous oppressors that the grandparents had suffered in the ghetto and the camps had led to a defusion of libido and aggression. Both sexuality and rage remained too available for them; temporary solutions to the problem of inappropriate impulses were found in fluctuating externalizations onto Felicity's mother. The continuing impact of this pattern of the grandparents' functioning made healing of Felicity's mother's own psychic wounds impossible. She had spent the years from 2 to 4 in highly charged, confusing circumstances. The normal toddler developmental tasks of libidinal fusion and resolution and integration of ambivalent feelings could not be accomplished in those years. Without mastery of those tasks, her loyalty conflicts between mother and foster mother were irreconcilable.

When Felicity entered the corresponding stage in her development, her mother was unable to be available in the ordinary way to absorb her aggression and carry an appropriate constant narcissistic and libidinal investment for her. For Felicity's mother to be a good-enough mother to her own children would have necessitated *her* making the unbearable, unspeakable, impossible reproach to her own mother. Only in analysis, in the context of a transference situation in which Felicity saw the analyst, on the one hand as the abandoning natural mother and the good foster mother, and, on the other hand as the abandoning foster mother and good natural mother, could she say, "I hate you for saving my life." On the foundation of owning her rage, Felicity could build towards the reinternalization of her affects and impulses, fusion of instinctual drives, resolution of her ambivalence, and integration of the split representations of the good and bad mothers. Rather than making a direct translation of her mother's story into Felicity's development, we had become able to know about her individual psychological history. Auerhahn and Laub, in likening dream translation to defenses against knowing, said, "When we interpret, as opposed to translate, a dream, we follow the threads. . . . The meaning we derive is neither above nor beneath the text, but rather is a hidden organization of that text that does not replace it" (1985, p. 192).

Felicity began her last session with a happy account of being "out and about" the day before. A pause brought thoughts of a friend's last day of therapy, when the therapist had asked if the patient had any questions about him. Felicity felt she used to have so many, but they didn't seem so burning now. As she mused about this, she realized that her questions were more about herself—Did the analyst think she was intelligent? Did the analyst like her? She felt she no longer needed to ask, because she felt sure of her own qualities. She pulled out a copy of Harry Mulisch's novel, *The Assault*, about the continuing impact of wartime experiences on a young boy, saying, "I thought a lot about this and decided I wanted to give it to you. You know how important it is to me." The analyst thanked her. After a silence Felicity remarked that she had been afraid that she might have a negative reaction after talking about the story she was editing for publication, but she had told only a few people she really wanted to share it with, and it felt fine. The day before she had worried momentarily because she hadn't worked on it, but then realized she would. She had noticed on the book jacket that Harry Mulisch had become an important writer in his fifties. With tears in her eyes and a beaming smile, Felicity ended her analysis by remarking happily, "Some people just take longer to do it than others."

PART IV
TECHNICAL INTERVENTION

11   TALKING WITH TODDLERS

In this chapter we will describe some clinical work with a toddler and her parents to illustrate a somewhat neglected area of preventive intervention. In Chapters 2 and 3 we described the early disturbance of the pleasure economy as an initial layer of sadomasochistic pathology. Here the case of a toddler illustrates this layer before the addition of subsequent phase-linked transformations, which would organize her painful experience into a sadomasochistic fantasy. Work with the G. family gave rise to some questions and thoughts regarding the role of speech in early object relations and ego development, and to an attempt to amalgamate puzzling clinical phenomena with psychoanalytic knowledge and research in infant development.

Gina, age 16 months, was brought by her parents for an evaluation because she had been waking in the night crying inconsolably for up to an hour. During these episodes she did not appear to be fully awake; she would not accept comfort from her father at all, did not seem to respond to her mother with recognition, but cried and kicked until she "wore herself out."

Needless to say, her parents were also worn out and very distressed by Gina's suffering and their inability to intervene effectively. Gina's parents were devoted, conscientious, middle-aged schoolteachers who had tried for many years to conceive their own child. They adopted Gina when she was 4 months old and adored her from the first moment, even though she arrived at the airport screaming furiously and refusing a bottle. She cried angrily in the same way when frustrated or in pain thereafter and the parents felt that there was grieving in her tone at such moments. Gina suffered repeated ear infections, which led to her having tubes inserted surgically in her ears at the age of 13 months. Soon thereafter Gina began to have repeated spells of crying at night and displayed signs of lowered frustration tolerance by banging her head or pulling at her hair when thwarted. She clung to Mother more frequently at times of transition to her familiar babysitters or when Father took his regular turn at childcare. Within ten days of the outpatient surgery on her ears, Gina developed a bladder infection which was resistant to the first medication tried. This eventually led to a full urinary tract investigation, including catheterization.

By this time, Gina presented the picture of a very angry, willful 15-month-old. When the parents said "no," Gina laughed and defied them. Because all her gross motor milestones had been delayed compared with fine motor and cognitive skills and she was not yet walking, and also, perhaps, because of the helplessness her anger was arousing in her parents, a full neurological workup was done. No organic problems were found and Gina was assessed as functioning well above her age level in fine motor and social/emotional development, and at the 12-month level in gross motor development, which was within normal limits of variation. Gina began to walk between her parents' first phone call to me (KKN) and our actual appointment; this step seemed quite literally to relieve much of her frustration, and the self-directed aggressive behavior faded out. When I saw her, it was therefore only the night crying that remained as a mysterious and disturbing behavior. The parents reported that her speech, which had been precocious (single words at 8 months, phrases at 1 year), had appeared to diminish as she began walking, but they could accept that this was normal behavior for an infant concentrating on a new developmental task.

Gina was sitting in her mother's lap, pacifier in her mouth, looking around alertly at the pictures in my waiting room when I went to meet them. Safe in her mother's arms, she responded with a shy smile to my greeting and looked with quick responsiveness and pleasure at the pictures I named for her. Gina indicated most definitely her unwillingness to walk with us into the playroom by holding her legs off the floor, but made no protest at Mrs. G. carrying her, and indeed she seemed eager to look around as long as Mother held her. Mrs. G. was apologetic that Gina was not more forthcoming, but was easily reassured and relieved by my remark that Gina was absolutely right to take her time with a complete stranger.

I will describe the playroom and the toys I had set out, so that we may better assess Gina's subsequent choices. The playroom was fairly large, all carpeted, with a wool hanging patterned with stars on one wall and a shiny mobile of fish hanging in one corner. There were two large cushions on the floor, one covered with smooth cotton, the other with velvety corduroy, as well as a small table and chairs. I had put out a stacking ring toy, a baby doll with a toy bottle, a Fisher-Price bus with little people, and some cloth blocks. Visible on a shelf, but out of Gina's reach, were a rag doll, some hand puppets, and a toy telephone. Mrs. G. and I sat down on the floor with Gina. At her mother's mild request, Gina carefully put her pacifier into the top of Mother's handbag, then checked twice to make sure it was there. She did not ask for it again during the session. Gina watched us each play with the stacking rings, listened while her mother named their colors, then ventured to lean out from Mother's lap to put them on their peg. She smiled at our praise and gurgled with laughter when I dumped them off for her to do it again. Over the next few minutes she warmed up gradually and began exploring the space immediately around her mother. She played a peek-a-boo game with me, hiding behind her mother's back, then disclosing herself with glee. Gina leaned over her mother's shoulder repeatedly to show me her mother's earrings, and was pleased when I responded by showing her mine. She detoured to the baby doll and fed her with the bottle for a while, but returned again and again to show me her mother's earrings. After about seven repetitions, she pointed to her own ears and I said, "Those are Gina's ears, like Mommy's and Mrs. Novick's. Gina does not have earrings. Those are Gina's nice ears; there are Mommy's [I pointed] and here are Mrs. Novick's." Gina led me through the sequence again, then pointed her little index finger and shook it. Mrs. G. exclaimed, "Oh she wants to tell you her poem!" Gina's "poem" turned out to be a song with accompanying gestures, which is commonly sung in mother–toddler classes and playgroups: "Five little monkeys jumping on the bed, one fell off and bumped his little head, mother called the doctor and the doctor said, 'NO MORE MONKEYS JUMPING ON THE BED!' Four little monkeys . . ." and so on. The doctor's caveat is accompanied by finger wagging in the familiar gesture of scolding. Gina made the appropriate gestures as her mother chanted the words, and then she went to the toy shelf and pointed at the toy telephone. Mother assumed she wanted to play calling Grandma, which is a frequent game and real event at home, so the mother held the phone and spoke "talking to Grandma" dialogue. Gina listened patiently, then handed me the phone.

I pretended to call her, said hello, and asked how she was. Gina wagged her finger and handed me the phone again. Then a hypothesis began to crystallize; I tested it by pretending I was calling the doctor to ask how Gina's ears were. I reported from the phone that the doctor said Gina's ears were very nice and very good, that Gina was very nice and very good, and that she had tubes in her ears to take the hurt away. Gina pushed the phone into my hands again and again. Mother's eyes filled with tears as I repeated the doctor dialogue and we both became convinced that Gina had connected her medical difficulties with being a naughty, disobedient girl. I added to the phone conversation that now the hurt was gone, so Gina wouldn't have to wake up crying in the night anymore, and Mommy and Daddy wouldn't have to call the doctor so worried again. Gina turned to pick up the dolly and feed her once more, then got down on hands and knees, crawled to Mother's handbag for her pacifier, and settled with a sigh against Mother's lap.

When Mr. and Mrs. G. came together with Gina a week later, they reported that the night crying had ceased from that day and had not recurred. In the second session Gina made a beeline for the toy telephone and pushed it eagerly into my hands. After two or three repetitions of the doctor dialogue she turned to the baby doll and fed it tenderly with the toy bottle. Gina offered me a turn with the doll and I took the opportunity to tell a story about how the doll's ears had hurt, like Gina's, and the doll's wee-wee had hurt, like Gina's, but the doctor had said they were lovely ears and wouldn't hurt anymore. I looked at the doll's diapers, smiled a lot, and said the dolly's wee-wee wouldn't hurt anymore either and what a nice wee-wee the dolly had.

I met with the parents for one further session, to talk to them about talking to Gina. Both parents had stimulated her intellectually, reading books to her from the beginning, but they had stayed on a concrete, naming level. It had not occurred to them to make causal connections for Gina yet, and certainly not to attempt to link events and feelings. Between the second session with Gina and the parent session, however, both Father and Mother had made an effort to take the time and trouble to explain things to Gina. They reported with affecting astonishment how much more tractable she had become. In addition to the phenomenological expansion of Gina's cognitive horizons, they were including the crucial element of feelings. In the supermarket they talked with Gina about being tired and how hard it was to wait; they extended their conscientious naming of objects into the realm of intangibles. Their increased joy in their child and Gina's relief made me feel confident of their capacity to manage the subsequent developmental hurdles more easily.

DISCUSSION

The brief clinical contact described above was gratifying to all concerned, but it raises many questions. The first area to be investigated involves understanding how Gina used what she had available to her to attempt to master overwhelming, probably traumatic, events and sensations. Here we will look at what we know about the intellectual development of infants before expressive speech is evident. The second has to do with trying to understand the parents' role in the psychological events that were reconstructed, and this introduces the meaning in the parent–child relationship of different stages of the infant's intellectual development.

The current explosion of research on infants includes much investigation of infant learning; this work has moved forward from the constraints of strictly Piagetian or anti-Piagetian studies to include a fuller view of the functioning child as a feeling, thinking, and doing person. Jerome Bruner (1983) provides a creative multifaceted account of the speech development of two little boys, which illuminates both sets of questions posed by Gina's problem and its resolution. Bruner examines particularly the games of the first year—peekaboo, object exchange, and hide-and-seek—as they arise in the context of the mother–child relationship and provide a setting for the development of speech.

Bruner describes the appearance of pointing from the age of 6 months on and notes that the child's ability to comprehend the adult's point preceded his own ability to perform the action consistently by one or two months. This is a pattern that recurs in various infant studies. We should keep in mind that Gina and her peers are taking in meaningful material well before they can express similar content communicatively. By 11 to 13 months, the infant becomes capable of "indexicals," which relate a sign to an immediate element of nonlinguistic context; these are the pointing and naming games of the young toddler. Once these are in the repertoire, the infant can move on to relating words to other words. Mr. and Mrs. G. reported that Gina was in this stage by 11 months.

McCall proposed that "although the predominant character of mental performance changes from stage to stage, mental behavior at every age serves two functions—the acquisition of information and the disposition of the organism to influence the inanimate and animate environment, the latter notion being similar to White's (1959) concept of effectance" (1979, p. 728f). Earlier, McCall described stages in the developmental function of mental behavior, with major transitions occurring at 2 months, 8 months, 13 months, and 21 months.

> The major cognitive event hypothesized to occur at approximately 8 months . . . is the separation of means from ends. . . . At approximately 13 months, stage IV marks the onset of complete sensorimotor decentering. The infant can appreciate the independence of entities in the world and understand that they carry with them their own properties, including their potential to be independent dynamic forces in the environment. . . . This cognition enhances information acquisition and influencing by permitting consensual vocabulary. [1979, pp. 729–730]

We know from her parents' report that Gina had been putting words together before the medical interventions at 13 months, so she was capable of intellectual manipulation of her experience, but not yet practiced at assigning appropriate meaning to those experiences. Means–end thinking was rapidly being transformed into cause-and-effect hypotheses, but the nature of the connecting links remained obscure.

What made Gina put together the specific poem about the monkeys jumping on the bed with her efforts at mastery of invasive procedures? We could suggest several alternatives, weighting the cognitive aspect, in the coincidence of the word "doctor" appearing in Gina's little poem, or upon the experiential aspect of being scolded for defiant toddler behavior and the doctor in the song scolding the disobedient monkeys, perhaps someone affectionately called Gina "a little monkey." A more sophisticated possibility would be using the song as a defense against anxiety aroused by helplessness and aggressive retaliatory impulses in the medical setting. The song was associated with fun with Mother and thus stood for completely contrasting affective experience; the reversal defenses are specific to the anal phase, and the thoughts underlying Gina's behavior and symptom may well represent the beginning operation of defense mechanisms. In blaming her own naughtiness for the doctor's intervention, Gina may have been protecting her parents from her hostility; it is not inconceivable that a child this age would have reparative impulses. We have all seen toddlers pat hurt peers or adults consolingly.

Any of these possibilities is plausible, but they still beg the question of why the particular connection was made. The answer probably lies in the direction of multidetermination. It is difficult, perhaps impossible, to know why one thing means more to a baby than another, but it is clear from current research on infancy that cognition cannot be divorced from emotion. The affective life of the child is central to his development in all areas and informs his intellectual development at every point; Anny Katan's (1961) elegant exposition of the role in ego development of the verbalization of feelings is a seminal psychoanalytic statement of this point. The importance of the mother–child relationship has not always been as self-evident to researchers as to parents, and so it is still possible to be pleasantly surprised by Bruner's (1983) decisive placing of language development in the context of the mutual attention of mother and child. He says,

> Language acquisition "begins" before the child utters his first lexicogrammatical speech. It begins when mother and infant create a predictable format of interaction that can serve as a microcosm for communicating and for constituting a shared reality. The transactions that occur in such formats constitute the "input" from which the child then masters grammar, how to refer and mean, and how to realize his intentions communicatively. [p. 18]

We think that Gina chose to make the connections she did because of the multiplicity of links available between the monkey poem and her experiences around doctors, some of which we can describe, others of which are probably inaccessible to us and perhaps to Gina. There are many traceable links: the verbal occurrence of the word doctor, the behavioral sequence of the parents' telephoning in both poem and life, the pain in the head of the monkeys and Gina, scolding going on in life and the poem, physical adventurousness beginning for Gina as it was for the monkeys, and so forth. There is, however, another kind of multiplicity here, what we may call affective charge. Gina tried to master overwhelming events and sensations; to do this, she brought to bear material loaded with the most powerful affects available to her at the time, all connected to her parents. There was powerful negative charge in the scolding, the pain, the anxiety palpable in the parents' telephone calls to the doctor during the night and the day. On the other hand, great pleasure and gratification accompanied her performance of the poem for her mother, talking to Grandma on the phone was a praised activity, while parents had been urging her positively toward gross motor progression. Berta Bornstein (1935) described a similar condensation of experiences, impulses, and affects in the development of symptoms in a 2½-year-old child and observed how "complicated" is the mental life of a little child.

We must not forget, however, that Gina's efforts to make sense of her experience were taking place invisibly, in thought. She was not communicating the intellectual structure she was creating to her parents because she couldn't talk very much yet, and it didn't occur to them that she might be trying to. Indeed, her heroic mental attempts to master the traumas were failing, and she developed the symptom of night terrors. Luckily, her parents were people who could hear that Gina's crying meant something, even if they didn't know what. But this brings us to the second set of questions mentioned above, those involving the meaning in the parent–child relationship of this transitional and momentous phase in the child's mental development.

It is something of a truism that scientists are now demonstrating things about tiny babies that mothers have always known, for example, that infant's facial expressions denote differentiated affects, or that babies recognize their mother's face or voice. It looks as if, at least in the field of infant personality development, science follows life. But when we come to cognitive and language development, common knowledge lags curiously behind scientific observation. Most parents don't assume understanding in their babies or toddlers and few adults advise parents on the basis of babies' capacity for comprehension, whether it be pediatricians helping the frequent management problems of this age group or mothers talking over the toddlers' heads in the supermarket. We ought to be wondering why this is so in general, just as we wonder why Gina's loving, involved parents never thought to talk to her about anything that was done to her. Bruner (1983) gives us a clue when he says, "One special property of formats involving an infant and an adult is that they are asymmetrical with respect to the knowledge of the partners—one 'knows what's up,' the other does not know or knows less. Insofar as the adult is willing to 'hand over' his knowledge, he can serve in the format as model, scaffold, and monitor until the child achieves requisite mastery"

(p. 133). The crux is the adult's willingness or unwillingness to hand over knowledge. We have seen that Gina was well able to think verbally, that is, that there were specific verbal elements in the theory she built to account for her experiences. But her parents resisted recognition of this capacity for independent intellectual functioning. Their resistance may have stemmed in part from the implications of intellectual independence—a child who can think has a separate life. Mr. and Mrs. G. had grappled with adoption and a difficult beginning to build a genuinely close relationship and foster excellent development in Gina. It was not easy for them, nor is it easy for any parent who has enjoyed the bliss of mutuality in the first year to give it up in favor of the uncertain communicative negotiations of the second year. Katan (1961) describes how much more difficult it is for parents to guess at the child's feelings than to respond to a pointed finger.

It is not only the independence of the toddler that parents may find difficult to accept and manage; the anal phase brings with it aggressive impulses and feelings that arouse powerful counter-reactions in others. Parents may respond by hostile suppression of the toddler's defiance and rage, which carries with it suppression of accompanying tendrils of ego growth, or they may respond with their characteristic defenses against their own aggressive impulses, which serve equally to blot out perceptions of what is going on in the child.

Given good-enough parenting and good-enough stimulation, however, the child with adequate endowment will move inexorably toward thought and speech. Perhaps the "terrible 2s" are a creation of the adult world's resistance to joining and fostering intellectual mastery of the internal and external environments by the infant toddling toward autonomy. Gina became happier, calmer, and easier to manage when her parents could see that she could understand the explanations of the inner and outer worlds they began to offer her. Gina has shown us that toddlers will make theories to account for their experiences whatever we do or don't do. But if we want their theories to reflect our view of reality and become part of a more sophisticated shared reality leading to progressive development and enrichment of the parent-child relationship, then we must provide the necessary ingredients and talk to our toddlers.

The clinical intervention of verbalizing Gina's feelings and teaching her parents to do the same may have prevented a later generalization of her inability to master an overwhelming experience, whether from an inner or outer source. It brought under control of her developing ego the areas of painful sensation and painful affect represented in the disturbance of her pleasure economy and the beginning disruption of her relationships with her parents. The differentiation of affect and sensation and the ownership of her body could proceed to integration within a libidinally cathected self-representation. Without intervention, Gina's painful experiences might have remained split off from her ego, susceptible to co-option as part of a later sadomasochistic disturbance. The association of suffering, distress, and anger to her "naughty self" might have been included in her early superego development. In considering technical interventions in the analysis of sadomasochistic problems, Gina's treatment demonstrates the importance of verbalization of affects and sensations, as well as the usefulness of early preventive interventions.

12 NEGATIVE THERAPEUTIC MOTIVATION AND NEGATIVE THERAPEUTIC ALLIANCE[1]

For over a quarter of a century social scientists, including many psychoanalysts, have been engaged in large-scale, costly projects evaluating the results of psychotherapy. The guiding principle in most of these studies has been to define, measure, and predict success. The results of this vast expenditure of time and money have been uniformly disappointing. Not only are the research efforts beset by seemingly insurmountable methodological difficulties, but, more important, the salient dimension of success has proved almost impossible to define, except in an arbitrary, often superficial way. There is a similar emphasis on success in psychoanalytic writings, especially those concerned with the areas of termination, goals of treatment, and assessment of analyzability. Here too we find authors referring to "fragmentary and contradictory knowledge" (Namnun 1968) and "the lack of well-defined criteria" (Limentani 1972). In a study of termination (Novick

---

1. Earlier versions of this chapter were presented at meetings of the Association of Child Psychotherapists, London, January 1977, and the Michigan Psychoanalytic Society, October 1977.

1976) it was suggested that the criteria of success are irrelevant to clinical practice since they often reflect ideals of mental health rather than goals set in the context of the person's individual pathology. This study revealed the extent to which criteria reflected theoretical, cultural, and personal predilections rather than clinical perceptions. We would now go further and say that our training and experience are such that we are not especially well equipped to define, measure, or predict success. We are, however, experts in the area of failure. Our patients are products of failure and manifest varying degrees of failure in development and functioning. As Tartakoff (1966) demonstrated, even those privileged to have candidates as patients are dealing with failure. The treatment of failures often ends in a failure of treatment, for, as Freud (1937) said, "Analysis . . . [is] the third of those 'impossible' professions in which one can be sure beforehand of achieving unsatisfying results. The other two, which have been known much longer, are education and government" (p. 248). This emphasis on success may be partly, as Freud suggests, "a child of its time, conceived under the stress of the contrast between the post-war misery of Europe and the 'prosperity' of America, and designed to adapt the tempo of analytic theory to the haste of American life" (p. 216). We should add here the impact of the explosion of alternate methods of treatment promising quick results, success with relatively little cost in time, money, or psychic pain. The increasing role of third party insurance with its insistence on cost efficiency should not be underestimated as a factor leading to the emphasis on success.

The total immersion in failure has a devastating impact on psychoanalysts, leading many into areas of work, treatment, or theory which promise protection from such an onslaught on their self-esteem. This, of course, is not a recent phenomenon, and we would suggest that many of the early and later psychoanalytic dissidents were not only competing with the father Freud, but were also, if not mainly, dealing with their own experience of failure in their theoretical and clinical work. Freud (1937) saw

Ferenczi's therapeutic experiments as a response to the frustration of analytic work rather than as a rebellion. After outlining the many obstacles to treatment, Freud says, "From this point of view we can understand how such a master of analysis as Ferenczi came to devote the last years of his life to therapeutic experiments, which, unhappily, proved to be vain" (p. 230).

We have become convinced that failure is not only an area of expertise but a most fruitful area of investigation. Our research has come to include the question of the relation between failure and omnipotence, the role of failure in normal and pathological development, and the factors related to failures of treatment. In 1937, Freud suggested, "In this field the interest of analysts seems to me to be quite wrongly directed. Instead of an enquiry into how a cure by analysis comes about . . . the question should be asked of what are the obstacles that stand in the way of such a cure" (p. 221). One such obstacle Freud called the negative therapeutic reaction (1923). As with many of Freud's concepts, later writers have tended to expand the meaning and application of the term, a fact noted by many others (Brenner 1970, Olinick 1964, Sandler et al. 1973). Some use the negative therapeutic reaction as the explanation for any protracted resistance to or failure of treatment. Freud used this term to refer to a specific reaction in treatment—a negative reaction to progress or to words of encouragement. "When one speaks hopefully to them [the patients] or expresses satisfaction with the progress of treatment, they show signs of discontent and their condition invariably becomes worse" (1923, p. 49). It is thus a specific clinical response occurring during the course of treatment and following a period of "successful therapeutic management" (Moore and Fine 1967). Amending his original views on the subject, Freud (1918) later said that this reaction was more than "defiance towards the physician and . . . fixation to the various forms of gain from illness" (1923, p. 49). It was a moral factor, a sense of guilt. In 1924, he was more specific and saw the cause of the reaction in a "need for punishment," a clinical manifestation of moral masochism (p. 166). Freud viewed the negative therapeutic reaction as a powerful resistance to treatment, but not necessarily the most powerful. Further, it is but one of many factors leading to failure or protracted treatment.

In this paper we shall explore another factor contributing to failure in treatment—*negative therapeutic motivation*. Unlike the negative therapeutic reaction as described by Freud, the negative therapeutic motivation occurs long before the patient sees the analyst or has any idea what analysis is about. The negative therapeutic motivation is the motivation to go into analysis or therapy in order to make the analyst fail. Before we illustrate the phenomenon or try to elucidate some of the underlying mechanisms, it is important to point to a logical error that occurs most frequently in discussions of obstacles to treatment. We are accustomed to think of a continuity between normal and abnormal, between health and illness. The difference is, in Freud's terms, an economic one or one of degree. However, when we talk of obstacles to treatment, we often create "pseudospecies" of patients and call them narcissistic, borderline, or "negative therapeutic reactors" (Olinick 1970). In our view, a negative therapeutic motivation, that is, a wish to enter treatment in order to make the analyst fail, is part of every treatment, regardless of degree or type of pathology. The phenomenon is, of course, more visible in certain types of patients, such as those with severe masochistic disturbances, and at certain ages, such as adolescence.

NEGATIVE THERAPEUTIC MOTIVATION

We shall present illustrations of how the negative therapeutic motivation manifests itself in the treatment situation and is related to the defensive need of both patient and parent to maintain an idealized image of a loving, loved, and omnipotent parent.

A. was a 14-year-old boy referred because he was severely depressed, tearful, failing at school, and feeling increasingly socially isolated. He said he felt that his whole world was shattering. The referring psychiatrist believed that he was highly motivated for treatment. When the analyst saw A., it was evident that he was indeed experiencing a great deal of psychic pain and that he very much wanted to be helped. It was not evident, however, that at the same time there coexisted a need to turn the analyst into a failure. His parents were in the throes of a separation battle and the air was filled with accusations and blame. After the third session A. stopped talking and did not say a word during the next nine months of treatment. Although this resistance was multidetermined, it became apparent that a major impetus stemmed from A.'s conscious and unconscious wish to make the analyst fail in her therapeutic efforts. Interventions became effective only after the analyst recognized her own feelings of failure as a counterreaction to A.'s need to make her fail. Slow, but gradual change occurred after a lengthy period during which the analyst maintained a steady level of therapeutic composure, accepted and shared with A. her limited power in the face of his resistance, made very few but often accurate interpretations of his nonverbal expressions, and interpreted his silence as an attempt to make her fail and thus externalize and displace hated aspects of his self and object representations onto her. Further confirmation that this long period of silence was a manifestation of negative therapeutic motivation occurred years later when he referred to that silent period as "the greatest year of my life." It had been. The analyst had become the failure. His parents, especially his mother, had been restored to something approximating his view of their former perfection. Whatever her failings, they were not as great or as evident as the analyst's. In later years, when the analyst had become a transference object and could interpret the sadomasochistic battle with her, A. recalled that even before he had met her he had decided that he would not talk to her.

J., a 16-year-old girl, was referred to a colleague because of uncontrolled bouts of crying, severe depression, and pervasive feelings of inadequacy. In her initial session she presented a bright, cheerful facade and claimed that others said she did not need treatment. The slightest critical comment on her part about her mother was immediately followed by a statement that she respected her mother and that her mother was nice. After her second session she left feeling convinced that the therapist had rejected her and that evening she made a medically serious suicide attempt.

On the basis of such little information one could posit other determinants of the treatment failure more salient than a negative therapeutic motivation, including a lack of skill or sensitivity in the therapist. However, we do have much more information on this girl, because following her suicide attempt she was included in a psychoanalytic study of attempted suicide in adolescents (Friedman et al. 1972). She was seen five times a week for five years. The material from her analysis was part of the information obtained from eight such cases, four boys and four girls (Hurry et al. 1976). One major finding of this study, which was discussed in Chapter 8, is germane to the topic of negative therapeutic motivation. The suicide attempt in each of the cases was not a sudden act but the end point in a pathological regression. Suicidal thoughts had been present for a considerable period prior to the attempt. Although there were important differences in these patients, and especially between boys and girls, they all showed a similar pattern in the regressive sequence. The regression started with the experience of failure in the move toward independence from mother. The cause of failure was externalized and attributed to the mother, who was experienced both as a failure and as someone who rejected them and withheld the magical solution. The blame and the experience of rejection and failure were then shifted once more to themselves and then most decisively to an external object. In each case the immediate precipitant to the suicide attempt was the experience of rejection consequent upon the failure of an external object to meet his or her needs. One girl had told her friend at school of her wish to kill herself and she was told to go to a psychiatrist. A boy had pinned all his hope on being accepted at a particular university; when he was rejected, he felt that there was nothing for him to do but to kill himself; and J. construed her analyst's words as a rejection and left the session saying to herself, "What's the use, she doesn't care either" (Hurry 1977). It was only well into the analytic process that the unconscious need to make the object fail could be elucidated.

For example, the young man who was rejected by the university of his choice often came late or came extremely early to a session and then blamed the analyst for failing to see him immediately or for his full time. Once he canceled a session, but appeared anyway. Since the analyst made it a practice to be available even during cancellations, this attempt to make him fail did not succeed and they could begin to look at his own need to make people fail him. He then recalled that he had applied to the university of his choice after the deadline.

Once these patients succeeded in placing the blame and failure onto some person or thing other than their mothers, they could, without the inhibiting factor of guilt, put their suicidal wishes into action. These adolescents illustrated a phenomenon we have seen in many children, adolescents, and adults—the need to make objects fail as related to a need to defend the mother from their own aggression and maintain an idealized image of a loving, omnipotent mother. Struggling with lifelong intense feelings of failure in major areas of functioning, these patients oscillate between externalizing and internalizing the blame for this failure. Either solution is painful and terrifying, and they soon obtain relief by finding some object other than mother to blame, to hate, and then to reject by turning that person into a failure. The failed object represents the "significant other," people such as fathers, siblings, teachers, friends, who could draw the child out of the maternal orbit. With each failure of a significant other, the child becomes ever more intensely and pathologically tied to the mother. The analyst becomes yet another in the series of objects who fail, and the negative therapeutic motivation is the manifestation in analysis of the primitive mechanisms of externalization and displacement of negatively cathected parts of self and object onto the analyst.

Work with children and adolescents highlights an important feature of the negative therapeutic motivation—the fact that the need to make objects fail is a motivation shared by mother and patient. Both mother and child seek help from others in order to make those others fail. The fact that parents often interfere with and sabotage treatment is well known, and the causes and types of parental resistance have increasingly become a topic of research (Rinsley and Hall 1962). To the descriptions of the many kinds of parental resistances we would like to add the hitherto neglected, yet potent factor of the negative therapeutic motivation. It has been our experience with child and adolescent workers that once the concept is presented and defined, many cases spring to mind illustrating the phenomenon.

The following material is taken from a supervised case. At the insistence of their doctor the parents referred their 16-year-old boy, B., for treatment because of severe psychogenic chest pains and his fear that he would die. During the lengthy and detailed evaluation the parents were seen as forthcoming and cooperative, as was B. in his interviews. It was felt that his motivation for treatment was high, and that the parents would be supportive. It was an intact middle-class family, without any obvious signs of severe parental pathology. In addition to his anxiety, B. was also doing very poorly at school, was becoming increasingly abusive and physically aggressive toward others, especially girls, and was engaged in numerous delinquent acts.

He came to his first session with his shirt unbuttoned down to the waist, lolling over his chair, seemingly expecting a sexual response from his female therapist. He saw no difficulties with the times or frequency of sessions and spoke as if he had expected that he would be staying all day, every day. By the end of the first session he said that he was bored, and by the second session he said that everything had changed and he was feeling much better. During the third session he presented what we later learned was his mother's assessment of his difficulties and her solution. He said that his difficulties were entirely due to his boredom with school and the failure of his principal and teachers to meet his educational needs. The mother then convinced the school that he needed a special educational program and she also arranged for her sister to provide additional tutoring. The mother had the matter in hand, she had made all the arrangements, and now everyone felt better. He did not come for his fourth session, and the mother telephoned, saying that he refused to attend the sessions, and then added, "You must be so disappointed." The therapist did feel disappointed and that she had failed.

The analyst had weekly meetings with the parents, which continued for a period of four months. During these meetings the mother spoke of herself as the only one who could and did respond to the boy's needs. She said he had been a difficult and unmanageable child from birth, but she could always handle him. However, the time before the referral was a period during which she felt she could not cope with him, could not meet his needs, nor manage his increasing anger. Although she made no conscious connection with her feelings of failure, she added that this was also a period during which he had begun to make his sexual needs more apparent in the home in a manner similar to his behavior during the first session.

In analytic work with adolescents we have seen a number of cases where patients insisted that their parents had a claim on their sexual wishes, that their sexual aims, usually passive ones, should be gratified by their mothers. We have also seen parents of adolescents who feel that as perfect parents they should be gratifying their child's sexual needs. Unable to do so, and unwilling to allow anyone else the possibility, they encourage regression to pregenital modes of functioning, which they can gratify. Although we lack analytic data to confirm our speculations about this boy and his mother, it seems that the mother felt that, just as she had been the only one capable of meeting his other needs, so she should be the only one to gratify his sexual wishes. In that period before the referral the mother had had a serious gynecological infection that required surgical intervention. According to her, she had neglected the infection and had almost died. She was incapable of intercourse many months prior to the operation, and she was too frightened to have sex afterward. Her own motivation for continuing the weekly sessions was her concern about her sexual inhibitions and her feelings of sexual failure. The material from her sessions revealed that she felt that she had failed her child. She was no longer the perfect parent and B. would blame her and be disappointed. He did blame her, and his fear of dying represented a defense against his rage at his mother and his conviction that he could destroy her. She felt that to be accused of failure was a destruction, a death to be defended against by abandoning the object. The mother walked out in the middle of her last session with her therapist and then telephoned to say, "I know what you were going to say, you were going to say that I am a failure." She expressed her fury at the therapist, blamed her, and accused her of failing to deal adequately with the situation. She never returned to treatment. We can infer that B. might have felt that to accuse his mother of failure would destroy her and would lead to abandonment. To protect her and to stay part of her he took on the perceived failure, the mother's imminent death, and he became the one who was helpless and about to die. The internalization of blame and failure was equally terrifying. In a manner that must have represented a lifelong pattern, mother and child found relief and restored the idealized omnipotent unit by locating the failure, disappointment, and blame in the therapist, someone external to the closed world of their now purified omnipotent dyad.

There is a group of children and adolescents in whom the degree of disturbance is such that the parental role in the negative therapeutic motivation remains hidden. These are patients who are often labeled borderline. Common on referral are problems of overwhelming anxiety, with panic attacks and tantrums occurring frequently. Severe disturbances in drive and ego development are evident, and the extensive use of externalization and a tendency to confuse and fuse self and object representations are prominent. They often rule the house with tantrums and rages, making the parents feel helpless and terrified. The referral usually is made because of a fear that the child will kill or seriously hurt a younger sibling. In cases of this type, the initial period of treatment is marked by the immediate discharge of wishes into action, which presents severe management problems. The preadolescents often rage, shout, break things, and throw objects out of the window. One boy came in with a BB gun, shouting that he would kill the analyst. Adolescents sometimes also present management problems in treatment, but usually the analyst has to contend with their unrelenting, abusive attack in which he or she becomes the recipient of all the negatively cathected aspects of self and object representations. With both children and adolescents of this type, the analyst not only is accused of being a failure but also is turned into a failure as this relentless attack on his or her competence, skill, and experience is carried on for years. Even more devastating is the attack on the analyst's identity as a separate person, for during this lengthy period the analyst exists only within the narrow limits of their externalizations and everything else is denied. Then, possibly because he has survived this unceasing attack, these patients begin to perceive the analyst as someone other than the hated parts of themselves and their mothers. As they gradually perceive the analyst as a separate and valued object, they can begin to have a transference relationship to that object. It becomes evident then that the negative therapeutic motivation reflects, in part, a defense against the positive transference. At this point, when the analyst is acknowledged as a separate and valued object, an object of positive transference, the maternal negative therapeutic motivation becomes visible and operative. It is at this point that parents remove the child from treatment, often going to such lengths as changing jobs or professions and moving to another city. Or one or both parents may become depressed and show other signs of severe disturbances resulting from the disruption of the pathological family pattern (Brodey 1965, and see Chapter 5, this volume).

This case illustrates another reaction that once more underlines the relationship between failure, externalization, and the negative therapeutic motivation. C., a 15-year-old boy, had been in analysis since the age of 11. Originally he had been referred to his first analyst because of uncontrolled rages and attacks on his younger brother. He and his parents saw the first period of treatment as a total failure. He had spent each session reading comics, slowly sipping from a container of soda pop, and talking to his mother by calling her on the telephone. His first analyst moved away and he was referred to a second analyst. When first seen, C. looked more like an 11-year-old than an adolescent about to turn 16. Every area of functioning was a total failure. He had gone through a progressive school without learning anything, and it was evident that he could never pass a final high school examination. He had no friends, was bullied and teased by everyone, and showed severe disturbances in most facets of drive and ego development. In the sessions he shouted and raged at his new analyst, saying that analysis was a jail, that all his problems were due to analysis, and that everything would have been fine if he had not been sent to therapy. He said that he wanted his mother to be his therapist, and after each session he would use the pay phone to call her and tell her what had been discussed.

He knew that he had made the previous analysis fail, and he was conscious of his wish to do the same again. During this time the parents were very supportive and encouraged him to go to treatment. They would keep the analyst informed of the "terrible things" he said to them and they offered sympathy for his contempt and for the analyst's failure to change him. Gradually, however, C. began to develop a positive transference and a treatment alliance. Through the work together he began to change, but as each change became apparent or about to be translated into action, the mother would do something to obliterate the analyst's role and his, so that the credit for the positive change would become hers alone. For example, as work proceeded on his need to remain a little boy, not only mentally but also physically, he began to grow and mature. As soon as these changes began to appear, she took him to a "growth clinic" where he was given a course of hormone injections. He became physically mature and of average height, but he did not attribute these changes to something internal or to something possibly linked with the analytic work. He viewed the physical changes as something due entirely to his mother's intervention. Each further progressive step was taken over in a similar fashion by his mother. His desire to leave school and start work, his moving from his home and living in a youth hostel, his changing to a better job, and even his first sexual experience were matters arranged by his mother. Thus, each success became a source of failure—the analyst's failure and his—and he remained tied to an image of an omnipotent mother who could magically grant all his wishes.

The analyst represented the significant other, the father or teacher, the carriers of the reality principle curtailing his omnipotent fantasies and demanding active and sustained effort for the fulfillment of realistic wishes. Painful and difficult as this may have been, he probably could have made the shift had he not been simultaneously overwhelmed by the terror that his relation to the analyst would destroy his mother and leave him totally abandoned by her. She offered him safety from the terror of abandonment. By carrying her failure and by being the devalued, helpless, damaged parts of her, he became extremely important to her and she would not—in fact, could not—abandon him. By inducing him to be a passive failure and making others, like his analyst, fail him, she could then become the omnipotent source of everything good. To the end he retained the fantasy that he would become a famous writer, even though he could barely read, or a famous pop star, even though he could not play any instrument or sing. By being the passive, damaged infant, he felt he controlled the omnipotent mother and together they lived out the mythological fantasy of the golden age, the Garden of Eden, a purified pleasure dyad.

The analyst's contributions to his development were repeatedly denied by both C. and his mother. There was a collusion between them to nullify and obliterate the significance of therapy. This manifestation of the negative therapeutic motivation is a repetition of an established pattern where mother and child obliterate the significance of any object other than mother. The most important significant other is the father, and in most such cases the phenomenon of "the bypassed father" (Asch 1976) is evident. In the cases we have seen, the fathers were physically or emotionally absent. They were often passive, ineffectual men who were viewed by their wives and children as another damaged child rather than a father. In work with adults in whom the negative therapeutic motivation is often more subtle and difficult to perceive, the material relating to a bypassed father is often a warning concerning the operation of negative therapeutic motivation.

NEGATIVE THERAPEUTIC MOTIVATION AND THE REFERRAL PROCESS

Case material from a postgraduate seminar for child psychoanalysts revealed how often referrals from other professionals are made, not at a point of crisis or treatment readiness in the patient, but at a point of actual, imminent, or feared failure on the part of the referring person. The referral is then made in a highly ambivalent manner containing both magical, omnipotent expectations and actions designed to make treatment fail. Analogous to the parental negative therapeutic motivation, professionals may also, at times, unconsciously wish for a failure in order to externalize their own feelings of failure and remain an idealized, omnipotent figure for the patient. Like the parent, the referring professional may be unconsciously conveying the message that if he cannot succeed with the patient then no one can.

A 16-year-old obese girl was referred after a suicide attempt. She had been known to the hospital since birth and had been to every department except psychiatry. When her obesity became life-threatening, she was referred to the obesity clinic, where she managed to lose considerable weight. She then attempted suicide and was referred to psychiatry. In terms of her own readiness for treatment, this was the least propitious moment for referral, but it was the moment of maximum failure for the referring physician because the medical department now worried that the girl would succeed in killing herself and they would be blamed. Psychiatric treatment was viewed and presented to the girl as a panacea, the magical cure for all her problems. At the same time the referral to the child analyst read as follows: "Once weekly treatment for a trial period of six weeks with the play lady."

The unconscious negative therapeutic motivation of the referring professional reinforces the patient's negative therapeutic motivation, and many premature terminations, especially during the early phases of treatment, can be traced to the unconscious intensification of a negative therapeutic motivation by the referring professional. This can occur even when the referral is from a psychoanalyst, as illustrated with one of our own cases.

At the time when I (JN) was planning to leave England, I referred a young woman for continuation of analysis to a colleague. The patient and I had agreed that she required further treatment, and she asked me to suggest someone she could see. For a variety of reasons we decided she should meet the new analyst while she was still in treatment with me. After seeing him she decided that she could not work with him, and the attempt to arrange further treatment failed. She blamed herself and felt that she had failed me after all my efforts to find a suitable person. My colleague also felt that he had failed and, at first, her description of the interview made me think that indeed he had. Of course, it was all too comfortable, and my own tinge of pleasure at being considered the only one and the best one alerted me to the collusion. The patient and I had created a purified pleasure dyad. I was loved for finding such a good substitute for me and doubly loved because he was not as good as I was. All this was to avoid the woman's intense rage at me for failing her both as an omnipotent, idealized object and as an analyst, since I was in reality stopping her treatment before she was ready.

Termination involves the relinquishment of a transference relationship stemming from all levels of development and having both positive and negative qualities. A forced termination, one in which a premature termination is initiated by the analyst, adds further reality-based complications to the transference relationship, particularly the real failure of the analyst to meet the legitimate needs of the patient. The defensive need of the mother and patient to externalize the failure and retain the illusion of an idealized, purified pleasure dyad has its counterpart in the situation of a forced termination. In addition to the usual working through necessary, in the case of a forced termination both patient and analyst have to come to terms affectively with the real failure of the analyst. This is extremely difficult and painful for both and the above case illustrates how a referral at the point of termination can, in addition to other determinants, have a negative therapeutic motivation in which patient and analyst unconsciously create an external failure to maintain an idealized patient–analyst relationship. In the particular case referred to and in others undergoing a forced termination, we have found it best to avoid making a referral and to leave the responsibility for this decision to the patient. Thus the question of further analysis and the means for attaining further help becomes analytic material similar to other major decisions such as career or marital choice.

In the case of the failed referral the patient and I realized the defensive collusion, the mutual unconscious wish to have the other analyst fail, and through this we could both acknowledge and feel my real failure, the real broken promise. The intense rage, disappointment, and hurt had to be experienced, survived, and integrated. At the end she decided, and I concurred, that although there was much work still to be done, she needed a period without analysis, to mourn and integrate what she had achieved. She wrote to me about a year later and it was evident that this had been a good decision as she not only maintained the analytic achievements but also continued to grow in many areas. She told me that certain areas remained unchanged and that she was considering further analysis but she did not ask me for a referral. About a year after this I received a New Year's card from her with a note that she had reentered analysis and after an initial difficult period was settling in and making progress.

THE NEGATIVE THERAPEUTIC ALLIANCE

We have described the negative therapeutic motivation as one among many motives within the patient, as something shared with the mother, and indicated how this motivation to have treatment fail can be shared and reinforced by the professional person making the referral. Similarly, one can speak of a *negative therapeutic alliance,* an unconscious collusion between the therapist, the patient, and others to produce a failure. This is not due to the analyst's deficiencies of skill or training or to the countertransference reactions produced by particular patients. As do the patients we have described, the analyst also carries the seed of failure with him into the treatment situation; his need to make the therapeutic enterprise fail relates, as in the patients, to issues of omnipotence, magical expectation, failure, and externalization of blame. The negative therapeutic alliance often becomes manifest in an overvaluation or a devaluation of the analyst's own skill, his importance as an object, and his therapeutic effectiveness. We shall highlight just a few of the effects of these attitudes.

Overvaluation is often part of an omnipotent quest based on the fantasy that there is a perfect mother with a perfect technique who can kiss away all the pain, create what Balint termed "a new beginning" (1968), and Kohut (1977) refers to as "the restoration of the self." Anna Freud (1969) said that the view that the analytic setting fosters a regression to the original mother–child dyad, and the possibility of undoing the primary "basic fault," is one that does not warrant much belief. This approach, however, often involves a direct clash with the patient's external or internalized omnipotent mother, one in which the mother–child duo is more powerful. The result will often be failure of treatment.

Another effect of the omnipotent quest for success is the overvaluation of technique. Omnipotence is a human fantasy, but it is not a human attribute. Only nonhuman objects such as machines can begin to approach omnipotent perfection. The quest for therapeutic omnipotence often leads to an overemphasis on technique, as a result of which the analyst may become an inhuman interpretive machine. As noted earlier, the negative therapeutic motivation functions as a defense against the positive transference by denying any human attributes of the analyst. The analyst's technical fervor may thus reinforce the defensive aspect of the negative therapeutic motivation and obscure the possibility of the emergence of a transference relationship.

Finally, we would like to emphasize the analyst's failure to detect the quality of sham and deceit in the negative therapeutic motivation of certain cases. These patients survive by becoming what others want them to become, by confirming the mother's externalization. They have become experts at counterfeit; they have become what one adult patient described as "an empty canvas waiting for you to paint a picture." Another adult patient described herself as a hologram produced by the intersecting projections from both her parents. She may look real, she may seem three-dimensional, but, like the hologram, she is nothing more than the intersection of two projecting beams. These are the patients who can do anything we would like them to do. They confirm our omnipotence, they can become a success for us, they can validate our theories. They are very quick to pick up our expectations, and in this way they can control us, retain us, and ultimately destroy us. Abraham (1919) and Riviere (1936) described this type of compliant, cooperative, pleasant patient as one who can speak of the resolution of the transference before the transference itself has ever been broached. To summarize: by overvaluing our importance, our technique, and our therapeutic effectiveness, we can enter into an open clash with the omnipotent mother, collude with the patient's need to avoid the human contact by becoming an omnipotent interpreting machine, and fail to see the sham and deceit behind the seeming cooperation and progressive development of certain patients.

The relation between the negative therapeutic alliance and a devaluation of one's skills, importance, and technical effectiveness is more apparent as the patient's need to make the analyst fail meets with a readiness on the part of the analyst to fail. The feature we would like to highlight is the extent to which we allow others to dictate the conditions of our work and the hesitancy we have in giving treatment the priority it deserves. This is apparent in child and adolescent work where we often see therapists giving after-school activities and even television programs priority over treatment. It is not unusual for parents urgently to seek help and then argue with the therapist about the frequency or time of the sessions because it would interfere with the child's swimming or music lessons. We have had psychologically sophisticated parents express their gratitude for the help we were giving them and their child, and in the same breath say that they were going to cancel a session for a visit to grandmother or because it was the last day before a vacation, there was so much to do and it didn't matter anyway. Some of these requests seem very reasonable, but, in our experience, to accede to them without timely comment may strengthen the negative therapeutic alliance.

Patients often set a time limit for treatment, and this is usually a manifestation of the negative therapeutic motivation. We have referred to this as the "unilateral termination plan," which exists before the start of treatment, is the condition for entering treatment, and the means by which treatment is avoided (Novick 1976). Describing the analysis of a 17-year-old where the unilateral termination plan was a way of avoiding the transference and becoming even more tied to the omnipotent mother, it was suggested that "at some point in the treatment, the patient must be confronted with the seriousness of his disturbance and the necessity of giving himself up to the analytic process by relinquishing the plan for unilateral termination. Analysis cannot become terminable until it is experienced by the patient as interminable" (p. 411). We would now add that what we called the unilateral termination plan is a manifestation of a negative therapeutic motivation. It is a need to make the analyst fail and a defense against a transference relationship with the analyst. As such it becomes a part of the analytic process to be dealt with in the appropriate technical manner. However, to accept the patient's rationalization as reasonable, to agree, for example, that university is more important than treatment, is often a collusion with the patient's negative therapeutic motivation, the formation of a negative therapeutic alliance, and the production of a misbegotten child—the therapeutic failure.

THE VALUE OF FAILURE

Beyond the clinical phenomena of the negative therapeutic motivation and alliance is a larger, more general issue of the role of failure and omnipotence in normal and pathological development. To many patients the alternative to omnipotence is abject failure and total inadequacy. In their striving for omnipotence and their total intolerance of failure, the mothers we referred to have become inhuman objects producing inhuman children. As analysts we can provide these patients with the experience of acceptance of human limitations and failure. Patients can see that we are not destroyed by failure and that failure often leads to positive growth and development. The "good enough mother" knows this and she slowly becomes less available to the child; she gradually increases the degree to which she fails the child, and this helps the child move beyond her body to the larger world of other objects.

The history of psychoanalysis provides us with a model for the adaptive response to failure. Each change in psychoanalytic theory and technique was a response to failure. It was the failure of patients to respond to hypnosis that led to the changes in technique, that culminated in free association and the psychoanalytic method of inquiry. It was the failure of Freud's seduction theory that led to the discovery of the Oedipus complex, instincts and their vicissitudes, and in general the intrapsychic world of instinctual drive derivatives and fantasies. Finally, it was the failure of patients to respond in an expected way to encouragement and praise that led Freud to describe the negative therapeutic reaction, relate this clinical phenomenon to the operation of the superego, and from this make the major theoretical change from a topographic to a structural point of view. So it is with Freud's comment on his own failure that we would like to end this chapter. In a letter of September 21, 1887 to Fliess, Freud said,

> I no longer believe in my *neurotica*. [He detailed the reasons for rejecting his seduction theory and then wrote,] I might be feeling very unhappy. The hope of eternal fame was so beautiful, and so was that of certain wealth, complete independence, travel, and removing the children from the sphere of the worries which spoiled my own youth. All that depended on whether hysteria succeeded or not. Now I can be quiet and modest again and go on worrying and saving, and one of the stories from my collection occurs to me: "Rebecca, you can take off your wedding gown, you're not a bride any longer!" [1950, pp. 215–218]

13   DECIDING ON TERMINATION: THE RELEVANCE OF CHILD AND ADOLESCENT ANALYTIC EXPERIENCE TO WORK WITH ADULTS

In recent years analysts have acknowledged the centrality of a developmental point of view; many emphasize that psychoanalytic theory is, above all, a developmental psychology (Meissner 1989, Pine 1985). Psychoanalysts have studied the development of the individual mainly through reconstruction from work with adults and through direct observations of infants and children. Reconstruction with adult patients of significant aspects of the past was central to the earliest work while psychoanalytically informed infant and child observation has a long history from Freud's own work with children (Novick 1989) to the current explosion of infant research (Lichtenberg 1985, Tyson 1989). Child analysis has been a third source of data contributing to our concepts of the development of the personality. Anna Freud (1970) described the initial pervasive excitement over the potential of child analysis to confirm the findings of adult analysis and her subsequent disappointment that this early promise had not led to greater collaboration and overlap between child and adult work. Almost a century of psychoanalytic work with adults has produced a vast body of clinical material and technical precept, and analysts have tried to integrate new data from infant and child observation as it has become available. It is our impression, however, that child and adolescent psychoanalysis remains a rich but relatively untapped source of insights into psychoanalytic process and technique, at every stage of treatment.

In our previous work we have used child and adolescent clinical material to examine a variety of topics including termination (Novick 1976, 1982a,b, 1988, 1990a). This clinical focus led to a theoretical paper on the application of child and adolescent termination experience to the end phase of adult analysis (Novick, 1990b). In that paper it was noted that, "three features stand out in a survey of the child/adolescent literature on termination: (1) the high percentage of premature terminations, (2) the involvement of parents in termination considerations and (3) the presence of developmental forces, which gives prominence to the overarching termination criterion of restoration to the path of progressive development" (p. 433). These three features are said to differentiate child and adult analysis, but it was argued in that paper that they may all be fruitfully applied to the understanding of termination issues in adult analysis. Particular attention was paid to Anna Freud's (1965) criterion of "restoration to the path of progressive development," and it was suggested that this concept requires further refinement and elucidation. "Perhaps we can begin the refinement of this concept by saying that during the pretermination phase the balance between progressive and regressive forces along a number of dimensions is assessed and a judgment is made as to whether the stress and strain of setting a date will lead to severe regressions or will be mastered in such a way as to promote progressive development" (Novick 1990b, p. 430). Several intrapsychic and interpersonal dimensions were suggested, including progressive shifts in sources of self-esteem. Here we will make use of clinical material from child, adolescent, and adult analyses to elucidate this developmental criterion and demonstrate its applicability to adults.

THE PRESCHOOL CHILD IN ANALYSIS

Goals of analysis at any age have always included resolution of the Oedipus complex, as figured forth in the transference neurosis. Most of what we know about the course of the Oedipus complex during analysis comes from work with adults. Child analysis has played an important confirming role since Little Hans, but, as Anthony (1986) has noted, child analysis has not added much to our understanding of this phase and its resolution. The analysis of preschool children almost always involves the passage of the oedipal phase and entry into latency, so examination of the termination of preschool analyses provides a window into criteria for judging resolution of the Oedipus complex.

Even without the accretions of later phases, the Oedipus complex of the preschool child is not simple. The normal Oedipus complex contains not only the familiar constellation of drive impulses, anxieties, and defenses, but also carries with it the inevitable narcissistic insult of facing the reality of physical inadequacy to fulfill oedipal wishes. This humiliation about the adequacy of the self echoes the child's helplessness in earlier phases to get the object to understand and gratify his wishes. In a good-enough mother–child relationship the child's inborn capacities to elicit an appropriate response provide an experience of effectance, which accumulates throughout development to counterbalance feelings of helplessness. The normal passage into latency draws upon this store of competence to direct the child to sources of self-esteem in his achievements, rather than seeking narcissistic supplies solely in his relationships to objects.

The Oedipus complex becomes traumatic when it is experienced as a continuation of an impaired mother–child relationship, in which feelings of helplessness have not been offset by experiences of competence, but have rather been defended against by magical omnipotent fantasies. Fantasies fill the gap between the real and the ideal and, for the normal child, they refer usually to the self-representation. Hence the surge in early latency of day-dreams of glory and fame. Such dreams can become the initia-tors of latency activities and so fantasy can lead the child back to competence as a source of pleasure and self-esteem. For other children the gap is between the real and the ideal mother; then fantasy is aimed not at enhancing the real capacities of the self but at denying and transforming the pain and inadequacy of the mother–child relationship. Unable to make use of real capacities to elicit appropriate responses from mother, these children fall back on magical control of the object to maintain their self-esteem.

The oedipal and preoedipal elements in the treatment of pre-school children are not different in themselves from those seen in patients of any age, but one quality stands out particularly viv-idly. Narcissistic sensitivity reaches a peak and we can see most clearly in the analysis of preschoolers the importance of the ter-mination phase to the adaptive transformation of the narcissistic economy. Let us look at material from the termination phase of a little boy who started five times per week analysis at the age of 3.

By the time Robert was 6¼, there had been consistent good reports from home and school for some while. In the analysis there had been an extended period of fruitful work on his preoedipal and oedipal conflicts. He spoke of having few prob-lems left and wondered what would happen when they were all gone. Termination was clearly on everyone's mind and the possibility had been raised by the parents. The analyst felt that Robert's self-esteem was sufficiently rooted in reality achieve-ments to allow for the beginning of a termination phase. Enjoy-ing himself as a 6-year-old boy in the second grade, however, meant giving up the omnipotent idea of being his mother's oedipal partner. Robert's genuine pride in his real achieve-ments was easily engulfed by defensive feelings of omnipotent triumph as he retreated into a magical narcissistic state, in which he imagined that he kept mother alive and powerful by giving her things to do. To this end he clung to a food fad, which kept him home from school at lunchtime while his mother busied herself making him special meals. His realistic appreciation of his achievements was difficult to maintain and easily slipped into a fantasy of grandiose oedipal triumph. As Robert grew tall and strong, he called the analyst a "squashed man" and "fatso"; as he experienced his own independence, he spoke of the analyst as useless. He had learned how to type, gave the analyst a card with his name and address, and said that the analyst could come to his house or telephone him if he wished to continue work. Verbalization of this pattern, where his accomplishments rendered the analyst useless, was followed by a reversal, in which Robert characterized the analyst as all-knowing and himself as helpless and full of problems. The same pattern was occurring at home with his mother. Repeated interpretation of his secret oedipal fantasy that he alone kept both analyst and mother powerful and alive by being a baby with problems finally led him to confront his mother. He told her he was through with all his problems except one, and that was her. He said that a little bit of her wanted him to stay a baby. Mother agreed that this was so, but emphasized that most of her wanted him to be a big boy, and that she and Daddy enjoyed his big boy achievements.

Robert reacted with relief and a spurt of forward movement. However, he could not maintain his realistic view of himself, and he invoked magical means to deny the reality of his status as a child excluded from the parental sexual relationship and his helplessness in controlling his mother. His magical omnipotent fantasies derived from many levels, as he imagined eating up the whole world, fooling everyone and poisoning them, strengthening his bones as the analyst's bones softened. The analyst contrasted Robert's infantile feelings of helplessness with the realistic power of his increasing competence. They understood together why Robert had felt that magic was the only route open to him, but that he could now feel good in other ways. Robert responded with renewed self-confidence and told the analyst that he had been able to put his face in the water at swimming. He alluded repeatedly to a wish to reduce the frequency of sessions and the analyst agreed that he was ready, but would leave it to him to decide when.

Robert worked in that very session to choose which day to drop, but asked the analyst to tell Mother, because "she'll be frightened out of her wits and you know what wits are. Wits are the widths in the swimming pool and she is so frightened she can't even swim a width, but I can swim a whole width with the board." When they reached the waiting room, Robert proudly announced that he was dropping a day. His mother later told the analyst she was sure that there was a clear connection between the reduction in frequency and Robert's learning to swim; he did four widths that afternoon, and fell asleep with a grin on his face. Soon after, it was mutually decided that the analysis would end in three months.

Termination is a reality which is hard to deny. To Robert's competent self, termination represented an accomplishment of which he could be proud. To his helpless infantile self it represented an imposition by the powerful analyst/mother, which challenged his omnipotent defenses to create more powerful magic at the expense of his realistic achievements. Thus, Robert felt that he had to produce more and more problems, deny the pleasures of school and imagine that he could thereby keep the powerful analyst at his command forever. By the termination phase, however, the failure of magic did not leave Robert prey to helpless anxiety; rather, he had available alternative reality-based sources of self-esteem.

What we learn from this examination of the termination of a preschool child's analysis is: that it takes the work of the termination phase to complete the work of the analysis; that the resolution of the Oedipus complex includes transformation of the narcissistic economy; and that the start of a termination phase is not when the conflicts are resolved, but when the patient is sufficiently rooted in realistic pleasures to put up a good fight against the regressive pull of fantasy solutions. The same issues arise in work with adults, but more subtly, because of the impact of intervening developmental transformations. Therefore, we will defer our discussion of omnipotent narcissistic defense in the termination phase of adult patients until we have described some issues that arise in latency and adolescence.

THE SCHOOL-AGED CHILD IN ANALYSIS

Anna Freud (1965) described the goal of analysis as the restoration of the child to the path of progressive development. The concept evokes a sense of momentum regained and implies that termination is appropriate when the child and family can continue the growth process independently of the analyst. Every child or adolescent patient ends treatment as an unfinished product; there is much development remaining. The same is true of adult patients, although the stages of development may be less clearly defined and the rate of change slower. Thus, child analysts know that termination can and should occur in the midst of a dynamic growth process, which has been reestablished by the work of treatment.

At any age the work of analysis is aimed at resolving preoedipal regressions to allow for the resolution of the Oedipus complex. Once the patient is sufficiently established at the oedipal level, a termination phase can be started in which working through, synthesis, and mourning can take place. This allows for consolidation at the age-appropriate phase. As one of the criteria to start termination with the preschool child we highlighted the role of the transformation of the narcissistic economy from a base in magical omnipotent fantasy to one in striving toward reality achievements.

School-age children brought for treatment are faced with similar tasks in analysis, since typical symptom-formation usually presupposes incomplete or inadequate resolution of the Oedipus complex.

Erica came into analysis at 8 years of age with panic attacks, fear of her parents dying, fear of using strange lavatories, fear of monsters, bedtime rituals, headaches, stomach aches, frequent falls and accidents, difficulty in falling asleep, open masturbation, baby talk and babyish behavior, lack of friends, intense unhappiness, anger, discontent and rages, intense jealousy, constricted speech and movement, and a learning disturbance. Most of these symptoms abated or disappeared in the course of the first year of analysis. Some of this was due to structural change, but most of the improvement was a consequence of Erica's use of the analysis for fantasy gratification of her preoedipal and oedipal wishes. When the analyst interpreted Erica's use of the analysis, she wanted to stop treatment, and used her symptomatic improvement as the rationale to try to convince her parents. The analyst's working alliance with the parents preserved the treatment in the face of Erica's resistance.

Two years later, when Erica was 11, the possibility of termination became apparent to Erica, her parents, and the analyst. A date was chosen and a termination phase began. As with Robert, one of the criteria for deciding on starting the termination phase was that the major source of Erica's pleasure was shifting appreciably to competence and effectance. For some time it had been clear that Erica was enjoying her high-level functioning at school and with friends. One day she and the analyst talked about wishes and she said that whenever she was asked for wishes, the "baby wishes," like the wish for a magic wand, immediately flashed into her mind, but these were not really her wishes any more, since she knew that she couldn't make them come true. She said she would tell the analyst her "grown-up wishes" and then the baby wishes. The "grown-up wishes" were to have a yacht and that the house and garden would be finished; the "big wish" was to be a ballerina, be able to do pottery, play a musical instrument, and have four monkeys and two cats. The analyst wondered if she had the wish to be a grown-up, be married, and have babies. Erica said, "That's a baby wish. I used to have it, but I don't any more. I had it when I was doing poorly at school and hated school. I would think to myself that grown-ups don't go to school, so I wished to be a grown-up. The baby wishes were to have a magic wand, to have wings, and to be a grown-up."

Work with the school-age child highlights the issue of postoedipal consolidation at the appropriate phase. For Erica this was latency, with its emphasis on work and play. We have already discussed the importance of the shift of the source of pleasure from the illusion of omnipotence to experiences of effectance. The schoolchild underscores the additional factor of change in the quality of pleasure and how to assess its manifestations.

Pleasure should become evident consistently, and we look for reports from home and school of more widespread enjoyment. Erica's parents began to envisage termination because they noted that she was frequently "beaming from ear to ear," which made her father aware that she never used to smile at all. So, consistent reports of pervasive and lasting pleasure are an important factor, but external change can have many meanings and roots; a genuine analytic termination must be decided on the basis of internal criteria. This is where we must look to add substance to the abstract goal of "restoration to the path of progressive development" (A. Freud 1965). Progressive development implies change along each of the metapsychological dimensions. We suggest that the functioning of the working alliance within the treatment relationship provides a barometer of these changes. The working alliance appears particularly vividly in the analysis of latency children, because their age-appropriate tasks include the development of the capacity to enjoy work.

At the time in Erica's analysis when everyone was aware of her much happier functioning at home and in school, she described herself as having few problems remaining and discussed the possibility of cutting down to four times a week. After some talk of the advantages and disadvantages of this, Erica produced a series of thoughts, which seemed to be a working through both of old problems that had been dealt with at length and issues that had received only some attention but that she seemed to have worked through on her own.

First, Erica talked about having always been afraid of her sister Lou's jealousy. She said it didn't bother her any more. "I mean it's really up to Lou if she wants to copy her friend Jill and be someone else. I mean it's her problem. If she's jealous of me and wants treatment, then she should speak to Mommy. It's silly to make myself go down just because Lou is jealous. That won't help Lou and it won't help me." Then, of Lou's attempt to be like Jill, Erica went on to say that one shouldn't try to be like someone else, one should be oneself. "I mean there's only one Erica and Erica is not like anyone else and if I try to be somebody else then there's no Erica." She followed with the comment that she had always felt that she must be just like her mother otherwise her mother wouldn't like her. "But I'm not like Mommy, I don't look like Mommy, I don't feel like Mommy, I'm myself, a completely different person and I want to be myself. I enjoy being myself."

The analyst wondered how Mommy might feel about Erica's being herself and Erica talked about Mommy having been in the center of her worries, but that Mommy didn't know that. Erica then wondered when her problems had started and suggested that it was when her sister Lou was born. She thought there may have been something before, "but it was just a titchy little bit and then when Lou was born I really felt they thought I wasn't good enough, that they weren't satisfied with me so they got somebody else, so from then on I had to be better than somebody else, better than Lou and I think that's when

I thought I had to be better than Mommy." She took out her baby album, which she had been keeping in the treatment room, and wondered if walking at 10 months was early. When the analyst said that it was a little early Erica said, "Maybe I was a little wrong to say it was just a little titchy bit of a problem before Lou was born because, you see, I'm walking early and maybe I already felt I should be better than Mommy because I wanted Daddy's approval, you see." When the analyst wondered about getting Daddy's approval now, Erica said, "I don't know quite how it's changed but it's really not that important to me now, other things are." She said that her worries had been very important when they were there, but now they were gone and they were really not important.

In this material we can see derivatives of instinctual wishes and defenses that had appeared repeatedly in the course of the analysis, such as Erica's rivalry with her sister and mother, her wish to please the analyst as the oedipal father in the transference, and the need to deny continuing difficulties. The material also shows the significant changes that had taken place. In addition to the remaining problems and the progress, however, the level of the working alliance reflects the achievement of a new pleasure in ego functioning. This pleasure is not relief or moral satisfaction in obedience to the superego, or omnipotent sadistic triumph over envied others, but a gratification from the functioning of ego capacities fostered by the analytic work.

In the above example, Erica is making effective use of her memory, conceptual ability, reality testing, time sense, and ability to tolerate uncertainty. All of this allowed for the flowering of her creative capacity, which we can see in operation here as she arrived at independent insights about, for instance, her defensive identification with her mother. With Erica not only do we see the shift in the source of pleasure from omnipotence to achievements but also, and most important, we see that this pleasure resides increasingly in the exercise of ego functions, as well as in the achievements themselves; that is, work itself becomes as much a pleasure as the results. Thus, it is in the working alliance that we may see Erica's beginning consolidation in the stage of latency. This criterion for the start of a termination phase applies to patients of all ages. Ego pleasure in the work of analysis ensures an adaptive response to the painful work remaining to be done. Elsewhere we've described application of this criterion to the timely start of a termination phase in an adult case (Novick 1988). The way this adult patient worked on a dream closely paralleled the ego pleasure we have described in Erica.

THE ADOLESCENT IN ANALYSIS

In the main, adolescents find it very difficult to leave their parents or their therapists in a mutually respectful manner that reflects a state of internal readiness and acceptance of a growth process. Most adolescents terminate prematurely, either provoking the therapist to force an ending or surprising the therapist with a unilateral termination plan. When this occurs near the end of treatment it may involve a regression from a differentiated to an "externalizing" transference, in which the therapist represents the helpless, depreciated, and rejected child discarded by the now-powerful adolescent.

In Chapter 6 we provided a detailed case example of a 15-year-old boy who attempted a unilateral premature termination. This, and many similar instances, led to the hypothesis that this adolescent form of premature termination may occur in the analysis of adults. A precondition for the start of a proper termination phase with adults may be prior work on the reemergence of the adolescent form of premature leave-taking (Novick 1976, 1988, and see Chapter 6 this volume).

If not premature, the termination of adult analysis may be unnecessarily prolonged, and here too we may use experience in the termination of adolescent patients to highlight some obstacles to the timely start of a termination phase. As we have seen, restoration to the path of normal development implies consolidation in the age-appropriate phase. This is easier to define in childhood and adulthood than in adolescence, which is normally characterized by flux and uncertainty. Compounding the appropriate uncertainty of the adolescent's life can be the analyst's counterreactions of anxiety about the patient's readiness for independent functioning. The analyst's overprotective impulses can be a formidable obstacle to starting a termination phase; the clarification of this counterreactive ingredient in the decision to start termination with adolescent patients alerts us to a similar, if more subtle, temptation to retain adult patients in a futile attempt to deal with every uncertainty and unfinished developmental line.

THE ADULT IN ANALYSIS

Termination of adult cases can be premature, timely, or interminable. We would like to share some preliminary thoughts on the problem of interminable analysis, an area that has thus far received scant attention in the vast and ever-increasing literature on adult termination. It is surprising that there are so few references to the issue of interminable analysis, since one of the first cases reported by Freud, that of the Wolf Man, might be considered such a case and may have contributed to the pessimism of Freud's "Analysis Terminable and Interminable" (1937). Some of the articles that refer to the topic may be including those patients who failed to respond to analytic treatment despite lengthy and heroic efforts of the analyst with those who do respond positively but seem unable to terminate (Anzieu 1987, Burgner 1988, Klauber 1977). The issue is often masked by the reluctance of analysts to admit that they have patients who have been in analysis for over ten years. Others may be concerned that they and the method may be seen as fostering a pathological dependence, so they set a time limit at the outset of treatment or force a termina-

tion of interminable patients by saying that analysis offers the
patient too much passive gratification and so must end.

Mr. M. first came to treatment at the age of 25. He had been
turned down as a training case because he was considered too
disturbed. He had been diagnosed as "borderline" and at his
first session he began to cry, pound the couch with his arms
and legs and plead, "I can't stand it. Please! Get it over with.
Punish me—beat me!" Since graduating from university he had
wandered in a fog of unfocused anxiety and tension, supported
himself with occasional house painting jobs, and found temporary relief in a series of relationships with equally disturbed
women, who were initially allowed to play the role of a controlling mother and then driven into a state of helpless rage
by his passivity and covert sadism. The initial period of work
brought a beginning sense of order and meaning to his life,
which gave him immediate relief, since he placed the analyst
in the role of the longed-for good mother who could respond
to his pain and kiss away the hurt. He felt so much better at
the first summer vacation that he thought he would soon be
able to end his analysis. The feelings of pride, pleasure, and
competence did not last long. He was soon locked in a relationship where he saw the analyst as the powerful mother responsible for all his psychic and physical states of pain or relief while he felt like the innocent victim of events. Covertly,
he worked to defeat all therapeutic efforts. The intense sadomasochistic transference reflected a "screaming" relationship
with a severely depressed, alcoholic mother and underscored
the patient's masochistic pathology and his lifelong addiction
to pain. Manifestations of these fantasies and functions were
figured forth in the transference, and constant attention to the
many determinants and functions of his active pain-seeking
behavior led to slow but steady progress. Mr. M. had been in
five times per week analysis for over ten years, and by all external and most internal criteria he was ready to stop. He was

happily married, joyfully anticipating the birth of a child, and successful in his career; for a considerable period of time he had worked hard and fruitfully at his analysis. All that remained was to pick a date and do the working through, mourning, and consolidating of the termination phase, but this proved to be a lengthy and seemingly impossible task. The work, of course, could have ended had the analyst taken responsibility for picking the date, and Mr. M. tried in every way to have the analyst do so. When this failed he became depressed, and it emerged that he lived by an eleventh commandment—"Thou shalt not leave your parents or your analyst." How could Mr. M. justify his lifelong need to prove that he was right to remain angry at his parents for leaving him when he was now planning "selfishly" to leave his analyst? The same situation had arisen at adolescence: when he and his friends went to Europe after graduating from high school, he broke down and had to return home.

With this link to Mr. M.'s adolescence we return to Mary, whose treatment helped the analyst understand and deal with Mr. M.'s inability to end his analysis.

Mary was taken into analysis following a medically serious suicide attempt. In Chapter 8, material from her analysis was used to test and extend the findings from a study of seven such adolescents and confirmed that the suicide attempt, contrary to popular myth, was not a sudden impulsive act, but the end point of a pathological regression that started in each case with the experience of failure to separate from mother.

At the beginning of Mary's analysis, as we have seen in Chapters 2, 3, and 8, the main concern had been that she would become irretrievably psychotic or that she would kill herself. Eight years later the analysis ended by mutual agreement, with some shared sadness but mainly pride at what was achieved and confidence that she was on the path of progressive development. She had become an attractive, happy person fulfilled in the areas of work, love, and play.

As a steady background to her many and varied conflicts was Mary's delusion of omnipotence and her desperate need to cling to an omnipotent self-image. Such fantasies defended against and compensated for lifelong feelings of helplessness, envy, jealousy, and rage. They allowed her to feel that she did not have to experience any of these painful affects since she was above it all, neither male nor female, neither child nor adult, but a being superior to all who could, if she so desired, do anything she wished to. Such fantasies can flourish relatively unchecked during latency but adolescence brings internal and external challenges that force disturbed children, such as Mary, to even more desperate measures, such as suicide, to retain the delusion of omnipotence.

Mary started treatment helpless, dependent, and seemingly incapable of a single age-appropriate activity. Yet, quite consciously, though secretly, she felt omnipotently superior to all because she believed that she, unlike most people, including her depressed mother, could really kill herself. Like the other adolescents we studied before and since (Laufer and Laufer 1984 and Chapter 7, this volume), Mary felt that her suicide attempt was a powerful, brave action that brought about important changes in her parents and her world. To her, suicide was a powerful, magical solution to all her conflicts and a manifestation of an omnipotent self-image. As the work progressed it became clear that Mary's primary pathology was not depression but an underlying severe masochistic disorder that subsumed both her depression and suicidal behavior. The view we put forward concerning the formation of masochistic fantasies in the early school years (see Chapters 1 and 2 this volume) was confirmed in Mary's case, underscoring the point of view that such fantasies involve omnipotence. Masochism and omnipotence are two sides of the same coin—the delusion of omnipotence can be maintained by masochistic, pain-seeking behavior such as suicide (see Chapter 3). As Mary worked through the complex layers of functions and determinants of her masochism she could experience and maintain pleasure for longer periods of time outside her analysis. The conflicts around pleasure became centered almost entirely in the analysis. She would feel happy, proud of some achievement, until she walked in the door and then would feel gloomy and bad.

There were many parallels between Mary and Mr. M. The analysis of Mr. M. had also opened up the range of positive affects, and for him too these remained outside the analysis. Even close to the end, he could maintain a cheerful, positive attitude no further than the threshold of the consulting room and by the time he was on the couch he was tense, confused, and depressed. As did Mary, Mr. M. reacted to the end of his analysis with a series of pain-seeking fantasies and actions aimed at simultaneously keeping and leaving, loving and hating, destroying and keeping the analyst safe. As with Mary, the multiple determinants and functions of his masochism became focused in the imminence of really leaving during the terminal phase. He was terrified of facing the world alone as he once more externalized all his own functions of control, containment, and purpose onto the analyst. He idealized both the analyst and the relationship so that leaving was imbued with fantasies of unbearable pain and irreplaceable loss. In Mary's case, after working through the adaptive, defensive, and instinctual determinants of the masochism, we were left with the final motive for clinging to pain—her unwillingness to take leave of her omnipotent, magical self. It was this experience with Mary— and, by now, many suicidal and otherwise masochistic adolescents—that alerted us to the final determinant in Mr. M.'s interminable analysis. It took years to work through his inability to leave; finally, he could accept that he could do so without further trauma. We could then see more clearly that, ultimately, termination meant leaving his magical, omnipotent self. To leave analysis was to relinquish his omnipotent fantasy that he could have it all, do everything, and never have to choose. Because he was in analysis, he imagined that he could live an active, responsible adult life outside and still be a passive, irresponsible, angry child. Because he still experienced pain in the session, he felt entitled to live outside social expectations and even reality restrictions. He could be loving and still allow himself to be sadistic, he could be an adult man and a sulky child, he could be male and female—in sum, he could maintain the delusion of omnipotence.

For Mr. M. and for Mary, omnipotent fantasies were defensive responses to lifelong feelings of helplessness, especially in eliciting appropriate caretaking responses from their mothers. To both of them the converse of omnipotence was complete helplessness, blackness, and nothingness, whereas the opposite of omnipotence, in fact, is competence. Competence is rooted in the child's inborn capacity to elicit a caretaking response from mother: the child's smile makes others smile, the child's cry of hunger makes the mother lactate and present her nipple. This is not a fantasy, a delusion of omnipotence; this is the root of competence, effectance, and self-esteem. Both Mary and Mr. M. received intermittent love and care sufficient to keep them tied to people but not in a way that would enhance a feeling of confidence in the ability to elicit a necessary response from mother. Their mothers smiled only when they emerged from a depressive state and felt like smiling, not in response to the child's smile.

At least as important as a mother's empathic response to her child's signals is the capacity of the couple to tolerate and then repair the inevitable breaches in the empathic tie. Inevitable mismatches are reacted to by an "aversive response" in the infant (Lichtenberg 1989) or an angry response by the older child; with her love the ordinary mother can absorb and transform the anger into a dialectic for growth. In both Mary and Mr. M.'s cases these aversive, angry responses to mother's lack of empathy occasioned ever-increasing spirals of rage, guilt, and blame so that in the end these children were made to feel omnipotently responsible for mother's pain, helplessness, and inadequacy.

Mr. M. described what he called a typical pattern of interaction between himself and his mother. He would come from school and put his books on the dining room table. She would shout that he is driving her crazy with his deliberate messiness and now she has such a blinding headache she'll have to take to her bed, they will have to make do with leftovers, and it's all his fault. He tells her that her cooking is so lousy he prefers leftovers. She collapses in tears, wails that she is totally inadequate and might as well kill herself. Terrified and guilty, he tries to make amends. He apologizes and takes his books to his room; she follows him, working herself into a fit of rage as she tells him he won't get away with it that easily, wait till Father comes home. She recites a list of misdeeds that stretches back to infancy when he was, according to her, "a whiny, demanding brat." By this point, young Mr. M. would become enraged and ask her why she couldn't be as cheerful and resourceful as the mother of his best friend. This remark, he knew, would devastate his mother, but the particular occasion he was recalling was one in which she had found a way of overpowering his most powerful weapon. She responded by saying that he had not only ruined her life and driven her to depression, suicide, and hospitalization but he had also ruined her marriage and she and Father were discussing divorce. From that time forth he felt that he really could force them to divorce and then he would have to declare publicly which parent he wanted to be with.

Earlier, we described children, like Mary and Mr. M., for whom omnipotent fantasies serve to fill the space between the real and ideal mother. The fantasies are not aimed at enhancing the real capacities of self but at denying and transforming the pain and inadequacy of the mother–child relationship. Unable to elicit a smile with a smile, both Mary and Mr. M. identified with mother's pain and imagined a special, unique relationship based on shared unhappiness. Only they understood mother's pain and without them mother would be alone, unconnected to anyone. This omnipotent fantasy was a thread through the labyrinth of the analysis and emerged most clearly as the end of treatment approached. The analyst had learned from Mary that it is useless to challenge such fantasies directly, and Mr. M. illustrated this point by saying that the analyst might not realize the unique nature of the relationship since he was probably at the peak of his health and success, but one day the analyst would get old, sick, and enfeebled and then realize that no other patient can understand and empathize with his pain as Mr. M. can. Pain is the "open sesame" to this magical world, and through the experience of pain the omnipotent self can live on, a masochistic fantasy enshrined in the major religious systems.

Not to be omnipotent is, in Mr. M.'s words, "to be a piece of junk floating forever in the endless blackness of space." Any little action or interchange in treatment can be incorporated in an omnipotent fantasy to maintain power. So both Mary and Mr. M. needed to stay in analysis to confirm their omnipotence, and then as omnipotent figures they carried the awesome responsibility for the well-being and survival of the analyst. For them, the only way to terminate was to make themselves the victim of the analyst's sadistic attack. A forced termination would actualize their masochistic fantasies, relieve them of responsibility and guilt, and confirm their omnipotence, as we have seen repeatedly with adolescent patients who provoke their therapists to end the treatment (see Chapter 2).

How then can we bring about a growth-promoting end to a seemingly interminable situation? It would be simpleminded to propose a simple solution, especially in an analysis that extends beyond ten years. No one phase of development or set of conflicts carries the solution, and a multideterminant and multifunctional epigenetic approach, as attempted in our developmental study of masochism, is one we would recommend in order to capture the complexity of interminability. However, looked at from the vantage point of work with adolescents, the need to cling desperately to the fantasy of omnipotence stands out as an important factor in the interminability of analysis.

Our experience with adolescents such as Mary has convinced us that a major reason that termination is so frightening for adolescents is that these young people have not only the task of leaving infantile relationships with other people but must also take leave of the omnipotent self. We consider this to be a major task of adolescence; the avoidance of and regression from reality demands often seen in late adolescence relates to an inability to relinquish the omnipotent self and find pleasure and assurance in competent interactions with reality.

Mary, like everyone at the end of analysis, had to mourn the loss of the analyst as an object of desires from all levels of development and also as a real person who represented all her newfound accomplishments. But for Mary the most poignant and difficult task of mourning related to the loss of her omnipotent, grandiose self. This was the last battleground for her pathology and a final determinant for her conflict around pleasure. The experience of pleasure was a threat to her magical, omnipotent self. To have pleasure was to give up magical fantasies of control of the object and to interact in a real way with the real world. The real and the magical, the competent and omnipotent selves became competing systems. As she allowed herself ever-increasing feelings of pride and pleasure, as she felt the relief and comfort of being in the real world, her omnipotent self receded.

Mary began playing basketball in the evenings, which she had done as a child. One day, after she had talked of her professional plans and the way they could be integrated with being married and her wish to have children, she said that she had decided that she didn't need basketball anymore. It turned out that while playing basketball she imagined she was Magic

Johnson, that it was the final of the NBA championships, and she was putting in the winning basket. That night she dreamed of being in a championship game: *she was jumping high, getting every ball, and putting in slam dunks—but she was very small, and each time she put the ball through the hoop her whole body went through.* As she told the dream Mary began to cry. "That little person was wrong," she said, "that little person made me miserable all these years, but I'm going to miss her. I'm happier now but she could do things I can't do anymore. She could win championship games and she could cut her wrists."

In analysis the inability to relinquish omnipotent fantasies of control over others will become manifest in either premature termination or interminable analysis.

Mary and Mr. M. had not been able to shift the source of pleasure from omnipotent fantasy control of others to realistic achievements, as Robert did in the process of resolution of his Oedipus complex, nor had they achieved consolidation in the latency phase, as we saw in Erica's capacity to enjoy the exercise of her ego functions in the working alliance. Without these alternative sources of pleasure and self-esteem, Mary and Mr. M. coped with the reality demands of adolescence by recourse to pain-initiated omnipotent fantasies.

The fact that termination of adult cases may require prior work on the adolescent pattern of premature leave-taking has been noted, and now, with Mary's material in mind, we would suggest that the interminable analysis of adults such as Mr. M. involves the patient's having to do what was not done in adolescence—take leave of an omnipotent self, give up the impossible task of controlling people magically, and find pleasure in the exercise of real skills in a real world. Omnipotent fantasies will not be relinquished easily, if at all, but through analysis we can allow for the emergence of a competing system of pleasure and self-esteem alongside the omnipotent system based on pain, avoidance of reality, and delusion. As Mr. M. said near the end of his analysis, "It's my life—I have only one life and I have to choose. It's hard to admit that I was wrong, hard to admit that my pain buys me nothing but aspirin. But then I never knew that I had a choice, that I could choose to live a real life, with real pleasure."

14 TERMINATION: A CASE REPORT
OF THE END PHASE OF AN
"INTERMINABLE" ANALYSIS

Ralph Greenson, a most prolific and influential writer on psycho-analytic technique, never published anything on the subject of termination. This is not surprising since very little was written on that topic until after his death. Despite Freud's (1913) expressed interest in termination, neither he nor his early followers had much to say about termination as a phase of treatment. The view that a standard psychoanalysis has three phases, a beginning, a middle, and a termination phase, was first proposed by Glover (1955) and did not become widely accepted until the late 1970s. Writing in 1950, Annie Reich could find only two papers on termination and in 1966 Rangell commented on the scant literature. But in the past fifteen years a vast literature has appeared, providing psychoanalysts with many useful suggestions on how to get into, through, and beyond a termination phase. Our own prior work (Novick 1982b, 1988, 1990b), as well as reviews by Blum (1989), Firestein (1978, 1982), and the Shanes (1984) cover most of the issues. The current emphasis on termination as a subject of study and clinical mastery is in sharp contrast with the prewar cavalier attitude toward the ending of an analysis.

The intensity of focus may have reached a peak and there are indications that a counterreaction to the plethora of articles may be occurring, with some authors suggesting that the importance of the phase may be overemphasized (Blum 1989), that termination can occur without a formal setting of a date (Goldberg and Marcus 1985), that termination is a misleading word and does not reflect what actually occurs (Pedder 1988), and even that a termination phase in and of itself need not be differentiated since termination is an issue from the very start (De Simone Gaburri 1985).

Nevertheless, work continues on this phase of treatment, with follow-up research raising interesting questions about goals of treatment and the role of self-analysis in the post-termination phase (Kantrowitz et al. 1990). In prior work we have looked at the timing of termination and the factors related to premature or delayed termination (Novick 1982, 1988). An extension of this work has led to a focus on the problem of "interminable analysis."

In the previous chapter we discussed the issues of interminable analysis and described the pretermination phase resistance to choosing a date and entering a termination phase. We illustrated our formulations with the case of Mr. M., the 25-year-old single man who was referred because he was seen as too disturbed to be a training case. What follows is an account of the termination phase of his "interminable" analysis.

THE TERMINATION PHASE

Mr. M. was in his eleventh year of analysis. After a year of work on his resistances to picking a date he finally decided upon, and I (JN) agreed with, a date in the middle of a working week fourteen weeks away.

In the spirit of this "postmodern age," in which no one theory or school is predominant—in art, literature, or psychoanalysis —and in which a text can be read many different ways with infinite meanings that depend on the reader, I will present the material as follows. In the right hand column are Mr. M.'s words, quoted directly or summarized, and my interventions, which are in italics; the left hand column contains my running commentary, kept to a minimum to allow the reader space to respond.

WEEK 1

He can experience, acknowledge, and contain the ambivalence, a major achievement.

Tension had always been a signal for rigid defense or rage. He had the fantasy that life should be without tension. He now speaks of using tension to initiate work.

Idealization of analyst barely covering up disillusionment and anger.

After making a firm commitment to a finishing date, Mr. M. reported that everything continued to go well in his outside world of work and family. But coming here now felt like a disturbance. "I had seriously considered the idea," he said, "of selecting a date one month earlier, to get it over with. But I thought the tension is worth working with."
"My first thought about finishing is that I'm not you. The fantasy, as you know, is that I would become you and be able to free-associate and get in touch with my deeper feelings. I find that very hard. I need this kind of situation to be able to do it." As he became visibly tense and angry he said, "I can get to my anger but it's not smooth, efficient, effective." After some mumbling and more self blame he went on to say, "In the back of my mind are some blaming feelings. I'm blocked. I can tell

by the way I'm talking—stammering, substituting words."

I said that he was angry at himself and me for not making him into the perfect, magical person he imagines me to be.

The fantasy persists that I can give him the magical power.

"After all this time," he said, "shouldn't I leave as the bar mitzvah king, carried off on everybody's shoulders? If I don't, aren't you kicking me out?" The next day he reported a dream. "Some big guy was arguing against six other big guys. I was just watching. Suddenly the guy grabbed me and said I was a hostage and he said, 'this guy is weaker than you guys.' My first thought is that I am weak, I'm a coward, and I envy the big guys." He then related another dream of a bat coming at him. He is startled but doesn't panic. He related the dream to his recent experience of competently handling a bat in his house in contrast to a few years ago when he lost control and panicked when a bat flew in. He noted that he is not captive to his fears anymore but he can still work himself up into a panic.

I asked why he would do that here, with me.

"To explore the fear more fully but also to say 'I'm not in control.' Watch me fall apart and then you'll rescue me."

I said that the bat dream reflected his competent handling of a realistic danger, whereas the hostage dream reflected his fantasy that by becoming weak, helpless, and fearful he will magically become powerful and protect himself from a deeper terror.

I interpret the masochism but I'm also looking for the underlying trauma.

He responded, "My mother and me. We can beat the other four or six big guys—the other members of my family. And here is where it gets out of control. This is my strategy. I'm just standing there having a drink and then I become the decisive force. With me, this guy can fight off the other six. I'm the one who tips the balance. I make my mother or father strong. It's all magical and it gets out of control."

Here is a major theme of the termination phase. Through his masochism, that is, his active pursuit of weakness and victimization, he omnipotently restores the object and thus ensures his own omnipotence.

Week 2

He started the week by talking of his wish that during these last three months I would come up with one last trick that would fulfill his magical wishes. The wish was to be like me and he listed a set of idealized thoughts concerning my ability to do self-analysis easily, smoothly, without effort or obstacles.

Disillusionment is a necessary part of the termination process (Novick 1982, Pedder 1988).

I said that he was clinging to an idealized image because he was beginning to face his disillusionment with me and the analysis.

He said, "There's also the other idea. You work so hard, you don't have time for your kids." At first this seemed like a fleeting thought but he returned to this idea and then said, "Calling into question what you do calls into question what I do. We both like to work, we both like to make decisions, we both enjoy going to the office. But the parallels are with my dad. He would come home late at night. It's hard even now to get beyond the boundaries you set up. You're this dynamic guy who teaches, writes, does service for the community, that's great! That's how I felt about my dad. He's president. That's great! I'm so proud of you. But that covers up my feeling of

Still protecting me by sharing the sin.

The feeling of disillusionment is experienced,

pushed away,

and then returns.

being left out and deprived. But I don't feel that, I feel proud!" He paused, then in a sad voice he said, "I wanted more involvement, not a big, exciting dad. Even as I tell the story I'm falling short of criticizing my dad. The aura of perfection is there for protection. What I hang onto with my father is the feeling of excitement when I'm around him. But my memory is of not being around him. I suspect that it's not only that you're not perfect but that you're not perfect for me. My image of my father is a caricature. I don't really know my dad. With my mom or granny or [housekeeper] I had a gut to gut relationship, with my dad it was smile to smile—like with you." These thoughts were accompanied by a deep sadness and by anger. The anger emerged in the transference as he spoke of his feeling hurt and excluded by my vacations.

I said that he kept me perfect to protect me from his anger.

"Yes. I'm afraid my anger will destroy the happy family."

WEEK 3

Defenses still operative but no longer unconscious. Present, analytic past, and historical past are condensed in his words. He knows it and knows that I know.

"I'm not facing things—your deficiencies, dad's deficiencies. I'm overlooking things, idealizing things, compartmentalizing so the criticism flows to my mom. As a child I needed to do that. It was necessary to have happy, good parents. Now it's a protection for me. Protects me from my anger."

A shared poetic language of allusion and shared myths, part of a terminal phase.

"My goal in life, my mission, is to have a happy family. In that light my anger causes me nothing but trouble."

He then spoke, with deep feeling, of his memories of being yelled at by his mother. "I vowed never to do that to anyone," he said.

A further working through of trauma, an essential part of a termination phase. See the interesting work by Kinston and Cohen (1988) and Cohen and Kinston (1989) on the danger to the patient if the trauma is not worked through.

I said that the anger was overwhelming, devastating to the core.

He said, "My anger isn't shut off but I'm scared of it. I was yelled at daily and I would yell back. I know what it feels like to have someone berate and belittle you, and I know what it feels like to have anger as the biggest feeling I have—to have it consume me, to be totally out of control." He went on to say that his father was never angry, in fact he was afraid of anger.

I said that he had held back his anger at father and me for fear it would overwhelm us.

He responded, "I hope you never heard such fights. Real hate, real destruction—we would rip up the relationship. I wouldn't want to do that to you or my dad. I definitely did have the capability of responding with an all out attack. Vicious! I don't want you to see me this way. I don't know if you'd collapse, but you'd be terribly disappointed." The next day he forgot the check and he realized that he was angry at me. "Yesterday I said I would risk my own survival to avoid anger at you. Today I'm saying you're as bad as my mom, just as controlling and inflexible. My anger feels palpable, as real as if you had really done something I didn't like." He spoke with powerful feeling about getting what he had paid for but not what he had hoped for. He had

He is very angry but he can step back, observe, and work with feelings. In the termination phase the working alliance is at maximum efficiency.

given up so much to idealize me, to protect me from his anger, so he should now get his magical wishes fulfilled: "so now I'm not paying you, I'm getting back at you, pathetically."

WEEK 4

He started the week by trying to control his anger, his disappointment. He spoke in the conditional but soon the conditional became the present. What he could feel he did feel, and he was shaking with rage as he expressed his need to control and boss. "The moral is I can provide for myself but the wish is you'll do it for me. I'll break down at the bottom of the street. You'll see me and you'll come and give me the best pep talk I've ever heard. The rescue will make all the angry feelings go away. You're not the depressed, incompetent mother. Look at what you can do and you're doing it for me."

Parental incompetence as a source of trauma, which makes the disillusionment of the termination phase extremely difficult to face.

I said that his anger and his wish to build me up through his own failure follows his disillusionment.

Though critical, this is actually a subtle form of fantasy that I really can give him what he needs, and that through his masochistic presentation he can force me to do so.

"I was just thinking how I needed feedback." He continued to complain about the lack of feedback, that I could give him more and that the analyst who first interviewed him did give him more feedback. Later he returned to what he perceived as my imperfections. "Seeing your imperfections derails me. You work too hard. I'm deeply ashamed, I'm afraid to invite my friends home. I'm responsible for how you are. We're back into my feelings of shame and responsibility. Why can't I accept your imperfection? So you're not Mickey Mantle or Willie Mays—so what?"

I said he might be afraid that my imperfection would make him so angry he would ruin over ten years of work. How hard it is for him to fuse imperfections with the good things.

WEEK 5

He continued to focus on his struggle over facing my incompetence. He said, "I don't have to deny my mother's incompetence but I have to protect you and my dad." He spent some time talking about his agreeing to tape a program for his father. It made him furious that his father couldn't do it himself. He wanted to deny his disappointment and rage, or become totally incompetent himself.

I said that this was a struggle he was now having with his feelings about me.

During termination the analyst's associations are more likely to be right on target and can be shared easily.

I was reminded of a fantasy he had reported a number of years before, when on passing my office during a vacation he imagined he would see me on the roof with power tools.

I told him my association and suggested that separation seemed to intensify his need to protect me.

During termination old dreams or fantasies are reworked with new elements added, sometimes, as in this case, memories of reality events.

He recalled that fantasy and the work we had done especially in regard to the sexual associations and his feeling excluded from my "powerful sexuality activities." But now that fantasy had a concrete reference to his father's inadequacy. He said "that image reminds me that as a kid I noticed that my father couldn't hammer a nail or use any tool. He couldn't make

toast or coffee. My mother's incompetence made my father
look good. That's what I do. I
build you and my dad up by
being incompetent."

WEEK 6

Mother's failure was a theme
throughout analysis; father's
failure was not fully experienced until termination phase
work focused on disillusionment with analyst.

He continued to talk about his
father's incompetence, he had
never seen it so clearly. For
years he had wondered why his
father had stayed with his
mother and he now understood
that his father needed his
mother in order to feel superior. He went on to speak of a
seemingly unrelated event,
when a friend had needed the
name of a therapist and he had
been too ashamed to give him
mine.

*I asked him to associate to why
he felt shame.*

His masochism was understood
throughout as including elements of identification with
his "damaged and masochistic
mother" and receptive feminine longings for his father. In
the end phase transference it

His first thought was shame to
reveal that he was seeing a
therapist, then that his fantasy
that we have the "perfect happy
relationship" would be exposed
and shown to be false and with
this I would be exposed as an
"incompetent fraud." He went
on "so I must believe that if I

becomes emotionally clear to him that his "feminine masochism" is part of an omnipotent fantasy of denying and repairing the father's failure.

Reenactments of a central developmental trauma probably occur throughout treatment, but the terminal phase allows the analyst the possibility of quickly recognizing and verbalizing transference-countertransference reenactments of what may be a developmental trauma.

The analyst cannot plan it, it just happens, but the analyst can learn to expect it and even welcome it as an important means for working through during the terminal phase. See Sandler's (1976) concept of role responsiveness as related to the process I am describing.

expose you I would destroy you so I protect you by being incompetent, by fumbling and bumbling. I become weak, a failure, a woman, a homosexual who takes it up the butt so you can feel superior."

Then there occurred one of those split second reenactments of a central transference countertransference drama. The next session I started to hand him my yearly vacation schedule. I hesitated when I realized he did not need it and I asked if he wanted it. He asked, "How far does it extend?" and I told him. The whole exchange took 10 seconds yet he immediately saw that I had made an error. There was no need to give him a vacation schedule as he was stopping in seven weeks. As he said, either I had forgotten or I did not want him to finish. But in a split second he asked how far the vacation schedule extends. By now, after ten years of analysis, he knew that the schedule extended for a full year and, furthermore, the question was irrelevant since he knew that he was finishing before any usual vacation date. He spent the next two sessions struggling with intense feelings of sadistic excitement and power, opposed by an equally intense wish to protect me by making himself the confused person who has to be rescued by me.

I noted that what he had presented as a possibility was something now deeply felt in the relationship. He had seen my incompetence and could feel the excitement and the wish to protect me.

He recalled the time he broke down in college and had to return home. He said "the excited wish to devastate can take secret paths. I broke down, came home, and my parents had to rescue me but my breakdown devastated my parents."

I said that his wish to break down was also a wish to devastate me.

He said, "If I've sacrificed so much of my life for you and you're still not perfect then I have a right to rant and rave and devastate you."

WEEK 7

A week during which he could experience a forward surge in all areas, a week of integration, one in which he reported feeling "really good about my life, all of it: my work, my wife, my child."

In the sessions he continued to work on the theme of being able to destroy me by exposing my incompetence and the wish to protect me by becoming the damaged woman. He took it further through a piece of a dream in which a woman asks him to speak at a seminar.

I interpreted his joining the woman to attack me, his father.

The traumatic experience of seeing the analyst's incompetence can now be put into words and worked through. His word "catastrophe" during terminal phase work alerts us to the fact that termination can often result in failure, or worse (Novick 1982). Cohen and Kinston (1989) review the work on catastrophe and termination. They suggest that "catastrophe usually means that the

He said that his mother could build up his father but she also took every opportunity to tear him down. "We're getting close," he said. "Seeing my mother nuts is bad. Having her attack me is horrible but to see her tear my father apart is catastrophe. So I make myself the target to preserve my family, preserve you." The price he paid for clinging to his omnipotent fantasy was central to our trauma of the patient's life is being directly relived . . . [this] may lead to growth or it may lead to a personal catastrophe such as illness, accident, death" (Cohen and Kinston 1989, p. 5).

An example of what Greenson called "working through"—something we would expect in the termination phase.

Sometimes the power of positive parental feelings is the only force which can stand up to the self protective delusion of the omnipotent system.

pretermination work and had enabled him to enter into a terminal phase. This week he saw clearly how it could and did affect his relationship with his baby boy. At a play group his baby was involved in something other than what the teacher wanted and Mr. M. felt disappointed with his baby, began to get angry, and then withdraw. He suddenly connected this sequence with how he reacted to me when I disappointed him and he realized his anger was due to the fact that he felt he could not magically control the baby and make him do his every bidding.

Later in the week as he spoke again of ending analysis and what he thinks he will lose, he said, "I'll lose the magic, my fantasy that I can and should control your life. Like my breakdown in college and return home, there's a powerful pull back to the world of magic where I am king, I control everyone's life. It's quick, easy, and exciting. But now I can see that the price includes my baby's life for he too has to become a willing subject."

WEEK 8

His wife had decided to return to work and put the 6-month-old baby in day care. His first response was to think that his boy would feel, as he still feels, rage at parents for finding something else more important than being with him. He kept calling his reactions "neurotic" and said that this was the price of clinging to magic. He was afraid that he wouldn't face reality and do what is right for everyone.

It is becoming clear that the analytic method has become part of his masochistic perversion. At this point I know it but I am still pulled in by my own counterreaction, my need to rescue the baby.

I said that calling his reactions neurotic left him helpless and in need of rescue. I then reminded him that he had said that they were introducing a new relationship in the baby's life.

"Did I say that? I didn't think of that but only of my baby's anger. The reality then is my jealousy, my being excluded. I can't stand people being separate. This is my neurosis."

I said that he is again dismissing his feelings as neurotic and so avoids looking at reality.

The next day he said, "I see that I have a choice. This 'neurotic' stuff is a defense against being a real person. Usually I feel I can't help it, but yesterday I saw I had a choice. You were saying that when I act neurotic I can use that as a signal that I'm staying away from being real and seeing things realistically. I have a choice! I can be neurotic and that's a choice or I can be competent and realistic. But I have a fear that I can't do it without you."

I said that last week he had said he would give up the magic; this week he is showing us he won't. Being neurotic is his way of being helpless and getting me to rescue him. But why? So that he doesn't have to look at me or his wife realistically. Why did I give him the schedule? Why does his wife want to change her relationship with the baby?

"As long as I keep things blurred about me, I don't have to look closely at you," he said. "You ask the price. The price is the same as the method. I

play dumb and I become dumb.
I give up the good feeling of
clear insight."

WEEK 9

During the first part of the week
he seemed overwhelmed by his
feelings. At the same time he
could observe and report his
reactions. For example, he said,
"I'm losing it. I'm mad without
justification. I'm angry but I'm
not using it as a signal. I'm depressed, angry, feeling overwhelmed. I don't want to deal
with this, it's too much. I'm not
being honest with myself."

*I again focused on his denial of
something he perceived.*

He shouted, "Why does she
want to go back to work?" The
next day he could tell her that
he was angry and disappointed
but he quickly assumed the
blame by talking of his neurosis, his high expectations of
motherhood.

*I reminded him that he had said
her decision to return to work,
"made no rational sense."*

"I do blur things," he said. "The point is I don't think it makes sense but she does." He again fell into helpless despair but then could say, "I know there's something I'm avoiding." Finally he told me that the baby had not settled into a sleep pattern and his wife was up every 2 or 3 hours to feed him. It was clear that she felt helpless, unsupported by Mr. M., and enraged at both him and the baby; she wanted to return to work in order to run away from her own feeling of failure. This was so close to his image of his incompetent mother that he was terrified of facing it. Having now done so, he could use what he had gained over the years to understand the situation and put his understanding into action.

Once again he had been rescued by the analyst.

He spoke to his wife, together they agreed on a plan for helping the baby, and within two nights the baby was sleeping through the night and the crisis was over.

I wondered what he was denying about me.

"The fact is I've been trying to convince you to change your mind, to see that I'm not ready. But the fact is, you're going to let me go. My magic won't work."

That's about you, I said, what about me.

"I'm not sure. The big issue now for me is staying in contact afterwards. I have little boy insecure feelings, you won't want to hear from me."

I wondered what kind of person I'd be to do that.

He said, "A bad person, cold and uncaring."

WEEK 10

The baby continued to sleep through the night and Mr. M. and his wife were feeling back together again. He was proud of his baby but also proud of the work he had done. He said, "I saw a side of my wife I don't like to see so I gave up and forgot that I had ever seen it. In that way I can deny my mother was ever mean or my wife is ever mean."

I wondered if he had allowed the crisis to build up so that he could avoid feelings about leaving.

"I'll miss you," he said.

"Yes, but you're afraid I won't miss you." I answered.

The helpless feeling of being unloved covered up by the omnipotent fantasy defense.

The link to resistance to separating/terminating.

He said, "That's a chilling thought. Most painful is the idea that all these years you didn't like me, you tolerated me. It feels like a new idea. What's new is the thought that my mother was looking forward to my going. I always emphasized how devastated she would be if I left her but it's not a big jump to see the reverse, that my mom not only didn't want kids, couldn't cope with kids, she was eager to get rid of me. I have the fantasy of overhearing you saying to your wife that you're glad I'm going, glad to be rid of me. Why didn't I want to leave? The answer is clear now. Leaving is the moment of truth. If I have an inkling that you want me out of here, it will be seen

He is now focusing on contact after termination. It sounds reasonable but, in addition, it is a fall-back position for the need to hang on to the omnipotent fantasy of control.

when I leave. But I also want to keep in touch. You're an important person to me. Do you reciprocate?"

WEEK 11

He started the week by noting that all the pressing things were cleared out and he could now concentrate on his analysis. "Only four weeks left. I feel numb." He proceeded to talk of his sadness and pain, and he went over the realization of last week that "leaving is the moment of truth."

I wondered if he was avoiding looking at the feeling that analysis had not fulfilled his expectations.

He said that he still expected that he should leave without conflicts. He returned, however, to the "pressing" question of keeping in touch after therapy. "I wonder about how often I should call you and would I be charged? I imagine I would be, especially if I did it on a regular basis. Let's say 6

He is not aware as yet that he is trying to enact a fantasy. Friday evening refers to a dream he had two years earlier in which he meets me when I'm visiting his hometown and he invites me home for a Friday meal. Behind the hospitality was hostile fantasy of control of my life.

o'clock on a Friday evening." He went on to say that he always had difficulty leaving and that the struggle was to put together the old stuff and the new. How could he go to college and still maintain relations with his family? "I need rules," he said. "I need a model for separating. I never had a clean, good feeling kind of break." As he noticed that he was feeling angry and demanding he said, "I have to be careful I don't turn this into a fantasy that I can have all this free time and money and still have my analysis."

I asked what came to mind about "6 o'clock Friday evening."

He responded "You light the candles. It's the old analogue of keeping you trapped. Oh yes! The dream of [my home town]— you thought you could get rid of me. Well you haven't. I'll show you. I'll invite you home for dinner. I'll break down and call you on Friday night and keep you under my control and take you away from your family and going out." He paused,

The use of vivid images and metaphors is often a feature of the termination phase and is indicative of the increased creativity due to analytic work. At the start of his analysis his thoughts were almost concrete and unimaginative and his words were stilted and colorless.

In Chapter 3 we noted the many resistances to relinquishing the omnipotent system and living in the world of realistic, competent interactions. Mr. M. illustrates the humiliation and feared helplessness when making such a move.

sighed, and said, "Clearly there's more to separation than phone calls. It's one dot in the whole picture but I'm closing in on it so it occupies the whole space. What am I blotting out?" He spoke of the lifting of internal constraints, the new freedom, and the new opportunities. As yet he doesn't feel the excitement, he wondered why. What he feels now is that it is a "humbling, humiliating feeling. The opportunities were always there. Most people enjoy the freedom. If I take this step I want to be the first! I feel as if I'm going into a different country and all my tricks aren't going to work in this new land. I need to be the first, to be the king, but in this new land I feel my identity blotted out. The same image of a dot of paint on a canvas. My feeling is that I'm a very special person but if I give up the magic then I'm afraid I'll become this vanilla guy disappearing among the million dots. This is clear when you compare me with my sister. Strip away my grandiosity and she can claim more attention than I can. What distinguishes me is that I'm the king, I'm the

victim, and I am angry. I'm not
engaging or attractive. I've established relationships by distortion, guilt inducement,
tricks, and manipulation. I'm
giving up a system. Like a great
basketball player switching to
soccer. I want to play soccer but
with basketball rules."

This interpretation is in the
nature of a "mop up" operation, returning to deal with remaining pockets of resistance,
a reworking of conflicts typical
of end phase analytic work. If
excitement remains exclusive to
the magical system then there
is little to induce a person to
live in dull reality.

*I noted that he had said that he
doesn't feel excited about ending or the opportunities in store.
I suggested that excitement, for
him, belongs to the magic system, an indication that the
magic system is at work.*

"Yes," he said. "Still, for me,
excitement has to do with something dropping out of the sky—
unexpected, dramatic."

*I suggested that his wish to keep
in touch might also be a wish
to keep alive the hope of experiencing the excitement of having all his wishes granted.*

His wish for closeness is a derivative of his sadomasochistic
wish to be the woman who sub-
mits to me and thus controls
me and takes all my power. As

"I never thought of that," he
said. "For me it's a feeling of
closeness, camaraderie. But
there is something in what you
say. There is a feeling that if I
break contact I'll be out there

a school child he had a day dream of sitting atop a flag pole with Indian princesses dancing around him. The fantasy was worked over from all angles and reference to it denoted the complex masochistic fantasy with all its determinants and functions.

working for what I want. What is lost is the aura of possibility. Without you I'll be left with what I am."

WEEK 12

He started the week by talking of "trade-offs," what he imagines he gains and what in fact he loses by living in his magical system. He said, "I always felt it would take tremendous effort to live by reality, but the other night I realized that it's much easier to live in reality, to see what I can and what I cannot control and not waste my life trying to control what I can't." He spoke again of the "trade-offs," of the cost.

During the termination phase it gradually became clear that his sado-masochistic stance had moved from the physical (pain, tension, heart attack, going blind) to the emotional (trapped in feelings of intense anger, or envy, or fear) to ego functions (figuring things out, remember-

I said that now we can't avoid seeing that the major cost is what he does to his mind in order to retain the fantasy that he can get me to rescue him with my magical powers. I said that in the recent work on his baby's sleep problem, I had merely repeated what he had

ing, differentiating, analyzing).
The fantasy of rescue became
realized when I responded to
his confusion by acting as his
memory, reminding him of
what he had said or what we
had understood at some earlier
time. It is easy and tempting to
be "brilliant" during the end
phase and the clue to my collusion was the pleasure I had in
these "brilliant rescues."

Interpretation of his rescue fantasies was effective for both patient and analyst.

*told me but he had experienced
my words as brilliant insights
and miraculous solutions.*

He said, "This is the cost. I give
up my ability to think and work
things out. I let you screw me
in the butt, mock me, and I kid
myself into thinking it's exciting. You did it! You dropped
from the sky and solved my
problem. What I do pales in
comparison."

This took place in the middle
of the week and from this point
there was a surge of hard work
in the sessions and effective action outside. I had not planned
to do so, but it felt right to remain silent for the rest of the
week, in fact till the end of the
analysis, which was three weeks
away.

WEEK 13

He had been thinking of the
"flag pole" fantasy and that behind that conscious day dream
was a secret fantasy of having
sex without growing up. "What,"
he wondered, "is my secret
fantasy about you? The goal
of analysis was to become you.

In the omnipotent magic system people are never lost and so mourning need never occur.

An attempt to abort the mourning process by moving back into the omnipotent system. Pain, deprivation, and justified anger open the doors to the world of fantasied hostile control over others.

One of the signs of being "on the path of progressive development." The regressive pull of the omnipotent system has lessened, the progressive pull of the competent, reality system has increased, a sign we look for when considering termination.

But now, there is a glimmer of a feeling that I can leave here and have learned from you but I'll become me. The hope is, I can leave here and recall you as human size and not a billboard size man, to leave here and not want to become you without feeling I'm rejecting you. I don't need to be you. I can incorporate things but I'm not you. I don't want to be you." He sighed and after a few moments of silence said sadly, "but then I'm faced with leaving, with the end. I can feel the mourning setting in. I can imagine the end. I thought of it last night and felt a real heartfelt missing of you and what I had here." This was followed by an attempt to convince us that he cannot do without me. "The thing I get here," he said, "is confirmation. I find that so important." He was on the verge of complaining about my lack of "feedback." He said, "You haven't said anything for over a week. It's less hard. That's not what I wanted to say. Why the slip? I wanted to say it's harder if you don't summarize, confirm. But I carry it too far and make your comments more impor-

(See Chapter 12 for further discussion of criteria for termination.)

tant than doing it myself." He brightened, his voice was firm, and he said, "There's excitement in finishing, in being challenged and rising to the occasion. I can feel it. There's excitement in the idea that I'll be worthy of dealing with life's problems. I now know when something feels right. It would be tremendous to have the validation in myself." He said that he realized that what I was doing was allowing him to find his own feelings about ending. "This is my leaving," he said. "It doesn't affect us the same. You remain the analyst, I become someone who does his own analysis. I'm going to take the last day off from work, make it a special day. No need for you to do that." Silence, then in a subdued tone he said, "But I want to wait for you. I want you to join me and if you don't I'll think that my leaving is not important. Reminds me of my first dream. I'm running the race, way out in front. I stop. I've gone too far. I have to wait for the others to catch up. We've talked about this dream many times but I have to recognize this desire. It's a

Reconstructed from his material and then confirmed. But this had happened at 2½; he is referring to what Freud (1918) called "deferred action" and Greenacre (1950) called the latency trauma.

contrived desire. I don't need you to validate the importance of the last day. I feel, honest to God, that there's something in me from way back that knows from inside what's right. I can recall a "show and tell" in kindergarten. The other kids brought toys and dolls to show and I just stood up and told everyone what I had planned to do after school. I had no hesitation in speaking out and saying what I wanted. Somehow this got overlaid by your feelings, my parents' feelings. My feelings had to be covered up. Another example, one we've talked about, a baby is born dead and everyone is sad and I'm happy. This is my leaving, it's special for me." Again he began to sputter, mumble, lose his train of thought, and then he spoke of how he doesn't "beat himself up" as much as he used to. I felt the urge to speak and confirm his hints that beating represented the masochistic fantasy that through pain he could keep the object. However, I remained silent and he rescued himself. He said, "There's a good feeling creeping back in," and he

Termination is usually a time of review.

again recalled the "show and tell" incident in kindergarten. He then talked of this being the last weekend and he reviewed the importance of weekends and vacations through the course of analysis.

Week 14

Something I encourage people to do. The first date they choose is often one that allows them to deny the significance of the ending. The first date he had chosen was a Friday and his mother's birthday.

This was the last week, a short week since three months ago he had decided to end on a Wednesday so that the ending would stand on its own and not be just like another weekend.

He started the week by talking of a television interview with the 80-year-old mother of a 60-year-old sports celebrity. The mother said that she worries that her son will catch cold. He wondered about himself and his child, his parents, and me. He said, "When my baby is 40, I'll be able to let him go, I'll know that he can take care of himself and I can take care of myself. I'll be sad when my parents die but I can take care of myself. As a dad I can let go and I've reached a point where I can let myself go. So I'm letting go of you and you can let go of me.

The thought of his parents dying used to be cause for a major panic.

At the end one not only relinquishes the object but, more important, an image of the self as the omnipotent controller of objects (Chapter 12, this volume).

It's a letting go of the relationship but also a letting go of the hope that on the eve of the last session something magical will happen. I know that—take away the pretense, there is excitement and freedom. But something keeps nagging at me. The idea of Respect. It's more respectful to feel that there is something more important than waking up every day and saying, 'it's my day'; something more important than my needs. There is US to consider, we will do it together, that is my mistake. Letting go of you is letting go of this fantasy that I'm not in charge of me but I'm in charge of the world as I conceive it: you, my sister, my wife and baby. I'm on the verge of having a life that is mine. I don't know how many years I've said it but I know I can work toward that, though I'm not there yet. I'm excited but I want to say, 'Forgive me for being glad for all I've accomplished, forgive me for being less attentive to you than I should be.' Again the idea from last week, it's my analysis and finishing is mine. Whatever feelings you have are different than mine. I can grieve, or be excited, or both. This kind of excitement and freedom keeps poking up but gets covered by clumsy, distorted, mumbled thoughts that there is a higher purpose, doing something for US. It's a crock, but these clumsy arguments carry a lot of force. I want them to carry force. All this reality stuff is not right. I want to take the easy route, the kingly route, which, again, gets me into trouble." He then told me that he had thought about a gift for me, that he has a wish to thank me, that so much has changed in his life, and that he wanted me to know that he was grateful for my patience, for my confidence in him when he didn't have any himself, and for my support and judgment. He then tried and quickly saw his repeated attempts to feel that in losing me he was losing something he could never do for himself, could never replace with others, in fact something magical. He was left then with the loss of me as a separate person who had been very important but whom he had now outgrown. "I'm just sad," he said.

As part of treatment, important human needs to communicate, share, and be understood are released and experienced with the analyst. It is important that during termination the person can realize that these needs can and should be gratified with others (Bergmann 1988, Novick 1990b).

Fantasies of bringing a gift at the last session are common (Calef and Weinshel 1983). Actually bringing a gift is seldom reported as occurring, though it is not unusual in work with children. He is the only one of my adult patients to have done so.

He can now experience the excitement and contain the ambivalence.

On the last day of a ten-year plus analysis the patient is still

"I can take away the memories and feelings of accomplishment but I'm sad. You're a friend, you won't be there for me. I feel close and part of feeling close is wanting to be around. But, that doesn't mean I can't replace that, in part." He left in tears.

On the last day he brought a gift, a beautiful sweater, with a card thanking me for helping him find his own way.

I thanked him but said nothing regarding the meaning of the gift. He said, "I feel all choked up. I've tried in the last few weeks to tell you how appreciative I am, I didn't want my feelings to pile up." He began to cry and then spoke of his gratitude to his wife and to his parents for their support. "I'm sad and I'm excited," he said. "It's a beginning as well as end." Again, he cried and said, "Sad seems to be the bigger feeling at the moment." He went on, "I'm lying here expecting my feelings to come gushing out but there's been a lot of work preparing for this day. I dreamt last night that one of the big guys in my field on the couch, still bringing dreams and using his self analytic skills. He is continuing to do analysis to the very end. Many analysts vary the technique at the end but the material of this case suggests that it is advisable to analyze to the very end.

Review of the shared analytic history is a frequent occurrence during the termination phase and is part of the mourning process.

The gift can and does have multiple meanings but just as the patient continues to work after the analysis is terminated so too can the analyst keep wondering and learning. The gift represents something that words alone could not encompass. It felt like an enactment

was impressed with an impromptu remark I made at a conference. It was a good feeling. My work felt good to me and was judged good by others. That's the way I feel here. I feel good about what I've accomplished and I think you feel good too. But I won't stop there, I still have a lot of work to do. I know my wish to hang on to my delusions and fantasies, but I also know the good feeling of knowing what I've really accomplished and that the choices are mine. The idea that somehow the great insight will occur has passed. It's a silly idea and if a great insight should occur it would mean I was not ready to leave." He went on to recall our first meeting and the many life events he had shared with me. He wondered again about keeping in touch, especially to tell me of further major events. He then spoke of the gift, the fact that it was uncalled for and was a "drop in the bucket" compared to all the money he had paid over the years. He realized that there were many motives, some of them magical but, "I had fun looking for the sweater. You of his deepest wish and fear, to be intimate yet separate. The sweater was my size, color, and style and not his.

Again this points to the importance of deidealization and disillusion before the working alliance can be transformed into a self analytic function.

Some things cannot be worked through until the termination phase but there may also be many things that cannot be worked through until the analysis is over.

know I hate shopping but I really wanted to do it, my heart was in it. I feel sad now, but it's a warm sad." He spoke again of his joyful anticipation of the next phase of his life and then said, "One of the things I've been thinking about is the way I used to come down on myself for not doing analysis by myself as well as I did it with you. But analysis is work! It's not easy. You're skilled and trained so you could give those turns and prompts, which are important. It was a great relief to realize I wasn't a failure for needing your skills and now these are skills I can take with me." He then turned his thoughts to the analytic work he will carry on alone after termination. "I feel the next few days and weeks I'll understand better what leaving means. I think it's going to be possible to be running my own life when I'm away from here. Being here I'm always trying to compromise. Leaving here is the moment of truth. It's going to college only this time I'm prepared and I'll take advantage of my being on my own. I'll seize the responsibility, something I can't do

He can now accept the reality and limits of psychoanalysis.

Again, the importance of finding someone else to meet those paraverbal aspects of the analytic situation, the safety, holding, containing, sharing, supporting, reflecting.

Erna Furman (1982) quotes Anna Freud as saying that "a mother's job is to be there to be left." In her beautiful paper Furman looks at the mother's ability to be left throughout the course of development. Mr. M. alerts us to the possibility that the analyst's job too is to be there to be left.

while I'm here. All the talking and working things through won't help if I'm here waiting for miracles."

He spoke again of our having shared his deepest moments, how much he relied on my presence, and then said, "I've not thought about a different support system for myself. My wife is the person I can now share things with but I've been so wrapped up here that I've let things slide. I would like someone I could lean on. I'm thinking of friends where the potential of a warm, meaningful relationship is possible. It'll take work but worthwhile work."

"There's one request," he said. "You don't have to respond. If you move, I'd like to know. I'd like to know how to get in touch with you. It's easier to hold on to what I've got from here knowing I could get in touch. Maybe I'll get to the point where I don't need that, but I feel I need it now." It was near the end of the hour, he sighed and said, "It's like saying goodbye to a grandparent who is dying. This is like a death.

This relationship will be no more. I'm left with memories."

Termination experienced as death has been mentioned in the literature (Stern 1968, Laforgue 1934). Here it seems to be closely related to accepting reality, including our helplessness in relation to death.

I said, "It's time to end."

He got off the couch, shook my hand, and at the door turned to look at me. He smiled, tears running down his face, and said, "Thanks."

I too was very moved.

CONCLUSION

There has been relatively little written on the topic of interminable analysis despite the fact that Freud's case of the Wolf Man (1918) would fall into that category. Difficulty with the Wolf Man was probably one of the motivations for Freud's rather pessimistic paper, "Analysis terminable and interminable" (1937). The fiftieth anniversary of the publication of that paper was commemorated at the 1987 International Psychoanalytic Congress in Montreal and a number of articles appeared (Anzieu 1987, Berenstein 1987, Blum 1987, Burgner 1988) that addressed some of the pertinent issues and questions. First, it is important to recognize that many analysts are reluctant to admit that they have cases that have been in analysis for over ten years. They may be afraid of being accused of fostering a pathological dependence; at a time when there is a great deal of professional and third party pressure to shorten therapy, to admit openly that a course of four to five times per week psychoanalysis can last for over ten years might be considered by some professional suicide. It would confirm the worst fears of most people looking for a therapist—adding substance to the wishes of insurance companies who want to deny payment for psychoanalysis—and it would be a windfall for anti-analytic mental health professionals who offer a smorgasbord of fast, painless cures. In 1987, *New York* magazine published an article entitled "Prisoners of Psychotherapy" and the cover had a photograph of a woman tied by thick ropes to the couch.

It is our impression that there are many long-term (over ten years) psychoanalytic cases out there; perhaps this report may encourage others to share their material. Patients like Mr. M. often bring about a premature termination as part of the sadomasochistic transference and the accompanying negative therapeutic reaction (Asch 1976) or negative therapeutic motivation (see Chapter 12). We need reports of long-term cases to differentiate among the many factors involved.

There are patients who seem to respond well to treatment but relapse soon after termination. The Wolf Man was one such case (Freud 1937) and the case used by Greenson (1965) to illustrate difficulties in working through is another. Perhaps closer attention to termination issues and criteria would be helpful. Some of these are suggested in Greenson's paper and in the work of Cohen and Kinston (1990) and Kinston and Cohen (1989) whose formulations are especially relevant to cases that break down or relapse after treatment. There are evidently patients who can never terminate, where therapy of some sort will be needed throughout life. Perhaps, if we could accurately isolate those who fall into this category, we could apply the method of "intermittent analysis" recommended by Mahler and others for use with children (Kramer and Byerly 1978). These cases could then be of briefer duration, with the expectation that analysis will resume in the future and intermittently for many years.

There are also a large number of patients who reach a stalemate after making substantial progress. The stalemate may be due to intense resistance in the patient and/or countertransference issues and technical limitations in the therapist. Mr. M. might be viewed as such a case, for by his eighth year he was, by most criteria, ready to stop. He was happily married, planning a family, and successful in his career. There are many analysts who would have suggested termination at this point and picked a date (Brenner 1976). Had I done so, the analysis could have ended two years earlier. There are many who might claim that my leaving the decision to the patient is a technical error that unnecessarily prolonged the length of treatment. In Chapter 13 we described Mr. M.'s attempt to have the analyst choose the date and his subsequent reactions when his attempt failed. Having him take responsibility for setting the date allowed for the clear emergence of his omnipotent fantasy. We would suggest that Mr. M. falls into the category of patients who take a long time to change and to work through conflicts and trauma, especially around issues of independence, change, separation, and termination. Such patients need time and the analyst must have patience and trust. When Freud first turned his attention to the problem of working through he said, "This working through of the resistances in practice may turn out to be an arduous task for the subject of the analysis, and a trial of patience of the analyst" (1914, p. 155). His recommendations to the analyst apply to the pace of material of people like Mr. M. "The doctor has nothing else to do than to wait and let things take their course, a course which cannot be avoided nor always hastened" (p. 155).

After over ten years of analysis what is left to do during the terminal phase? Having accomplished so much and having finally accepted that the analysis must end, would it be preferable to avoid prolonging the agony and end it quickly, as was once the practice, perhaps at the long summer break, with a handshake and a glint in the eye indicating that it is all over (Gardiner 1983)? We think Mr. M.'s material illustrates the importance of the terminal phase regardless of the time spent before it. If the timing is right (Novick 1988), if the phase is started not when the goals of analysis have been achieved but when progressive forces are in the ascendant (Chapter 12), then the terminal phase can be a most stimulating and fruitful period of work for both analyst and patient. As illustrated by Mr. M.'s material, the reality of an ending date intensifies and revives conflicts and anxieties. At the same time the working alliance is at peak efficiency and both analyst and patient have much more available to resolve conflicts and work through potentially traumatic events. The termination phase is a time when the analytic achievements can be seen and tested. A large range of affects can be experienced, owned, and used as a guide and spur to further action. Affects such as disappointment, disillusionment, and sadness are particularly intense during this phase and detailed work on defenses against and working through of these affects allows the patient to endure and grow from the experience. In particular a mourning process sets in, during which the working alliance can be internalized as a self analytic function, the crowning achievement of the analysis and the main outcome of the work done during the terminal phase of treatment.

15 SADOMASOCHISM AND THE THERAPEUTIC ALLIANCE: IMPLICATION FOR CLINICAL TECHNIQUE*

In our work with severely disturbed children, adolescents, and adults, and our infant and toddler observations, we have been exploring sadomasochism, the beating fantasy as its essence, and externalization as a major mechanism in its development and functioning. In working with the sadomasochism of our patients we found, as have others from Freud on (Freud 1909, 1940, Meyers 1988), that the analyses were long and arduous because of the self-destructive character of the pathology, its roots at every level of development, and the intense countertransference reactions it evoked. This led us to wonder about the nature of the resistance. In an earlier discussion of these problems we noted that while we find derivatives of each phase in sado-masochistic patients, there is a delusion of omnipotence that infuses the patients' past and current functioning like a thread linking knots of fixation points at oral, anal, and phallic phases (see Chapter 3).

---

*First presented at the New York Freudian Society, Washington, DC, October 8, 1994.

Up to that point we had more or less accepted and worked with the classical formulation of the development of omnipotence and its role in normality and pathology as described by Freud and Ferenczi (Ferenczi 1913, Freud 1911, 1915, 1917). Their view was that the child is born feeling omnipotent and only gradually, and reluctantly, under the impact of failure of the omnipotent system, turns to and accepts reality. In the course of our work on sadomasochism we have come to feel that there are inherent difficulties in the traditional formulation, which lead us to describe the development of omnipotence rather differently.

Looking at the development of the delusion of omnipotence in this new way implies a separate line of pathological development, in contrast to the development of normal systems of self-esteem regulation based on an economy of pleasure from competence at each phase. We have described two systems of self-esteem regulation, the competent and the omnipotent. We think that these are aspects of distinct pathways of development that may be traced through the life span, helping us to understand the overdetermination of pathology at any point in development.

This is different from the formulation that pathology represents a solution to conflict that involves regression to an earlier normal state. The traditional approach has been to view pathology as either an exaggeration of normal traits or the persistence or reemergence of normal infantile behavior in a later phase when it is no longer appropriate. Many widely accepted terms and concepts—the symbiotic phase, infantile omnipotence, the paranoid and depressive positions, the anal-sadistic phase, normal feminine masochism, adolescence as a normal phase of disturbance—exemplify this view of pathology. To generalize from pathology to normality can be seen as an epistemological stance that has proven its value, but, like all positions, it too has its drawbacks. Recently we noted that such generalizations now may prove to be more of a burden in our work than an aid (deVito, Novick, and Novick 1994).

In this chapter we explore the possibility that there are two distinct paths of development, two distinct types of solutions to conflict, and we consider the implications of thinking in this way for working with sadomasochistic pathology. We assume that conflict and conflict resolution are universal but neurosis is not. Neurosis is one of the pathological solutions to conflict. It would follow then that the normal mother–infant bond is not symbiotic, the anal phase is not necessarily sadistic, the oedipal period need not be experienced as traumatic, latency is not a period of arid repression, masochism may be pervasive but it is not normal, and normal adolescence is not a period of emotional turbulence that is akin to a severe emotional disorder. These formulations assume a path of "healthy" or "adaptive" solutions to conflict that may be achieved throughout life. Psychoanalysis is a psychology of conflict resolution and we are often called upon to judge whether a particular conflict resolution is pathological or not. Our main criterion for making this judgment comes from a knowledge of the range of normal development and is contained in Anna Freud's stated analytic goal of restoration to the path of progressive development (A. Freud 1965). We suggest that omnipotence does not play a role in normal development. Rather, the presence of omnipotent functioning is a sign of pathological solution to conflict.

The omnipotent and competent systems of self-regulation do not differentiate people, that is, they are not diagnostic categories. Rather, they describe potential choices of adaptation *within each individual at any point in development* and allow for a matapsychological, or multidimensional, description of the components of the individual's relation to himself and to others. The treatment goal of restoration to the path of progressive development refers to restoration to the path of reality-rooted competence, pleasure, and self-esteem (see Chapter 13). We have concluded that sadomasochism is not a separate diagnostic category, but is an integral part of all pathology. Omnipotence is a hostile defensive component of sadomasochism. Most simply, in all pathology there is sadomasochism; in all sadomasochism, there is an omnipotent fantasy. We may liken it to a Russian doll: the largest doll represents psychopathology, the one next in size sadomasochism, the next is omnipotence as a response to helplessness and a solution to conflict, and the smallest one inside is a helpless, traumatized child.

Many theorists have described omnipotent fantasies as a part of borderline disorders. Borderline patients were first described in 1884 in the journal *Alienist and Neurologist* by Hughes and Russell. They referred to such patients, however, as "borderland patients," which seems clinically very apt (Hughes 1884, Russell 1884). We too prefer describing a place to labeling a person. When a patient is labelled "borderline" there is an implication of difference from us, with an assumed scale of superiority ranging from normal down to neurotic, borderline, and then psychotic. But when a person is operating in a borderland we can join him there if we have the bravery, skill, and desire to do so. If we are secure in our original identity, we may safely travel and explore, trying to see the other place through this person's eyes. The sadomasochistic aspect of pathology, imbued with the quality of omnipotence, resides in the borderland. Experiences of helplessness, that is, traumatic experiences that overwhelm the ego, can lead anyone to take up residence in the borderland, choosing an omnipotent solution in the absence of a sense of alternative possibilities. Our choice to join a patient in his magical borderland is safely undertaken only with the help of our numerous ties to reality, the support of colleagues and institutions, training, and experience (Panel 1987). Our theories, too, provide us with conceptual tools and techniques for staying anchored in reality while ranging through such foreign territory. The clinical field may be surveyed through a number of lenses; it is the same field whether we look at it through the lens of transference, defense, object relations, or, as we propose to do in this chapter, the lens of the therapeutic alliance.

The importance of a therapeutic alliance for the successful pursuit of an analysis is a notion that was stressed in technical discussions during the 1960s and 1970s. The term was first introduced by Zetzel in 1956 and, in a major paper, Greenson (1965) suggested naming it the "working alliance." The concept had roots in Freud's ideas concerning the positive transference and the analytic "pact" (1913, 1916–17, 1937, 1940), Fenichel's (1941) concept of the rational transference, and Sterba's (1934) views about the therapeutic split between the observing and experiencing parts of the ego.

Greenson noted the contributions of Stone (1961) and Loewald (1960) and elaborated his own views in a further series of papers (Greenson and Wexler 1969, Greenson 1970, 1971) where he emphasized the importance of the "real relationship" between patient and analyst. Therapeutic alliance was a concept that allowed for new ways to look at psychoanalytic technique, particularly aspects relating to analytic setting, transference and non-transference elements in the therapeutic relationship, and issues in termination. It also highlighted the difference between Kleinian and classical analysis. There was general agreement that the working alliance should be distinguished from transference and that each is equally important for analytic work. Further, most authors said that the working alliance was based on the conscious and rational wish to be rid of suffering. Greenson (1971) wrote that the core of the working alliance was the "real relationship" between analyst and patient.

There were some who began to question these views, most notably Friedman (1969), who said that the alliance concept served the needs of the therapist rather than those of the patient, and Loewenstein (1969), who noted that the willingness to work and the wish to get well were not necessarily coterminous; there were some patients who were willing to work but not get better and there were those who wanted to get better but not work. Using a child analytic case, one of us (J. Novick 1970) demonstrated that the alliance was not stable, was not based solely on rational motives, and was not distinct from transference. This inclusion of irrational motives for the alliance led to a further study where we illustrated, again using child and adolescent material, the action of a negative therapeutic motivation and the formation of a negative therapeutic alliance (see Chapter 12).

Nevertheless, the concept of the therapeutic alliance as a rational, nontransferential motive for change persisted until 1979, when critical articles by Brenner, Curtis, and Kanzer seemingly succeeded in rendering the term obsolete. Brenner, for example, argued that the working alliance cannot be distinguished from transference and is therefore of no value. He said that the distinction between alliance and transference "is a specious one and its consequences for analytic practice are, generally speaking, undesirable" (1979, p. 155). This view was echoed a few years later by Weinshel (1984), who said that the concept of a working alliance can be a potentially harmful or confusing guide. The almost total dismissal of a formerly central technical idea is reflected in the current official psychoanalytic reference to terms and concepts, where the working alliance is described as "both ambiguous and controversial" (Moore and Fine 1990, p. 195). A recent issue of the *Psychoanalytic Quarterly* (1990) was devoted to the psychoanalytic process without a single reference to the concept of therapeutic or working alliance.

It is ironic that, just when psychoanalysts have dismissed the concept of therapeutic alliance as ambiguous, unnecessary, or even harmful, research in the adjoining fields of psychiatry, counselling, and psychotherapy finds that the quality of the working alliance is a critical factor in predicting outcome (Frieswyk et al. 1986, Gelso and Carter 1985). Karon (1989) states that this phenomenon is so robust that it seems to work no matter which measure is used.

Although many criticisms of the concept remain valid, we too find that we cannot do without some attention to the techniques needed to get a person into treatment, get him to stay and work, and help him leave when it is appropriate; therefore, we continue to find the therapeutic alliance a significant concept for all age groups. In a series of presentations and publications (K. K. Novick 1991, J. Novick 1992) we turned our attention to a revised theory of the therapeutic alliance that reflects the complexity of the concept, acknowledging that Greenson and others were responding to the reality that the therapeutic relationship cannot be taken for granted at the start, nor at any time throughout the course of treatment. However, what others refer to as components of the therapeutic alliance, we see as long-term treatment goals, applicable at the beginning of analysis probably only to the analyst. Patients come to treatment because they are unable to use their capacities to be with or to work together with others. The more impaired their capacities, the more important becomes a focus on the therapeutic alliance as we hope to reformulate it—as a dynamic, integrated, and fluctuating component of the whole therapeutic process.

In a paper titled "The Therapeutic Alliance: A Concept Revisited" we said that the alliance is not separate from transference, but is "a lens which highlights certain features of the therapeutic field . . . rather than being irrelevant or undesirable, [the alliance] is useful in delineating therapeutic tasks central to each phase of treatment" (1992, p. 97). We have come to view the alliance, as does Hanly (1994), as a necessary but not sufficient agent of therapeutic change. Our current thinking can be summarized as follows:

1. The therapeutic alliance is not separate from other technical perspectives, or lenses, such as transference, resistance, defense analysis, and the like.
2. All patients have the *capacities* necessary for a therapeutic alliance. Individual differences among patients lie in the motivational sphere. Our experience with severely disturbed patients of all ages has been that they are able to build and maintain an alliance when that effort is made an integral part of the therapeutic work.
3. The various motives for the alliance may be rational or irrational, conscious or unconscious.
4. The therapeutic alliance is not stable, but varies at differ-

ent stages of treatment and, more microscopically, with each successive emergence of a conflict and its object, drive, and affective components. The fluctuations of the alliance enable the therapist to see, share, and interpret conflict, defenses, anxiety, and transference in a way the patient—even a young child—can understand. Fluctuations in the alliance may be used as a barometer of conflict, resistance, and change.

5. The therapeutic alliance is a relational concept and thus requires input from all parties to it. Minimally and usually this includes patient, therapist, and parents or significant others, each of whom has complementary phase-appropriate therapeutic alliance tasks. The therapeutic alliance tasks of each phase of treatment persist through all subsequent phases, but the primary task highlighted in each phase relates to the progression of the therapeutic work and provides a measure of that progress.

6. The concept of the therapeutic alliance can serve to bridge the gap between the therapist's knowledge and the patient's experience, by providing for an understandable shared formulation of goals and ways to measure progress towards them.

7. We find it useful to distinguish between two fundamental therapeutic modes, the mode of active intervention and that of receptivity. The therapist's receptivity operates throughout the treatment to put him in touch with the deep current of the patient's unconscious wishes and feelings. We think that this knowledge may best be used for interpretation when the analyst has actively engaged the patient around the therapeutic alliance issues.

8. It follows that the initiative for creating a therapeutic alliance lies with the therapist and not the patient.

The consequence of this approach is to shift the locus of problems from outside to inside the therapeutic setting. It is our view that the greatest danger in treatment, even greater than premature termination, is the patient's submission to an authoritarian system of unfounded statements, interpretations that carry the weight of irrational authority rather than of a shared evidentiary base. In work with patients whose main way of relating is to try to engage the analyst in a sadomasochistic interaction, it is particularly important to focus joint attention on fluctuations around a baseline of mutually agreed phase-specific therapeutic alliance tasks that serve as a barometer of dynamic issues. Attention to the therapeutic alliance allows us to create a field within which valid interpretations may be made, heard, and used. Here we will look at clinical material through the lens of the therapeutic alliance to illustrate how useful this approach can be in highlighting sadomasochistic elements in the interaction at each phase of treatment. Staying mindful of the therapeutic alliance aspects of the relationship allows for collaborative work by patient and analyst on the sadomasochistic pathology that is often the most powerful resistance to analytic progress.

EVALUATION

The purpose of an evaluation is assessment of whether a patient can benefit from therapy. But this decision is often made de facto by the referrer or the patient, and initial contact slides quickly into therapy without explicit evaluation, joint decision-making, or a shared working agreement by patient and therapist about goals and methodology. The specific task of the therapeutic alliance during the evaluation phase is the initiation of several *transformations*. Transformation is a developmental task at each point of transition, whether from one phase of treatment to another or from one phase of development to another. Transformation will be an alliance task at each transition during analysis, but it is during the evaluation phase that transitions between modes of being may be experienced particularly vividly, with obstacles and conflicts made especially visible.

The patient comes in a state of need, looking for an authoritative person to relieve distress. The underlying transference may be to a powerful, omniscient parental figure. This sets up a conflict between the wish for and fear of dependent submission. There is an immediate imbalance in the power relationship, part of which is real and necessary, part of which is the patient's transference. The patient really needs someone competent, who knows what can help, but there can be a confusion in both people between authoritative competence and authoritarian dominance. Analysts may collude with the patient's fantasy wish and make intrusive formulations for which there is no shared data base, thus setting up from the very beginning a situation of therapeutic compliance, or they may bend over backwards to avoid this danger and be so tentative and passive that the patient has no feeling of safety.

The evaluation phase is a time of anxiety for the patient and the analyst and both are vulnerable to invoking omnipotent defenses. We think that the conceptual framework of the therapeutic alliance tasks of evaluation can be used for withstanding transference pressures that are not yet fully known or understood, but that operate from the first contacts with the patient.

Mr. G., who was introduced in a vignette in Chapter 4, was a highly successful professional, married man with two children. He telephoned asking if the analyst had available treatment time. The analyst said that she had time to meet and talk about Mr. G.'s situation so that they could come to a preliminary understanding together about what was going on and what would be of most help. Mr. G. seemed somewhat nonplussed, said he was certain he needed therapy, probably twice a week, but agreed to come to explore the issues. He began the first evaluation session by saying that he had been given a number of names and was shopping around; he wanted to know the analyst's theoretical orientation and policy around missed sessions since he traveled frequently.

Such a situation creates an intense pressure on the analyst to sell himself, to be the preferred item on the shopping list, by deviating from his habitual policies or style. Another way out of this anxiety is to submit quickly to the patient's treatment plan or immediately to impose one's own. But that carries other dangers. In this case the analyst used the transformation tasks as a reality guide for herself and was able to say that, without hearing the patient's story, she could not know whether she could be of genuine help.

> Mr. G. began to talk about his relationship with his wife. He had sought treatment after she threatened to leave him because he had thrown dishes at her. He presented a list of abusive behaviors, described with a certain bravado and a barely concealed challenge to the analyst to reprimand him. After the analyst said to Mr. G. that, despite the fact that he was so hard on his wife, he seemed to value the relationship, Mr. G. began to cry and said he felt he couldn't live without his wife, that he needed treatment in order to keep her. Mr. G. and the analyst had arrived together at a description of Mr. G.'s internal conflict between his wishes to control his wife and his anxieties about losing her. As their joint capacity to accomplish this transformation of an external problem into an internal one became clear, they began to discuss treatment once again. Mr. G. argued about everything the analyst presented—days, times, who sat where, and so on. The analyst noted this and asked, "Is arguing a big part of your life?" Mr. G. detailed the wrangles he got into at work, arguments with friends, constant bickering with his wife, battles with his children. As he talked, he remarked, "I guess I could use more than twice a week." The analyst agreed and they started an analysis.

BEGINNING

Analysts are understandably reluctant to categorize patients or to schematize phases of treatment. Each patient forms a unique relationship with each analyst, who in turn changes with and is changed by each patient. The course of each analysis is also unique, unpredictable, and perhaps more amenable to chaos theory than to two-dimensional linear regression coefficients. At the same time, dating from Freud's early distinction between passive and active seductions (Freud 1895) and his recommendations to analysts for the beginning of analysis, the heuristic value of categorization has been accepted. Freud discussed the beginning phase of analysis and referred to the middle and end phases, but it was Glover (1955) who explicitly expounded a tripartite division of analysis into beginning, middle, and termination phases. If we keep in mind that the phases of treatment are not mutually exclusive, nor are they mechanical checkpoints in a sequence, then the schema can be useful for highlighting certain tasks, resistances, and techniques.

At the beginning of treatment each patient has an individual way of functioning; some struggle to begin, others overflow with material. But, with all patients, the analyst really does not yet have enough sure knowledge to make interpretations. His insufficient information is one impediment that will be removed with the passage of time. Another, more significant impediment resides in the patient's resistances to engaging in the process. We think that delineating the therapeutic alliance task illuminates resistances, which then allow for defining the terms of conflicts. Once we have a sense of a particular conflict, the progressive and regressive forces at work within it can be identified. This creates a loop or cycle in which focus on the therapeutic alliance allows for keeping the work internal to the patient and the therapy. Acting out, such as self-mutilation, suicide attempts, dangerous behavior, drug and alcohol abuse, and so on, can be brought into the context of the treatment relationship.

In the beginning phase of treatment the patient's therapeutic alliance task is to be with the analyst; the analyst strives to feel with the patient. The analyst intervenes actively when obstacles to being together arise in the patient, from the environment, and from the analyst himself. These tasks of *being with* and *feeling with* persist throughout treatment but predominate at the beginning. The model for this attunement is the early mother–child relationship. Fluctuations in attunement draw upon and relate to issues of mother–child attachment during infancy and toddlerhood. Disruptions and deviations in *being with* are our first indicators of resistance to engaging in the therapeutic process and direct our attention to the conditions under which the patient can be with the analyst.

Even before we know the full history or dynamics of the pathological relationship, we may quickly engage the patient in noticing feelings about *being with*, what he does to make himself comfortable, and begin to wonder together what he gives up in the service of maintaining a sadomasochistic interaction.

> The focus at the beginning of Mr. G.'s analysis was his life-long tendency to provoke battles and his sense of the self-destructive nature of this pattern. He started by talking about his battles at work and his wish to argue with the analyst, especially about the vacation schedule. He recounted his growing up in a home where the men were, as he put it, "sadistic bullies" who dominated and brutalized the women. As his history unfolded and was reexperienced in the transference, he saw clearly the relation between his feeling of helpless anxiety and his reaction of identification with his shouting, verbally abusive father. When he was angry, he felt a rush, an excitement, a feeling of power and indestructibility. Mr. G. gave many examples of acting recklessly in states of anger and made it clear that he attributed all of his many achievements to his lack of inhibition of rageful, bullying behavior. He thought his voice was overwhelmingly powerful and that he could get anything he wanted by shouting.
>
> The analyst tracked Mr. G.'s good feelings in the sessions, noting when he enjoyed coming and using his mind, and when he felt good about the analyst's meeting of his normal ego needs to be listened to, understood, and respected. Mr. G. recaptured

early memories of his grandmother who had loved him and treated him as a worthy individual. Through this transference, he recovered a loving, joyful aspect of himself, which constituted the other side of the conflict with an omnipotent, magical, destructive self. The omnipotent defenses made him feel safe and powerful; his love left him feeling vulnerable, especially to abandonment. Focus on his feelings around being with the analyst allowed for full experience of his conflict between two ways of functioning. In his external life, particularly at work, where his organizational and research activities were notably successful, there was a gradual expansion of pleasure from competence.

The omnipotent fantasies enacted in Mr. G.'s provocative argumentativeness had become restricted to hostile interactions at home with his wife, and, more subtly, with his older child. He mentioned these battles with his wife in passing, always with self-justifying evidence, and never really engaged with the issues involved until later in his analysis.

MIDDLE PHASE

All the therapeutic alliance tasks coexist throughout the course of treatment: transformations begun during the evaluation continue to be worked on to the end of analysis and beyond; the experience of being together and the interferences and conditions related to it are intrinsic to every phase of the work. But each phase of treatment has its own therapeutic alliance task that seems specifically highlighted as the process unfolds. For the middle phase of treatment the therapeutic alliance task is *working together*. From the very first phone contact, the analyst has implicitly and explicitly presented a model of *working together* with the patient. Both work to effect the beginning transformations of the evaluation phase and to elucidate the conditions for being together at the start of the treatment process. Increasingly, working together becomes central, and we begin to track fluctuations in the patient's willingness to engage in the work. Just as we saw in earlier phases, staying mindful of the relevant therapeutic alliance task illuminates resistance. The source of resistance may be traced to the operation of defenses; here we will examine the contribution of omnipotent defenses to resistance to working together in the middle phase of analysis.

Mr. G. continued to relate to the analyst as a supportive, admiring grandmother, and used the analysis to keep his work free from debilitating power struggles. His battles were confined to weekends with his family, when he provoked his wife, accused her of being stupid, and forced her to submit physically and sexually to his demands, all of which was rationalized in terms of "If you really love me, you will be happy to do whatever I want." He recounted a perverse sexual practice, in which he made his wife wear a prosthesis during intercourse and pretend she was a cripple. This was his central sadomasochistic fantasy: either he or the woman had to be a cripple. But Mr. G. did not seem bothered by or wish to change the fantasy or the practice, indeed he did his best to keep it out of the analysis.

He continued to expand his intellectual and social activities and often remarked with pleasure on his increased enjoyment of his mental functioning, especially his memory. As memory was essential to his occupation, he had always employed a vast array of mnemonics; now, with pride, he began to speak of his "steel trap mind." In the third year of his analysis, when Mr. G. arrived for the last session of the month the day before the analyst's vacation, the analyst waited a few minutes before noting that Mr. G. had not given her the check, as was their custom. Mr. G. said that he had forgotten that it was the last session of the month and then said in a flat tone, "I guess I must be angry at you for taking a vacation." He went on to recount details of his current life events. When the analyst noted Mr. G.'s sliding past the question of the check the patient dutifully ran through all the transferred wishes they had uncovered, especially those of wanting to deny and destroy the envied father. Mr. G.'s tone of helpless resignation and the analyst's own feelings—ranging from helplessness to a wish to argue—alerted the analyst to the possibility that Mr. G. had externalized his internal conflict onto the treatment relationship.

His memory lapse, the provocation of a sadomasochistic battle, and the invoking of material about his father all defended against Mr. G.'s experience of helplessness at being unable to control being left by his analyst/wife/mother. The analyst's vacation challenged Mr. G.'s omnipotent fantasy of complete control. He reconstituted his omnipotent fantasy by turning the tables and making the loved objects be the ones rejected, abandoned, forced to feel helpless or overwhelmed. He imagined the analyst desperately clinging to him for survival, safety, and love.

These defenses were still operating in Mr. G. when the analyst returned from vacation; the analyst became aware of her own moments of sudden sleepiness, a sharp drop in awareness. She tracked those occurrences and found that they came in conjunction with material related to separation. It is useful not only to follow closely the operation of the patient's ego functions, but also to monitor those ego functions the analyst uses for *working together*. The analyst realized that her feeling was one of being dropped, suddenly feeling all alone. She began to remark to the patient at those times, for instance, "I feel you're not here today." Mr. G. responded in a definite way: "Yes. Now that you mention it, I notice that I'm talking to you, but I'm somewhere else." This was the inception of a long, painful, halting period of work that led eventually to the reexperiencing and reconstruction of his mother's reactions to any success on his part. Mr. G.'s mother focused her attention on him only when she worried that he was crippled; an able child did not need her and she dropped him instantly. Against the backdrop of the alliance tasks of being together and working together, Mr. G.'s defensive omnipotent fantasy—that being crippled would ensure attachment, control, safety, special powers, and sexual excitement—clearly emerged. During the middle phase of Mr. G.'s analysis the multidetermined levels and functions of his sadomasochism and its omnipotent fantasy could be more clearly elucidated, from his early attachment to a mother who worried constantly that he was damaged and deformed to the organization at adolescence of a perverse sexual fantasy that included his identification with a verbally abusive father.

Genuinely nonexploitative, joint work threatens a stable sadomasochistic character organization that seeks to turn analysis into a never-ending perverse gratification. Sadomasochism has determinants from all levels of development, serves multiple functions, and is a most difficult pathology to deal with. Hostile omnipotent fantasies form a triumphant, self-protective shell in sadomasochistic disorders and patients may go to extreme lengths, even to suicide, to avoid relinquishing them. The therapeutic alliance and its tasks provide an alternative to this omnipotent way of relating. As such, the alliance is a major means for helping people battle with perversions, but it also constitutes a major threat to an omnipotent system of mental functioning. This is the reason that the therapeutic alliance tasks appear so centrally in conflict at each stage of treatment.

PRETERMINATION PHASE

This phase of treatment is seldom discussed or delineated, but recent intensive study of termination has made it clear that there is a distinct set of tasks to be addressed before a termination phase can be started. The tasks for the patient are *to maintain progres-*

sive momentum, take increasing responsibility for the joint work, and *translate insights into effective actions.* Each of these tasks may arouse intense resistance, as they clash directly with features of an omnipotent system of defense and self-regulation.

The pretermination phase is marked by a clinical sense that termination has become a genuine rather than a fantasied possibility. The real possibility of readiness to end is based on the reestablishment of progressive momentum in the patient's life in and out of treatment (see Chapter 13). This impels a departure from the timelessness of the middle phase and actively imports the reality dimensions of time and change. But the reality of time challenges the omnipotent denial of change, growth, generational differences, and mortality, and triggers resistances to forward development. The patient's increased involvement in working together, which was the focus of the middle phase, has led to recovered capacity to take responsibility. But this runs counter to the old way of relating in which the other (in this case the analyst) appears to be all-powerful, while the patient presents himself as a helpless, passive, or compliant victim. Such a sado-masochistic relationship has been an important organizer of otherwise unintegrated experience for the patient, functioning rather like a religion, in which the analyst is cast in the role of omnipotent God while the patient retains secret control, able to get God to do or be exactly what he wants him to be through the power of prayer.

Putting insight into action directly challenges the omnipotent assumption of the magical power of thought. The patient who manages to achieve brilliant insights but never changes is denying the pleasure of achievement and reality for the sake of maintaining a delusion of the power of his thoughts and wishes. He will never want to move on to setting a termination date, because any action implies accepting the distinction between fantasy and reality.

From the very start of his analysis Mr. G. had a treatment plan that included being in control of termination. Each year he secretly decided that analysis would end at Christmas or just before the summer break. When he finally told about his plan it could be viewed as a characteristic way of defending against feeling rejected and left. He planned to surprise and overwhelm the analyst by suddenly announcing the end of treatment and part of his omnipotent fantasy was to make the analyst feel like a helpless, abandoned child.

This represented the type of externalization we have described elsewhere (see Chapter 7) as a prime mechanism of an omnipotent system of self-regulation, and as an instance of the emotional abuse that underlies the concrete events of sexual and physical abuse. In relation to termination, we have earlier described regression from a differentiated to an externalizing transference (Novick 1988, 1990, and see Chapter 6, this volume). The analyst's sense of being dropped, rejected, or treated with contempt was often the signal that Mr. G. was planning a unilateral termination. One internal measure of having achieved the pretermination phase was that the secret plan was no longer a feature of Mr. G.'s thinking.

Things were going well for Mr. G. on all fronts, even at home, where he had longer periods of genuine pleasure and love for his wife and children. Both Mr. G. and the analyst felt it was time to consider what further work was needed to begin a termination phase. There followed a time of fruitless stagnation with a strong sense of no forward momentum. With both people's acknowledgment of this phenomenon, Mr. G. recognized that he was fighting against doing the work necessary to start the process of saying goodbye. He said that his only way of saying goodbye was to be angry, to provoke an attack and then react with justifiable hostility. He said he would never be able to leave if he felt loving. "I'd rather be mad than sad." He clung to his omnipotent fantasy, rather than feel vulnerable to being left by the loved one but gradually it became clear to him that his attempts at hostile control of others destroyed his love and concern. He faced the incompatibility of the omnipotent system of hostile control of others and the competent system with its love and respect for separate individuals.

Sessions alternated between these two systems. On Mondays and Fridays Mr. G. was dull, withdrawn, his lip curled in an unmistakable sneer. During the middle three days he was engaged, active, and clearly enjoying the working of his mind and the fullness of the treatment relationship. When the analyst asked if he had noticed his two ways of being in the sessions, Mr. G. said he was trying to prove that he could have it both ways; he needn't choose, for he could be both a controlling vengeful God and a loving, respectful human being. He planned to stay in analysis forever, never grow older, never get sick, and never die. Since his earnings had increased substantially during his time in treatment he now felt he was, as it were, paying nothing.

Even his thoughts about contact after termination had an omnipotent quality. He could not imagine ever seeing the analyst again; when treatment ended, the analyst would disappear into a black hole. As underlying feelings of traumatized helplessness emerged, he tried to reassert the reality of his omnipotent fantasy. The most fiercely defended element was his belief that he had the power to force others to love him, that this was a real power and not a magical delusion. The fixity of such a delusion is reinforced by childrearing methods that use expressions of love to mold behavior, and by exploitative cultural forces that extol methods of making someone love you by driving the right car, wearing a certain perfume, and so on.

Mr. G. initiated a crusade to prove that he could force another person to feel and be a certain way. He sensed impatience in the analyst, expressed his fear that the analyst would kick him out, and then said that he would be totally devastated, destroyed, "rubbish, floating out to sea." The analyst commented that they seemed no longer to be functioning as two adults working together to help him get ready for the next step, but had shifted into a magical destructive system where the analyst had been given life-and-death power over the helpless patient. This intervention about the lost therapeutic alliance helped Mr. G. gain perspective on his destructive rage. He said that his anger made him forget how much time they had spent together, what they had achieved in understanding, and how much he had come to value thinking things through. Mr. G. felt he was acting as if he were still the helpless 2-year-old who had been suddenly removed from his parental home and sent to live with strangers because his mother had been hospitalized.

From all this work Mr. G. arrived at the base of his sadomasochism and the core of his omnipotent fantasy: he had clung to the magical belief that his pain and rage could make his mother be a good-enough provider for his developmental needs. "So there it is," he said. "I have to put aside the idea that my mother could love me in the way I needed and get on with all the good things I now have. Or I can destroy all that I have worked for and go on thinking that there is something I can do to force them to do my bidding. You said there's a lot of work to saying goodbye. I can feel that now, but I think I'm ready to do it."

TERMINATION

The therapeutic alliance tasks of each phase persist throughout treatment, overlapping and interacting with each other. So, the highlighted tasks of the previous phase lead into and inform the termination phase. Similarly, while the patient's tasks in the termination phase—*relinquishing infantile fantasies, mourning, and internalization of the alliance*—are not new, indeed they have been part of the work throughout the treatment. But they take on new prominence and character in light of the reality of ending. During the pretermination phase process of choosing the date the analyst is entirely flexible, stipulating only that the date be independent of other anniversaries and that the patient and analyst take time to explore the connotations of any particular date proposed by the patient. In contrast, once the date has been jointly determined, we remain firm about holding to it. This implies including reality in the treatment process in a somewhat new way. The reactions of both people elucidate conflicts over the integration of reality and the role of the ego function of reality testing in the overall working of the patient's personality. There is an opportunity to examine hitherto hidden pockets of fantasy functioning and to test the therapeutic alliance in new directions. Particular aspects of omnipotent fantasy functioning inform resistances to alliance tasks in this phase.

> Mr. G. picked a date and the termination phase began. By the end of the first week, he mounted a major effort to get the analyst to rescind the agreement, do away with the ending, or, at the very least, defer it for another year. It was a powerful demonstration, including a weekend binge of drugs and drinking, sexual abuse of his wife, and threats to fire his entire staff. Mr. G. insisted that these events proved that the analyst was wrong, that he wasn't ready to finish, in fact he might never be. The analyst too wondered if she had been mistaken, but then wondered aloud about the function of the furor. Did the intensity of that impulse indicate that Mr. G. was back to fighting off the painful task of putting aside his fantasy that he could use his troubles to force the analyst to do his bidding? Mr. G. sighed, saying he had always hated change; as a child, he had turned every routine into an unalterable ritual, and now he had made analysis into his protective ritual. With analysis, he would never get sick, old, or die; in analysis he could imagine he was still young and slim with a full head of hair. With this understanding—that the ending date was a reality confronta-

tion with his omnipotent fantasy system—Mr. G. could again experience the end date as a helpful anchor point.

Over the next few weeks, however, he tried to provoke the analyst to become more active. He claimed he couldn't think, associate, observe, or recall, that the analyst knew everything anyway. The analyst remarked that Mr. G. was not really giving up his fantasy of omnipotence but handing it over to the analyst while retaining the secret fantasy that he could force the analyst to use that power. This had been worked on earlier and Mr. G. recalled his religious phase when, as a child, he had believed he had special prayers that could make God do various things like "smite mine enemy Johnny who called me a nerd." His sexual perversion of making women pretend to be crippled, then forcing them to perform certain acts, had emerged at each phase of treatment with Mr. G. attempting to get the analyst to forbid these practices. In the termination phase, after he had failed to get the analyst to agree to change the date, Mr. G. escalated his provocations. He began to tease and humiliate his younger son quite brutally. The analyst asked why, at a time when Mr. G. had all the skills to direct his own analysis, he was trying to force the analyst to intervene actively in his life by, perhaps, calling Protective Services. Mr. G. was shocked. He hadn't realized how far he had gone. He said, "I'm having a temper tantrum. I don't want to work, to be responsible, to grow up. It's some kind of fantasy, no, it's more, it's a delusion that I can control the world by being a boorish, sadistic, shouting asshole. I believe it when I'm doing it. I feel strong and powerful then, but look at what I almost did." He began to cry, "I love my son and yet I was willing to destroy him to hang on to this craziness." From this point on Mr. G. began to mourn the imminent real loss of his analysis and his analyst.

This was not the end of the work on Mr. G's omnipotence, however. He became cloudy and dull and the analyst wondered if he was again turning away from some reality. Mr. G. said,

"I'm turning away from my disappointment. I've changed a lot—I'm happy and creative. But I came into analysis not to be a better me but to be someone else, like my blond, blue-eyed brother. Then I wanted to be like you, but now I wonder about you. You work too hard. Are you like my parents, always busy, never time for your kids?" He found his disillusionment unbearable and switched back for a few days to omnipotent functioning: he was furious with everyone and shouted that he had suffered so much for so many years. "Shouldn't I now be acknowledged as the king, shouldn't you and everyone else obey my every whim and command?" His oscillation between the omnipotent and competent systems could be seen even within the same session. In his rage he lost all his analytic skills, but, as he regained his capacity for self-analysis with little or no intervention from the analyst, he could put aside the omnipotent demands consequent on his rage. After his furious criticisms of the analyst, he stepped back and reflected that he must be terrified if he reacted so strongly to seeing a possible flaw in the analyst, that it must have made him think it would be as it was with his parents, where things so quickly went from bad to worse to chaos. "It was a good analysis, you are a good analyst, and I can acknowledge that you're human, you have your faults. I don't have to panic and then protect myself by becoming a fire-breathing dragon."

Internalization is the outcome of an adaptive process of mourning the loss of real valued relationships, feelings, or experiences. Treatment includes a unique way of working, specific to the relationship created by particular individuals and productive of its own satisfactions. When it ends, there is a real loss, accompanied by sadness. A normal grieving process, with mourning and eventual internalization, allows the patient to keep the positive aspects of the therapeutic alliance inside, available for his own use.

Throughout treatment there has been a struggle within the patient between the wish to hold on to past infantile solutions with the hope of magical gratification and the progressive forces that represent realistic relations with others and the world, mediated by competent functioning and yielding genuine, predictable pleasure. Relinquishing infantile wishes from all levels of development, including magical omnipotent images of the self and others, seems a frightening and painful loss for the patient. But the work of the earlier phases has allowed for the establishment of alternative sources of security and self-esteem in realistic achievements and representations. Much of the work of the termination phase involves drawing the distinction between the illusory loss of unreal fantasy gains and the real loss of the setting, the analyst, and the special therapeutic relationship. This contrast was drawn first during earlier exploration of the patient's fantasy fears that the end of therapy means total loss of the analyst, that the analyst will die or disappear into a black hole. The hostile wishes contained in these fears, and the assumption of omnipotence of thought, demand continued and repeated work at each phase of treatment. We differentiate between, on the one hand, panic and fears of abandonment, which imply hostility, and, on the other, sadness and missing, which come from loving feelings and are intrinsically part of them. The intensity of fantasies of omnipotence becomes evident in the termination phase when the patient persists in thoughts that the analyst will cease to exist after the end of treatment, or that patient and analyst will become friends, colleagues, or lovers. This in turn gives rise to material about what will or should happen after termination. We are careful to explore these thoughts in detail, as they often contain the hidden remnants of defensive fantasies and other conflicts underlying them.

The reality of the imminent ending adds a special intensity to these conflicts. Denial bolstered by fantasies of omnipotence is a common response to the experience of helplessness in the face of reality. When the patient has in fact been traumatized in the past by cruel and overwhelming reality events, there is an even greater likelihood that all aspects of reality, such as the passage of time, change, loss, and death, will be experienced as hostile personal attacks to be resisted with all possible psychic power, including delusional fantasies of omnipotence.

Remnants of his omnipotent fantasy emerged in Mr. G's thoughts about the last day and afterwards. The tasks of the posttermination phase were discussed explicitly throughout the termination phase. When Mr. G. became fearful about his independently achieved insight about searching for his dead father, he and the analyst looked together at his anxiety about surpassing the analyst. The analyst pointed out that the work of treatment continues after the end date and suggested that what they had done together allowed Mr. G. not only to maintain momentum himself, but to go beyond what had already been done. Mr. G. seemed pleased at first, then said he was angry at the idea that the work would continue after the finishing date. He still wished that life could be free of conflict, effort, or work, that treatment would be the suffering that "opens the pearly gates of passive bliss." He wanted to know if he could contact the therapist afterwards; should they fix a specific time, like every Sunday morning? Mr. G. laughed as he associated this thought to material of many years earlier in which "early Sunday morning" referred to his hostile wish to interfere with and control parental sexual activities. After this understanding of transference wishes, the analyst explored with him the importance of integrating his therapeutic gains with his ongoing life, and the usefulness of keeping the analyst available as a therapeutic resource to be remembered or recontacted if needed, in contrast to his omnipotent fantasy of turning the analyst into his best friend.

As they neared the ending, the analyst asked Mr. G. what his thoughts were about the upcoming last day. Mr. G. said he was planning to bring a gift that he would rather not discuss, as he wanted it to be a pleasant surprise. He talked of his pleasure in thinking about it, as he was sure the analyst would enjoy it. The analyst acknowledged the positive feelings behind the impulse, but said that, in a therapy in which both had agreed to think, to associate, and to talk rather than act, the thought of ending with an action was worth exploring. At first Mr. G. protested, became angry, and accused the analyst of being a rigid, orthodox Freudian, but then he began to associate to his idea of bringing a gift on the last day. Yes, it was an expression of his love and gratitude—he had been planning to give a book he had referred to, one he knew the analyst would enjoy. But it would have been a surprise, a shock, like his teenage suicide attempt, which caught everyone unaware. The analyst would have been helpless, not knowing what to say, left with the feeing that whatever she said or did would be wrong. Mr. G. also imagined the analyst reading the book after the end, thinking of Mr. G., and missing him. This related to his deep, painful worry that the analyst did not like him, was happy to get rid of him, and would forget him when he was gone. The book would force her to remember.

Work on the multiple meanings of Mr. G.'s idea of a gift at the last session was part of the analyst's alliance task of *analyzing to the very end.* To fulfill this task, the analyst must resist his own pull to assuage the loss by changing the relationship. This is only possible when the analyst has allowed himself to acknowledge his loss at the end of a treatment and to mourn the passing of a unique working relationship. Then he may remain available as a therapeutic resource.

Children, adolescents, and adults finish good-enough treatment with the potential for adaptive transformations in response to the vicissitudes of life. From the alliance task of *being with* comes confidence in the capacity to be alone with oneself, to value oneself, and to cooperate in a trusting, mutually enhancing relationship with others. The new level and range of ego functions used to *work together* in alliance with the analyst can be used for living and for self-analysis whenever necessary. The explicit inclusion of self-analysis as a goal arises in the context of the pre-termination phase focus on issues around *independent therapeutic work*; self-analysis may thus be seen as one of the tools for living that will be available to the patient after finishing. Each therapeutic alliance task accomplished and internalized equips the patient in specific ways.

The internalization of the therapeutic alliance tasks of being with, working together, relinquishing magical fantasies, and carrying on adaptive transformations throughout life strengthens the competent, reality-attuned mode of self-regulation and so equalizes the forces in the life-long struggle against developmentally determined and culturally reinforced hostile sadomasochistic omnipotent solutions to the vicissitudes of life.

REFERENCES

Abelin, E. C. (1975). Some further observations and comments on the earliest role of the father. *International Journal of Psycho-Analysis* 56:293–302.

—— (1980). Triangulation, the role of the father and the origins of the core gender identity during the rapprochement subphase. In *Rapprochement*, ed. R. F. Lux, S. Bach, and J. A. Burland, pp. 151–169. New York: Jason Aronson.

Abraham, K. (1919). A particular form of neurotic resistance against the psychoanalytic method. In *Selected Papers on Psycho-Analysis*, pp. 303–311. London: Hogarth, 1927.

—— (1924). A short study of the development of the libido. In *Selected Papers on Psycho-Analysis*, pp. 418–501. London: Hogarth.

Alvarez, A. (1971). *The Savage God.* London: Weidenfield & Nicholson.

Anthony, E. J. (1986). The contributions of child psychoanalysis to psychoanalysis. *Psychoanalytic Study of the Child* 41:61–87. New Haven: Yale University Press.

—— (1987). Introduction. In *The Invulnerable Child*, ed. E. J. Anthony and B. J. Cohler, pp. 3–48. New York: Guilford.

Anzieu, D. (1987). Some alterations of the ego which make analyses interminable. *International Journal of Psycho-Analysis* 68:9–20.

Arlow, J. A. (1991). Methodology and reconstruction. *Psychoanalytic Quarterly* 60:539–563.

Asch, S. S. (1976). Varieties of negative therapeutic reaction and problems of technique. *Journal of the American Psychoanalytic Association* 24:383–407.

Baechler, J. (1979). *Suicides.* New York: Basic Books.

Bak, R. C. (1946). Masochism in paranoia. *Psychoanalytic Quarterly* 15:285–301.

—— (1968). The phallic woman. *Psychoanalytic Study of the Child* 23:37–46. New York: International Universities Press.

Balint, M. (1968). *The Basic Fault*. London: Tavistock.

Berenstein, I. (1987). Analysis terminable and interminable, fifty years on. *International Journal of Psycho-Analysis* 68:21–35.

Bergler, E. (1948). Further studies on beating fantasies. *Psychiatric Quarterly* 22:480–486.

—— (1949). *The Basic Neurosis, Oral Regression and Psychic Masochism*. New York: Grune and Stratton.

Bergmann, M. S. (1988). On the fate of the intrapsychic image of the psychoanalyst after termination of the analysis. *Psychoanalytic Study of the Child* 43:137–153. New Haven: Yale University Press.

Bergmann, M. S., and Hartman, F. R. (1976). *The Evolution of Psychoanalytic Technique*. New York: Basic Books.

Bergmann, M. S., and Jucovy, M., eds. (1982). *Generations of the Holocaust*. New York: Basic Books.

Bieber, I. (1966). Sadism and masochism. In *American Handbook of Psychiatry*, ed. S. Arieti, pp. 256–270. New York: Basic Books.

Bion, W. (1958). On hallucination. In *Second Thoughts*, pp. 65–85. New York: Jason Aronson, 1967.

Blos, P. (1980). The life cycle as indicated by the nature of the transference in the psychoanalysis of adolescents. *International Journal of Psycho-Analysis* 61:145–151.

Blos, P., Jr. (1985). Intergenerational separation-individuation. *Psychoanalytic Study of the Child* 40:41–56. New Haven: Yale University Press.

—— (1991). Sadomasochism and the defense against recall of painful affect. *Journal of the American Psychoanalytic Association* 39:417–430.

Blum, H. P. (1974). The borderline childhood of the Wolf-Man. *Journal of the American Psychoanalytic Association* 22:721–742.

—— (1980a). Paranoia and beating fantasy: an inquiry into the psychoanalytic theory of paranoia. *Journal of the American Psychoanalytic Association* 28:331–362.

—— (1980b). The value of reconstruction in adult psychoanalysis. *International Journal of Psycho-Analysis* 61:39–52.

—— (1987). Analysis terminable and interminable: a half century retrospective. *International Journal of Psycho-Analysis* 68:37–48.

—— (1989). The concept of termination and the evolution of psychoanalytic thought. *Journal of the American Psychoanalytic Association* 37:275–295.

Bonaparte, M. (1953). *Female Sexuality.* New York: International Universities Press.

Bornstein, B. (1935). Phobia in a two-and-a-half-year-old. *Psychoanalytic Quarterly* 4:93–119.

—— (1949). The analysis of a phobic child: some problems of theory and technique in child analysis. *Psychoanalytic Study of the Child* 3/4:181–226. New York: International Universities Press.

Boswell, J. (1988). *The Kindness of Strangers. The Abandonment of Children in Western Europe from Late Antiquity to the Renaissance.* New York: Pantheon.

Brenman, M. (1952). On teasing and being teased: the problem of moral masochism. *Psychoanalytic Study of the Child* 7:265–285. New York: International Universities Press.

Brenner, C. (1959). The masochistic character: genesis and treatment. *Journal of the American Psychoanalytic Association* 7:197–226.

—— (1976). *Psychoanalytic Technique and Psychic Conflict.* New York: International Universities Press.

—— (1979). Working alliance, therapeutic alliance, and transference. *Journal of the American Psychoanalytic Association* 27:137–157.

Brinich, P. M. (1984). Aggression in early childhood. *Psychoanalytic Study of the Child* 39:493–508. New Haven: Yale University Press.

Brodey, W. M. (1965). On the dynamics of narcissism: I. externalization and early ego development. *Psychoanalytic Study of the Child* 20:165–193. New York: International Universities Press.

Bruner, J. (1983). *Child's Talk.* New York: Norton.

Burgner, M. (1988). Analytic work with adolescents—terminable or interminable. *International Journal of Psycho-Analysis* 69:179–187.

Busch, F. (1992). Recurring thoughts on unconscious ego resistances. *Journal of the American Psychoanalytic Association* 40:1089–1115.

—— (1995). *The Ego at the Center.* Northvale, NJ: Jason Aronson.

Cain, A. C. (1961). The presuperego "turning inward of aggression." *Psychoanalytic Quarterly* 30:171–208.

Calef, V., and Weinshel, E. M. (1983). A note on consummation and termination. *Journal of the American Psychoanalytic Association* 24:425–436.

Chasseguet-Smirgel, J. (1984). *Creativity and Perversion*. New York: Norton.

—— (1985). *The Ego Ideal: A Psychoanalytic Essay on the Malady of the Ideal*. New York: Norton.

Cohen, J., and Kinston, W. (1989). Understanding failures and catastrophes in psycho-analysis. Paper presented at the 36th International Psycho-Analytical Congress, Rome, July. Copy available on request from W. Kinston.

Cooper, A. M. (1984). The unusually painful analysis: a group of narcissistic masochistic characters. In *Psychoanalysis: The Vital Issues*, ed. G. H. Pollock and J. E. Gedo, pp. 45–67. New York: International Universities Press.

—— (1986). Narcissism. In *Essential Papers on Narcissism*, ed. A. P. Morrison, pp. 112–143. New York: New York University Press.

—— (1988). The narcissistic-masochistic character. In *Masochism: Current Psychoanalytic Perspectives*, ed. R. A. Glick and D. I. Meyers, pp. 117–138. Hillsdale, NJ: Analytic Press.

Curtis, H. C. (1979). The concept of the therapeutic alliance: implications for the "widening scope." *Journal of the American Psychoanalytic Association* 27:159–192.

—— (1983). Construction and reconstruction: an introduction. *Psychoanalytic Inquiry* 3:183–188.

Daldin, H. (1988). A contribution to the understanding of self-mutilating behavior in adolescence. *Journal of Child Psychotherapy* 17:61–66.

deMause, L. (1974). The evolution of childhood. In *The History of Childhood*, pp. 1–73. New York: Psychohistory Press.

—— (1991). The universality of incest. *Journal of Psychohistory* 19:123–164.

Demos, E. V. (1985). The elusive infant. *Psychoanalytic Inquiry* 5:553–568.

De Simone Gaburri, G. (1985). On termination of the analysis. *International Review of Psycho-Analysis* 12:461–468.

deVito, E., Novick, J., and Novick, K. K. (1994). Interferenze culturali nell'ascolto degli adolescenti [Cultural interferences with listening to adolescents]. *Adolescenza* 3:1–14.

Docherty, J. P., and Fiester, S. J. (1985). The therapeutic alliance and compliance with psychopharmacology. *Annual Review, American Psychiatric Association* 4:607–632.

Eidelberg, L. (1934). A contribution to the study of masochism. In *Studies in Psychoanalysis*, pp. 31–40. New York: International Universities Press, 1952.

—— (1958). Technical problems in the analysis of masochists. *Journal of Hillside Hospital* 7:98–109.

—— (1959). Humiliation in masochism. *Journal of the American Psychoanalytic Association* 7:274–282.

—— (1968). *Encyclopedia of Psychoanalysis.* New York: Free Press.

Escalona, S. K. (1968). *The Roots of Individuality.* London: Tavistock.

Feigelson, C. I. (1976). Reconstruction of adolescence (and early latency) in the analysis of an adult woman. *Psychoanalytic Study of the Child* 31:225–236. New Haven: Yale University Press.

Feigenbaum, D. (1936). On projection. *Psychoanalytic Quarterly* 5:303–319.

Fenichel, O. (1941). *Problems of Psychoanalytic Technique.* New York: Psychoanalytic Quarterly, Inc.

—— (1945). *The Psychoanalytic Theory of Neurosis.* New York: Norton.

Ferber, L. (1975). Beating fantasies. In *Masturbation from Infancy to Senescence*, ed. I. M. Marcus and J. J. Francis, pp. 205–222. New York: International Universities Press.

Ferber, L., and Gray, P. (1966). Beating fantasies: clinical and theoretical considerations. *Bulletin of the Philadelphia Association of Psychoanalysis* 16:186–206.

Ferenczi, S. (1913). Stages in the development of the sense of reality. In *First Contributions to Psychoanalysis*, pp. 213–239. New York: Brunner/Mazel, 1980.

Firestein, S. K. (1978). *Termination in Psychoanalysis.* New York: International Universities Press.

—— (1982). Termination of psychoanalysis: theoretical, clinical, and pedagogic considerations. *Psychoanalytic Inquiry* 2:473–497.

Freud, A. (1936). The ego and the mechanisms of defence. *Writings* 2:3–191. New York: International Universities Press.

—— (1958). Adolescence. *Writings* 5:136–166. New York: International Universities Press.

—— (1960). The child guidance clinic as a center of prophylaxis and enlightenment. *Writings* 5:281–300. New York: International Universities Press.

——(1962). Assessment of childhood disturbances. *Psychoanalytic Study of the Child* 17:149–158. New York: International Universities Press.

—— (1965). Normality and pathology in childhood: assessments of development. *Writings* 6:3–273. New York: International Universities Press.

—— (1969). *Difficulties in the Path of Psychoanalysis. Writings* 7:124–156. New York: International Universities Press.

—— (1970a). Problems of termination in child analysis. *Writings* 7:3–21. New York: International Universities Press.

—— (1970b). Child analysis as a subspecialty of psychoanalysis. *Writings* 7:204–219. New York: International Universities Press.

——(1978). The principal task of child analysis. *Writings* 8:96–109. New York: International Universities Press.

Freud, S. (1886). Letter to W. Fliess, December 6. In *The Complete Letters of Sigmund Freud to Wilhelm Fliess*, ed. J. M. Masson, p. 207. Cambridge, MA: Harvard University Press, 1985.

—— (1895a). Project for a scientific psychology. *Standard Edition* 1:283–397.

—— (1895b). Draft H. paranoia. *Standard Edition* 1:206–212.

—— (1895c). Studies in hysteria. *Standard Edition* 2:3–335.

—— (1897). Letter to Fliess [December 12]. In *The Origins of Psychoanalysis*, p. 237. New York: Basic Books, 1954.

—— (1899). Screen memories. *Standard Edition* 3:303–322.

—— (1901). The psychopathology of everyday life. *Standard Edition* 6:1–310.

—— (1905). Three essays on the theory of sexuality. *Standard Edition* 7:125–243.

——(1908). On the sexual theories of children. *Standard Edition* 9:207–226.

—— (1909a). Letter to Jung. In *The Evolution of Psychoanalytic Technique*, ed. M. S. Bergmann and F. R. Hartman. New York: Basic Books, 1976.

——(1909b). Notes upon a case of obsessional neurosis. *Standard Edition* 10:155–318.

—— (1910). "Wild" psycho-analysis. *Standard Edition* 11:221–227.

—— (1911a). Psycho-analytic notes on an autobiographical account of a case of paranoia (Dementia Paranoides). *Standard Edition* 12:3–82.

—— (1911b). Formulations on the two principles of mental functioning. *Standard Edition* 12:215–226.

—— (1913a). On beginning the treatment. *Standard Edition* 12:123–144.

—— (1913b[1912–13]). Totem and taboo. *Standard Edition* 13:1–161.

—— (1914a). Remembering, repeating and working through. (Further recommendations on the technique of psychoanalysis II). *Standard Edition* 12:145–156.

—— (1914b). On narcissism: an introduction. *Standard Edition* 14:73–102.

—— (1914c). On the history of the psychoanalytic movement. *Standard Edition* 14:7–66.

—— (1915a). Instincts and their vicissitudes. *Standard Edition* 14:117–140.

—— (1915b). The unconscious. *Standard Edition* 14:159–215.

—— (1916–1917). *Introductory Lectures on Psychoanalysis*, Lecture 15. *Standard Edition* 15:228–239. Lecture 16. 16:243–256. Lecture 27. 16:431–463.

—— (1917). A metapsychological supplement to the theory of dreams. *Standard Edition* 14:217–235.

—— (1917[1915]). Mourning and melancholia. *Standard Edition* 14:239–258.

—— (1918[1914]). From the history of an infantile neurosis. *Standard Edition* 17:7–123.

—— (1919). A child is being beaten. *Standard Edition* 17:175–204.

—— (1920). Beyond the pleasure principle. *Standard Edition* 18:3–64.

—— (1922). Some neurotic mechanisms in jealousy, paranoia, and homosexuality. *Standard Edition* 18:221–232.

—— (1923). The ego and the id. *Standard Edition* 19:12–59.

—— (1924). The economic problem of masochism. *Standard Edition* 19:157–170.

—— (1925a). Negation. *Standard Edition* 19:235–239.

—— (1925b). Some psychical consequences of the anatomical distinction between the sexes. *Standard Edition* 19:248–258.

—— (1925c[1924]). An autobiographical study. *Standard Edition* 20:7–70.

—— (1927). The future of an illusion. *Standard Edition* 21:5–56.

—— (1930[1927]). Civilization and its discontents. *Standard Edition* 21:64–145.

—— (1931). Female sexuality. *Standard Edition* 21:223–243.

—— (1933). New introductory lectures on psychoanalysis. *Standard Edition* 22:5–182.

—— (1936). A disturbance of memory on the Acropolis. *Standard Edition* 22:239–248.

—— (1937). Analysis terminable and interminable. *Standard Edition* 23:209–253.

—— (1940[1938]). An outline of psychoanalysis. *Standard Edition* 23:141–207.

—— (1941[1938]). Findings, ideas, problems. *Standard Edition* 23:299–300.

—— (1950). *The Origins of Psychoanalysis*. New York: Basic Books, 1954.

Freud, S., and Pfister, O. (1963). *Psychoanalysis and Faith*. New York: Basic Books.

Friedman, L. (1969). The therapeutic alliance. *International Journal of Psycho-Analysis* 50:139–153.

—— (1983). Reconstruction and the like. *Psychoanalytic Inquiry* 3:189–222.

Friedman, M., Glasser, M., Laufer, E., et al. (1972). Attempted suicide and self-mutilation in adolescents: some observations from a psychoanalytic research project. *International Journal of Psycho-Analysis* 53:179–183.

Frieswyk, S. H., Allen, J. G., Colson, D. B., et al. (1986). Therapeutic alliance: its place as a process and outcome variable in dynamic psychotherapy research. *Journal of Consulting and Clinical Psychology* 54:32–38.

Furman, E. (1973). The impact of the Nazi concentration camps on the children of survivors. In: *The Child in His Family*, ed. J. Anthony and C. Kupernik, 2:379–384. New York: Wiley.

—— (1980). Transference and externalization in latency. *Psychoanalytic Study of the Child* 35:267–284. New Haven: Yale University Press.

—— (1982). Mothers have to be there to be left. *Psychoanalytic Study of the Child* 37:15–28. New Haven: Yale University Press.

—— (1984). Some difficulties in assessing depression and suicide in childhood. In *Suicide in the Young*, ed. H. S. Sudak, A. B. Ford, and N. B. Rushforth, pp. 245–258. Boston: John Wright.

—— (1985). On fusion, integration, and feeling good. *Psychoanalytic Study of the Child* 40:81–110. New Haven: Yale University Press.

Furman, R. (1986). The father–child relationship. In *What Nursery School Teachers Ask Us About*, ed. E. Furman, pp. 21–34. New York: International Universities Press.

Galenson, E. (1988). The precursors of masochism: protomasochism. In *Masochism: Current Psychoanalytic Perspectives*, ed. R. A. Glick and D. I. Meyers, pp. 189–204. Hillsdale, NJ: Analytic Press.

Gardiner, M. (1983). *Code Name "Mary."* New Haven: Yale University Press.

Gelso, C. J., and Carter, J. (1985). The relationship in counseling psychotherapy. *The Counseling Psychologist* 13:155–244.

Glenn, J. (1984). A note on loss, pain and masochism in children. *Journal of the American Psychoanalytic Association* 32:63–73.

Glover, E. (1955). *The Technique of Psychoanalysis*. New York: International Universities Press.

Goldberg, A., and Marcus, D. (1985). "Natural termination": some comments on ending analysis without setting a date. *Psychoanalytic Quarterly* 54:46–65.

Goettsche, R. (1986). Reconstruction of adolescence in adult analysis. *Psychoanalytic Study of the Child* 41:357–377. New Haven: Yale University Press.

Gray, P. (1982). "Developmental lag" in the evaluation of technique for psychoanalysis of neurotic conflict. *Journal of the American Psychoanalytic Association* 30:621–655.

Greenacre, P. (1950). The prepuberty trauma in girls. In *Trauma, Growth and Personality*, pp. 204–223. New York: Norton.

Greenson, R. (1965a). The working alliance and the transference neurosis. In *Explorations in Psychoanalysis*, pp. 199–224. New York: International Universities Press, 1978.

—— (1965b). The problem of working through. In *Drives, Affects, Behavior*, vol. 2, ed. M. Schur, pp. 277–314. New York: International Universities Press.

—— (1970). Discussion of "the nontransference relationship in the psychoanalytic situation." *International Journal of Psycho-Analysis* 51:143–150.

—— (1971). The "real" relationship between the patient and the psychoanalyst. In *Explorations in Psychoanalysis*, pp. 425–440. New York: International Universities Press, 1978.

Greenson, R., and Wexler, M. (1969). The nontransference relationship in the psychoanalytic situation. In *Explorations in Psychoanalysis*, pp. 359–386. New York: International Universities Press, 1978.

Greven, P. (1991). *Spare the Child: The Religious Roots of Punishment and the Psychological Impact of Physical Abuse*. New York: Alfred A. Knopf.

Grossman, W. I. (1986). Notes on masochism: a discussion of the history and development of a psychoanalytic concept. *Psychoanalytic Quarterly* 5:379–413.

Grotstein, J. S. (1981). *Splitting and Projective Identification*. New York: Jason Aronson.

Haim, A. (1974). *Adolescent Suicide*. New York: International Universities Press.

Hanly, C. (1987). Review of "The Assault on Truth: Freud's Suppression of the Seduction Theory," by J. Masson. *International Journal of Psycho-Analysis* 67:517–521.

—— (1994). Reflections on the place of the therapeutic alliance in psychoanalysis. *International Journal of Psycho-Analysis* 75:457–467.

Hanly, M-A. F. (1993). Sado-masochism in Charlotte Bronte's *Jane Eyre*: a ridge of lighted heath. *International Journal of Psycho-Analysis* 74:1049–1061.

Hartmann, H. (1939). *Ego Psychology and the Problem of Adaptation*. New York: International Universities Press, 1958.

Heimann, P. (1952). Certain functions of introjection and projection in early infancy. In *Developments in Psycho-Analysis*, ed. J. Riviere, pp. 122–168. London: Hogarth.

Hughes, C. H. (1884). Borderland psychiatric records: prodromal symptoms of psychical impairment. *Alienist and Neurologist* 5:85–91.

Hurry, A. (1977). My ambition is to be dead: part I: a case study. *Journal of Child Psychotherapy* 4(3):66–83.

—— (1978). My ambition is to be dead: parts II and III: past and current findings on suicide in adolescence. *Journal of Child Psychotherapy* 4(4):69–85.

Hurry, A., Laufer, E., Novick, J., et al. (1976a). *Attempted suicide in adolescents.* Center for the Study of Adolescence, London, England.

Hurry, A., Novick, J., and Laufer, M. (1976b). *A study of eighty-four adolescents who have attempted suicide.* Report to the Department of Health and Social Security. Center for the Study of Adolescence, London, England.

Isay, R. A. (1975). The influence of the primal scene on the sexual behavior of an early adolescent. *Journal of the American Psychoanalytic Association* 23:535–553.

Jacobs, T. J. (1987). Notes on the unknowable: analytic secrets and the transference neurosis. *Psychoanalytic Inquiry* 7:485–510.

Jacobson, E. (1964). *The Self and the Object World.* New York: International Universities Press.

Jaffe, D. S. (1968). The mechanism of projection. *International Journal of Psycho-Analysis* 49:662–677.

Joseph, E. D., ed. (1965). *Beating Fantasies: Regressive Ego Phenomena in Psychoanalysis.* New York: International Universities Press.

Kahr, B. (1991). The sexual molestation of children: historical perspectives. *Journal of Psychohistory* 19:191–214.

Kantrowitz, J. L., Katz, A. L., and Paolitto, F. (1990). Follow-up of psychoanalysis five to ten years after termination: 1. Stability of change. *Journal of the American Psychoanalytic Association* 38:471–496.

Kanzer, M. (1979). Book essay: developments in psychoanalytic technique. *Journal of the American Psychoanalytic Association* 27:327–374.

Karon, B. P. (1989). The state of the art of psychoanalysis: science, hope, and kindness in psychoanalytic technique. *Psychoanalysis and Psychotherapy* 7:99–115.

Katan, A. (1961). Some thoughts about the role of verbalization in early childhood. *Psychoanalytic Study of the Child* 16:184–188. New York: International Universities Press.

Kernberg, O. F. (1987). Projection and projective identification. In *Projection, Identification, Projective Identification,* ed. J. Sandler, pp. 93–115. Madison, CT: International Universities Press.

—— (1988). Clinical dimensions of masochism. *Journal of the American Psychoanalytic Association* 35:1005–1029.

Kernberg, P. (1974). The analysis of a fifteen-and-a-half-year-old girl with suicidal tendencies. In *The Analyst and the Adolescent at Work*, ed. M. Harley, pp. 232–268. New York: Quadrangle.

Kestenberg, J. (1982). Survivor-parents and their children. In *Generations of the Holocaust*, ed. M. Bergmann and M. Jucovy, pp. 137–158. New York: Basic Books.

Kinston, W., and Cohen, J. (1988). Primal repression and other states of mind. *Scandinavian Psychoanalytic Review* 11:81–105.

Klauber, J. (1977). Analyses that cannot be terminated. *International Journal of Psycho-Analysis* 58:473–477.

Klein, M. (1932). *The Psycho-Analysis of Children*. London: Hogarth, 1950.

—— (1946). Notes on some schizoid mechanisms. In *Envy and Gratitude and Other Works 1946–1963*, pp. 1–24. New York: Delacorte Press/Seymour Lawrence, 1975.

—— (1955). On identification. In *New Directions in Psycho-Analysis*, ed. M. Klein, P. Heimann, and R. E. Money-Kyrle, pp. 309–345. New York: Basic Books.

Kohut, H. (1977). *The Restoration of the Self*. New York: International Universities Press.

Krafft-Ebing, R. von. (1886). *Psychopathia Sexualis*. 7th ed. Philadelphia: F. A. Davis, 1892.

Kramer, S., and Byerly, L. J. (1978). Technique of psychoanalysis of the latency child. In *Child Analysis and Therapy*, ed. J. Glenn, pp. 205–236. New York: Jason Aronson.

Krystal, H. (1978). Trauma and affects. *Psychoanalytic Study of the Child* 33:81–116. New Haven: Yale University Press.

—— (1982). The activating aspects of emotions. *Psychoanalysis and Contemporary Thought* 5:605–648.

—— (1988). *Integration and Self Healing*. Hillsdale, NJ: Analytic Press.

Laforgue, R. (1934). Resistance at the conclusion of analytic treatment. *International Journal of Psycho-Analysis* 15:419–434.

Lamb, M. E. (1976). The role of the father. In *The Role of the Father in Child Development*, pp. 1–63. New York: Wiley.

Lampl-de Groot, J. (1937). Masochism and narcissism. In *The Development of the Mind*, pp. 82–92. New York: International Universities Press, 1965.

Laub, D., and Auerhahn, N. C. (1985). Prologue: Knowing and not knowing the holocaust. *Psychoanalytic Inquiry* 5:1–8.

Laufer, M. (1965). Assessment of adolescent disturbances: the application of Anna Freud's diagnostic profile. *Psychoanalytic Study of the Child* 20:99–123. New York: International Universities Press.

—— (1976). The central masturbation fantasy, the final sexual organization, and adolescence. *Psychoanalytic Study of the Child* 31:297–316. New Haven: Yale University Press.

Laufer, M., and Laufer, M. E. (1984). *Adolescence and Developmental Breakdown*. New Haven: Yale University Press.

Lerner, H. (1993). Self-representation in eating disorders: a psychodynamic perspective. In *The Self in Emotional Distress*, ed. Z. V. Segal and S. J. Blatt, pp. 267–287. New York: Guilford.

Lerner, P., and Lerner, H. (1995). Dissociative disorders, omnipotence, and sadomasochism. Unpublished manuscript.

Lichtenberg, J. D. (1984). Continuities and transformations between infancy and adolescence. In *Late Adolescence*, ed. D. D. Brockman, pp. 7–27. New York: International Universities Press.

—— (1985). *Psychoanalysis and Infant Research*. Hillsdale, NJ: Analytic Press.

—— (1989). *Psychoanalysis and Motivation*. Hillsdale, NJ: Analytic Press.

Limentani, A. (1972). The assessment of analysability. *International Journal of Psycho-Analysis* 53:351–361.

Litman, R. E. (1967). Sigmund Freud on suicide. In *Essays in Self-Destruction*, ed. E. Shneidman, pp. 324–344. New York: Science House.

Loewald, H. W. (1960). On the therapeutic action of psychoanalysis. *International Journal of Psycho-Analysis* 41:16–33.

Loewenstein, R. M. (1957). A contribution to the psychoanalytic theory of masochism. *Journal of the American Psychoanalytic Association* 5:197–234.

—— (1969). Developments in the theory of transference in the last fifty years. *International Journal of Psycho-Analysis* 50:583–588.

Lush, D. (1968). Progress of a child with atypical development. *Journal of Child Psychotherapy* 2:64–73.

Mahler, M. S., Pine, F., and Bergmann, A. (1975). *The Psychological Birth of the Human Infant*. New York: Basic Books.

Mahon, E. J. (1991). The "dissolution" of the Oedipus complex: a neglected cognitive factor. *Psychoanalytic Quarterly* 60:628–634.

Maleson, F. G. (1984). The multiple meanings of masochism in psychoanalytic discourse. *Journal of the American Psychoanalytic Association* 32:325–356.

Malin, A., and Grotstein, J. S. (1966). Projective identification in the therapeutic process. *International Journal of Psycho-Analysis* 47:26–31.

Markson, E. R. (1993). Depression and moral masochism. *International Journal of Psycho-Analysis* 74:931–940.

Masson, J. (1984). *The Assault On Truth: Freud's Suppression of the Seduction Theory.* New York: Farrar, Straus and Giroux.

McCall, R. B. (1979). The development of intellectual functioning in infancy and the prediction of later IQ. In *Handbook of Infant Development*, ed. J. D. Osofsky, pp. 707–742. New York: Wiley.

McDougall, J. (1985). *Theaters of the Mind: Illusion and Truth on the Psychoanalytic Stage.* New York: Basic Books.

Meissner, W. (1989). The viewpoint of the devil's advocate. In *The Significance of Infant Observational Research for Clinical Work with Children, Adolescents, and Adults*, ed. S. Dowling and A. Rothstein, pp. 175–195. Madison, CT: International Universities Press.

Meltzer, D., Bremner, J., Hoxter, S., et al. (1975). *Explorations in Autism.* Perthshire, Scotland: Clunie Press.

Meyers, H. (1988). A consideration of treatment techniques in relation to the functions of masochism. In *Masochism: Current Psychoanalytic Perspectives*, ed. R. A. Glick and D. I. Meyers, pp. 175–189. Hillsdale, NJ: Analytic Press.

Miller, A. (1983). *For Your Own Good: Hidden Cruelty in Child Rearing and the Roots of Violence.* New York: Farrar, Straus and Giroux.

Modell, A. H. (1989). The psychoanalytic setting as a container of multiple levels of reality: a perspective on the theory of psychoanalytic treatment. *Psychoanalytic Inquiry* 9:67–87.

Moore, B. E., and Fine, B. D. (1967). *A Glossary of Psychoanalytic Terms and Concepts.* New York: American Psychoanalytic Association.

—— (1990). *Psychoanalytic Terms and Concepts.* New Haven: Yale University Press.

Mulisch, H. (1985[1982]). *The Assault.* New York: Pantheon Books.

Nagel, J. J. (1994). The paradox of performance anxiety in musicians: the disillusionment of omnipotence. Paper presented at the I. S. Gilmore International Keyboard Festival, Kalamazoo, MI, May.

—— (1995). Injury and pain in performing musicians: a psychoanalytic diagnosis. Paper presented at the International Arts and Medicine Association. Tel Aviv, Israel, June.

Namnun, A. (1968). The problems of analyzability and the autonomous ego. *International Journal of Psycho-Analysis* 49:271–275.

Niederland, W. G. (1958). Early auditory experiences, beating fantasies, and primal scene. *Psychoanalytic Study of the Child* 13:471–504. New York: International Universities Press.

Novick, J. (1970). The vicissitudes of the working alliance in the analysis of a latency girl. *Psychoanalytic Study of the Child* 25:231–256. New York: International Universities Press.

—— (1976). Termination of treatment in adolescence. *Psychoanalytic Study of the Child* 31:389–414. New Haven: Yale University Press.

—— (1977). Walk-in clinics for adolescents. *Journal of Child Psychotherapy* 4:84–89.

—— (1980). Negative therapeutic motivation and negative therapeutic alliance. *Psychoanalytic Study of the Child* 35:299–320. New Haven: Yale University Press.

—— (1982a). Varieties of transference in the analysis of an adolescent. *International Journal of Psycho-Analysis* 63:139–148.

—— (1982b). Termination: themes and issues. *Psychoanalytic Inquiry* 2:329–365.

—— (1984). Attempted suicide in adolescence. In *Suicide in the Young*, ed. H. S. Sudak, A. B. Ford, and N. B. Rushforth, pp. 115–137. Boston: John Wright.

—— (1988). Timing of termination. *International Review of Psycho-Analysis* 69:307–318.

—— (1989). How does infant research affect our clinical work with adolescents? In *The Significance of Infant Observational Research for Clinical Work with Children, Adolescents, and Adults*, ed. S. Dowling and A. Rothstein, pp. 27–39. Madison, CT: International Universities Press.

—— (1990a). The significance of adolescent analysis for work with adults. In *The Significance of Child and Adolescent Analysis for Work with Adults*, ed. S. Dowling, pp. 81–94. Madison, CT: International Universities Press.

—— (1990b). Comments on termination in child, adolescent, and adult analysis. *Psychoanalytic Study of the Child* 45:419–436. New Haven: Yale University Press.

—— (1992). The therapeutic alliance: a concept revisited. *Child Analysis* 3:90–100.

Novick, J., and Holder, A. (1969). The simultaneous analysis of two brothers. (Unpublished manuscript).

Novick, J., and Hurry, A. (1969). Projection and externalization. *Journal of Child Psychotherapy* 2:5–20.

Novick, J., and Novick, K. K. (1970). Projection and externalization. *Psychoanalytic Study of the Child* 25:69–95. New York: International Universities Press.

—— (1972). Beating fantasies in children. *International Journal of Psycho-Analysis* 53:237–242.

—— (1991). Some comments on masochism and the delusion of omnipotence from a developmental perspective. *Journal of the American Psychoanalytic Association* 39:307–328.

—— (1992). Deciding on termination: the relevance of child and adolescent analytic experience to work with adults. In *Saying Goodbye*, ed. A. Schmukler, pp. 285–304. Hillsdale, NJ: Analytic Press.

—— (1994). Externalization as a pathological form of relating: the dynamic underpinnings of abuse. In *Victims of Abuse: The Emotional Impact of Child and Adult Traumas*, ed. A. Sugarman, pp. 45–68. Madison, CT: International Universities Press.

Novick, K. K. (1988). Childbearing and child rearing. *Psychoanalytic Inquiry* 8:252–260.

—— (1991). The therapeutic alliance in work with parents. Paper presented at the annual meeting of the American Psychological Association, San Francisco, August.

Novick, K. K., and Novick, J. (1987). The essence of masochism. *Psychoanalytic Study of the Child* 42:353–384. New Haven: Yale University Press.

—— (1994). Postoedipal transformations: latency, adolescence, and pathogenesis. *Journal of the American Psychoanalytic Association* 42:143–170.

Ogden, T. (1979). On projective identification. *International Journal of Psycho-Analysis* 60:357–373.

Olinick, S. L. (1964). The negative therapeutic reaction. *International Journal of Psycho-Analysis* 45:540–548.

—— (1970). Report of panel: Negative therapeutic reaction. *Journal of the American Psychoanalytic Association* 18:655–672.

Orgel, S. (1974). Fusion with the victim and suicide. *International Journal of Psycho-Analysis* 55:532–538.

Otto, U. (1982). Suicidal behavior in childhood and adolescence. In *The Child in His Family*, vol. 7, ed. E. J. Anthony and C. Chiland, pp. 163–169. New York: Wiley.

Panel (1956). The problem of masochism in the theory and technique of psychoanalysis. M. Stein, reporter. *Journal of the American Psychoanalytic Association* 4:526–538.

—— (1972). Indications and contraindications for the psychoanalysis of the adolescent. M. Sklansky, reporter. *Journal of the American Psychoanalytic Association* 20:134–144.

—— (1981). Masochism: current concepts. N. Fischer, reporter. *Journal of the American Psychoanalytic Association* 29:673–688.

—— (1983). Reanalysis of child analytic patients. A. L. Rosenbaum, reporter. *Journal of the American Psychoanalytic Association* 31:677–688.

—— (1984). The relation between masochism and depression. J. Caston, reporter, *Journal of the American Psychoanalytic Association* 32:603–614.

—— (1985). Sadomasochism in children. Vulnerable child discussion group. Midwinter meetings of the American Psychoanalytic Association. Dec. 1985. (Unpublished).

—— (1987). Issues in psychoanalytic treatment of a borderline/severely neurotic child. R. Galatzer-Levy, reporter. *Journal of the American Psychoanalytic Association* 35:727–737.

—— (1990). Sadism and masochism in neurosis and symptom formation. F. M. Levin, reporter. *Journal of the American Psychoanalytic Association* 38:789–804.

—— (1991a). Sadism and masochism in character disorder and resistance. M. H. Sacks, reporter. *Journal of the American Psychoanalytic Association* 39:215–226.

—— (1991b). Sadomasochism in the perversions. S. Akhtar, reporter. *Journal of the American Psychoanalytic Association* 39:741–755.

Papousek, H., and Papousek, M. (1975). Cognitive aspects of preverbal social interaction between human infants and adults. In *Parent–Infant Interactions*. New York: Associated Scientific Publishers.

Pedder, J. R. (1988). Termination reconsidered. *International Journal of Psycho-Analysis* 69:495–505.

Petzel, S. V., and Riddle, M. (1981). Adolescent suicide: psychosocial and cognitive aspects. In: *Adolescent Psychiatry*, vol. 9, ed. S. Feinstein, J. Looney, A. Schwartzberg, and J. Sorosky, pp. 343–398. Chicago: University of Chicago Press.

Piaget, J. (1952). *The Origins of Intelligence in Children.* New York: International Universities Press.

—— (1954). *The Construction of Reality in the Child.* New York: Basic Books.

Pine, F. (1985). *Developmental Theory and Clinical Process.* New Haven: Yale University Press.

Plath, S. (1965). Lady Lazarus. In *Ariel*, pp. 16–19. London: Faber and Faber.

Pumpian-Mindlin, E. (1969). Vicissitudes of infantile omnipotence. *Psychoanalytic Study of the Child* 24:213–226. New York: International Universities Press.

Rangell, L. (1966). An overview of the ending of an analysis. In *Psychoanalysis in the Americas*, ed. R. E. Litman, pp. 141–165. New York: International Universities Press.

—— (1989). The significance of infant observations for psychoanalysis in later stages of life: a discussion. In *The Significance of Infant Observational Research for Clinical Work with Children, Adolescents, and Adults*, ed. S. Dowling and A. Rothstein, pp. 195–211. Madison, CT: International Universities Press.

Rapaport, D. (1944). The scientific methodology of psychoanalysis. In *The Collected Papers of David Rapaport*, ed. M. M. Gill, pp. 165–220. New York: Basic Books, 1967.

—— (1950). The theoretical implications of diagnostic testing procedures. In *The Collected Papers of David Rapaport*, ed. M. M. Gill, pp. 334–356. New York: Basic Books, 1967.

—— (1952). Projective techniques and the theory of thinking. In *The Collected Papers of David Rapaport*, ed. M. M. Gill, pp. 461–469. New York: Basic Books, 1967.

—— (1960). On the psychoanalytic theory of motivation. In *Nebraska Symposium on Motivation*, ed. M. R. Jones, pp. 173–247.

Rapaport, D., and Gill, M. M. (1959). The points of view and assumptions of metapsychology. *International Journal of Psycho-Analysis* 40:153–162.

Reed, G. (1990). A reconsideration of the concept of transference neurosis. *International Journal of Psycho-Analysis* 71:205–217.

—— (1993). On the value of explicit reconstruction. *Psychoanalytic Quarterly* 62:52–73.

Reich, A. (1950). On the termination of psychoanalysis. *International Journal of Psycho-Analysis* 31:179–183.

Renik, O. (1990). The concept of a transference neurosis and psychoanalytic methodology. *International Journal of Psycho-Analysis* 71:197–204.

Rinsley, D. B., and Hall, D. D. (1962). Psychiatric hospital treatment of adolescents. *Archives of General Psychiatry* 7:78–86.

Ritvo, S. (1966). Correlation of a childhood and adult neurosis. *International Journal of Psycho-Analysis* 47:130–150.

Riviere, J. (1936). A contribution to the analysis of the negative therapeutic reaction. *International Journal of Psycho-Analysis* 17:304–320.

Rosenfeld, H. (1965). *Psychotic States.* New York: International Universities Press.

Rubinfine, D. L. (1965). On beating fantasies. *International Journal of Psycho-Analysis* 46:315–322.

Russell, I. (1884). The borderlands of insanity. *Alienist and Neurologist* 5:457–471.

Rycroft, C. (1968). *A Critical Dictionary of Psycho-Analysis.* London: Nelson.

Sandler, J. (1962). Research in psychoanalysis: the Hampstead Index as an instrument of psycho-analytic research. *International Journal of Psycho-Analysis* 43:287–291.

—— (1976). Countertransference and role responsiveness. *International Review of Psycho-Analysis* 3:43–47.

—— (1992). Reflections on developments in the theory of psychoanalytic technique. *International Journal of Psycho-Analysis* 73:189–198.

Sandler, J., Holder, A., and Dare, C. (1973). *The Patient and the Analyst.* London: Allen & Unwin.

Sandler, J., and Rosenblatt, B. (1962). The concept of the representational world. *Psychoanalytic Study of the Child* 17:128–145. New York: International Universities Press.

Sandler, J., and Sandler, A. M. (1984). The past unconscious, the present unconscious, and the interpretation of the transference. *Psychoanalytic Inquiry* 4:367–399.

Schafer, R. (1968). *Aspects of Internalization.* New York: International Universities Press.

Schimek, J. (1987). Fact and fantasy in the seduction theory: a historical review. *Journal of the American Psychoanalytic Association* 35:937–965.

Schmideberg, M. (1948). On fantasies of being beaten. *Psychoanalytic Review* 35:303–308.

Shane, M., and Shane, E. (1984). The end phase of analysis: indicators, functions and tasks of termination. *Journal of the American Psychoanalytic Association* 32:739–772.

Shapiro, T. (1977). Oedipal distortions in severe pathologies: developmental and theoretical considerations. *Psychoanalytic Quarterly* 46:559–579.

—— (1981). On the quest for the origin of conflict. *Psychoanalytic Quarterly* 50:1–21.

Shapiro, T., and Perry, R. (1976). Latency revisited. *Psychoanalytic Study of the Child* 31:79–105. New Haven: Yale University Press.

Shengold, L. (1989a). Further thoughts about "Nothing." *Psychoanalytic Quarterly* 58:227–235.

—— (1989b). *Soul Murder: The Effects of Childhood Abuse and Deprivation.* New Haven: Yale University Press.

—— (1991). A variety of narcissistic pathology stemming from parental weakness. *Psychoanalytic Quarterly* 60:86–89.

Shirley, L. (1981). Teen suicide. *Ann Arbor News,* May 7. Ann Arbor, MI.

Silver, D. (1985). Prologue. *Psychoanalytic Inquiry* 5:501–507.

Simons, R. C. (1987). Psychoanalytic contributions to psychiatric nosology: forms of masochistic behavior. *Journal of the American Psychoanalytic Association* 35:583–608.

Smith, S. (1977). The golden fantasy: a regressive reaction to separation anxiety. *International Journal of Psycho-Analysis* 58:311–324.

Solnit, A. J. (1994). A psychoanalytic view of child abuse. In *Victims of Abuse,* ed. A. Sugarman, pp. 25–44. Madison, CT: International Universities Press.

Spence, D. (1982). *Narrative Truth and Historical Truth.* New York: Norton.

Sterba, R. (1934). The fate of the ego in analytic therapy. *International Journal of Psycho-Analysis* 15:117–126.

Stern, D. W. (1985). *The Interpersonal World of the Infant.* New York: Basic Books.

Stern, M. (1968). Fear of death and neurosis. *Journal of the American Psychoanalytic Association* 16:3–31.

Stone, L. (1961). *The Psychoanalytic Situation.* New York: International Universities Press.

Sugarman, A. (1991). Developmental antecedents of masochism: vignettes from the analysis of a 3-year-old girl. *International Journal of Psycho-Analysis* 72:107–116.

Tartakoff, H. H. (1966). The normal personality in our culture and the Nobel Prize complex. In *Psychoanalysis—A General Psychology,* ed. R. M. Loewenstein, L. M. Newman, M. Schur, and A. J. Solnit, pp. 222–252. New York: International Universities Press.

Tronick, E. Z., and Gianino, A. (1986). Interactive mismatch and repair. *Zero to Three* 6:1–6.

Tyson, P. (1989). Two approaches to infant research. Introduction: the significance of the data of infant observational research for clinical work with adolescents. In *The Significance of Infant Observational Research for Clinical Work with Children, Adolescents, and Adults,* ed. S. Dowling and A. Rothstein, pp. 27–39. Madison, CT: International Universities Press.

Tyson, P., and Tyson, R. L. (1990). *Psychoanalytic Theories of Development.* New Haven: Yale University Press.

Valenstein, A. F. (1973). On attachment to painful feelings and the negative therapeutic reaction. *Psychoanalytic Study of the Child* 28:365–392. New Haven: Yale University Press.

—— (1989). Preoedipal reconstructions in psychoanalysis. *International Journal of Psycho-Analysis* 70:433–442.

Waelder, R. (1951). The structure of paranoid ideas. *International Journal of Psycho-Analysis* 32:167–177.

Weinshel, E. M. (1984). Some observations on the psychoanalytic process. *Psychoanalytic Quarterly* 53:63–92.

Weiss, E. (1947). Projection, extrajection, and objectivation. *Psychoanalytic Quarterly* 16:357–377.

Winnicott, D. W. (1960). The theory of the parent–infant relationship.

In *The Maturational Processes and the Facilitating Environment*, pp. 37–55. New York: International Universities Press.

—— (1965). *The Maturational Processes and the Facilitating Environment*. New York: International Universities Press.

—— (1969). Adolescent process and the need for personal confrontation. *Pediatrics* 44:752–756.

Wurmser, L. (1990). The way from Ithaca to Golgotha—some observations about clinical masochism. *Jarbuch Psychoanalyse* 26:135–214.

—— (1993). *Das Ratsel des Masochismus* [*The Riddle of Masochism*]. Heidelberg: Springer Verlag.

Zetzel, E. R. (1956). Current concepts of transference. *International Journal of Psycho-Analysis* 37:369–376.

CREDITS

The authors gratefully acknowledge permission to reprint material from the following sources:

"Beating Fantasies in Children," by J. and K. K. Novick, in *International Journal of Psycho-Analysis*, vol. 53, pp. 237–242. Copyright © 1972 by the Institute of Psycho-Analysis.

"Varieties of Transference in the Analysis of an Adolescent," by J. Novick, in *International Journal of Psycho-Analysis*, vol. 63, pp. 139–148. Copyright © 1982 by the Institute of Psycho-Analysis.

From "Lady Lazarus," in *Ariel*, by Sylvia Plath. Copyright © 1963 by Ted Hughes. Copyright renewed. Reprinted by permission of HarperCollins Publishers, Inc., and Faber & Faber Ltd., UK.

"Attempted Suicide in Adolescence: The Suicide Sequence," by J. Novick, in *Suicide in the Young*, ed. H. S. Sudak, A. B. Ford, and N. B. Rushforth, pp. 115–137. Copyright © 1984 Butterworth-Heinemann.

"Talking with Toddlers," by K. K. Novick, in *Psychoanalytic Study of the Child*, vol. 41, pp. 277–286. Copyright © Yale University Press.

"Negative Therapeutic Motivation and Negative Therapeutic Alliance," by J. Novick, in *Psychoanalytic Study of the Child*, vol. 35, pp. 299–319. Copyright © 1980 Yale University Press.

Chapters 1 and 5 form part of a research project entitled "Childhood Pathology: Impact on Later Mental Health," conducted at the Hampstead Child Therapy Course and Clinic, London. The project is financed by the National Institute of Mental Health, Washington, DC, grants no. MH-5683-09 and MH-5683-07. We would like to express our gratitude to the many child analysts who generously made available case material for this study, and are grateful for Anna Freud's many helpful suggestions. We also thank Dr. J. Sandler and members of the Index and Clinical Concept Group for their insightful suggestions.

INDEX

Omnipotence, infantile, 21, 50–51
Omnipotent,
 mother as, 271, 277, 282–
  285, 300
 system, 68, 339, 354, 369
Orgel, S., 27, 54, 200
Otto, U., 174

Pain, clinging to, 64, 169, 303
Pain, seeking, 19–20, 23, 31,
  33, 49, 150, 300, 302–303,
  306
Paolitto, F., 311
Papousek, H., 61
Papousek, M., 61
Passivity, 10, 31, 141, 300
 feminine, 5, 8, 9, 13, 140
Pedder, J. R., 311, 315
Perry, R., 85
Perversion, 13, 48, 51, 63, 93,
  369, 375
Petzel, S. V., 174
Phallic-oedipal phase, 34–37,
  76–77, 214, 225, 355
 in adolescent, 142–143, 145–
  146
 and beating games, 8–10, 13, 16
Piaget, J., 50, 103
Pine, F., 50, 287
Pleasure, 62, 64, 169, 309, 355
 in competence, 57, 68, 354, 366
 conflicts around, 24, 66, 307
 economy, 17, 52, 264
 principle, 101, 103
 source of, 290, 294, 297, 298,
  307, 366, 377
Preoedipal phase, 5, 12, 44, 293,
  294
 conflicts, 124, 139, 144, 290

Primal scene, 8, 34–35, 83, 136,
  137, 145
"Primary fault," 22, 282
Projection, xiv, 97–126, 102, 106
Projective identification, 167–168
Psychoanalysis, xi, xii, 265, 287–
  288, 355
 intermittant, 350
 treatment phases, 310, 311
 and "working through," 326
Psychosis, 24, 49, 59, 156, 174,
  176, 177, 195, 301
Puberty, 13, 38–39, 42, 83, 224
Pumpian-Mindlin, E., 50
"Purified pleasure dyad," 30, 57,
  198, 275, 278, 280, 281

Rangell, L., 71, 310
Rapaport, D., xi, 97, 98, 101,
  105
Reality, 84, 220, 354, 374
 principle, 50, 101, 277
Reconstruction, 56, 81–82, 89,
  93, 287
Reed, G., 71, 82
Regression, 200, 213, 246, 270,
  301, 339
 in adolescence, 274, 307
 during termination phase,
  288, 298
 pathological, 182, 186, 195
Reich, A., 310
Renik, O., 71, 89
Resistance, 49–50, 69, 88, 267–
  269, 350
 and analysis, 88, 145, 236,
  336, 365
 to communication, 73, 102, 134
 and conscience, 132, 135

Suicide sequence, 60–61, 181–
197, 270–271
Superego, 41, 52, 76, 77, 133,
286
conflicts, 78, 79, 81, 246
formation of, 8, 35, 37, 84, 85
precocious, 124, 264
functions of, 38–39
Symbolic thinking, 204, 207, 213

Tartakoff, H. H., 266
Termination, 144, 243–245,
265, 288, 357
adolescent, 89–90, 128, 298–
299, 350
unilateral, 146, 284–285,
371
adult, 274, 299–309, 373–380
interminable, 310–352
forced, 280–81, 299–300, 306
preschool age, 289–293
school-age, 293–298
Therapeutic alliance, xiv, 310–
311, 353–380, 356, 361–
363
beginning phase, 364–366
middle phase, 366–369
pretermination phase, 369–
373, 380
termination phase, 373–380
Toddlerhood, 25–34, 54, 214,
219, 253–264
Transference, 218, 234, 238–
239, 359, 378
in adolescence, 127–146
defense against, 18, 276, 285
(*see also* Resistance)

differentiated, 298, 371
externalizing, 165, 298, 368,
371
fantasies in, 12, 38, 64, 229
masochistic, 46–47, 66
rational, 357
as reenactment, 17, 37, 154,
158, 237
sadomasochistic, 300
Transformations, 85–86, 149,
253, 292, 293, 361, 379–
380
Transposition, 245–247
Trauma, 34–35, 148, 216–217,
222, 225, 317, 325–326
infantile, response to, 178,
200
the latency, 84, 341
Tronick, E. Z., 20, 21, 25
Tyson, P., 59, 77, 287
Tyson, R. L., 77

Valenstein, A. F.. 22, 45, 48, 53,
71
Verbalization, 124, 260, 263
Victim role, 59, 79, 80, 168,
300, 314
in sexual abuse, 151–153, 241

Weinshel, E. M., 345, 358
Weiss, E., 98
Wexler, M., 357
Winnicott, D. W., 88, 92–93
Wolf Man, the, 42, 58, 299, 349
Wurmser, L., 63

Zetzel, E. R., 356–357